Matter: Material Processes in Architectural Production

Matter tracks the recent generational shift in design culture from the pure abstraction of representation towards new practices that are engaged in the tactile world of matter. Introduced through a series of four interviews, it serves as a catalog of the new methodologies that have emerged out of this shift. The projects and essays presented are organized according to a variety of issues that have been impacted by these developments, ranging from material detail to sensation and ecology. As a collection, this book serves as a brief snapshot of contemporary practice and thought surrounding materiality, fabrication, and architecture. Its diversity, both of method and outcome, is intentionally broad to illustrate the variety of approaches and topics that are in development today.

Beautifully illustrated with a great deal of technical information throughout, this is not a coffee table book with no explanation of how, nor a theory book with no descriptions of the projects. The book shows work, technical technique, and process and marries this with the theoretical reasoning for making certain material decisions. It gives the student a complete package with which to address materiality in their designs.

By assembling a range of voices across different institutions and generations, this book offers a multifaceted portrait of material design today and is an excellent resource for the studio and classroom. Students and design professionals alike will find this collection of both project- and process-based discussion to be an essential guide for understanding this increasingly important aspect of design and for insights into the forces that shape architecture.

Gail Peter Borden is principal of the Borden Partnership and an Assistant Professor of Architecture at the University of Southern California. His numerous awards and publications include the Architecture League of New York Young Architects Prize; 2011 AIA Young Architect Award; an artist-in-residence at the Chinati Foundation, the Atlantic Center for the Arts, and the MacDowell Colony; a Graham Foundation Grant; and the Borchard Fellowship.

Michael Meredith is a principal in the architecture office MOS, and an Associate Professor of Architecture at the Harvard University Graduate School of Design. His writing has appeared in *Artforum, Perspecta, LOG, Praxis, Domus,* and *Harvard Design Magazine,* along with many others. The work of MOS has been widely published and received numerous awards. In 2009, MOS was awarded the PS1/MoMA Summer Pavilion.

First published 2012
by Routledge
2 Park Square, Milton Park, Abingdon, Oxon, OX14 4RN

Simultaneously published in the USA and Canada
by Routledge
711 Third Avenue, New York, NY 10017

Routledge is an imprint of the Taylor & Francis Group, an informa business

British Library Cataloguing in Publication Data
A catalogue record for this book is available from the British Library

Library of Congress Cataloging in Publication Data
Matter : material processes in architectural production / edited by Gail
Peter Borden & Michael Meredith.
p. cm.
Includes bibliographical references and index.
1. Building materials. 2. Building. 3. Architecture. I. Borden, Gail Peter. II.
Meredith, Michael, 1971-
TA403.M386 2011
721'.044--dc22
2010040684

ISBN: 978-0-415-78028-5 (hbk)
ISBN: 978-0-415-78029-2 (pbk)
ISBN: 978-0-203-82702-4 (ebk)

Typeset in Typeset in Garamond Premier Pro and Univers
by Gavin Ambrose

Printed and bound in India by Replika Press Pvt. Ltd.

Matter: Material Pro[cesses in] Architectural Produc[tion]

Edited by Gail Peter Borden and Michael Meredith

Routledge
Taylor & Francis Group

LONDON AND NEW YORK

Contents

Notes on Contributors

Phillip Anzalone is the Director of the Building Science and Technology Sequence and the Director of the Avery Digital Fabrication Laboratory at the Graduate School of Architecture, Columbia University. As Director, he leads research and curriculum related to applied and experimental building science and technology, digitally based design, fabrication and assembly techniques, as well as numerous creative constructed projects at the School. He teaches classes related to computer-based fabrication, building structures, advanced material studies, industry collaboration and architectural detailing, as well as graduate level design studio. Anzalone is a Registered Architect with experience as a curtain wall consultant for R. A. Heintges & Associates, as an architectural designer with Greg Lynn Form, and is currently a partner of Atelier Architecture 64 (aa64) with Stephanie Bayard. He holds a Masters of Architecture from Columbia University and BPS Architecture from SUNY Buffalo.

W. Andrew Atwood is an Adjunct Assistant Professor at the University of Southern California where he teaches graduate and undergraduate design studios and courses in physical computation and materials and methods. In 2009, he started his own design firm ATWOOD, based in Los Angeles, CA.

Stephanie Bayard teaches design studios and history/theory seminars at the Graduate School of Architecture and Urban Design at Pratt Institute. Her teaching and research involve modernist housing in Europe and the United States, emphasizing the relationship between design and construction methodologies. Her current research involves the integration of technology, material exploration and new modes of manufacture in architectural theory, education and practice. She founded Atelier Architecture 64 (aa64) with Phillip Anzalone, as an experimental practice focusing on design, digital fabrication and material construction with built projects in USA, Europe and Korea. She received her Architecture Diploma with distinction from Paris La Villette, France, and her MsAAD from Columbia University. aa64's work has been published and exhibited at the AIA NY Center for Architecture.

David Benjamin is co-founder, with Soo-in Yang, of The Living and the Living Architecture Lab (www.thelivingnewyork.com). The practice and the lab emphasize open source research and design. Recent projects include Living City (a platform for buildings to talk to one another), *Living Light* (a pavilion in Seoul that displays air quality and public interest in the environment), *Proof* (a series of design studios that apply testing and evolutionary computation as exploration techniques), and *Architecture Bio-Synthesis* (a hands-on research initiative about synthetic biology, DNA manipulation, and innovation in buildings). Before receiving a Master of Architecture degree from Columbia, Benjamin graduated from Harvard with a BA in Social Studies.

Lawrence Blough is principal of GRAFTWORKS, an interdisciplinary design research office in New York City, and is Associate Professor and Coordinator of the Intermediate Design sequence at Pratt Institute School of Architecture. Before founding GRAFTWORKS, he worked in the offices of Peter Eisenman, Antoine Predock and was a Senior Associate in a non-profit architecture and urbanism foundation in New Haven. His work and collaborations have been exhibited at Locust Projects in Miami, CAUE 92 in France, Yale University and Pratt Institute among others, and in 2005 GRAFTWORKS was a finalist in the P.S.1/MoMA Young Architects Program. Blough is the recipient of a New York State Council on the Arts 2010 Independent Projects Award to develop an innovative aerated concrete assembly system. His current fabrication and tectonic research has been presented at the Acadia 2010 conference at the Cooper Union, the Input_Output symposium at Temple University, and the Material Matters conference at USC.

Gail Peter Borden is principal of the Borden Partnership LLP (www.bordenpartnership.com), and an Assistant Professor of Architecture at the University of Southern California. His numerous awards and publications include the Architecture League of New York Young Architects Prize; an artist-in-residence at the Chinati Foundation, the Atlantic Center for the Arts, and the MacDowell Colony; a Graham Foundation Grant; and the Borchard Fellowship. His first book is entitled *Material Precedent: The Typology of Modern Tectonics* by Wiley. In 2010, he was selected to exhibit *Light Frames* at Materials & Applications Gallery. He holds five degrees from Rice and Harvard University.

Michael Carroll is an Assistant Professor at Southern Polytechnic State University School of Architecture (SP_ARC) where he lectures on building technology and directs the SP_ARCs Materials Library. He has also taught at Syracuse University School of Architecture and McGill University School of Architecture. He is a founding partner of atelier BUILD, a design/build firm based in Montreal. Atelier BUILD was awarded the Canadian Prix de Rome of Architecture in 2004. A monograph on the work of atelier BUILD was published in spring 2010 by TUNS Press of Halifax, Nova Scotia, Canada. Atelier BUILD's work has been published in North America and Europe and exhibited in a series of group shows in the United Kingdom, Canada, the United States, and Japan.

Dale Clifford's work is aimed at advancing qualitative systems thinking across traditional disciplinary boundaries of science, engineering, and architecture. To forward this goal, Clifford directs the Bio_Logic Lab at Carnegie Mellon University, an open source collaborative enterprise convened to transfer knowledge from the field of biology to the domain of the built environment. Clifford has applied his interests in biomimetics to the medical and aeronautical industries under the direction of Dr. Don Ingber at Molecular Geodesics, with designs for wing interiors, drug delivery devices, medical instruments, implants, and Space Shuttle tiles. The common thread is that all were inspired from the geometry and performance of natural systems. He is a founding member of the Emerging Materials Technology Program at the University of Arizona and has worked on grants, contracts to forward structural and biomimetic research with Buro Happold, IDEO, NASA, DARPA, DOE, and Carnegie Mellon University. Clifford is principal of Binary Design, a research-based architectural practice in Pittsburgh and NYC.

Jenna Didier is in pursuit of a new approach to the built environment. A lifelong interest in the creation and use of public space led her to Los Angeles and a career in water feature design and public art. In 2002, to explore the development of immersive public spaces further, Didier founded Materials & Applications, a non-profit organization dedicated to pushing forward new and underused building technologies and collaborative methods. She formed the art and technology team, Didier Hess, with Oliver Hess in 2004. Didier Hess creates interactive artworks for public places. They discover invisible but powerful forces influencing a site and make them tangible through responsive lighting, fog, water, sound or mechanical effects.

John Enright and Margaret Griffin established their Los Angeles-based studio, Griffin Enright Architects, in 2000. Their collaboration is a fusion of collective interests in experimentation, innovation and a desire to explore cultural complexities relative to the built environment. Their versatility is evident in the scope of their projects that range from furniture design and gallery installations to large-scale commercial and residential commissions. They are the recipients of numerous design awards including the American Architecture Award from the Chicago Athenaeum, and have been featured in local, national and international publications. In addition to their practice, they have taught design studios at Syracuse University, USC, the University of Houston, Cal Poly Pomona, and UCLA. John Enright is currently Undergraduate Program Chair at SCI-Arc, and Margaret Griffin currently teaches design studios and seminars on materiality, also at SCI-Arc. Griffin received a BArch from Syracuse University, and an MArch from the University of Virginia. Enright received a BArch from Syracuse University and an MArch from Columbia University.

Thom Faulders, architect, leads Faulders Studio, which creates projects on a wide array of building scales, exploratory architectural proposals and speculative exhibitions. The office pursues architecture as performative research, and proactively situates architecture in a dynamic interplay between artificial and natural phenomena. Faulders' work is included in the Permanent Architecture and Design Collection at the San Francisco Museum of Modern Art, and has been included in numerous international exhibitions, including *Dentelles d'architecture* at the Maison de l'Architecture et de la Ville in Euralille, France; *Case per Tutti* at the Fondazione la Triennale di Milano, Italy; *Safe: Design Takes on Risk* at the Museum of Modern Art in New York; and *Experimentadesign* at the Lisbon International Biennal. He received an Emerging Voices Awards from the Architectural League of New York, and an SFMOMA Experimental Design Award. He is an Associate Professor in Architecture at the California College of the Arts in San Francisco.

Jeremy Ficca, AIA, is an Associate Professor of Architecture and founding Director of the Digital Fabrication Laboratory (dFAB) in the School of Architecture at Carnegie Mellon University. His award-winning teaching, research and practice focus on the convergence of tectonics, materiality and digital technologies. His professional practice and research operate across multiple scales, from object to building and utilize emergent digital workflows to explore opportunities for a reinvigorated understanding of architecture's material, structural and spatial conditions. He has spoken widely on the topics of digital design, materiality and pedagogy, and his work has been exhibited throughout North America and recognized with two AIA design awards. Ficca's teaching innovation and excellence have been recognized with an ACSA National Young Faculty Teaching Award; an NC State University College of Design Teaching Award; and a Carnegie Mellon University Henry Hornbostel Teaching Award. He holds a post-professional Master of Architecture from Harvard University and a Bachelor of Architecture from Virginia Tech. Prior to joining Carnegie Mellon University, he was an Assistant Professor at North Carolina State University.

Laura Garófalo's research and practice focus on the conjunction of natural and architectural systems. Her work proposes emergent ecologies that use architecture as an active instigator for new relationships between people, buildings and landscape. Her firm, Liminal Projects, has been exhibited at the Architectural League of New York, and the National Building Museum, and was selected by the Architectural League of New York as Notable Young Architects. Recent design competition entries include First Place in d3 Housing Tomorrow competition, a winning proposal for the "What if New York City ..." Post-Disaster Housing Design Competition, a Gold Spark Award, and an ACSA Faculty Design Award.

Oliver Hess has a wealth of experience and insight into construction in the computational world and real world. His own work leaps between mechanical effects built out of necessity to bring a virtual concept into the built environment, and virtual animated worlds created to bring physical concepts into the expansive algorithmic realm of the digital. Through his work with Didier Hess, he collaborates on large-scale permanent public art projects, exploring the transformation of forces to the human scale to create unique public spaces. As Co-Director of Materials & Applications, Oliver provides visionary ideas for the development of its structures and programming. He is also an Instructor at the Art Center School of Design.

David Hill, AIA, is an Assistant Professor of Architecture at North Carolina State University where his research and teaching focus on architectural prototype design and production in contemporary practice. He has worked on award-winning projects with Hashim Sarkis Studios, Pearce Brinkley Cease + Lee Architecture, and Tonic Design. Hill has presented his work at numerous professional and academic conferences, and he has received grants to study architect George Matsumoto's post-WWII demonstration houses. He has been recognized with an ACSA Faculty Design Award and honors in several design competitions, most notably his winning entries for the AIA New Home on the Range (with PBC+L) and "What if New York City ..." Post-Disaster Housing Design Competition (with Laura Garófalo and Nelson Tang).

Eric Höweler, AIA LEED AP, is founding principal of MY Studio and Höweler + Yoon Architecture. He received a Bachelor of Architecture and a Masters of Architecture from Cornell University. He is currently a Design Critic in Architecture at the Harvard Graduate School of Design. He is the author of *Skyscraper: Vertical Now* (Rizzoli/Universe Publishers, 2004). Höweler + Yoon Architecture/MY Studio was awarded the Architecture League's Emerging Voices Award in 2007 as well as *Architectural Record*'s Design Vanguard in the same year.

Florian Idenburg, RA, AIA-IA, is partner of Solid Objectives – Idenburg Liu, a New York office that produces work in the realms of art, architecture and urbanism. SO – IL currently is working on projects in New York, Athens, Seoul, and Beijing. SO – IL was the 2010 winner of the MoMA/PS1 Young Architects Program and the AIA-NY Young Practices award. Idenburg is the Brown-Forman Visiting Chair of Urban Design at the University of Kentucky as well as Adjunct Assistant Professor of Architecture at Columbia's GSAPP and Design Critic at the Harvard G.S.D. He is a frequent lecturer, panelist and critic at universities and institutes throughout the USA and abroad. His writings appear regularly in magazines such as *Abitare*, *Domus*, *A+U*, and *Mark Magazine*. He is writer and editor of two books: *Learning from Japan* (Lars Müller, 2009) and *Relations* (PostMedia, 2010). He holds an MSc from Delft University.

Lisa Iwamoto and Craig Scott. Lisa Iwamoto is partner of IwamotoScott, a practice formed in partnership with Craig Scott. Committed to pursuing architecture as a form of applied design research, IwamotoScott engages in projects at multiple scales and in a variety of contexts consisting of full-scale fabrications, museum installations and exhibitions, theoretical proposals, competitions and commissioned design projects. IwamotoScott's work has been published widely nationally and internationally. Iwamoto is the author of *Digital Fabrications: Architectural and Material Techniques*, published by Princeton Architectural Press as part of their series, Architecture Briefs. She is an Associate Professor in the Department of Architecture at the University of California, Berkeley, where her research focuses on digital and material techniques for architecture.

Andrew Kudless is a designer based in San Francisco where he is an Assistant Professor at the California College of the Arts. In 2004, he founded MATSYS, a design studio exploring the emergent relationships between architecture, engineering, biology, and computation (www.matsysdesign.com). He has taught at the Architectural Association, Yale University, and the Ohio State University where he was the Howard E. LeFevre Fellow for Emerging Practitioners. Kudless has a Master of Arts in Emergent Technologies and Design from the Architectural Association and a Master of Architecture from Tulane University. Prior to forming MATSYS, he worked as a designer for Allied Works Architecture in Portland and New York, and as a digital design consultant for Expedition Engineering in London.

Keith Mitnick, Mireille Roddier, and Stewart Hicks founded the collaborative design practice Mitnick Roddier Hicks in 2002. Their work has been featured as part of the Emerging Practices series in *Architectural Record* as well as the On the Boards series in *Architecture Magazine*, and *Mark Magazine* and has been exhibited in Chicago, Boston, San Francisco, New York, and Paris. The firm has received numerous awards including the 2004 Young Architects Forum award from the Architectural League of New York, The "Unbuilt Architecture" award from the Boston Society of Architects, and an Honorable Mention for their entry to the San Francisco AIDS Memorial Competition. Their recently constructed *Split/View Pavilion* is on permanent exhibition on the grounds of the Philbrook Museum in Tulsa, Oklahoma, and was included in the publication *XS Green: Big Ideas, Small Buildings*. Mitnick Roddier Hicks are among ten international firms featured in *Architectural Record*'s 2005 Design Vanguard award issue and they have been selected to build several installations in France and the United States, including the Chaumont-Sur-Loire international landscape competition, the Montpellier Festival of Architecture and the Los Angeles Forum for Architecture + Urbanism. Keith Mitnick and Mireille Roddier are Associate Professors at the University of Michigan, and Stewart Hicks is currently Assistant Professor at the University of Illinois, Urbana-Champaign.

Kiel Moe is an architect and Assistant Professor at Northeastern University as well as a Rome Prize Fellow and author of *Thermally Active Surfaces in Architecture* and *Integrated Design in Contemporary Architecture* (both from Princeton Architectural Press), and co-editor, with Ryan Smith, of *Building Systems: Technology, Design, and Society* (Routledge, 2011). He is currently developing a manuscript on lower-technology, higher-performance architecture. He has received awards recognizing his scholarship, teaching, and design from the ACSA and AIA, among other organizations. His research has been funded by competitive grants by the Boston Society of Architects Architectural Research program, the AIA RFP grant program, the AIA UPJOHN grant program, the Northeastern University Provost Faculty Development program, and the Gorham P. Stevens Rome Prize in Architecture from the American Academy in Rome.

Dwayne Oyler received a Bachelor of Architecture from Kansas State University and a Master of Architecture from Harvard University Graduate School of Design. He was awarded the Skidmore, Owings, and Merrill Traveling Fellowship in 1996. In 2000, with Jenny Wu, he established the office of Oyler Wu Collaborative. He has also worked in the office of Toshiko Mori, Architect, and has collaborated with Lebbeus Woods on numerous projects. Oyler has taught at the Southern California Institute of Architecture (SCI-Arc), and the Research Institute for Experimental Architecture in Vico Morcote, Switzerland. Prior to relocating to Los Angeles in 2004, he taught in the Thesis Design Studio program at Cooper Union for the advancement for Arts and Sciences in New York City. He currently heads the Undergraduate Thesis Design Studio at the Southern California Institute of Architecture (SCI-Arc). He is a licensed architect in the State of California.

Jason Payne is principal of Hirsuta LLC, an architectural practice located in Los Angeles, California. Hirsuta pursues both built and speculative projects with a commitment to the synthesis of research and practice. The office is a full service architectural, interior, landscape, and object design firm specializing in advanced form and the integration of emerging technologies in construction. Payne has worked as project designer for Reiser + Umemoto/RUR Architects and Daniel Libeskind Studio and co-partnered the award-winning office Gnuform, best known for the *NGTV Bar* (2006 AIA Design Award) and the 2006 PS1 entry *Purple Haze*. With the launch of his new office, Hirsuta, Payne continues to promote a new materialism with a distinctly sensate bias. Informed by intensive research and an experimental approach, his work engages material dynamics in the production of form to create a direct appeal to the senses.

Santiago R. Pérez is an Assistant Professor and 21st Century Chair in Integrated Practice at the University of Arkansas, Fay Jones School of Architecture, developing new initiatives related to "Craft + Advanced Digital Fabrication in Architecture." Pérez has published and lectured widely on the relation between craft and digital fabrication. His essay entitled, "Cardboard: Structural and Material Innovation in Architecture," was published in *Outside the Box: Cardboard Design Now*. Pérez was an invited panelist in the *Design Life Now: National Design Triennial* at the Contemporary Arts Center in Houston, and was an invited lecturer at the University of Oregon's Distinguished Speakers Series on "The Digital Imagination: Art, Design and Computing." Pérez received a Master of Architecture with Distinction from the Harvard Graduate School of Design in 1991. As a recipient of the Tamaki Fellowship, he was a researcher in residence in the office of Tadao Ando in Osaka, and the AMORPHE office in Tokyo, headed by Kiyoshi Sey Takeyama.

Axel Prichard-Schmitzberger is currently teaching as Associate Professor at California State Polytechnic University. Prior to this engagement, he has taught at various academic institutions in Los Angeles in the areas of architecture, multimedia, and graphic design. He received his architectural master degree from the Vienna University of Technology, Austria, and practiced in various architectural design offices on internationally recognized projects. In 1999, he founded hostcell to pursue interdisciplinary projects with wide recognition, such as the interior design for the Austrian national broadcast agency ORF, and has been recognized for his contribution to *+rosebud* magazine. After his reallocation to the United States and a three-year engagement with Morphosis Architects, he founded and currently manages the practice 11.1 design | research along with partner Arshia Mahmoodi, exploring contemporary built architecture at all scales; the firm's most recent project is the construction of a high-end residence in Hollywood Hills. In 2009, his firm hostcell transformed into the graphic design enterprise, starfish-prime, as a collaboration in contemporary graphic design with partner Ice Lee.

Heather Roberge is a practicing architect and educator in Los Angeles. She is the founder and principal of murmur, a practice that studies the spatial, structural, and atmospheric potential of emerging digital design and manufacturing techniques. She is Associate Vice Chair of the Department of Architecture and Urban Design at UCLA, where she teaches graduate courses in design and digital fabrication and is Director of the Undergraduate Program in Architectural Studies. Her work has been included in *A+U*, *Praxis*, *Metropolis*, *Japan Esquire*, *Architectural Record 2*, *Log*, *306090*, *Form Magazine*, the *New York Times,* and the *Los Angeles Times*. In 2006, as co-founder of Gnuform, she participated in MOMA's Young Architects Program with the submission of a project entitled *Purple Haze*. Her work has been displayed in exhibitions including *Gnuform: Hairstyle, Patterns: Cases in Synthetic Intelligence, Temporalism*, and *Matters of Sensation*. murmur's current projects include the *Vortex House* under construction in Malibu, CA, and *Caipora*, a new Brazilian lounge in Los Angeles.

Rhett Russo is partner and co-founder of Specific Objects, Inc. in New York. His firm specializes in architectural and industrial design. He is a graduate of Columbia University's Master's of Architecture program, where he received the McKim Award for Design Excellence, and the SOM Fellowship. He has also received the Dinkeloo Prize, from the Van Alen Institute and the Young Architect's Award from the Architectural League of New York. In 2009, Russo became an Associate Professor and the Graduate Curriculum Coordinator in the College of Architecture and Design at the New Jersey Institute of Technology where he teaches courses in architectural design. He has taught previously at the University of Pennsylvania, Columbia University's Graduate School of Planning and Preservation, Pratt Institute, and Cornell University.

Hilary Sample is an Associate Professor at the Yale University School of Architecture. She has been selected as a MacDowell Colony Artist in Residence, a visiting scholar at the Canadian Center for Architecture in Montreal, and is currently completing the project Sick City, and Maintenance Architecture. She is also a founding principal of MOS with Michael Meredith. The firm has been published widely and is the recipient of numerous awards, most recently the 2010 American Academy of Arts Letter's Academy Award, and the New York Architecture League's Emerging Voices Award in 2008. MOS' work has been showcased at PS1/MoMA's

Young Architecture Program, the 2010 Venice Biennale, and is held in the collection of the Art Institute in Chicago. She holds a BArch from Syracuse University and an MArch from Princeton.

Blair Satterfield is a co-founding principal of HouMinn Practice (with Marc Swackhamer), an Assistant Professor of Architecture at the University of British Columbia, and a co-founding member of the web-based modern plan company Hometta. Satterfield has worked for Atelier Fei Chang, Visable Weather, and Bricker + Cannady Architects, where he served as Director of Design. His work has won multiple AIA and national SARA awards for architecture, landscape, and urbanism. HouMinn has been published and exhibited extensively throughout the world and has garnered such honors as the 2008 R&D Award from *Architect Magazine* and the Best in Environments award from *ID Magazine*. Satterfield has taught at Rice University, the University of Houston, and the University of Minnesota. He holds degrees from the University of Illinois at Urbana-Champaign and Rice University.

Marcelo Spina and Georgina Huljich, Argentinian architects and educators, are the co-principals of P-A-T-T-E-R-N-S, a design research architectural practice based in Los Angeles. P-A-T-T-E-R-N-S' original approach to design and architecture integrates sophisticated digital tools and techniques in the understanding and conception of form, tectonics, and materials. In pursuit of a synthetic real, their architecture operates in close proximity to the material forces that influence the life of the body and its physical environment. Part of a so-called digital generation, what sets P-A-T-T-E-R-N-S apart is not only its overt ambition to materialization but the quality and extent of built work. Recently completed projects includes *FyF House* in Argentina, *Prism Contemporary Art Gallery* in Los Angeles, *Chengdu Fluid Core-Yard* in China and *Jujuy Redux Apartment* in Argentina. Exhibited and published worldwide, P-A-T-T-E-R-N-S' first comprehensive book monograph entitled *Embedded* is forthcoming by ACDCU. Marcelo Spina is a Design and Technology Faculty at SCI-Arc. In addition, he has taught at the Universities of Harvard GSD, Angewante Vienna, Berkeley, Tulane, Washington, and Innsbruck, after holding a position in the National University of Rosario and the Di Tella University in Buenos Aires, Argentina. Georgina Huljich is Design Faculty and JumpStart Program director at the Department of Architecture at UCLA. She has previously taught at UC Berkeley, where she was the recipient of the Maybeck Fellowship, and at the University of Southern California.

Marc Swackhamer is an Associate Professor of Architecture at the University of Minnesota and a co-founding principal (with Blair Satterfield) of HouMinn Practice, an interdisciplinary design firm. HouMinn's work has been published and exhibited all over the world. Their residential construction research has won national awards from *ID Magazine* and *Architect Magazine*. At the University of Minnesota, Swackhamer researches the relationship between performance and ornament through the lenses of digital production and fabrication. In his teaching, Swackhamer has developed coursework on the topic of biomimetics, which won AIA COTE (Committee on the Environment) National Education Honors in 2007. Swackhamer was a chair of the 2008 National ACADIA (Assoc. for Computer Aided Design in Architecture) Conference and now serves on ACADIA's Board of Directors. He holds degrees from the University of Cincinnati and Rice University.

Warren Techentin, AIA, is an architect and urban designer who runs his own firm, Warren Techentin Architecture (WTARCH) – a multi-disciplinary office based in Los Angeles and engaged in a number of architecture and design projects of varying scale. He is also an Adjunct Associate Professor at the University of Southern California where he teaches design and researches urban issues.

Kentaro Tsubaki, RA, is an Assistant Professor at the Tulane School of Architecture where he explores the tectonic implication of materiality and logic of construction. His practice, STUDIO KT, is a vehicle to investigate its potential implementation as an architectural solution. Tsubaki holds a BS in Physics from Kyoto University, an MArch I from University of Colorado, and an MArch II from Cranbrook Academy of Art. He is a registered architect in the State of New York where he honed his practice as an Associate at PKSB Architects, P.C. from 1997 to 2006. His considerable professional experience along with the phenomenology-based education at Cranbrook and his background in experimental physics laid the groundwork for his empirical approach to architectural investigation, the subject of his numerous papers and presentations.

Jason Oliver Vollen, RA, is the Associate Director at the Center for Architecture Science and Technology, Associate Professor at Rensselaer Polytechnic Institute, and researcher focused on emerging material technologies, the development of next generation building systems, dynamic and environmental simulation, and digital fabrication. Vollen's work has been funded by the Boston Society of Architects, the AIA's Upjohn Research Grant. He is an ongoing research investigator on various NYSERDA and DOE research grants. He is a co-winner of *Architect Magazine*'s 2009 R&D awards and in 2010 was awarded a citation by the New York Center for Architecture for his entry in the Innovation Curtain Wall Design competition. Vollen's pedagogical work focuses on design strategies based on the integration of next generation technical systems. He is a founding partner of Binary Design, a collaborative research and practice endeavor focused on energy-effective design with projects ranging from 100 SF modular residential units to commercial and institutional projects.

Tom Wiscombe founded EMERGENT, an internationally recognized design office operating at the forefront of digital design, in 1999. EMERGENT's work stands out in terms of its use of biological models in the synthesis of form, pattern, color, and technology. In particular, EMERGENT is known for its ability to blend aesthetic and engineering issues into singular, irreducible constructions. EMERGENT has developed an international reputation through competition entries, exhibitions of work at major institutions, and publications in over 250 books and magazines in 50 countries. *ICON Magazine*, in its May 2009 issue, named Wiscombe one of the "top 20 architects in the world who are making the future and transforming the way we work."

Jenny Wu received a Bachelor of Arts from Columbia College and Master of Architecture from Harvard University Graduate School of Design. She was awarded the Clifford Wong Prize in Housing Design while at Harvard and was a Skidmore, Owings, and Merrill Traveling Fellowship finalist. She was the project architect at various offices in New York and Los Angeles, including Architecture Research Office and Gluckman Mayner Architects. She founded Oyler Wu Collaborative in 2001 along with her partner, Dwayne Oyler. They are currently based in Los Angeles, CA. Their projects include: gallery installations in Los Angeles, Boston, and New York; a 23-storey residential tower in Taipei, Taiwan; and residences in Los Angeles, Boston, and Inner Mongolia. She currently teaches design studios at the Southern California Institute of Architecture (SCI-Arc) and has previously taught at Rensselaer Polytechnic Institute (RPI). The first office publication entitled, *Pendulum Plane*, was published in August 2009. Oyler Wu Collaborative was the recent winner of the 2010 Arch Is Competition sponsored by the Los Angeles AIA.

J. Meejin Yoon, RA, is founding principal of MY Studio and Höweler + Yoon Architecture. She received a Bachelor of Architecture from Cornell University, and a Masters of Architecture in Urban Design from Harvard University. She is an Associate Professor at Massachusetts Institute of Technology where she is the Director of the Undergraduate Program in Architecture. She was the recipient of the United States Artists Award in Architecture and Design in 2008, and the Athena RISD/Target Award in 2008. Recent publications include *Expanded Practice: Projects by Höweler + Yoon Architecture/MY Studio* (Princeton Architectural Press, 2009) and *Public Works: Unsolicited Small Projects for the Big Dig* (MAP Book Publishers, 2009).

Acknowledgements

Matter first came to form as a conference held at the University of Southern California in the fall of 2008. Without the initial support of Marlene Davis and the ACSA in hosting this event, and the discussion that emerged from those who were in attendance, this present text would never have been possible.

That discussion has continued to evolve and develop thanks to the commitment, time, and focus of each of the contributing authors. The editors are particularly indebted to Stan Allen, Neil Denari, Michael Maltzan, and Nader Tehrani whose insightful conversations significantly expanded the initial framework of the project.

The editors would also like to thank Fran Ford, Georgina Johnson-Cook, and Ben Woolhead at Routledge for their editorial input and support in realizing the project.

Among the many others who contributed to the development of this book, the editors would like to thank Marrikka Trotter for her work editing the Introduction, "Foreign Matter," Bryan Norwood for his work editing the conversations with Stan Allen and Nader Tehrani, and Matt Eshleman for his help in the final stages of making the book a reality.

Most importantly, the editors would like to thank Brooke, Frieda, and Gail Calvin for their unequivocal love and support, and Hilary for her support and comments since the book's inception.

Introduction
Foreign Matter

Gail Peter Borden and Michael Meredith

In "Regarding Economy,"[1]Adolf Loos argued that the "old love of ornament" should be replaced by a love of material. In proposing materiality to replace ornamentation, he was advocating the exposure of "inherent qualities" of materials, which has remained an enduring, at times nostalgic, approach towards materiality in architecture. This correlation overlooks Loos' deeper argument of societal values and taste toward materiality, which must therefore be constantly reevaluated and questioned. Our difficulty with this formulation today is twofold.

First, we understand that we can no longer endlessly extract, polish, and arrange blocks of some pure material so that their surfaces conform to shared standards of privilege; we know that those standards, at a large and ever-increasing scale, are unsustainable.[2] There are no obvious untapped resources to be easily exploited. Before the Industrial Revolution, material extraction rates were constrained by the expense and difficulty of transport, along with the technological limitations of local craft. These pressures constrained the formal and effectual traditions of vernacular architecture. Wood was harvested from local trees with certain desirable characteristics, bricks were fired from area clays with unique strengths and limitations, and stones were quarried locally. The relationship between the material and the act of making was constructed locally. The Industrial Revolution seemed to modify this relationship of the construction of materials and the construction of buildings in scalar as well as proportional terms. Transportation infrastructures combined with large urban working populations and the development or redevelopment of technologies such as steel and concrete created a long-term illusion of endlessly abundant materials that could be moved about and employed without regard for regional application traditions. The architect was suddenly presented with a *palette* of materials. Architecture became less hermetic, more democratized, selection could be based on considerations of cost, structural limits, form, and effect that had been completely rescaled and detached from material sources. Material properties themselves became expressive (an expression that was also manufactured much like the materials); the way façade related to structure or frame related to enclosure was regulated not by necessity, but by tasteful artfulness. With performance and technological development as the architect's only limitations, the composition of architecture became bound with the selection, application and detailing of materials.

Over and above our fundamental socio-ecological shift, new fabrication and construction technologies have severed the equally illusory tie between the "natural," so-called inherent properties, and architectural applications. In other words, compressive strengths, bendability, tensile limits and other "innate" physical properties no longer define our relationship to a dwindling material palette. The mediation of fabrication technologies has multiplied and fragmented what had seemed to be stable application-traditions: when tree trunks cease to be automatically understood as cylindrical fibrous bundles and can instead be conceived as stacks of veneer sheets laminated without consideration of wood grain, or sawdust molded and pressed together with chemicals to achieve dimensional stability, we find that our nostalgic default material understanding has

----

been fundamentally destabilized. In the context of our reluctant comprehension of scarcity, we have eschewed the presumed link between performance and the pseudo-science of natural material properties. (Performance has become a method of rationalizing expressionism.) This is a necessary attempt at countering our shrinking ecological and economic purchasing power. Our expanded technical abilities have allowed glass, steel, plastic and concrete to become almost endlessly malleable, engineered lumber accumulates smaller members into any shape and span, woodchips and sawdust are recycled as OSB and MDF, and even masonry has found new formal and technical applications. The emergence of digital fabrication processes has similarly driven a needed expansion of our methods of production and fabrication. Anything can be cut with ease and precision. Materials can be bent, rolled and cast with seemingly infinite flexibility. The design application limits of a particular material are no longer seen as inherent within the material itself, but rather as functions of surrounding processes. Tools and materials have become inseparable and indistinct from one another. There is no material that is unmediated.

Twenty plus years ago, the notion of "material" was aligned with the so-called humanist tradition of the craftsperson. Material consideration was not "avant-garde" or recognized as a part of a conceptual project. Instead it was relegated to a technical discourse in which the history of architecture was reduced to a pedantic history of building, of materials used and the repertoire of joinery and construction techniques. Because this narrative was seen as appropriated by capitalist production and commodification, some sought to eliminate the agency of material in architectural signification: to produce architectural meaning capable of amortizing physical considerations. This was how architecture could become "conceptual." The hope of "cardboard architecture"[3] was that a formal language divorced from material immanence could uniquely negate capitalist appropriations of aesthetic power. This position is no longer tenable. Today we must come to terms with our knowledge that there is no clear objective mind–body split, that we are part of the fields of matter, materials are matter, and matter is always connected to all other matter, the notion of negating materiality is no longer ontologically possible. Architects and architecture are part of mutually interdependent material networks composed of neurons, trees, electricity, finance, et cetera, all together. We operate in the context of simultaneous and dynamic forces to which all matter is subject and with which all matter participates, amplifying and mitigating and being amplified or mitigated in turn. Today, we have to learn to look at the old "normal," "natural," and "traditional" as just as artificial as cardboard architecture, and at cardboard architecture as just as inescapably "real" – composed of real matter – as the rest. In other words, we can no longer locate the avant-garde in the myth of ephemerality; since "what is not there" is always actually "there," architecture cannot seek resistance in refusal. Today, we need to construct an inclusive architecture through matter.

The past decade has shifted towards a more practical model of architecture. Pedagogy has engaged a new literalism of architectural technique and production that focuses on material performance, to work through the real instead of ignoring it. As the architectural discipline begins what we can again term a more direct relationship with materiality, however, we continue to lack a way of understanding materials as protagonists rather than subservient to form. Our disciplinary challenge today, therefore, is to invent new narratives which help us make sense of denaturalized, destabilized, and contingent matter-as-material, matter-as-social, and matter-as-fabrication-technologies. Our re-emerging interest in physical form and visceral effects is a way of playing with a post-postmodern need for realism and a post-digital need for quantifiable techniques and evaluation.

What does it really mean to say that we operate within mutually interdependent networks of matter? Would we not see innovation today as fundamentally manipulative rather than extractive and/or constructive: that it is about deploying altering sequences within existing relationships? Understanding the interface of design and process *as manipulative* helps establish a new series of operational logics in which matter-as-material, matter-as-human, and matter-as-fabrication are all identified participants. Grouped under three primary collections, their loose identifications are: *monolithic* (planes and surfaces with continuous, there-or-not-there integrity), *unit* (aggregation, chunking, and field effect), and *vector* (bone, member, trajectory). An equivalent trifecta of material, process and assembly logic in each of these approaches permits design and form to be generatively synthetic, resulting in a new conceptualism that positions materiality as a procedural medium in which and through which we work. Understanding the interface of design and process as manipulative also requires us to revise our traditional scalar narratives. When transitions from element to element and position to position are no longer ignored as givens but instead problematized as creative potential, part-to-whole systems of composition are scrutinized. In other words, the singular scale of an image is exposed as incomplete: part, whole, surface and unit become equally available for consideration at multiple scales, and Beaux-Arts overarching compositional models are undermined in favor of scalar and discrete situational relationships.

These emergent and required reorganizations of architectural thinking and action through matter, reveal both our current opportunities and our mounting debts with greater clarity. In responding to these issues rather than avoiding their implications, the practices and projects highlighted in this book propose the possibility of a conceptual architecture of substance, of matter – accepting that there was never another alternative – by manipulating and deploying an array of innovative interactions with, through and in our unavoidable material circumstances.

Organization of this book

Matter is a text focused on the pedagogy of material exploration as the premise for the making of architecture. By confronting the question of what are shared current architectural obsessions between various practices and contemporary pedagogy and beginning with material, the book revolves around physical material making and design decisions that emerge from material interaction.

Focusing on matter as the premise of design exploration, this text identifies and graphically illustrates how material and modern tectonics have defined the formal and conceptual premise for the making of architecture. As a catalog consisting of diverse viewpoints emerging from the modernist sensibilities, the articles illustrate contemporary formal and spatial repercussions emerging from the physicality of material manipulation and the intrinsic design decisions that emerge from material interaction. As a catalog of thought and methodology, it presents material as the matter of architecture – that which makes the form, the space, the performance and ultimately the experience that is architecture.

The book is organized into discrete categories to try to bundle conceptual underpinnings of the diverse authors, into nine parts. Identified for primary trajectory, not to be divisive or singular in reading, the work in any one topic contains lateral similarities and hybridizations that run across the diverse classification allowing for specific and collective readings.

The new relationship established through the re-conceptualization of material roles is the premise of this book. An anthology of contemporary practices, this book establishes a generation of architects that are operating along similar allegiances. Varied in technique and scale, method and intent, their collective connection to the physical translation of idea into matter makes them a generation fascinated with thinking through making. Challenging technology and physicality to further the relationship of material to architecture, their convictions on the inter-relations of material to space and experience with equal importance allow their work to have the litmus of the actual. Their design method does not necessarily require a constructed resultant, but the physicality of the real rather is ingrained in their thinking and process. The method of working is ultra real, demanding a physical response to the outcome and challenging the thinking out of the abstract and into the bluntly real. The delicacy and intelligence of this translation are the efficacy of their thinking. The foresight of this generation of emerging practitioners stems from their innately digitally savvy design methods allowing a synthetic engagement and permitting their work to move beyond the formalist trapping of method and technique. The result is the derivation of new boundaries, techniques not grounded in virtual but physical media, engaging craft and technology to hybridize architecture and making. This direct relationship allows an interest in the material proper, the process of its manipulation and the assembly technique, all as issues to produce from an effect. The collection of participants included is an elite group of designers. Each selected for their design excellence and their material affinities, the conceptual spectrum presented includes case studies in process, effect, tectonic systems, digital methods, pedagogy, and experience.

- - - - - - - - - - - - - - - - - -

Categories of thought

The book is framed by four conversations: Stan Allen, Neil Denari, Michael Maltzan, and Nader Tehrani. Each establishing a collective vision of the issue, their perspectives offer an eloquent overview of their own work and thinking, bridging academia and practice with ease.

The sub-categories of: **Matter Design**, addressing the formal and functional implications of building materials as process applications and the formal implications of material composition; **Matter Processes**, that engages fabrication, technology and making directly; **Matter Precedent**, that deploys case studies in material application and conceptual detailing of design; **Matter Detail**, as the relation between pieces through connections; **Matter Ecology**, as the material and issues of sustainability; **Matter Pedagogy**, an examination of the role of materiality in design education; **Matter Sensations**, as the role of affect and effect; each illustrate the sub-themes of materiality, and **Matter Surface**, the role of information, responsive materials, and responsive skins.

As a collection, this book serves as a brief snapshot in contemporary practices and thought surrounding materiality, fabrication and architecture. Its diversity, both of method and outcome, is intentionally broad to illustrate the variety of approaches, topics and methodological veins. These case studies represent a distinct opportunity for architects who think and work through an architecture constructed of Matter.

Notes

1   Adolf Loos, "Von der Sparsamkeit," in Bohuslav Markalous, ed., *Wohnungskulture*, 213, 1924.

2   See Peter Sloterdijk, *Terror from the Air*, trans. Amy Patton and Steve Corcoran (Los Angeles: Semiotext(e), 2007), pp. 88–96. [Originally published in 2002 as *Luftbeben* by Editions Suhrkamp, Frankfurt.]

3   Peter Eisenman, "Cardboard Architecture: House 1," in *Five Architects* (New York: Wittenborn, 1972).

Part I
Matter Conversed

These fireside chats discussing the role of materiality began a conversation with significant designers on both the east and west coasts. In order to break down the traditional formalities and pre-prepared answers of an introductory or framing essay, these interviews were employed to ignite a conversation about materiality. These figures were identified as fore-fathers of the issues and the generation of thought that the text represents. Attempting to address the communities of themes, methods and participants within the book, each of the conversations represents a distinct touchstone of materiality: theory, systemization, representation, application, discourse, and effect. Though each of these issues is similarly discussed as themes in each conversation, their significance and approach present a distinct vantage of each architect and their approach to materiality. In each conversation, however, the role of materiality proves to be a universal almost spiritual connector among the collective community of architects as intrinsically rooted in the shared craft of the profession, but is locally and individually taken with disparate vantages and agendas. These conversations reveal the themes of contemporary practice and reveal the position and interest of the participants, they spark the issues of the collection and illustrate the dialog and thinking that have led us to where we are and hint at where we are going.

Stan Allen
Neil Denari
Michael Maltzan
Nader Tehrani

Interview 1

SA = Stan Allen; MM = Michael Meredith.

MM: We are trying to frame a certain pedagogical discourse that is of a particular moment, and perhaps a particular generation, where there is a return to thinking about materiality. If materiality was at one point the enemy of the formal, humanist project, it is not any more. It is probably closer to an avant-garde trajectory, that is to say, materiality is now used to find new methods of non-composition through rethinking the part to whole relations of "tasteful" composition. Materiality provides ways to destroy the objectness of architecture. It is a tool for undermining the status quo. There are now many different groups in relation to material. There is the Aalto-esque camp, there are those who are looking for new kinds of logics within materials, and there are those who are looking for new ways of thinking about organization through material.

SA: What I found refreshing about looking over the table of contents of this book is that it has a generational frame, and it seems that most of the people in this current generation do not see the opposition between material and form as a dilemma. By contrast, that opposition certainly framed my thinking when I was trying to formulate ideas about what I came to call "material practices" back in the early 1990s. At that time, there really was an opposition between the points of view of, on the one hand, someone like Kenneth Frampton, Peter Zumthor, or Juhani Pallasmaa, for whom materiality, the concrete, the haptic, and the tactile were ends in themselves. These people were completely skeptical of any form of abstraction. On the other hand, the opposing camp of Eisenman and even, at that time, Hejduk in a certain sense, thought the fundamental building blocks of architecture were formal, or representational, and not material. And it's important to remember that at that time, the lingering notion that you could do architecture without ever building anything was still a viable, alternative route.

MM: I still think it is a viable route. Even just to be thinking about material, you are already part of what Hal Foster calls the real; you are already dealing with life, not just abstract representation.

SA: Well, partly why I hesitated with the Hejduk example is that. It is true that Hejduk built very little, but everything he drew was buildable in comparison to, let's say, the Libeskind *Micromegas*, which were impossible to construct.

MM: They were pure representation.

SA: The opposition between an architecture of pure representation, on the one hand, and the Frampton critique of representation in favor of materiality, on the other, in my mind, is just non-productive. And to me it is refreshing that most of the people of your generation do not see this as a tremendous dilemma to be resolved. They are very comfortable toggling back and forth between the actual and the virtual. I do not want to just assign that comfort to the emergence of digital technology; the change of thinking is more important than the change in technology. Nonetheless, engagement with the tools of computation has certainly facilitated the intellectual agility of toggling back and forth because that is exactly what you do with a computer. I think the other cause of this refreshing change is the critique of what I call discursive practice: architecture as built discourse that holds itself up to the criteria of other media. These other forms – film, writing, video, and so on – are much more transparent in their means of communication than architecture. If you try and hold architecture up to the criteria of these fluid, discursive forms of media, it is always going to come up short. You are going to feel like you are working with a tool that is very blunt, and if you do not take account of architecture's bluntness, slowness, and lack of transparency as a discursive medium, then you are always going to feel hobbled.

MM: But discourse on architecture is not always meant to clarify the architectural object. For example, the avant-garde of architectural production was all about film – you can link Tschumi, Eisenman, and Koolhaas through a desire to create an architecture of film. The problem, of course, with this craft-oriented analysis is that film was a formal condition of repetition for some, and for others is was a visceral event. For Koolhaas, film was a surreal experience, a way of overlapping multiple realities. The form of the craft was used to communicate very different kinds of content. There could be even more ways of thinking about film today through material. If we flatten discourse in order to find clarity, what is produced? a horrible equivocation of everything. At that moment we hit a frictionless dead end. Then, inevitably, we just build. I am not willing to give up the discursive; I do not want to turn in to a *mere* craftsman, although I am a craftsman, of sorts.

SA: There is another issue here, and it is not so much about specificity of disciplines as it is about paying attention to the capacity of the discipline to produce certain concepts. For a lot of people – Greg Lynn, Sanford Kwinter, myself – in the early 1990s, Deleuze was a very important figure, and the shift from Derrida, who is a philosopher of language, to Deleuze, who is a philosopher of matter, had a great impact. People looking at "Field Conditions"[1] from the outside may think it is just another part of the larger movement of post-structuralism. If they do, they did not pay attention to the difference between Derrida and Deleuze. For us, at that moment, it was a very important difference. Thinking about Deleuze's books on cinema, for example, I am going to build on your comments on film for a moment. For Deleuze, the goal is not to apply philosophical concepts to a reading of cinema, but instead to pay attention to the way cinema – through its own internal rules and procedures and methods – actually produces philosophical concepts. You can still be deeply theoretical and discursive about your discipline, but you do not have to fall back on what, to me, is a suspect intellectual construct – some vague corpus of ideas called theory, which you then make specific relative to architecture, film, painting, or whatever. Deleuze suggested that every discipline is capable of producing its own theoretical and philosophical concepts through means that are specific to each discipline, and thus you end up producing different ideas in architecture than in film or painting. This methodology breaks down the false dilemma between the discursive and the practical, in that you pay very close attention to the capacity of architecture to produce ideas, rather than applying or importing ideas from the outside.

MM: I once had a conversation with Eisenman about what he did, and he said: "It was very easy for me because I had a PhD first." I thought, that is the most depressing thing I've ever heard: I had my theory figured out first and then I did the work. Theory and work should be much more fluid – more like criticism. Practice and theory are strangely concrete categories. If practice is slow, I think theory should be fast, but the reverse seems to be true right now. I love Eisenman, but I am also very troubled by him.

SA: I think that is his role in the field.

MM: For me, Eisenman is not one to listen to but rather to watch. He operates much differently from what he says, and the way he operates is far more interesting.

SA: This generation has a great deal of facility in working with and manipulating form, which they, in some ways, learned from Eisenman. At the same time, they are skeptical of Eisenman. Famously – going back 40 years now – for him, the drawing, the model, and the buildings were just one among many possible representations of an idea. So it did not matter if the building was built out of cardboard, and when the photograph of the finished building was confused with a photograph of a model, he was fine with that.

MM: Architecture was somehow separated from embodiment. It's a horrible idea. Inevitably you *have* to think of material, even if you are just drawing. Not that material is inherent in drawing, but that it is in some way stuck to it.

SA: I think it works the other way around too. I have been reading Richard Sennett's book on the craftsman.[2] There is one particular point where Sennett talks about the loss of craft in architecture, and he blames digital technology. I am part of a generation that learned digital technology very late, so I cannot call myself an expert at all, but to say that there is no craftsmanship in digital technology is crazy. I can look at computer models done by different people in my office and see that some of them are beautifully crafted while others are a mess. Exactly the same concepts of a craftsman organizing his or her workspace, taking care with execution and finish, as well as the idea of making your own tools to perform a job apply in digital work. In a shop, somebody makes a jig to hold a model piece, and in the digital realm there are people who write routines to manipulate form. They are the same. You can see the exact same values operating in the digital medium.

MM: If anything, there is the craft to understanding the actual world's material properties in digital modeling, but then craft is still a word that makes most people cringe. I get a little nervous about it. When you take Frampton, and the avant-garde – Eisenman, Hejduk – and you put all of them together, you end up with this new, strange soufflé of ways of working. Most of us do not think about it that deeply while working. Maybe there is something nice about finding tools that nobody else knows how to use and exploiting them. This soufflé produces a new generational methodology, but the discourse of craftsmanship is still a tricky thing.

SA: Maybe it is a question of parsing the generations too finely. I belong to a generation that was pretty much educated by Eisenman, Hejduk, Libeskind, and Tschumi in the 1980s, when there was this huge sense of doubt and skepticism and, in a material sense, very little work. We tended to do speculative work, competitions, early on and have only more recently made the transition to practice.

MM: This current generation is more interested in practicing first.

SA: But this is what I am saying about parsing generations too finely because the generation *in between*, the early 1990s, moved very quickly to an entrepreneurial mode of practice. My sense of your generation is that you do not see a strong distinction between a gallery installation, a temporary construction, or a commission for a client – or, for that matter, working in digital media, film or drawing. All of those things are operating on a similar plane. There is less of a sense in the current generation that – as you get with SHoP – where you have a set of very powerful tools, learned from the previous generation, which are now going to be applied in a very concrete, real-world, market-driven situation.

MM: SHoP did open up territory for us, which is very important, but you can get too removed from a discursive mode, which is also problematic. You start to put everything into terms of money. I think that is a really bad place for architecture to be. I also think it is a problem if you put everything in terms of sustainability. I do not see it as an enemy, but rather want to temper it with other models that have been given to us through the avant-garde trajectory. For me the autonomy of architecture exists, but it is not formal. It's social. I am not interested in theory without images. I would probably be more interested in criticism than theory, ultimately, as a mode, because it cannot get rid of the object. The question everyone is debating now is just how influential the outside is on architecture. I think it is incredibly influential, but what I think is most influential is the art world, music, film, and writing – culture in general.

SA: Take a building like the *Seattle Public Library*. Clearly, you can have an incredibly well-developed conversation within the discourse about it, but part of the intelligence of OMA is their ability to operate simultaneously in multiple registers. We can have a complex technical discussion about the diagrid as a strategy for dealing with seismic loads, the move away from the free plan, the separation of the skin from the structure, and the integration of the structure into the skin. However, 99 percent of the people who use the library each day do not care about that. The success of OMA is their ability to deploy specifically architectural expertise in service of broadly legible effects – architectural, urbanistic, cultural, and social.

MM: And, frankly, most of those architectural strategies already existed in late modernism. Koolhaas and Herzog & de Meuron have arguably had more influence on thinking about materials: Koolhaas through large models, where you try to make it as close to real as possible – even if materiality is just a Xerox copy – and Herzog & de Meuron through prototyping, where everything is mocked up at full scale. These strategies have had incredible influence on a generation who have had to think outside of the American dilemma produced by Eisenman.

SA: This is one of the reasons why these figures make Eisenman so nervous.

MM: They should! There is always the sheer power of built architecture – the thing itself – regardless of discourse. Eisenman is not a builder type – he does not seem to care about making buildings, at any cost. He is happy with the grids. The desire for a non-figurative architecture is something that is still around as a faded trajectory of the avant-garde and as a strategy of non-composition, and it is something we are all still interested in, even the younger generation working with digital technology. Materiality, however, is a relatively new way to pursue the desire for non-figurative architecture, and a way to deal with architectural materiality that is not a craftsmanship or humanist model has not yet been completely figured out.

SA: Two things. First, I recently did an interview with Mansila Tunon, and they used a phrase that really stuck in my mind: "non-centralized expansive systems capable of becoming specific at any given point." Although a little bit awkward in the phrasing, this is actually quite provocative as a response to the grid. They describe their own work *MUSAC*, the museum they recently completed in Leon, as the moment they discovered this. They are an interesting test case in this discussion because they come out of Moneo's office. Their work has very often been seen in terms of materiality and tectonics, and they have an incredibly impressive record of getting stuff built in a super-convincing way. Yet their work method is also super-diagrammatic and very playful. The capacity to go back and forth between the diagrammatic and the material is remarkable. The other thing – what I would say particularly for *our* generation – is a suggestion: do not think about specific materials. Do not think about concrete, glass, or steel; think about material properties: think about heaviness, lightness, translucency, and transparency. Those kinds of properties are much more important than the particular stone you choose. The theoretical framework for this that is helpful for me is Gregory Bateson's discussions about information and information exchange. Oppositional readings would see form, organization, and material, on one side, and communication and information, on the other – Bateson collapses this difference. His famous definition of information as "the difference that makes a difference" continues to resonate with me, and gives you a way out of the form/content (or form/program) dilemmas that have haunted recent architecture. We can talk about the form of a form. For Bateson, form is information, and you can talk about a complex formal configuration as one with a high degree of embedded information.

MM: Could you describe the difference between information and text?

SA: Text requires a linguistic framework for translation, a series of agreed-upon conventions, which are in turn socially or culturally based. Information exchange, by contrast happens on a one-to-one basis, a more immediate and material basis, as in the opening or closing of a circuit. What for me is valuable about Bateson's model is that you can talk about something, for example, as familiar as the pitched roof: on the one hand, we could see it through the traditional semiotic lens as the symbol of the house, which is in turn deeply embedded in history and culture. Or we could simply think of it as a geometrical or material configuration with a certain performative capacity – let's say, to shed rain. The information model collapses this distinction. When rain falls on the roof, all the material characteristics of that roof – if it is porous, if it is rough, the steepness of the pitch – can be defined as embedded information, and there is in turn a process of information exchange between that embedded information and the raindrops falling on the roof. Or you could see the semiotic dimension too as part of an information exchange; Bateson was trained as an anthropologist, after all, and he saw this kind of exchange too as something that could be recorded and analyzed. You could see all that as information – cultural and material – in very abstract, almost calculable terms rather than reiterating the distinction between the material and the symbolic condition of the house. Bateson collapses the formal distinction between material information exchanges and semiotic information exchanges. It is the ability of Bateson's theory to cross the material and the semiotic that for me makes it very powerful, and it is not accidental that the origin of this theory and the cybernetic theories of the 1950s and 1960s are so closely related to computation.

MM: What is happening in architecture right now in terms of other cultural production? Let's take art production, which no longer has the same status in architecture as it did with Clement Greenberg, or even Colin Rowe. If there was an artistic medium for postmodern architecture, it was the planometric medium of painting. Those architects chose painting over sculpture as a medium to understand architecture, and that turned everything into a compositional picture plane. They understood architecture as essentially two-dimensional. Either it was façade as a two-dimensional composition, or it was plan as a two-dimensional composition. Consequently, they were never able to get to the discourse that was had in the 1960s on qualities, where architects considered, for example, the quality of weight in architecture in the same way Richard Serra did with sculpture.

SA: I actually wrote something where I made exactly the opposite argument. I am skeptical of the notion that architecture has a natural affinity to sculpture because both are three-dimensional and material. At some deep level maybe I do have an allegiance to Colin Rowe.

MM: I tend towards painting myself, in a certain way, but I am skeptical of this …

SA: My argument is that because of the abstract notational quality that painting and architectural drawing share, there is a common territory. Painting remains for me invested in some kind of transformation or translation, the suggestion of something beyond the actual material artifact, whereas with sculpture – admittedly not all contemporary sculpture – there is more emphasis on the artifact itself. That creates one of those impossible aspirations for architects – we will never achieve the immediacy and presence of certain sculptural works. Serra, in particular, seems to me a very suspect model for architects for precisely that reason. I am not only thinking about issues of use and construction, which always impose a complexity on architecture that would make the formal reduction of his work impossible to achieve, but the fact that we are always going to be dependent on others to execute our work and therefore in my mind, need to look toward art forms that are more abstract and transformational, like music or painting.

MM: But in the discipline at this moment, the plan is a kind of ghost. It really is unimportant to students at this moment and probably to lots of young practitioners. The diagram has trumped the plan.

SA: You are probably right. There is probably an equivalent generational break in the art world as well. My connections and affiliations in the art world tend to be painters, but there is a tremendous amount of very interesting production in the art world that simply does not take the inherited disciplines as a problem any more.

MM: I am very interested in how we locate architecture. If architecture has medium specificity, then how do we think about medium today? The only way I can produce a survey of architectural production at this moment is to say that everyone has turned to niches, and the only way I can describe these niches is through their status as mediums. There is always a problem in describing the medium of architecture because we do not produce the thing. Architecture is the most mediated of art forms. At a certain point, in academia but also in your generation (if you think of Scott Cohen or Office DA), you had to claim a medium. That was what you did. I'm geometry, I'm pattern, I'm digital blobs – you are claiming a medium status through which we can read your architecture, and the medium produced subjectivities, ways in which we look at and appreciate architecture. You could rewrite the history of the discipline through each specific medium condition. In our generation, we do not have that kind of specificity. We are much happier to sometimes do a video and sometimes do a painting or an installation. What does that mean? I think it means that material has a different status, and this new status becomes incredibly important if we think of material as a medium condition.

SA: The media theorist Friedrich Kittler has suggested that there is no such thing as "multi-media" any more because everything is now translated into bits and pixels. The materiality – and therefore the medium specificity – of the phonograph record or the celluloid film have been dissolved into an abstract and self-similar field of ones and zeros. In architecture, it does not matter if you are drawing on velum, mylar, or toilet paper, because media is now an output question, not a production question. I want to bring Alejandro Zaero-Polo into the discussion, partly because I have been thinking about the design research he is doing around the building envelope here at Princeton. It is a very interesting self-critique: he has suggested that the exclusive attention to the planimetric dimension and horizontal connectivity is insufficient as an architectural project, thus requiring him to turn his attention back to the vertical plane. Of course, there are a lot of things that go into it beyond that critique. It is a practical disciplinary question, an effort on his part to respond to the market conditions of architecture that very often give architects a volume and take away the plan. The marketing consultants and the technical people are going to define many of the variables that used to belong to architectural plan making. It is situated within a large political argument, too. He calls into question the naïve assumption that architects could ever make political boundaries disappear simply by wishing them away – which was the underlying assumption of the architecture of "flows" so prevalent in the 1990s. But it's also a reassertion of a very specific aspect of architectural expertise: the suggestion here is that if architects are expert at anything, they are experts at limits and boundaries.

MM: It is a kind of flattening ...

SA: It is a different kind of flattening – Alejandro's suggestion is that embedded in the thickness of the envelope are a whole series of social, political, economic or technical variables. It's not a paper-thin façade any more, but a thick, working membrane. I would say that's what differentiates his argument from Venturi's idea of the decorated shed.

MM: If anything, at the moment, we are part of this flattening of everything. What does it produce in the end? And where does it take us?

SA: In this context, what is interesting to me about it is that it suggests a return to the vertical plane: that architecture can once again take account of images icons and figures.

MM: Alejandro is not afraid of symbolism and iconography, which is interesting, because the 1990s were about destroying it. Distort it, repeat it, do whatever you can to avoid the image. The problem was that the product is still an image. I see students now who make things that they think are somehow avoiding semiotics, but they are just creating a different semiotic.

SA: Exactly. In terms of my own education, you are absolutely correct. Eisenman is incapable of thinking in any dimension other than plan, but Hejduk – who also, by the way, was a brilliant plan-maker – in his later work, became all about the iconic figure of the building on the landscape, elevations, and his famous silhouette drawings. I locate myself in a slightly different generation. I do not feel as capable of moving so freely between different media, although it is something I incorporate into the office by taking advantage of people who can do that. I have a huge distrust of animations, for example. My problem with animations is that as film they are generally pretty lame.

MM: I actually like animations, but I do not think they have properly been done yet. They are too commercial. I do think you produce subjectivities and constituencies through your representation. The biggest thing that most people have had to deal with recently is photography because the architectural world revolves around magazines, and the internet – primarily for bandwidth reasons – is still mostly images. But inevitably architects are going to have to deal with animation, moving images, as a way to communicate and build constituencies. I was just on thesis reviews at the GSD and I can tell you, the plans were horrible, but the images were stunning. So what do you do at that point? In China they would be okay with it – just hand in the images and they build it. Is that okay? I do not know what it means for us as a profession when we evacuate the plan.

SA: I think you are right about the need to come to terms with the moving image. The problem is that the development of animation technology has all been market-driven. All of the conventions for animations have developed in service to the client, even in the schools. Twenty years ago when I was in school, the drawings that you made for an academic presentation and the drawings you might make for a client presentation were completely different. They are almost identical nowadays. How can we make better use of this new technology without falling back into these familiar routines?

MM: Artificial light in computers really changed things because it makes everything so seductively real and polished – it looks like magazine culture, and that is where everyone wants to be. How these problems of representation affect materiality is a question that we're still figuring out.

Notes

1   Stan Allen, "Field Conditions" in *Points + Lines: Diagrams and Projects for the City* (Princeton, NJ: Princeton Architectural Press, 1999).
2   Richard Sennett, *The Craftsman* (New Haven, CT: Yale University Press, 2008).

Interview 2

ND = Neil Denari; GPB = Gail Peter Borden.

GPB: We are interviewing a number of architects, of which you are one, and including Michael Maltzan, Stan Allen, and Nader Tehrani, to discuss their relationship to the manifold aspects of materiality. Within this realm, there are many issues I would like to touch on: issues of scale, representation, tactility, space, geometry, ideas about pedagogy, although I'm not sure if this text draws too much into academia although almost everybody in it is in some way an academic. Again, this text is grappling with issues of materiality and contemporary architecture, and we've talked briefly about these generational waves of history, philosophy, digital media and now arriving at a manifestation of these in materiality. What is your take on the idea of material and associated with that a process as an architectural generator? Does that resonate with you as an architect?

ND: I'm not so sure I would be the first person one would think about *vis-à-vis* materiality, because historically this concern suggests a sensualist approach. I'm really at this point a geometric sensualist and a kind of material expediter in that the materials we typically work with are selected for their ability to accentuate form. For me, materials have three basic conditions, of which the first two are most important: the visual phenomena of the surface, its workability (cutting, bending, shaping, etc.) and finally, its tactility. When you get into issues of the way in which the visual works, let's say, in my work, which isn't about tactility but at the same time it is deeply tactile at the level of process to construct with: tools and people coming together in various locations and sites in order to assemble something. That couldn't be more tactile but it doesn't necessarily predict whether or not someone wants to run their hands over the surface.

GPB: For me, what's intriguing about your work, and in particular your unbuilt work through your books, especially *Gyroscopic Horizons,*[1] but going all the way back to *Building: Machines (Pamphlet Architecture),*[2] where there is a very strong agenda in terms of the media, that evolved from a manual agenda to a digital agenda, but in both of these realms there is an intense and really precise, consistent and relentless idea about tectonics. In all of those projects you never release it to just a formal investigation, there is always a relationship back to a handrail, to a corrugation, to a batten, and that kind of tectonic to me as a student and an architect has always been incredibly interesting, and to me that is one major reason that I think of you as a very material person because, given the hyperflexibility of the virtual realm, you still feel the burden or responsibility to somehow bring that with you. For me, I think that is a sophistication of your work being able to now bridge to a whole new chapter which is the built realm, which is really now where you are almost exclusively operating.

ND: That's just because basically I am a very concrete person. In terms of the experimental aspect of architecture, which I personally think is a very wide-ranging aspect, I could never bring myself to entertain the ambiguous or the obscure as a kind of deferring or delaying or forestalling of an inevitable facthood. And my deal was always about facthood as far as I could take it within any context, whether it was making a drawing, or using high-end software very early on to bring a phenomenological impact

---

to the image, even though it was less still about sensuality, since I didn't use texture mapping in the early digital work, but probably more about old school techniques of using light and shadow to dramatize surface. The surfaces themselves weren't super-articulated but how you might build them and obviously all the armatures and infrastructure were dead on in there. And for me that is a pretty personal thing because it wasn't like I was doing that to make a counter-proposal to the proposition of the day. I was just carrying out my interests, on one level, that's all I do as an architect. In that sense, the story is maybe becoming a little more revealed in reverse as I build. I always wanted to build. It's not a defensive point of view, but if you can read that into all of the work as being incredibly latent, because the other thing was, I never wanted to suffer a crisis of translation. All of this was not about forestalling. It was about annexing the future more and more to be able to get to the point of feeling professionally and architecturally aware and confident.

GPB: So you have clearly this intense formal agenda, this intense geometric agenda, what would you do if someone came to you with a material premise? Have you had a client, or if someone said I love block or I love Plexiglas, or whatever it would be, I'm curious, at what point that comes into play? You have a form, but you are always thinking of that form relative to physics. There is always this idea of how you can make a form or implement something, but it is still form first or geometry first. Has it ever happened? Or what would you do? Would you be prepared? Would you not want that? Would it be a positive thing? Or would you just be ambivalent, and suddenly the kind of parameters change but the agenda can still work with it? To me, the *High Line Project* in a way feels like it sets that up. I feel like when you presented that there were so many kinds of constraints that just came out of the condition, both programmatic and economic in this funky site with all of the contextual stuff you have to deal with and the realities of the structural envelope and the innate complexity, it feels like you were almost given all of this weight and you have to embrace it somehow. Is it jujitsu where you use the strength of your partner against them? It seems like all of those things got embraced and brilliantly brought into the fold in an incredibly articulate package but one that is unique to your work, meaning it is the next step, but also it is so grounded. It's not like you lost anything in any way, it only made it better somehow.

ND: Yeah, I think so. But going back to the earlier comment, if one were presented with a material agenda or in some of the research we will present ourselves with a material agenda like concrete, which is obviously not a limiting material.

GPB: But the formwork becomes one ...

ND: Yeah, of course, there is a limit on formwork and so forth and how you deal with curvature, to actually thinking about the way in which formwork goes together, because concrete's just concrete, it's all about what it flows into. But if somebody came and said I want you to make something out of concrete block, for instance, if it was essentially presented as a kind of limitation literally through and through, I would think that client would not come to me. First of all, I would say they're not taking advantage of our talent or research, so I kind of have to take that off the table. It's not a clever answer, in a way, it's more of a clear answer. If somebody said, I want you to build a concrete block box and you can do whatever you want with drywall on the inside, I'll do it in a second. At some level there is a project, and for sure I am interested in geometry, not at all costs and not at all levels of complexity, because I think what we do is relatively controlled. The apparent effect is so much greater than the control placed on it, and that's the hallmark in a way of what we do. Besides the fact that it is reductive in certain ways, it is expansive phenomenologically and expansive in terms of affect. That is something that if you are handing out advice, you'd say get to that point, because then you can potentially build a lot, given the fact that if you receive a commission you can carry it out and probably exceed expectations in that sense. And that has been the case with us. I think materiality is obviously connected to taste, speaking from the client side or speaking from the consumer side, it is clearly connected to taste or connected to certain ideas of status or familiarity or associations. I don't know if I mentioned Baudrillard and *The System of Objects,* but that has been a guidebook for me, which was written in 1968.[3] It explores the transition from wood and older materials to newer materials like plastic and glass and so forth and the one-off nature of an antique versus the productive nature of factory-assembled elements. I feel like right now our work isn't about producing the antique but producing the one-off and doing it with materials that are less connected to traditional concepts of warmth. The geometry at times kind of supplants, in an abstract way, ideas of embrace that materials traditionally do, like wood, for instance. That is also something that's been foregrounded since the installation in Gallery MA when the owner of Toto, the company that sponsored it, walked into literally the first thing I was able to build in 1996, he walked in and he said, "I don't know what it is but I feel very comfortable." That might have been noise to the avant-gardiest's ears, like, "Aren't you upset? Aren't you agitated?" The fact that there was some alien quality that could be compelling was a signal for me that, from the point of view of geometry, color, and abstraction, one could generate a sensibility that ultimately attracts rather than repels. In our banks we were asked to use wood as a means to generate comfort. In fact, we proposed almost every color you can imagine and it was always rejected because they asked that wood be used to be the mediator between the odd geometry and the humble but wealthy patron of the bank. I have to say, that at the moment, it was disappointing because we had never used wood in an interior and I thought we needed to uphold the project of resisting forms of tradition in that way. In other words, by over-coding it with the fluid geometry, we could produce conditions of attraction, embrace, and comfort through those means, and for some clients that might work, but they finally said they could not go that far. When I went to Nagoya to see the first project completed, what struck me was that the wood just seemed brown, a color, not a particular material. That reading came primarily from the fact that the wood is actually a thin veneer applied like wallpaper, which is about as close as can you can get to texture mapping, which is even more strangely artificial than if it would have been painted cyan. So that was a moment where materiality, especially as it is and as it was read graphically, it fell right into the agenda of what we were looking to do with color.

GPB: Why such a desire for such an otherworldliness like the movement away from the grain? Was the thought that it would interfere? Or that it was an issue that you didn't need for your agenda?

ND: I always relegated wood to being literally just the element that was pan-culturally referred to as warm.

GPB: So there was too much of that assumption coming in.

ND: Yes, basically, I wanted to reject that. That was my latent avant-garde project and having gone through it, it actually opened up the world of materials as a set of possibilities, although I am not somebody who just wants to dabble in materials for their own autonomous qualities. We will look at something, but I am still more interested in, for example, the profiles one can perforate aluminum with. So let's say geometry or something graphic to me is still a primary agenda as opposed to having pink shag carpet drive everything about the next project. In terms of geometry, then the frame is immediately invoked relative to structural systems, i.e. steel vs. concrete, and whether or not either of these materials will also operate as skin.

GPB: Or the process itself. The perforation process to you is not so interesting, it is more the geometry of the perforation, the effect of the perforation, it is not necessarily the control of the machine and the systemization of all that.

- - - - - - - - - - - - - - - - - -

ND: After understanding the capabilities of the machines, I'm personally more interested in the design possibilities than the spectacle of the fabrication process.

GPB: That brought up a couple things, one is this idea of color, which is really interesting. How do you approach that? It's been with you always, but really introduces itself in the jump from the hand to the computer. Isn't that the moment of introduction? Prior to that it is essentially black and white with at moments diagrammatic highlighting of red or orange or a splash, but really when it becomes dominant is in that moment. What was that? That's also the point at which you, correct me if I'm wrong, but that's when cortex and that language come into play. The color bar, I don't want to say graphic, because that graphic aspect has always been there, but the almost print graphic came into play and the idea of color really stepped up, and it's still present in the renderings, but it is also present in the wonderful *Alan-Voo House Addition*, like the subtle tone, it's something you don't shy away from while others do. What does color mean? How do you make those decisions? What is it? Is it effectual?

ND: I've always tried to see if there were ways in which you could outline a legitimate, culturally aligned conversation about color, even if for most this ambition would normally be superseded by issues of emotion or the unspeakable. Color, about which Sylvia Lavin has written very provocatively, does indeed have assigned values and forms of acceptance based on associations and contexts that may be recalled on an emotional level, but I believe it's possible to create logic for its use even if there are less "functional" aspects such as symbol or code attached to it.

GPB: But they are emotive, right? They are not cognitive mapping in the most simple way like the *Centre Pompidou* where the systems are somehow codified, there is I think coming back in the current generation, a lot of people with much more complicated systemizations of stress diagrams, those things are beginning to somehow reveal a latent information. In your work, it is much more atmospheric, it's about confusion with the sky, it's about a much more experiential agenda.

ND: Yes. In the case of the *Alan-Voo House Addition*, it is.

GPB: In our conversation you brought up two really interesting issues: one is that a lot of the generation that is included in this book is either on that cusp or headed quickly towards that cusp of translation from the small project, either the virtual project or the installation work, to a larger scale of architecture that suddenly has all these greater responsibilities of codes, and flashing and liability: bigger responsibilities. There are firms that are incredibly intriguing as a research-based office but when they became a practice-based office, so many of the ideas can't play through. I am curious if you have any ideas about the complexities that are now happening through extended software technologies like parametric modeling where we can hyper-customize, we can do things now that are so informationally heavy and so loaded and so complicated geometrically with much more ease. We are now able to translate that through fabrication technologies and a lot of manual labor at the same time, into intricate endeavors. There are certainly housings for this from PS1 to SCI-Arc Gallery to Materials & Applications, there is a constant flow of ever increasing complexities. Do you foresee a problem? Are we kind of the ship that is going to be dashed against the rocks as a generation in a way? The idea you mention of a "reality," I feel a great amount of kinship with in that a lot of my work, though unbuilt, I am still very much interested in 2x4 or a sheet of plywood and its module and so the sky is not the limit when it comes to form, there is an idea about an economy, existing technology, and the realities of finance and materiality that is essential. But that is not universal for our generation. I grapple with how much utopian idealism do you hang onto and how much pragmatism do you hold onto and at what point does that become baggage? I don't know, maybe I'm too puritanical in my thinking.

ND: On one level, the conversation is sort of about the way in which ideas can be applied *vis-à-vis* contexts, whether it's scale, budget or market. Those criteria, as well as the allowable conditions and parameters, obviously change from project to project. When I started developing the sheet geometry in the early mid-1990s, a lot of it was based on overcoming a whole set of references, ones that were very obvious in the work that I was doing in the 1980s, that relied on a kind of Baroque level of technical exoticism and so forth. I wanted to develop something that was not only going to overcome specific technological references, but to do it in an incredibly simple and economic way which wasn't reductive at the same time. There were historical precedents, but basically the trope of the continuous surface was just about building surfaces, and at the time I said no 3D curves. We only used developable surfaces, which are ultimately very simple planar surfaces, conic sections, cylindrical sections, and using the conic and cylindrical sections in a way to do the greatest amount of work to confuse a reference of the Cartesian. So, for me, it was an intellectual and geometric problem coming together. I knew if I could figure it out, it would be buildable, and it would be buildable at an economy that potentially would be indiscriminate to how much budget you had. You could build it better or worse but at some level it wasn't going to price itself out of the ball game. That was a very cautious decision that occurred at the convergence of a kind of focus on avoiding the crisis of translation from the digital to the material. As you inferred in the second part of your comment, it is not about getting bigger in scale, it is about whether or not at any scale you can physically craft what it is you are working on digitally or that your building simulations take into account the limitations, not just the possibilities of material properties.

GPB: But your work has always had to me a certain kind of smartness of being able to engage the physicality and I think it goes back to that conversation about representation. In those virtual renderings, that sense of materiality only helps. I equate it to Romantic paintings like a Caspar David Friedrich, where you'd have this massive natural landscape that was overwhelming and heroic, and always in the corner there was a small human figure, which gave you a sense of scale that made the larger composition even more impressive. To me, that's how I always found your drawings so inspiring, it was that you'd have something that seemed so evocative and maybe so unattainable, but then maybe there'd be a handrail or an outlet or whatever it would be that suddenly pulled it all back. Or you'd do an incredibly dramatic cut-away perspectival section, but then the building construction lines are pulled out so there is that relationship back always to an idea of making a real physical manifestation. A lot of other architectures, I think, paint themselves into preventing some of those things from ever entering the conversation, so that they kind of fall apart and you have to embrace that ugliness. I think that is two issues. One being the kind of more heroic agenda of the representation and one being the question, is there an architectural methodology that simply can't translate itself at some point? I mean, I think, there is right? Or it's so beautiful or so self-resolving in a way as is. It is only going to be hurt if you try to make it physical. I've seen a lot of architects grapple with that. It's been interesting they either have to reinvent themselves and find a new way of operating, or they have to retreat back from that and be fine with the making. I think *Gyroscopic Horizons* is so much like *Mask of Medusa* by John Hejduk,[4] totally different in terms of its agendas, but in terms of being a master catalog of unbuilt work which is so latent with thought and position and agenda and so influential to generations of practitioners directly or indirectly, which is incredibly exciting. So to see the next generation of your work, building all of these things now and redefining yourself is a whole new agenda, in a way. How do you grapple with that? Are there any discontinuities between the two?

ND: When I was a graduate student, I remember a Swiss architect came to lecture, I really can't remember his name and I don't know where he is today, but he was very open in saying he could design a scheme for a house in a really short amount of time and then spend eight months detailing it. In this case, there was a doctrinaire philosophy for designing and then craft becomes the really differentiated place of elaboration, probably coming from precedents and antecedents like Scarpa, and so forth, where craft and detailing become a dramatically fetishistic world, whether it is minimal or expressive. I remember thinking at the time, "that doesn't sound right." Here we are as students and we are spending all of our time and we haven't built anything.

GPB: And you are only in that first stage of design, not the immense follow-through of execution.

ND: Yes, and we as students didn't really know what detailing is, but I thought that it sounds wrong, that craft would be the content. Now, we have spent two years on some details on HL23, we literally have, just trying to figure out either from the issue of water or either in the issue of alignment, or how can we fabricate the pieces that make up a difficult condition. However, it doesn't mean that it is an over-determination of details relative to design. It really does talk a lot about craft and in the new monograph I am writing a piece concerning the topics craft and detailing, to be able to situate that obsession within the larger ambitions of the work. The text works off of ideas that were forwarded by a professor I had at Harvard, an Austrian ex-patriot artist named Paul Rotterdam. He taught in the visual studies program. And he had a simple idea where there is a world called *normal reality*, which let's say is the everyday, or the ordinary. After normal reality there is *craft reality*. Craft reality is a little bit more what we were talking about with the Swiss architect. There is a normal *parti*, make a house, but craft it to the extreme. After craft reality, great art had to go into a reality called *art reality* which is transcendent. But it had to pass through craft at some particular level. And then finally it went back through this loop back to normal reality. In other words, you had to understand the quotidian, you then had to kind of understand what it would mean to polish that world. In architecture it might mean polishing a modernist project. Then send it into art reality where it still could be suspended in a world of possibilities or potential, but he was saying if it didn't make its way back to normal reality, then it would be kind of suspended.

GPB: So it has to come full circle.

ND: That's one of the most important axioms we work by, to work at a high level of craft, but never to announce that in any way in which the craft would become foregrounded. I always say build it precisely so someone won't notice that it is, so that the aura of the project and the argument of the project are the thing that comes through. For architects, when it is done poorly you notice. When it is done well, you have a tendency to basically read the argument of the project. It is a pathway to get there and for me that is the most important role that craft plays. I have never been very interested in building even a reasonable approximation of an extreme idea, to build up experience through failure, which is the most normal way one becomes expert at something. I don't see why craft has to suffer in the experimental process.

GPB: Like I tried and that's enough … How do you do that? How do you literally do that? Because you get to this high level of sophistication but you don't necessarily have the fabricator across the street, you don't necessarily have the hundred buildings that you don't tell anybody about and then you pop out with one that has finally resolved all of these kinds of issues. And so many architects work in a more cumulative way, like I solved my baseboard detail in that house, and then I solved this detail over here, and then I got this great soffit detail, and those things start to come back and re-occur. So much so that those moments become almost little autobiographies when you visit a project you can see a history of things. There are re-occurring moments in your work like certainly the radius, but there's a lot of just it comes out perfectly baked in a way. How do you do that? How do you get the recipe just right on the first time?

ND: When we were able to start building a few things, the projects were commissioned by great clients who shared the same goals we did. So there was enough time and support to do the proper research on materials and construction systems. *LA Eyeworks*, the first project of NMDA, was only 1100 square feet but it took eighteen months to do it. That comes out to 2 square feet per day to worry about!

GPB: So you were on every aspect of the project?

ND: Of course. I worked with one person at the time, Duks Koschitz, who left the office in 2007 to get a PhD in computation at MIT, and we learned very quickly that the more we spoke to the people who were going to build the project, the more control we were going to be able to exert over its conceptual and spatial readability. For instance, we learned that we would have to use four kinds of paint to achieve the monochromatic abstraction that the design called for. That's just basic R+D, but in this case we used the reality of paint technology to create unreal effects, a reverse engineering of materials, as it were. When the clients saw how much we were into the realization process, they knew that our lack of building experience would be superseded by intelligence.

GPB: So they trusted you at that point.

ND: Yes, plus it was a small interior. It wasn't like we were doing a 50-storey building to launch the practice. Since we could completely control all aspects of the environment, it allowed us to make the project in its materiality and in its appearance look as close to the renderings as possible, which was basically no material and only color. As I said, the last eight years have seen an expansion of thinking about materials beyond abstracting them graphically. I have a greater appreciation for the sensual effects of materials independent of geometry, especially since the projects have gotten larger and more complex in terms of construction.

Notes

1   Neil Denari, *Gyroscopic Horizons* (Princeton, NJ: Princeton Architectural Press, 1998).
2   Robert McCarter, ed., *Building: Machines (Pamphlet Architecture)*(Princeton, NJ: Princeton Architectural Press, 1996, 2nd ed.).
3   Jean Baudrillard, *The System of Objects,* trans. James Benedict (London: Verso, 1996).
4   John Hejduk, *Mask of Medusa* (New York: Rizzoli, 1985).

Interview 3

MM = Michael Maltzan; GPB = Gail Peter Borden.

GPB: There is an emerging generation of practitioners, that span from their late twenties to early forties in age, that are all grappling with the issue of materiality in some way. In an era of post-digital fabrication issues that dominated the 1990s, there is a movement beyond that, that all those skills are now intrinsic in a way and the fascination with the process just as a process isn't as exciting, so now there is this idea of how we put some of those things into production. The goal of this book is to address a cross-section of practices as intriguing snapshots of current practice and give us a perspective on issues of materiality in contemporary architecture. Coming off of these generational waves: early 1980s history dominated, late 1980s, early 1990s philosophy started dominating, in the late 1990s digital media dominated, and now this generation has full skills in all of these areas and isn't necessarily obsessed with any one of them and is looking towards the idea of materiality. It is really trying to confront matter and physicality in some way. In some ways the economy has aided this in terms of opportunities as there are not the large-scale projects, and as a result it is creating a generation where people are looking at the installation or artifact in some way, not always buildings, but are interested in the physical making something as a way of thinking.

MM: You are talking about the timeline for these different architectural generations in smaller and rapid increments.

GPB: They seem to be accelerating ...

MM: The specific moments you were talking about, and other particular moments as well, have been generated, I think, often by downturns in the economy. When I was in school, a lot of the thinking about the making of things was also focused in areas not traditionally considered architectural. Not just as a reaction to modernism, but looking at the potential in other practices, especially artistic practices, writing practices, linguistic and semiotic practices, for ways to situate research, and to think about what architecture could be in the face of an architectural discipline that wasn't carrying the same kind of expressive possibilities that it did before. It is interesting that you're setting this conversation at a time when it feels that there is the potential for architecture to ask "What's next?" If you look at the last 10 or 15 years, architecture in some ways has become so incredibly "good" that it is hard to look at architecture and ask if there are any problems left. So one of the questions is "What's the problem?" What's the issue? It seems to me that that is part of the context of the questions that you're asking.

GPB: Absolutely, maybe to delve into that it seems like the issues surrounding tactility seem to be on the table. Issues of complexity and issues of physicality, and the inter-relationship of those three, because there is obviously a growing complexity. Parametric modeling allows now for hyper specificity through incredibly intensive models that I don't think we could have handled five years ago in terms of their sophistication. I'm curious as to how you think that comes back to physicality.

MM: I wouldn't want to generalize what other architects are thinking in that regard, but I do think that there is a distinction between material and modeling. I think that often when people talk about materiality, it becomes a catch-all for many parts of the discipline or making, so that ideas of technique, ideas of fabrication, ideas of digital competence and control, ideas of craft, are all made a part of that idea of materiality. But I'm not sure that those things are necessarily a part of materiality or a conversation about materiality. They might be, but I'm not sure that they are automatically part of that conversation. There have recently been a couple of conversations, including one I was involved in at Delft, where this idea of materiality and craft were combined, and I'm not convinced they are inevitably related. For me, materiality probably has less to do with techniques, or with the material in a technical sense, but has much more to do with the effects or the characteristics or the presence of material. Not so much in terms of its abstraction either, but really in terms of how it produces or amplifies experience. To some extent, I think that probably aligns my work more with the trajectory of material thinking that comes from a West Coast idea of artistic practice from the 1950s, 1960s, and 1970s, and you can see that that track of investigation had enormous effect on the architectural work made here in the 1970s and even the 1980s at the time when the rest of the debate about architecture, especially on the East Coast and in Europe, was more interested in the idea of representation through form. Representation, at that point in the work in Los Angeles, was not so much of an issue, it was not as significant an avenue of investigation, it was really more about these other qualities that material produced. It was curious when you asked me to participate in this conversation because I think of myself as having an ambivalent or agnostic relationship to material, at least in the way that most people think about it. I have a deep suspicion about the way that material is often used, especially in the cultural or societal expectations that material stands in for something. That's not the way I think about it, it's not the way that it relates to my work.

GPB: You touched on three or four great issues I am curious about. I think you are downplaying material because as an architect who builds first and foremost, you have been incredibly fortunate and productive. Your practice has always had the opportunity to be persistently engaged with building [execution] as tethered intrinsically to making. I agree that when looking at your kind of work there are clearly chapters, like the *Inner City Arts*, or the *Harvard Westlake*, or the *Pasadena Children's Museum* where it seems like the material is almost a kind of "whiteness." There is a subordination of the material, somewhat due to economy, but knowing that there is more of an interest in form, in light, in perception and sequence, and other complexities of architecture. But then it seems in more recent work like the *Marina del Ray Park* that is under construction, which to me is almost all material form, it is merging landscape and architecture, where the bandstand is so materially driven, or the *Benedict Canyon House* which has your great patterned wall still on display out in the parking lot, or the *Book Barn*, those things seem to be much more overt about the material. It seems like there is some sort of transition in there. Then there are these moments of the *Pittman-Dowell Residence*, which seemed like it was both in a way. That it had those kinds of issues of a parallaxing view and incredibly perceptual moments to it, but it still really celebrated these moments of material, like the flooring, there are moments where material became present in the composition. Or even the *Dark Side of the Moon*, which I thought was so material; I mean, to be anti-material you have to actually be on the cutting edge of materiality. I mean, Pawson and Chipperfield know more about materiality, to make it go away you need to know even more about the systems and it seems overt in your projects. I am curious about those chapters of your work.

MM: There are a number of important points for me in that. Those projects, at least in the sense of the groups that you put them in, seem arguably true. In each of those cases there were shifts in the amplifications and reconsiderations in the ways that I was thinking about the work; certainly there were important conceptual or philosophical accelerations in each of those successive stages in the work. As I've said, I have always been suspicious about how social and cultural representational qualities are often used as a short circuit for meaning, that it creates too easy a way to make cultural or social references, and the danger in that, for my work, has always been that in trying to produce intensely experiential relationship between the viewer and the architecture, that the material has the problematic possibility of over-accentuating one's apprehension of the physical, the visceral relationships that are possible.

GPB: Right, too many voices in the conversation, so instead of a limiting like Judd or Irwin deploy, there is a palette that is determined, then within that the effect is engaged …

MM: In the beginning, movement, and the choreography of movement, were an essential aspect of the way I was organizing and thinking conceptually about architecture. The experience unfolded for somebody participating in the architecture. In a lot of ways, for me, form was used as a way of creating a series of relationships, maybe even psychological relationships, which I realized over time had been primarily about space, about the qualities of space, as opposed to the qualities of the form. In much of that early work, material, and as you described it, "the whiteness of the material," was trying to create an extremely present neutrality as material, again as a method of prejudicing qualities of form relationships, and spatial intensities, and also I think that because the "whiteness" of those forms allowed me to produce a rip in the context, and in creating that rip in your expectations, that it put more pressure on the new architecture in its relationships to that context. It questioned whether there were other more abstract but perhaps just as characteristic ways of creating context relationships that didn't depend on a kind of mimicry or material conversation. So it wasn't that it was completely trying to deny its position, its character and relationship to the context, but it was trying to intensify and call into questions those relationships. As the work developed, for instance, like the roof of Fresno or the skin of Pirelli, I became very interested in a sense of surface to see if you could produce a kind of equivalent formal intensity that I had been exploring in the composition of three-dimensional forms of the early work to see if that kind of perceptual intensity could occur in the surface itself. In that group of work you begin to see a more complex intent to still produce a relationship between the viewer and the building, but to do that now using some level of thinness. In that way it is about surface, and about the tradition of façades and the communicating qualities.

GPB: There is a really large discourse, it seems like that surrounds that idea of skin and pattern and even ornament, and I don't mean that in a derogatory way, but what is intriguing to me about your work is that it adds on to that earlier agenda that is effectual, experiential, and spatial but other people aren't talking about it that way. There is this movement definitively in contemporary architecture away from the object and much more to the field. I think in some of the projects you mentioned, the same consideration is there, but you are not interested in it, well, you are as a total reading, but there seems to be again this effectual quality to it that seems to be rooted in an artistic approach, much more the kind of composition, the kind of control, the kind of calibration is much more sophisticated, even to the point of using the polished stainless steel, you even get depth, even in the thinness you bring the depth back.

MM: Yes, I think that's right, and there has been a conversation about producing these kinds of façades through an exploration of the field or through seriality, but you're right that my intent here is different.

GPB: Even now much more complex parametric models that can locally respond to these sorts of things.

MM: In a lot of that work there is an extraordinary complexity that is present, and I think that the goal is

----

often that high level of formal complexity, which is a valid avenue of investigation, but I'm not really interested in that kind of complexity. I'm interested in a perceptual or experiential complexity, which is the difference.

GPB: It allows for impressive calibration within those parameters.

MM: In some ways that is a technique that's really rooted in an understanding of the mind. I'm not interested in abstraction, I'm interested in experience, and when you were mentioning the stainless steel skin that is behind the perforated white skin at the *Benedict Canyon House*, that is really about the thinness of that surface, but is really about the space within the thinness of the surface which is emitting all of the effects, reflections, and qualities of light, and the context in that singular surface. In that way it is about both its flatness.

GPB: Its absorption, its projection ...

MM: It's meant to change quite radically in the course of the day, the year.

GPB: It is never the same twice ...

MM: As well as the way one approaches and moves around and through the building. I think that kind of approach does lead to a certain type of practice.

GPB: There is a real smartness there, a real intelligence there that is guided towards the effectual. I'm curious because it seems like there is a generation where we might even argue that material is the new theory. I can see the kind of precipitous nature of that definitively because I think it does read like an over-fetishization or an over-objectification. You are able to hold separateness from that. What is intriguing to me is that your work is held between a utopian ideal, I mean, there is a lot of utopian vision, but there is an incredible effectual nature, but with the same hand you really embrace the kind of messy reality of things in people, like sweat and dirt and even a lot of your clientele right now is the homeless, where most people may see them as the most problematic or confrontational clients in a way. But the work really is smart in a way and is able to bridge both things, in that it is not the overly precious object. For instance, I did an artist in residence at the Chinati Foundation, spending three months in west Texas, imbibed in Donald Judd. He has a hyper minimal, hyper refined attitude, but then at the same time there is this casualness where none of the spaces are conditioned or sealed, the antelope give birth in these concrete boxes, and it's kind of all okay, it actually kind of makes the work better, stronger. I feel like you are able to tap into that, but it's unique, very few people are talking about space these days. I mean, Moneo talks about space, you talk about space via experience and I would argue a highly visual, optical sensibility of space, but that is unique in many ways. So many other architects are interested in a formal vision, a sequential vision; I mean, sequence is a lot in your work too but always as a subordinate collaborator with the ideas of space.

MM: The work that I'm doing, that I'm interested in, negotiates many different types of projects, many different contexts. I am interested in seeing if architecture has the ability to exist at many different levels: socially, culturally, economically, and urbanistically. I think that one of the ways you're able to navigate that diversity is if your primary interest is in space, in the idea of space, then there is an extraordinary complexity that is both able to exist in that idea, but also needs to exist in that idea. Given a particular situation, at times, I feel more comfortable with the architecture being an armature for events and effects to take place. At times the architecture has to become much more prominent, much more insistent, for a variety of reasons, but it comes from a belief that architecture has the ability to be much more elastic in its ambitions.

GPB: How do you let go? I mean, how do you let go? You don't seem to be concerned with fussiness, of details. It's like moments can happen and it's okay, it's not the end of the world how the baseboard hits. There seems to be a bigger agenda where the details can roll with the punches in a sort of way. It's not the way that it is über-controlled that some architects require in a way because the gesture is so powerful. I think maybe the same is true of people like Koolhaas, the realities come into it but you embrace them and roll them into the greater agenda and it somehow becomes a collaborator of the space, it doesn't make or break the space. Whereas for someone like Piano, who I worked for, when one sprinkler head is out of line, it all kind of all falls apart. Like a ding in a Ferrari.

MM: I have an admiration for anyone who is able to sustain that kind of insistence in their work, but that's not ultimately what I'm interested in. Maybe it is a different attitude of what control in architecture is. What kind of dynamic does that actually produce? That question has evolved in my work. Going back to the idea about movement may help to describe that sensibility, especially when you were talking about an openness to admit imperfection in the work. Early on I was more interested in movement, and the choreography of the way that someone would experience work, because for me that was a way of rethinking the relationship between space and form. I was in school in a time when the debate between modernism and post-modernism was really in full throw, and I was always very interested in thinking about architecture's role in cities urbanistically, as well as its role in the complexities of public space in cultural settings and contemporary culture. I felt that much of the idea about the city that was being produced at the time was a kind of disconnected, very formal, planametric way of thinking about making the city. I became much more interested in ideas or strategies that would allow you to design in those contexts at the level of the city, of the viewer, which is where ideas like perspective and movement started to become the primary focus in the way I thought about making architecture. That led, in a lot of my early work, to a highly scripted, highly narrative way in which the user was meant to engage the architecture and form. In time, I became much more suspicious of that, about putting yourself in a position where you are forcing that much control over the experience and space of the architecture, and became much more interested in a highly discursive, horizontal, perhaps more democratic idea about movement. It wasn't that movement was less important, because it was still the thing that was animating the relationship between the architecture and the user.

GPB: It becomes more multivalent.

MM: Yes, it becomes much more dispersive, and that break in my thinking, that switch in my thinking was the moment where an idea about control at a totalizing level became much less of a concern for me. Even at the level of material and detail. I don't want to give the impression that those things aren't considered, but I think I've become much more confident even in the building process, that the reality of, as you called it "that messiness" actually produces and allows much of the effect of connection between the building user and the building. It is as much a part of how somebody feels that they are admitted to that conversation as being able to say quite literally that you're a part of that conversation.

GPB: I didn't mean to make it seem that any of that thing seemed casual. In fact, at moments in the *Pittman-Dowell Residence* you take the elliptical window that folds from ceiling to wall, which I can imagine is an incredible feat of detailing and I thought of the calibration that goes into something like that is incredibly articulate but it is also incredibly anonymous in terms of the final goal. It becomes more like Turrell, where the knife edge is hidden and the effect becomes incredibly pervasive but the understanding of it isn't. You talk about some of the Los Angeles artists in the 1970s and your lineage coming out of Machado Silvetti's office, which is incredibly intellectual, which is all head, and then Gehry's office, which is so instinctual, with an eye and visceral quality that you found this amazing hybrid of instinctual intellectual, which is the best of both worlds.

MM: [Laughs] I like that idea.

GPB: But it is really intriguing to me because it does come out of Irwin in his early works, he cleans his entire studio, and that's what it's all about. It is a return to these more primal experiential qualities in a way, which, for me, is really my interest in materiality is that it can produce these kinds of things. You have the privilege of doing it on a real scale; you are doing real architecture, which is always a hard bridge in some ways. Often young or small firms do incredible smaller projects but then jump to a building and it's a really hard transition for them. What they do might both be incredibly interesting but seeing how that evolution happens sort of changed in a way.

MM: I think that one thing that absolutely does have to do with material is something highly architectural, that's the reality of scale. It's something I'm very conscious of because of the very different scales that we often work at, and I think you're right, ideas in that sense of architecture don't necessarily translate scale easily. It's one of the reasons why the three-dimensional model, the physical model is still such important currency for me in the process of designing. There are a lot of techniques and ways in which we go about building models here that are trying to produce a kind of scalar equivalency, not only to the form, but very much to the effect of the material.

GPB: They are testing in a very literal way.

MM: That immediate physicality in the design process does have a significant relationship to our ability to negotiate those big, often radical, changes in scale. But it also means that the thing that we were just talking about, both the precision in certain moments of the work – you call it the calibration of certain moments of the work – and then the matter of fact, or the moments where it appears that there is less concern, that comes from a level of confidence that's been developed over time, knowing when and where the intensities are, where the moments of deepest resonance are in an architecture. Where it's important, the different threads of ideas, or the different realities of the character of what you are trying to produce, or the layering of context and material and form, where the pressure points in the ideas are. Very often those are the places where a real attention to this high level of conceptual as well as physical precision exist, because you know that those are the moments where they will be the most articulate, the most effectual.

GPB: Right.

MM: And I've realized over time, and I think that probably comes from having overworked things at times, that those moments, those articulate moments, have the ability to speak precisely.

GPB: They can carry the whole thing.

MM: Exactly.

GPB: You brought up the issue of representation, how do you deal with material representation in two-dimensional work, in three-dimensional work? At what point does that come into the process? There are moments in which, for example, at the *Benedict Canyon House*, where the idea of that super-reflective surface has to at some point become fundamental.

MM: It is true. It is always a little bit of a joke in the office because very often as the project is emerging, even our clients are constantly asking.

GPB: What's it going to be?

MM: Yeah, what's it going to be made of, and the fact is that very often I don't know until deep in the process. The reason for that is that material does not come out of an investigation in and of the material itself, for me, it comes out of the ambition for the material to be a part of the consistency of the overall trajectory of ideas. What I mean by that is that it is most times an answer to an ongoing set of questions and conversations that are borne out of these primary interests about form and space, movement and engagement.

GPB: It sounds like it can't really come in until you are ready for it.

MM: That's right, for instance, at the *Benedict Canyon House*, it was kind of excruciating as we were very late in the process and I was struggling deeply with the form of the building and in that case the pressure that the art, because it is a house that is very much about the collection of art, I was struggling with the fact that the art spaces had produced these large rectangular objects that I felt were not keeping up with their responsibility to produce that visual engagement that the form of our buildings often take. At that point, I became more interested in the question of whether I could produce an amount of formal movement, sculptural intensity, visual depth, in a surface four or five inches deep.

GPB: Shallow space.

MM: Right, and the idea, and that material really came out of that. It came out of beginning to think about moiré patterns and the way that thinness through two surfaces interacting can create all of that conceptual complexity. That idea of the material, the assembly, and fabrication could not have been produced earlier in the process. It did clearly relate to an ongoing theme in the office about the investigation of surface, but it couldn't have come along faster. In the office, one of the things I am trying to defeat in the physical models is their lack of a sense of scale or relational presence to the material, and sometimes all of the fabrication notations that get left on the model, the scotch tape, the cut marks, the process, gets left in the models, not because I am interested in seeing the process, I am actually not interested in that at all, but the detritus of the process stands in for the reality of another scale when things finally get manifested in the actual building.

GPB: You mean the need for expansion joints, or flashing, or the like ...

MM: Exactly, or the misalignment of panels, all of the realities of those things that are very much the condition of building practice and building scale and the visual language of the construction. That modeling process does end up in the making of a series of full-scale mock-ups of the material to test it for its buildability, its constructability, but more importantly, those are the first real tests of whether perceptual effects at a scale are real, and very often the tuning that we do at that point has less to do with the detailing, the physical detailing, and has more to do with the tuning of the character and the qualities of your perception of those materials.

- - - - - - - - - - - - - - - - -

GPB: So where do you think tactility, materiality, where does physicality go from here? It seems like the affect/effect argument is too limiting, but the tangibility and sensuality of the physical never seem to actually arrive in architectural discourse as much as it probably should. Where do you think things are going? I don't want absolutes, but what do you think the next step is? We started the conversation with the possibilities that now through media and representation are almost endless, the technology in terms of construction has advanced the material palette exponentially, almost anything is really possible now structurally if we have the budget and desire, and even being architects that practice in Southern California, we have weathering and so many other issues that aren't as aggressively in our foreground allowing us to unshackle a direct commitment to some of these things, so I am curious, where does the conversation go? How does the idea of that, of tactility, physicality, is there a merger in terms of space? So many of the things you talk about again to pull it back to some iconic artists, if you think of someone like Richard Serra, he makes a very similar conversation and dialog, but the materiality he chooses, the corten steel is essential. Even with Donald Judd, the fact that it is plywood, or aluminum or Plexiglas is essential in a way. It seems like that is a trajectory you are headed in, but one that is incredibly intriguing because of this merger between intellectual intention, perceptual experience and the physicality, the holy trinity in a way: the intent, the matter and material as a force of resistance, and the effect, the thing that is an emotion, less tangible.

MM: I wouldn't be presumptuous enough to say or know where that leads, I do know, and believe strongly, that we are at a real threshold moment, moving from one idea about architecture, and its presence in culture, to something else. I believe that there is still enormous power and room to investigate the potential in architecture's role in creating a kind of immersive and intense spatial experience. That it is in that realm that I think architecture has the capacity to engage social or political issues that we are confronting today. It is the place where architecture has the ability to be both confrontational and also deeply generous in the way in which it participates in that conversation. The artists that you are talking about do provide a clue for the role of material in that regard. All of the people you mention use material that we recognize but in almost no cases are they using those materials for their purely representational ability.

GPB: Absolutely, they disembody it.

MM: It doesn't mean Plexiglas. It doesn't mean corten.

GPB: In fact, they elevate it to a level of independent beauty.

MM: It has a different effect on you and that's why someone like Richard Artswager is such a resonant sculptural artist because of the way he uses material, in his case, through representations of prosaic materials like Formica and plastic laminates, but is always distorting our perception of things like scale, and reality, and the authenticity of the material to produce a completely different relational effect with the audience. I think in that work is a very authentic use of material three-dimensionally for the goal of creating a deep conversational relationship with the sculptural audience, and I think architecture has the potential to rediscover that ability. If the goal is to use the techniques of architecture and the manipulation of form in a more singularly self-referential way, I think it deeply limits our ability to have architecture be a real progressive voice, an adamant voice, in the importance of architecture's ability to steer, suggest, implore, change and progress in culture. I think that's really what is at stake in that part of the conversation.

GPB: The future is now.

MM: It has to be. I think architecture over the last fifteen or twenty years built up one set of expectations of what architecture is, and I think it's important that the discipline of architecture, the profession of architecture, continues to maintain its adamancy about having a role in that conversation. But I also think that it's important to constantly reexamine and question what those expectations are becoming as they get rebuilt, and whether they are continuing to have the same cultural effect they did fifteen or twenty years ago. There is a lot of debate that's possible in that, but I think that is the important conversation to have. I think it is happening.

Interview 4

NT = Nader Tehrani; MM = Michael Meredith.

MM: You participated in the intricacy project that Greg Lynn curated in 2003. Do you feel that you are still part of that project?

NT: We were part of the project, and Greg identified us with the category of "assemblage," for which he used the *Tongxian Brick* project as an example. He wrote a great essay on that project, but by the time he wrote it we were already involved in a host of other things, so we could have fit into other descriptive slots that were probably less convenient for his venue. I still think Greg's argument is strong, but I think our work has taken on other conceptual categories that preoccupy me more now. The intricacy argument is unable to identify the many hurdles, stumbling blocks, and frictions that come with the architectural process. For example, one of the most easily identifiable hurdles is how one introduces a threshold – like a door – into a material and geometric system that does not tolerate industry standards, on the one hand, nor the formal peculiarities of a system on the other. The door is a great issue that many people have taken on, some by transforming a system, and others by introducing an anomaly within the system. If you want to make a strong thesis, does that mean that everything should be designed, or does it mean that some objects *should not* be designed in order that some other architectural phenomenon can be foregrounded? These are tactical positions that we take every day, and they suggest a different kind of judiciousness to what we do. The intricacy project represses these tensions in favor of a seemingly complex but nonetheless harmonious whole.

MM: The contingencies of building certainly include how to absorb voided or normative figures, like doors.

NT: Yes, certainly, but how do we absorb these figures not merely as functional constraints, but as precise design problems that are a reflection of a transforming architectural culture – a culture with new media, new critical parameters, and evolving values? It is telling how architects can, on the one hand, lapse into specifying a door from the catalog, or, on the other, fall prey to their own invented system, which may, for example, produce a door consistent with the language of their building while totally disengaged with the mechanics of hinging, and bracket other architectural issues that may be at stake.

MM: It would be strange, though, if everyone started designing doors. If someone was the triangular door architect, or the circle door architect, and someone else was known for an amorphous door, the architectural environment would be populated with meaningless difference. I am glad that some things resist figuration. Doors may be the last holdout against the architect's desire for totalizing design. The door acts as a moment of silence in the designed object.

NT: The operation of silencing is an apt allegory for all of the things that happen in architecture. You are always silencing eight things in order to amplify one or two others.

MM: Do you think there is a scale shift evident in how we think about this silencing? How do you go from a proposal for an entire building to re-imagining pieces of material? The language of a building can often operate without material concerns. How do you go about the design process?

NT: We usually design a process that produces a head-on collision between urban or typological organizations, on the one hand, and material organizations, on the other. These ordering systems inevitably challenge each other, and at some point we have to figure out what, if anything, is of interest in the confrontation. We rarely have a project that develops linearly in which everything comes together happily. One of our recent projects, the *Taiwan Pop Music Center*, is such a large urban project that it is not reducible to a material unit, but obviously it still does engage material questions. In this project, the material palette is in the service of a larger urban proposition, and yet it also has its own set of tectonic potentials at a more intimate scale. We used large, foam and aluminum panels, whose initial motivation was to serve an acoustic function, muting the sounds emanating from the outdoor concerts. In turn, the perforations within the foam could also be scaled in varied ways, enabling the punching of openings for windows, thresholds, screens, and more solid surfaces. In this way, the material is transformed by the way it responds to different scales, while it does not impinge on the larger scale of canopies and elevations it serves.

MM: And there is a performative potential ...

NT: Obviously for a competition like this one, which is all about the large, iconic move, we relented on micro level specifications. Detailed questions of materiality and performance were abstracted for the competition even though they were important to us.

MM: I would read this project in a different way. The architecture is not driven by the material logic of folding perforated metal or the geometry of ruled surfaces, but rather appears to be about landscape, or perhaps an image of landscape, which evidences a much different concern. Landscape and material seem like two different ways of thinking about architecture, but maybe they can be synthesized?

NT: They do not necessarily need to be synthesized, as such; projects sometimes exist in their differences. This project is about Taipei itself, whose identity is defined by the relationship of the built and natural skyline; the juxtaposition of these two landscapes is salient in their contrast, not their similarity. Thus, we treat the urban edge with due attention to architectural orders, while also dealing with landscape within the medium of horticultural specifications of that terrain, all the while understanding the ambiguities that lie between them. These different conditions collide with one another within the context of the night markets, the alleyways we designed as part of the proposal.

MM: While some architects struggle with idealized forms (symmetry, for instance), it seems you are much more interested in the contingencies of architecture and their potentials. There is an inherent moment of choice in the relationship between these contingencies, where one thing is going to have to win over another. It may happen in small moves or in overarching decisions, but your value system will come down to what you are willing to give up. If someone said, "Look, we cannot do this project in bent metal" after you have already come up with a design in bent metal, "but we have to do it in wood instead," what do you do? Do you have to change the whole design?

NT: No, you cannot merely take wood and substitute it. You would need to make systemic changes. We are put in this position all the time. It is an incredible thing to have a project like Scott Cohen's *Tel Aviv Museum of Art*, FOA's *Yokohama Port Terminal*, or Toyo Ito's *Opera House* in Taiwan, where you develop a building organization that is able to maintain such a close parity between geometry, material systems and an architectural idea. Most projects are not able to do that. Scott Cohen's *Nanjing Performing Arts Center*, for instance, runs into many problems precisely as a result of not being able to negotiate issues of formal, spatial, and material difference.

MM: It has too many disparate, seemingly collaged, parts.

NT: The choice of an external fire escape that runs diagonal to the vertically organized windows is something that complicates the geometric clarity of that face, a moment where the contingencies overwhelm his ordering system, and where he loses control, as it were. In Tel Aviv, by explicitly separating the skin from the structure and the inside from the outside – and by not requiring many windows – he is able to control the breakdown of the paneling system, its geometry and its connections. Yokahama does the same thing for FOA. The absence of complex programming enables them to essentially create a sequence of vaults and ramps, and thus affords them a relative purity in dealing with steel, wood and glass systems. Ito's *Opera House* seems to be similar in this respect, but I know little about how it is developing as a material proposition. All these buildings share exceptional circumstances where one is not constrained by the contingencies that compromise the other 80 or 90 percent of architectural works.

MM: How would you describe the buildings that result from such moments? Do they always have a monumental form?

NT: They are often characterized by a singularity of function, monolithic formal qualities, and an escape from the scalar problems of small, medium, and large conditions — where one can instead focus just on the large conditions or just on the small conditions. Maybe Scott Cohen's *Tel Aviv Museum of Art* is an exception to this, as he negotiates a variety of other spatial conditions between the atrium and the skin. But, for example, with housing you can do most everything with small conditions, and great housing is able to dissolve scale, in the way Steven Holl does at MIT. What is amazing about Holl's MIT project is that it identifies the increments of housing modules by making them even smaller in scale. Not every project is able to do that. The moment you have small, medium, and large scales, you have to conflate the scales of systems, functions, and formal conditions that normatively do not want to play together well. That is why we are amazed when people are able to demonstrate this kind of leverage in more complex projects. I am interested in the *difficult* part of synthesis, and not synthesis at any cost. Synthesis would suggest the Fosters and the Pianos who somehow are able to encase everything in a broad formal, mechanical, and structural logic and erase the difficulties of programmatic misalliances, of complex urbanisms or architectural anomalies. They flatten everything down. Conversely, others like Aalto expose the possibility of more complex organizations, of scalar differences, and of difficult junctions – reconciling more sophisticated scenarios.

MM: When rethinking "matter" in architecture, the question of pedagogy inevitably comes up. How do we understand and work through the problems of architecture? Since the 1970s in particular, architecture has struggled with the problem of medium that results from the condition that architects are separated from the actual making of architecture. The domination of representation as the tool through which we understand architecture is disruptive. Architecture defined by representation means there can never be a clear, stable idea of architecture's medium because representation is constantly changing. One of the big shifts today in this inherently unstable field is that when you started practice, everyone had to claim a specific medium – Scott is geometry, you are materials or perhaps pattern – every participant had staked out a medium. More recently, we have become concerned instead with the contingencies of building. Within this realism-based or practice-based model, the diagram has taken over and deskilled architectural plan making; you could describe architecture in a single line with a couple of words on it and an image, thereby conveying it in two simultaneous extremes: a photorealistic image and a reductive, abstract diagram. This is probably still one of the major modes of working. The diagrammatic and realistic model has arguably deskilled architecture to such a degree that architects are disinterested in history, forsaking architectural self-consciousness for agency, function or performance. How would we rethink architecture now in this economy, after the realist/practice model?

NT: When I started practicing in the 1980s, "representation" had a certain value and dominance in architectural culture. It helped distance architecture from mere building, and thus connect it to deep traditions linked with drawing, perspective, and techniques of representation that have been central to our discipline. It was also a vehicle to link architecture to the production of meaning, this in a time when semiotics was on center stage within academia and other forms of cultural production. In this sense, the centrality of representation had a critical function to its era. By the time we got to work, we had seen the demise of architecture precisely because of the abandonment of its link to building traditions, tectonic culture and the state of the building industry, all of which we saw as central to the possibility of invention, and transformation of the discipline. The claiming of material culture as the basis of our initial preoccupation, of course, did not abandon other inquiries: spatial, programmatic and formal researches, for instance. Scott's claim on geometry, I believe, has not weakened him as a builder (in Tel Aviv, for instance) and so I also see a convergence in interests after these initial forays into focused media. In more recent years, the reliance on the diagram, on the one hand, and the startling advancement of realism via Photoshop have had their own merits and relative limitations – both somehow glossing over the complexities of building, but in turn advancing other issues – maybe less so on the realist front.

MM: Do you think the younger architecture offices today still operate within the same sense of the architectural discipline that you had? Do you think that BIG, for instance, would have that same self-consciousness or sense of the disciplinary project of architecture?

NT: I sense they have less angst about the weight of culture we carry on our shoulders, but I would be troubled that you would think that a firm like BIG does not have a consciousness of the larger historical framework in which it operates. I think Bjarke Ingels is very self-conscious of what he is doing, even though his dominant mode of communication is through diagrams. Of course, these diagrams have a rhetorical function, and a very successful one at that, but they do not necessarily supplant his knowledge of other forms of architectural knowledge. The fact that he does not show precedents does not mean that he is ignorant of architectural history.

MM: Well, I do not think history is even in Bjarke's way of thinking, he's more of a modernist than postmodernist. The difference between him and Koolhaas is that Koolhaas (at least in his early work) operates with a concern for history. Koolhaas is always thinking about architecture's history as the material that he is reusing and sampling. BIG is not thinking about history, they're thinking about function and performance instead. Bjarke, like a lot of architects, utilizes the diagram as his representational protagonist, in avoidance of history.

NT: You might say that the diagram avoids history, but in an information era where history is collapsed into one simultaneous set of overlapped events, it is hard not to think about it more intensely than before. Before this collapse we may have thought of history linearly; we may have thought, "These are the precedents and this is how we are going to extend them." More than ever, history is thought through synchronically, with forms, materials, spaces all available for immediate re-adaptation and play. I do not discount your opinions on Koolhaas, but I was merely suggesting that BIG can build on that with

- - - - - - - - - - - - - - - - - -

more ease, in essence, having internalized that culture, and now focused more on how to expose the instrumentality of Koolhaas' thinking.

MM: We do tend to think of history today as more of a flat playing field than a line. It is a topology. I agree with that, but the reality of architecture is that because there are so few differences between any of us, the way you distinguish is by the exaggeration of minor dissimilarities: the things people say about the things they produce as well as the things themselves. The little discursive moves people produce around their objects are incredibly important because they heighten, reframe, and produce values.

NT: I am not suggesting that we eradicate the discursive platforms on which we construct the architectural discipline. All that we really can rely on is debates and the nuanced differences between very similar things, but then the world of buildings, drawings and models are part of that very discourse, "building" arguments as vehemently as the words that are cast on them. However, what the diagram has perfected has little to do with the discipline in terms of materiality, of bricks and stones as such; it has to do with modes of communication that operate at a mass level. Diagrams are extremely effective advertising strategies because they bring to the foreground the necessity of clarity, synthesis, and irreducibility – much of which has also led to the dumbing down of discourse with its ultimate dangers being anti-intellectual in nature.

MM: Yes. The diagram may be clear and discursive, but it also facilitates the production of a series of students that have an incredibly particular perception of architecture. They don't understand the making of architecture as a physical, tectonic thing. The diagram is the product of the separation of real construction from representation. After the initial split of the building and its representation, the architectural medium bifurcated. Most of us chose representation, while some held out for construction. They usually lived in Switzerland. The entire American architectural world was divided up according to representational mediums. Then, in the "noughties" everyone got sick of representation and switched to documentation, so that all you could show were construction drawings and photographs. Right now we are in another moment. We have proliferated mediums, and they all coexist. Medium is pluralized into genres, and no one approach is dominant.

NT: I tend to flatten out a lot of these different representational tendencies by grouping them according to what they share and what they unveil. For instance, if you think of the problem of representation historically, what architects did was draw. Going back to the Académie Royale of the seventeenth century and through the Enlightenment shows how architecture evolved as a practice that uses drawing as a discipline, and eventually as a means to cultivate a social contract. What had been a rarefied discourse shared among elites was disseminated among a vaster population leading to the democratization of the discipline – the point being that the separation of building and drawing was central to this process. We are going through a similar shift right now. Those disciplinary peculiarities that were held in the academy can now be downloaded by anybody on the internet. Most anyone can learn geometry just as well as you, and they can begin to do presentations between Rhinoceros®, Illustrator, and PowerPoint almost as well as you can. For this reason, we are getting many more "participants" in the architectural field, some of whom are really good, and this has broken down the old hierarchies; in turn, it has also produced a good many dilettantes, for the ease that some of this media produces.

MM: Medium specificity is a disciplinary problem. Once we get into the discipline we have to talk about the speciation into multiple genres allowed by medium. Within genres we only have micro-discourses within different camps: the material people conspire together, the parametric people get together for shop talk, the sustainable people hold coffee klatches, etc. Of course, there is cross-pollination, but

- - - - - - - - - - - - - - - - - - - -

inevitably we basically understand architecture in terms of camps. Everybody coexists happily in our little tribes. There are no major wars, just the occasional spat.

NT: Medium is, in part, determined by those irreducible aspects that define a discipline, like grading and topography are to landscaping and aggregation and bonding are to masonry projects. The radicalization of certain techniques may lead to camps, but that is neither the goal nor the vocation of working within a medium. I would argue that camps, as such, are the results of a social contract designed to produce a security blanket for people of some delicacy, like a clique in junior high school, and by nature tend to be reductive. Camps are a dangerous way to reduce practices and individuals. If we think Koolhaas is a master at theorizing program, does this mean that the material agendas of the *Seattle Public Library* are uninteresting?

MM: I would argue that architecture now operates in a post-medium capacity. We are perhaps medium-less.

NT: Or medium-proliferate ...

MM: So where do we go from here?

NT: The interesting people dealing with material now are focused on the relationships between material and computation, material and landscape, etc. Conflicts and confluences are brought about as a result of these disparate relationships. The most typical question we are asked is "What is your fascination with the skin?" When the skin deals with architectural phenomena outside itself, program, performance, perception and a range of other architectural interests remain at stake.

MM: We could say the skin is a reaction against postmodernism's fascination with the façade. Even calling it a skin reframes the disciplinary problem.

NT: For me, skin versus façade does not say enough about material. For example, the postmodern façade may have dealt with the same concrete blocks as those we deal with today. The material is the same but the operations to which the material is submitted are vastly different, and so the perception induced and effects produced can be of significant theoretical difference. It is also different to compose a façade rather than developing a set of rules for it in an open process in which others can participate, including engineers, builders, and other designers. At one level, parametric design abandons the centered position of the author, while at another it also refocuses the author's vocation. That, to me, is what is of consequence. Whether that operation is a skin or a surface is a second-order issue.

MM: The one thing that would carry over from the notion of "façade" to the notion of "skin" is a sense of latent autonomy. For example, in Classicism, the façade is almost a separate project from the building.

NT: But that is also true in modernism. The stucco that Mark Wigley discusses is potent precisely because of its ability to erase the laminar and structural conditions that underlie it: its ability to dematerialize the presence of the slab, encase the insulation, and overcome waterproofing. All of these things are part of the evolution of the wall section. If you look at a Roman façade, do you say it is a masonry wall, a stone wall, a concrete wall, or a brick wall? You have brick formwork for concrete, stone cladding on top of that, and elaborate plasterwork on the interior. This is not like the modern façade of the 1930s, nor is it like the façade of today, which is "emancipated" from many of the material concerns of the 1930s. Rather it is encrypted, with a great deal of intelligence that addresses environmental conditions problematized today. We need to revisit the history of wall technology to reveal the architectural content hidden from ready visual assessment. There has always been a more complex ordering system under the surface. The distinction between "wall" and "skin" matters much less than the complex theoretical and material conditions that underlie each term. This goes back to your point earlier. It is one thing to identify the working parts of the wall, I suppose, but much harder to cultivate the complexity that lies within.

MM: That is because complexity is a disciplinary problem rather than a "mere" medium problem. If the medium came to stand in the place of the discipline in the 1970s, then the current post- or prolix-medium condition means that we have to rethink the discipline. We have yet to rearticulate the discipline of architecture because our criticism is still caught in a medium paradigm – in other words, we are still in a technique-based mode. We can deal with part-to-whole compositional problems, we can deal with scripting, and we can deal with positivist approaches to architecture, but it has become almost impossible to talk about the cultural project of architecture. Critics choose the factual and quantifiable discourses over the more qualitative, speculative and political ones, and tend to evaluate architecture based on its apparent methodological consistency. How many reviews have you been on where the critics actually talk about the work as situated within the cultural or historical problem of architecture? "How" has dominated our discourse.

NT: On the other hand, you have the generalists who, for lack of ability to engage in disciplinary specificity, start to evoke large global narratives like sustainability and global warming. That also remains very unsatisfying because the particulars of the architectural debate are totally glossed over in favor of large societal issues that can be called on as a referendum for what is relevant. The autonomy project is summarily decapitated at that point, and with it, the peculiarities and specifications of media are overlooked; in this sense, it is too easy to say we are operating in a post-media historical moment. You would need to demonstrate how various media weigh in on the traditional boundaries of the architectural discipline, but also you would need to show how certain traits, operations, and techniques are stubbornly bound to architecture at the same time, despite such radical shifts. You can't simply sweep the question of media under the carpet to speak to cultural questions.

MM: The formalist, autonomy project has devolved into a similar positivism. Eisenman's attack was brilliant when he set out because it was aimed at functionalism, which is a positivist project. This made his project cultural. However, the autonomy project proceeded to devolve into technique for the sake of technique, to the point where it was just about methodology. Now, where do all those people run when the autonomy project ends? Straight to sustainability, because it is the new pseudo-science. You can measure it, you can quantify it, and you can produce tautological arguments. Sustainability is based in facts, and these facts produce forms. So now you see a lot of formalists doing twists related to sun angles.

NT: I have yet to see designers establish a tense relationship between performance and form in a self-conscious way. Even Rahm, whose main thesis is to argue for the environmental basis for his formal interests, only reinforces the autonomy between form and performance. Tension is a very difficult phenomenon to activate and engage.

MM: In a way, sustainable positivism is broken into two camps. You are either earnest and naïve, or you are cynical and use it as camouflage for something else. Either way, the functionalist sustainability narrative ends in a sort of crisis.

NT: In a world where form is treated autonomously, the challenges of construction, engineering, budgeting, trades, and all of the other associated disciplines that tend to richly convolute the autonomy of

- - - - - - - - - - - - - - - - - -

practice end up being so relevant that if you do not lasso them in at the beginning, you are in danger of being overwhelmed by them – and effectively becoming their victim. It is the knowledge of and active engagement with those disciplines that sustain the project of autonomy, not their denial. In that way, there is a huge difference between Eisenman, on the one hand, and Sejima or Zumthor, on the other. Why? Because those other people become invested, almost obsessively, in these other systems, not because of their desire to celebrate them, but because of their insistence on erasing them – in order that some other notion about form, materiality, or space can be maintained as a resistance to culture at work, in the normative sense. Eisenman's buildings are infested with all of the signs of the "everyday" at work, a condition which winds up compromising the very condition of autonomy he is after. Thus, I am not so much here challenging Eisenman's intellectual project on autonomy, but rather pointing out that ironically his denial of the very technical and material means by which architecture is "mediated" results in the demise of his project; in turn, those who do not really articulate his thesis, may be more successful at the project of "form" precisely because of their alertness of the bureaucracy of material culture that surrounds our medium. Post-media? Maybe, but only if one has a deeply invested knowledge in the very relationships of what constitutes the foundations of the discipline. In contrast to Eisenman, Frank Gehry emerged into the discipline by building. It could be argued that he was never that interested in the building discipline as such, but he did radicalize certain building propositions as a result of a methodology that had to deal with the building industry. He challenged the sheet metal industry to do things that otherwise would not have been done. For example, roofers never worked with a façade; the roof and the façade were different trades. He collapsed disciplines and also redefined legal practices. The other thing that you cannot forget is that there was a moment when architects essentially could assemble all the associated disciplines under one roof. That is becoming harder to do, because the associated disciplines are operating at such an advanced level as specializations. You have to develop different collaborative models in order to maintain a relationship to the act of building. How the architect controls the means and methods of construction and gets around the questions of representation becomes our challenge.

Part II
Matter Design

Matter Design refers to processes that begin with a material and a system simultaneously. Engaging synthetically the formal and functional implications of building materials as process applications and the formal implications of material composition, matter design addresses the translation of material to process to form as a seamless dialog. The ensuing design work integrates at all steps the ideals of making and thus the effects and processes are integrally synchronized with the material engaged. These projects represent a belief that merges materiality with design and produces an application from the associated physical realities.

Jason Payne, Hirsuta
Lisa Iwamoto and Craig Scott, IwamotoScott
Gail Peter Borden, Borden Partnership
Florian Idenburg, SO – IL
Oliver Hess and Jenna Didier, Didier Hess

Chapter 1
Raspberry Fields

Jason Payne
Hirsuta

Kiwa hirsuta

A very strange new animal was discovered in 2005 living on hydrothermal vents 7200 feet deep along the Pacific-Antarctic Ridge 900 miles south of Easter Island. *Kiwa hirsuta* (Figure 1.1), a crustacean that is neither lobster nor crab is nevertheless dubbed "yeti lobster" or "yeti crab" for its resemblance to these animals. In fact, *K. hirsuta* constitutes not only a new species but a new genus and family (*Kiwaidae*) of which it is the sole member. Rarely do scientists find new organisms of such striking peculiarity to warrant this kind of distinction. Given *K. hirsuta's* strong morphological similarity to other lobster species, it seems surprising that it would require a new family for classification. One characteristic, however, is deemed so unusual as to thrust this creature through established hierarchies of biological order into its own unique taxonomic orbit: its hairiness.

　　Unlike any other crustacean, *K. hirsuta* has a full coat of silky blonde hair covering its legs and claws. Resembling a fur coat, this material's function is uncertain. It may be used to capture bacteria and other small organisms on which the animal feeds, or the bacteria may detoxify the poisonous minerals emitted from the hydrothermal vents. Or it may simply be a spontaneous, natural expression of material exuberance. Whatever the case, *K. hirsuta* is undeniably the most stylish crustacean currently crawling the ocean floor.

Figure 1.1 *K. hirsuta*

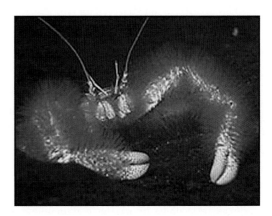

Hirsutism

Hirsutism describes the condition, usually botanical or medical, of hairiness (Figures 1.2–1.3). More generally, hairiness is a ubiquitous material condition that crosses a variety of disciplines and aspects of life. Despite this, hairiness has rarely been considered a subject of relevance for architecture. This seems odd given the ease with which one might begin to theorize the use value of hairy morphologies, mechanisms, and materials in an architectural context,[1] especially within current design discourses interested in moving from surface to texture, from geometry to atmosphere, and from mass to ornament.

Figure 1.2 Botanical hirsutism
Figure 1.3 Medical hirsutism

This text explores the undervalued material and organizational potentials of hair, or masses of flexible strands, for architectural application. We will approach what might otherwise be an unruly subject through two focusing lenses, one internal to our discipline, the thatched roof, and one external, the hairstylist's art. While different in history, scale, technique, material, and application, thatching and haircutting each constitute a relatively lowly material practice developed within guilds meant to satisfy pragmatic ends. While the prosaic humility of these crafts may at first seem limiting and not worthy of academic attention, it is this very quality that allows each the freedom to thrive in unusual, even irresponsible ways.[2]

Thatching

Thatching is one of the oldest building arts practiced in the world. Pre-dating even clay, stone, and wood, the massing of natural fibers formed humankind's earliest dwellings. Only caves are more primordial living structures and these, of course, come readymade. Over the course of centuries in various locales thatching evolved into a variety of tendencies and forms, some more complex than others, all linked by a basic reliance upon stranded, bundled, and woven morphologies. Unlike other building techniques such as masonry and post and beam construction, thatching has rarely sought to rise above its humble station, that of utilitarian material practice. Despite the evolution of a limited variety of ornamental flourishes that add a certain decorative flair to the thatched roof, this building method has sought neither metaphysical legitimacy nor ideological membership in the loftier strata of the architectural discipline. The most we can say for any higher aspirations of the craft involves its latter-day contribution to an agrarian picturesque, though this has been mostly accidental and after the fact. Thatching has always been about getting the job done, the job being nothing more than keeping the house warm and dry, using local materials and labor. More recent pastoral associations are largely a function of its durability, as a well-made thatched roof may last over 100 years when carefully tended. In villages where thatch still exists, it is often the sole physical evidence of a time gone by. Of course, the visual resemblance

Figure 1.4 Common illustration of a thatched cottage

between sloped, thatched courses and the furrowed fields of the surrounding countryside also lends a degree of pastoral resonance to the form but this, too, is accidental, arising from our general nostalgia over the move from an agrarian to an industrial/information economy. Thus, when we associate thatched roof cottages with former times and ways of life (that were not nearly as idyllic as we might imagine), we place undue burden on a material practice and morphological potential otherwise free of such responsibility (Figure 1.4).

While acknowledging the presence of this post-rationalized, picturesque affect, this author rejects its usefulness for the continued evolution of thatching and, by extension, more contemporary hairy architectures. Hobbits, trolls, and wizened English hermits are not our target audience. Instead, the arguments presented here advocate for combing through the physical properties and technical procedures that constitute the thatcher's craft to find novel ways forward. Exploring new styles, shapes, and textures in thatch reinvigorates this most ancient of material practices in ways that are truly contemporary. Indeed, if viewed in purely morphological terms this practice may be seen as primed for exploitation within a certain strand of current architectural discourse. Not only do the bundled, flexible lines of a thatched mat appeal to recent developments in architectural geometry[3] but, more importantly, move this idiom further toward materialization, quality, texture, and affect through their undeniable physicality. The lines and mats are, after all, made of something, specifically water reed or wheat straw, and with this something comes all the richness of specific material characteristics. Malleability, turgidity, brittleness, roughness, color, and optics, to name a few, lend a certain yet variable feel to the geometry of woven linework. Oddly enough, thatch may be the ideal test case for the polemical move from geometry to affect, form to atmosphere.[4]

Apex case: thatching technique in the United Kingdom

For those truly interested in actually learning this craft, the highest concentration of advanced thatched projects and expert thatchers is found in the central, southern, and south-western United Kingdom (Figure 1.5). While

Figure 1.5 The Cott Inn, Dartington, Devon, one of the oldest thatched inns in the UK

various forms of thatching are found in other locales, that of the British Isles stands unrivaled.[5] Despite its decline elsewhere, the United Kingdom maintains impeccable standards through guilds, the members of which pass technique on through successive generations. This centuries-old expertise as well as state-of-the-art methods from the region have been compiled in a single, large text entitled *The Thatcher's Craft,* published by England's Rural Development Commission.[6] Roughly analogous to a combination of our *Architectural Graphic Standards* (Ramsey/Sleeper) and *Building Construction Illustrated* (Ching/Adams) but a far more pleasurable read than either, *The Thatcher's Craft* clearly describes every aspect of thatching, from start to finish, according to proper English standards and is used as an on-site manual by all guilded thatchers in the United Kingdom. A second book, *How to Thatch a Small Roof* [7] is aimed specifically at those new to the craft, clearly illustrating the peculiar ingenuity of thatching. These two references are excellent resources on the disciplinary and material protocols of this strange, enduring practice.

Hairstyling

Upon recontextualizing thatch toward contemporary architectural applications we might then appeal to the outside discipline of hairstyling (cosmetology) for stylistic inspiration and technical knowledge. The mechanico-physical similarities between hair and thatch, and thus hairstyling and thatching, are obvious (Figures 1.6–1.8). So striking are these commonalities, in fact, that the tools involved in each practice are virtually identical – shears, combs, parting and tying devices, and the like are used in each. Their only significant difference lies in their necessarily different scales.[8] Beyond this, referencing a material practice and "lower art" extrinsic to architecture promotes a deeply materialist, empiricist polemic. It is not a question of "what does thatch wish to be?" but rather "how does thatch behave when worked?" And while the disciplinary incorporation of hairstyling may be unusual, it is not without precedent, however tenuous. Rococo painters mastered techniques for representing hair and soon thereafter their counterparts in architecture set about applying delicate tendrils of plaster across wall surfaces. Similarly, Art Nouveau architects and other organically inclined designers found fascination with botanical hairiness, expressed in the whimsical dynamism of excessive linework. Later still, Verner Panton styled his interiors with an even more literal furriness in the form of lush shag carpet and dangling, filamentous chandeliered ceilings. Perhaps the most direct example of an architect's desire to work with hair, however, is Leonardo da Vinci's *Study for the Head of Leda* (Figure 1.9) in which it is believed that da Vinci created the hairstyle himself.

      With the possible exception of da Vinci (of which little is known of his reasons for creating a new hairstyle for his model), each of these examples is linked not only through fascination with hairy motifs and effects but also through a conscious move away from higher metaphysical aspirations toward what Georges Bataille would later describe as "bring[ing] things down in the world."[9] Though few and obscure relative to larger canonical movements in architecture's history, these divergent moments provide some degree of precedent for arguments toward the contemporary use value of the cosmetological arts for architecture.

For an introduction to the remarkable (and, perhaps, surprising) expertise achieved in cosmetology there is likely just one best source: the Vidal Sassoon Academy. The methods and concepts developed by Sassoon (or simply "Vidal" to those within the discipline) and his school have elevated hairstyling to levels of virtuoso geometrical-material performance rivaling any found in the so-called "higher arts." Known in the world of cosmetology as the "Harvard of Hairstyling," Vidal Sassoon Academy has developed a rigorous methodology for the analysis and description of the morphological and material characteristics of hair and its compositional relationship to the shape of the skull. These principles are formalized in a comprehensive set of evolving manuals for hairstylists that are not unlike our own *Architectural Graphic Standards*. Much information of interest to contemporary architects of advanced form may be found in these volumes, perhaps the most compelling being an extensive collection of finely-drawn geometrical diagrams describing the mechanics of hair, head, and hairstyling technique.[10]

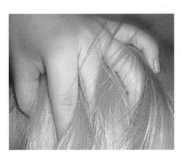

Figures 1.6–1.7 Separating bunches during thatching

Figure 1.8 Separating bunches during hairstyling

Figure 1.9 Leonardo da Vinci, *Study for the Head of Leda*, 1503–1507

Figure 1.10 "The Thatch"

Thatch cosmetology

Given the striking parallels between these two disciplines it really should have occurred to architects before now that a marriage of thatching (architecture) and hairstyling (cosmetology) is a match made in empirical-practice heaven. As it happens, it did occur to at least one person already: Vidal Sassoon. His 1972 collection included a cut named simply "The Thatch" (Christopher Brooker, stylist) in which the model's strawberry blond hair is treated and styled in a manner reminiscent of a classic UK thatched roof (Figure 1.10). Coming off as a witty take on superficial similarities between the model's hair texture and color and that of its reedy architectural equivalent, this particular moment of intersection was more insightful than it first appears. For Vidal Sassoon was formally trained in Bauhaus compositional principles and was especially fond of their application in building design. From this came a body of research, experimentation, and ultimately practice now known within cosmetology's academe as Vidal's "architecture of hair." No mere sloganeering, Sassoon's architectural prowess is expressed not only in the evolving set of principles and techniques taught in his Academy but is ultimately most evident in the work itself. Decades of hairstyle collections[11] show sustained compositional, material, and stylistic refinement through cuts of formal complexity rivaling our own best works in architecture.

The above arguments for a re-discovery of thatching through hairstyling notwithstanding,[12] it is this more generalized cross-pollination of practical and compositional principles so evident in advanced cosmetology that holds most promise for architecture. Vidal Sassoon and generations of subsequent hair designers under his influence have worked decades to advance the cause of an oft-overlooked material category – that of the humble hair. Volumes of built precedent now exist for inclusion within our own discourse – hairstyles so very close in character and concept to works of architecture ... each one a little building, really! For this effort we ought to return the favor with a nod to Vidal (and a wink to Semper) and move forward toward a hirsute architecture.

Raspberry Fields

The project that follows is included here to indicate a particular architectural expression of some of the potentials outlined above. While not thatched *per se*,[13] it is hairy (or furry, really), and does rely on certain construction methods and conceptual principles found in cosmetology. For example, shingles in certain key locations are heat-curled using a device similar to a curling iron (the shingles in the scale model were, in fact, curled with curling irons) and styled according to compositional principles outlined in Sassoon Academy's cut manuals.[14] This project began shortly after its principal designer completed a series of training seminars at the Vidal Sassoon Academy in Santa Monica, California, and thus represents the kind of disciplinary cross-pollination advocated above.

> Funk is not what is scripted
> Or what is expected ...
> It is what is felt.

(Al Sharpton, on James Brown, 2007)

Figure 1.11 *Raspberry Fields,*
schoolhouse symmetry and bipolarity

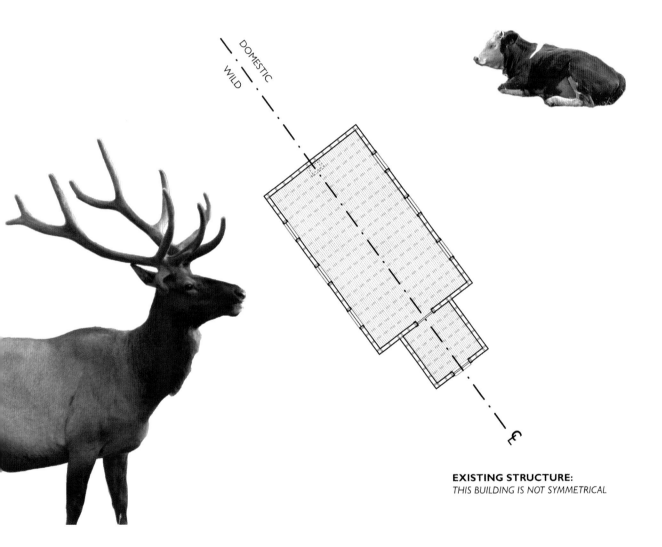

DOMESTIC

WILD

¢

EXISTING STRUCTURE:
THIS BUILDING IS NOT SYMMETRICAL

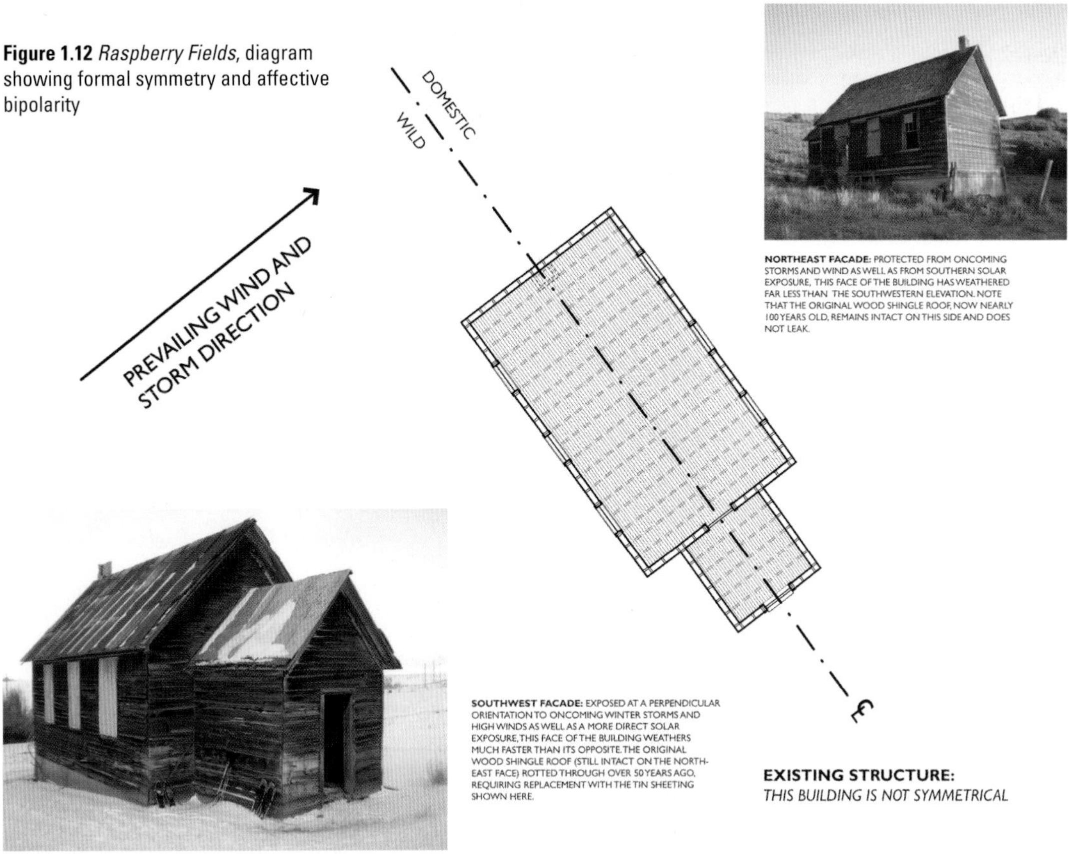

Figure 1.12 *Raspberry Fields*, diagram showing formal symmetry and affective bipolarity

DOMESTIC
WILD

PREVAILING WIND AND STORM DIRECTION

NORTHEAST FACADE: PROTECTED FROM ONCOMING STORMS AND WIND AS WELL AS FROM SOUTHERN SOLAR EXPOSURE, THIS FACE OF THE BUILDING HAS WEATHERED FAR LESS THAN THE SOUTHWESTERN ELEVATION. NOTE THAT THE ORIGINAL WOOD SHINGLE ROOF, NOW NEARLY 100 YEARS OLD, REMAINS INTACT ON THIS SIDE AND DOES NOT LEAK.

SOUTHWEST FACADE: EXPOSED AT A PERPENDICULAR ORIENTATION TO ONCOMING WINTER STORMS AND HIGH WINDS AS WELL AS A MORE DIRECT SOLAR EXPOSURE, THIS FACE OF THE BUILDING WEATHERS MUCH FASTER THAN ITS OPPOSITE. THE ORIGINAL WOOD SHINGLE ROOF (STILL INTACT ON THE NORTH-EAST FACE) ROTTED THROUGH OVER 50 YEARS AGO, REQUIRING REPLACEMENT WITH THE TIN SHEETING SHOWN HERE.

EXISTING STRUCTURE:
THIS BUILDING IS NOT SYMMETRICAL

Historical context

This project is a full renovation and restoration of an existing, one-room schoolhouse built in northern Utah in the early 1900s. Used as a school into the 1920s, the structure was then used sporadically to store grain through the 1950s and birth lambs in the 1960s, after which time it was abandoned for any formal use. Despite this decades-long lack of utility, the building has stood as a reminder to the local ranching community of their origins in this difficult, remote part of the country. Over the years, through seasons of hard winters and hot summers, the structure has remained straight, unbroken, and – true to its original design – absolutely bilaterally symmetrical. Or so it would seem.

Existing conditions

The long axis of the building is oriented at approximately 30° off of the east–west direction such that its south-west façade faces directly into prevailing winter storms as well as the southerly solar exposure. For this reason, the south-west side of the building has weathered significantly, having seen over a century of freeze-thaw dynamics (Figures 1.11–1.12). The north-east side, however, has remained nearly perfectly preserved. The effects of weathering (or lack thereof) are captured in the shape, texture, and color of the original wood cladding and shingles (Figure 1.13). On the north-east side all is in order, while on the south-west side the wood planks have curled with such force as to pry the nails from the studs and the shingles have long since blown away (Figures 1.14–1.16). Similarly, the protected side remains a deep, even brown, while the weathered side has become wildly striped with all manner of browns, blacks, grays, and even moments of bright greens and oranges where lichen have found purchase in the tortured surface. All of this is to say that this structure, while formally an exercise in perfect symmetry is phenomenally something quite different. In terms of both material dynamics and affective disposition, the two faces could not be more different.

Figure 1.13 *Raspberry Fields*, rendering of south-west façade showing stained and styled shingles

Design response: symmetry and bipolarity

The design for the renovation and restoration of this building stems from this synthesis of strong formal symmetry and radical affective bipolarity (Figure 1.17). The work seeks to reinforce and amplify this pre-existing dichotomy from both directions. The design of the interior becomes a nuanced play of symmetry-making and breaking, with certain elements aligning along the central axis or aligning against the two flanking edges, while others move off-axis in the age-old compositional play that pits idiosyncrasy against balance. In contrast to the formal-geometrical project of the interior, the design of the exterior addresses the affective material qualities of wood subjected to various degrees of weathering (Figure 1.18). The entire building is re-clad in wood shingles that, in the beginning, are all the same: 4" by 24" (with 12" exposed face) by 1/2" thick cedar stained a deep, almost black purple. On the day construction is complete, the building's massing and cladding will appear to be relatively flat, monolithic, self-similar, and more optically absorptive than reflective. Over time, however, the object's material and contextual bipolarity will be revealed, not only through the expression of natural weathering on the two different sides, but through an accelerated process brought about by unusual detailing. The long, slender shingles are attached intentionally improperly, with the bottom ends unfixed and the grain oriented more horizontally than vertically. This encourages premature curling of the kind already seen in the

Figure 1.14 *Raspberry Fields,* diagram showing asymmetrical weathering of existing structure

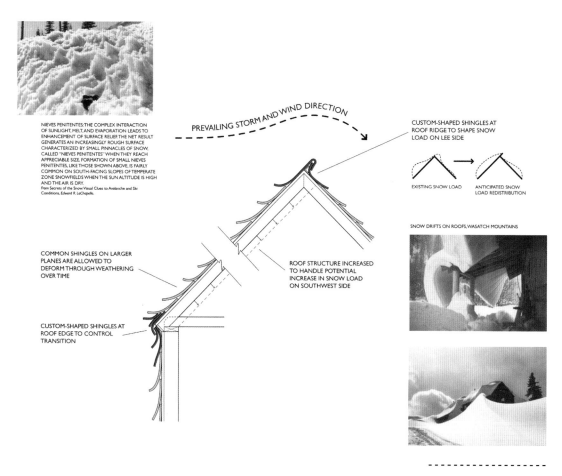

NIEVES PENITENTES: THE COMPLEX INTERACTION OF SUNLIGHT, MELT, AND EVAPORATION LEADS TO ENHANCEMENT OF SURFACE RELIEF. THE NET RESULT GENERATES AN INCREASINGLY ROUGH SURFACE CHARACTERIZED BY SMALL PINNACLES OF SNOW, CALLED "NIEVES PENITENTES" WHEN THEY REACH APPRECIABLE SIZE. FORMATION OF SMALL NIEVES PENITENTES, LIKE THOSE SHOWN ABOVE, IS FAIRLY COMMON ON SOUTH-FACING SLOPES OF TEMPERATE ZONE SNOWFIELDS WHEN THE SUN ALTITUDE IS HIGH AND THE AIR IS DRY.
From *Secrets of the Snow: Visual Clues to Avalanche and Ski Conditions,* Edward R. LaChapelle.

PREVAILING STORM AND WIND DIRECTION

CUSTOM-SHAPED SHINGLES AT ROOF RIDGE TO SHAPE SNOW LOAD ON LEE SIDE

EXISTING SNOW LOAD   ANTICIPATED SNOW LOAD REDISTRIBUTION

COMMON SHINGLES ON LARGER PLANES ARE ALLOWED TO DEFORM THROUGH WEATHERING OVER TIME

ROOF STRUCTURE INCREASED TO HANDLE POTENTIAL INCREASE IN SNOW LOAD ON SOUTHWEST SIDE

CUSTOM-SHAPED SHINGLES AT ROOF EDGE TO CONTROL TRANSITION

SNOW DRIFTS ON ROOFS, WASATCH MOUNTAINS

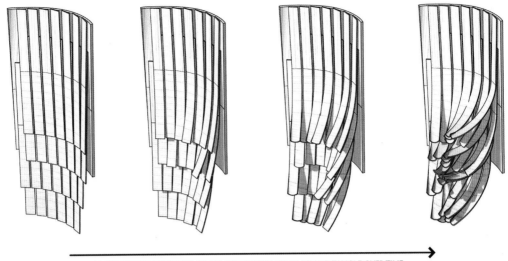

CONCAVE SURFACE ENCOURAGES SHINGLES TO OVERLAP AND TANGLE OVER TIME

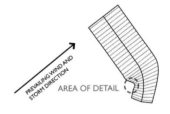

PREVAILING WIND AND STORM DIRECTION

AREA OF DETAIL

Figure 1.15 *Raspberry Fields*, common and custom shingle profiles
Figure 1.16 *Raspberry Fields*, detail of physical model showing curled roof shingles

existing south-western façade, only much worse due to the "impropriety" of the shingles. Adding to the drama, the undersides of the shingles on this side are stained much more brightly than the dark topsides, ranging in color from orange to purple to match the four colors of raspberry species indigenous to the site. Thus, when the shingles begin to curl, their undersides reveal a flamboyance that is in marked contrast to the darkened reserve of the initial skin. Over many years it is hoped that the shingles on the exposed side take on the character of fur, growing slightly fuller with each season. Meanwhile, the northeast side – the only façade subjected to local scrutiny due to the orientation of the building on the site – will remain reasonably straight and composed.

- - - - - - - - - - - - - - - - - -

Figure 1.17 *Raspberry Fields*, transverse building section

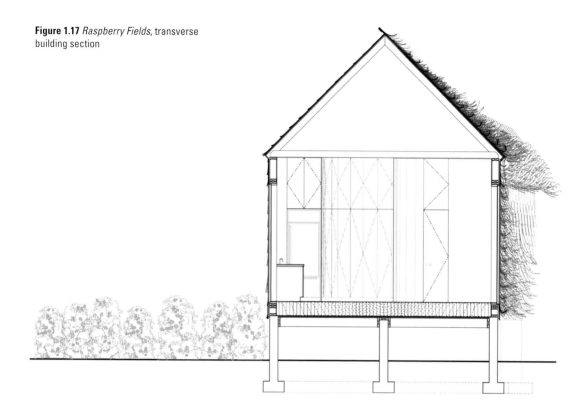

Figure 1.18 *Raspberry Fields*, physical model from north showing cultivated fields in foreground

Notes

1   For an example of just how easy (and fun!) hair and fur theory can be, see Gottfried Semper's *Style in the Technical and Tectonic Arts; or, Practical Aesthetics*, Vol. 1, Chapter 4, Section 28: "Furriery: A Recently Neglected Technique" (Los Angeles: Getty Publications, 2004, pp. 173–175).

2   Irresponsible, that is, to loftier ideological and disciplinary protocols.

3   Such as the recent idiomatic movement dubbed "intricacy" by Greg Lynn and other, more general tendencies toward compositions made of very large arrays of geometrical components.

4   Thatch also intersects current discourse in another, entirely unrelated way: thatch is green. It happens that a thatched roof has a significantly higher insulation value than any modern roofing technology. Further, thatch is an entirely natural, renewable material and is often locally-grown, eliminating the environmental impact of material transportation. While certain plant types perform better than others, most any long-stemmed species may be used. This material requires little in the way of processing and thatchers are usually local craftspeople. So compelling is the environmental argument for thatch that growing numbers of environmentalists are calling for renewed consideration of this nearly forgotten cladding technology. Thatch's green-ness, however, is of little relevance to the arguments presented here.

5   On this point, thatch should not be confused with the woven and braided structures found in certain African cultures which, while equally ingenious, are not technically thatched.

6   *The Thatcher's Craft* (London: Rural Development Commission, 1960).

7   Leo Wood, *How to Thatch a Small Roof: A Step-by-Step Illustrated Guide on Thatching Your Own Small Roof by a Master Thatcher of 40 Years* (www.thatch.org, 2006).

8   An almost comical example of this technical parallelism can be seen in the thatcher's comb, a giant version of that used in cosmetology.

9   Georges Bataille, "Formless," *Documents* 7 (December 1929): 382.

10   Mark Hayes, *ABC: Cutting Hair the Sassoon Way* (London: Vidal Sassoon Academy, 2000).

11   Analogous to those found in fashion design, a "collection" is defined as a series of hairstyles conceived and executed as a coherent family of cuts and styles. Vidal Sassoon typically produces three collections per year and each contains somewhere between three and twelve individual hairstyles.

12   And for the record: on the question of the natural affinity between thatch and hairstyle, Vidal got there first.

13   Nor should it be. Any good hairstylist will tell you that head shape and hair type largely govern what one can and cannot do with your hairstyle. In this case, the existing structure and material palette resist a thatched response.

14   Hayes, *ABC: Cutting Hair the Sassoon Way*.

Chapter 2
Voussoir Cloud

Lisa Iwamoto and Craig Scott
IwamotoScott

Building form and material operate at different scales. Form is large and singular; material is small and comes in parts. While perhaps a gross characterization, this simple distinction is increasingly evident in the arena of parametric design whose explorations have focused on material assemblies defined by modulated fields. One presumption is that such relational models will afford greater connectivity among various aspects of the architectural work. However, with a bottom-up cellular or modular approach, how these systems aggregate or subdivide is often conceived apart from overall building form. Predictable disjunctures often play out between form and skin – either a form is wrapped by a skin that adjusts to fit, as is the case both with conventional building materials and highly evolved parametric parts, or a skin makes an indeterminate form predicated on a modular system. It is not surprising therefore that finding effective translations between material and building scales is a growing architectural preoccupation.

Intermittently throughout architectural history, whether weighted toward constructive necessity or design agenda, architects, engineers and builders have employed structure as the imperative that connects material with form. From traditional masonry construction to geodesic domes, this method of form making is largely dependent on geometry, the single most important factor in determining structural performance. Arches, vaults, domes, thin shells, tensile membranes, cable nets and the like intricately unite material with surface structure. The ultra-thin concrete hypar roofs of Felix Candela and catenary domes of Heinz Isler, Eladio Dieste's sinuous brick walls, and Frei Otto's wood lath grid-shells and steel cable nets are modern examples that celebrate the coupling of material behavior with structural surface geometry. These architects employed extensive physical form-finding such as hanging chain models, plaster mesh casts, and cable nets loaded with weights carefully monitored by strain gauges to achieve optimized structural solutions.

In contrast to such structurally pure models, the power of computation has opened possibilities for at once muddying and synthesizing geometry, structure and material performance. Where the earlier twentieth-century experiments employed a more or less uniform tectonic based on symmetrical structural diagrams, contemporary analysis and design techniques can efficiently adapt a material system to address variable, localized, and non-symmetrical loading conditions. The seemingly ad hoc structural framework of CCTV designed by OMA and engineered by Arup serves as a good example of expressive structural modulation. The skin's diagonal bracing tightens, changes size, and sometimes disappears altogether based on forces generated by the two-way building cantilever. Foster Partners and Buro Happold Los Angeles offer a more stealth approach in the design of the Smithsonian Institution courtyard roof enclosure. The roof canopy is similar to a minimal soap bubble surface geometry, but is far more shallow and non-uniform in its overall configuration. The resulting irregular stress pattern is addressed with a variant structural diagrid whose segments swell and shrink according to localized forces while the overall diamond pattern remains intact. Both these projects characterized by non-optimized structural form register the impacts of geometry on material behavior with a deviated tectonic system.

IwamotoScott's design research does not explicitly pursue a tectonic agenda, but rather attempts to achieve a synthetic outcome by negotiating material and surface with environment and space, geometry and form. The work uses structure as a predominant, but non-determinative constraint. *Voussoir Cloud*, our installation at the SCI-Arc Gallery in 2008, extends this research and draws from the methodology of the abovementioned historic and contemporary precedents. However, rather than the design process being determined either by the structural and material optimization pursued by the architect/engineers of the mid-twentieth century, or by a deviated constructional system based on non-optimized forms in the latter examples, *Voussoir Cloud* began with research into material behavior. The original design intent was therefore not formally motivated, but evolved from empirical testing of a material and determining its salient relationships to geometry and structure. The material selection stemmed from a previous project, *In–Out Curtain*, which was made from folding micro-thin wood and paper laminate (Figure 2.1). For *Voussoir Cloud*, we were interested in de-familiarizing this normally common and basic material, wood, typically used either as decorative skin or trabeated structure, as skin and structure simultaneously. The unexpected combination of a wood product being paper-thin and having shear strength, translucency and the ability to fold propelled the qualitative aspects of the design.

Figure 2.1 *In–Out Curtain*, operable screen prototype, Ornament Exhibition, Chicago

The design process for *Voussoir Cloud* began similarly to *In–Out Curtain*, by folding sheet material into a three-dimensional modular component. In this case, however, we sought to explore the possibilities of folding along a curved seam. Small handmade models were used to test geometric relationships across the fold in plan and section (Figure 2.2). It was relatively simple to determine that the greater and more acute the curve in plan resulted in a higher degree of curvature in section, but finding accurate dimensional relationships between the two was significantly more complicated and became central to the digital design process. What also became apparent from these physical experiments was that any aggregation of the modules, or petals as we termed them because of their shape, produced a naturally curving surface. By assembling a number of small mock-ups from simple hand-drawn plan patterns using diagrid and Delaunay tessellations, it was evident that both types of triangulation resulted in overall arcing of the surface due to the outward bowing out of the flange along the curved seam (Figure 2.3). This vaulted nature ultimately dictated the overall form and design strategy.

From here the design process developed two parallel tracks. The first worked to translate the material behavior of a single petal into a digital script based on a set of geometric relationships, the second to determine overall form. In designing the form the project took on many variations, however, certain design

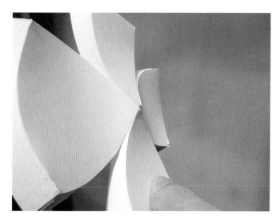

Figure 2.2 Delaunay triangulated and diagrid paper prototype assemblies

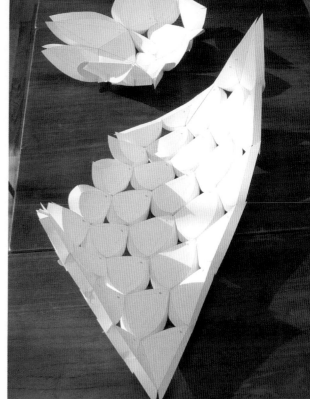

Figure 2.3 Delaunay triangulated and diagrid paper prototype assemblies

intentions remained consistent throughout. These included the desire to create an occupiable and atmospheric environment in the gallery rather than a discrete object, and to have the installation be equally compelling from above as from within. Driving this concern was that a primary view of the gallery space is from above via a frequently traversed walkway at mezzanine level which is open even during non-gallery hours.

The final design fills the gallery with a system of vaults whose billowing character and constructional system are revealed from above. The plan is based on the typology of the peristyle hall, but adapted here to produce scalar, spatial and tectonic affects. The columnar and volumetric organization takes advantage of the contemporary capacity to inflect as opposed to the static, regularized definition typical in both classical and modernist buildings. Using the edges of the gallery as spatial and constructional constraints, the vault edges are supported and delimited by the entry soffit and the two long gallery walls. The vaults modulate in scale and proportion, migrating to form greater density at the edges and toward the rear of the gallery forming a progressively compressed and varied space.

The geometry of each vault is structurally derived; however, the seemingly obvious connection between the vaulted surface of the petals, and a structurally vaulted form was not immediately apparent. It took multiple failed design attempts working with the curved surfaces as a structural panel system applied to a singular form to move to a process of structural form finding (Figure 2.4). Once this methodology took hold, the conceptual premise of the project became more focused in its aim to create a voussoir cloud. That is, reforming the expectations of a traditional vault made of massive wedge-shaped stone or brick into an ephemeral structure by exploring the structural paradigm of pure compression coupled with an ultra lightweight material system.

As a form-finding enterprise, the project draws significantly from the work of Frei Otto and Antonio Gaudi who used hanging chain models to find efficient form. Under their own weight hanging chains naturally

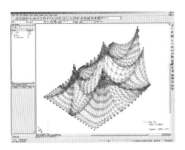

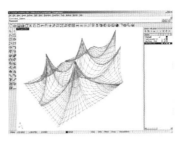

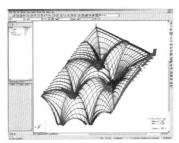

Figure 2.4 ROBOT hanging chain model

Figure 2.5 Overlaid original approximated and final catenary curves

Figure 2.6 ROBOT finite structural analysis of axial load paths

adopt a funicular profile with minimal internal stress; they are in pure tension with no shear or bending forces. If re-inverted, the tension becomes compression, creating a pure catenary arch. We worked closely with the engineering firm Buro Happold, Los Angeles, to arrive at a funicular configuration for the vaults through an iterative digital design process. Each version began with our office first creating a three-dimensional digital model articulating the vault edges with approximated catenary arches (Figure 2.5). This model was then given to Buro Happold, who literally turned it upside down to evaluate the curves as a network of digital hanging chains. The engineers used the structural analysis program ROBOT to form-find the new catenary geometries using non-linear analysis; this allowed the curves to deform under a uniform self-weight computationally mimicking a hanging chain. For the final curves, the displacement between the initial and the form-found geometry was up to 12 inches, and the form-finding process reduced the bending and deflections in the structure by 90 percent. IwamotoScott used the pure catenaries from Buro Happold to generate the surface geometries of the vaults. These surfaces were first approximated in Rhinoceros, then shaped into funicular shells using another form-finding script in Maya (Figure 2.6).

Structurally, the vaults rely on each other and the three gallery edges to retain their pure compressive form. This overall system is stable because adjacent vaults are in equilibrium at their intervening seams; the outward thrust of one vault is balanced by the equal and opposite force of the vault adjacent. The seams also function as a pathway for the compressive force in each vault to travel down to the gallery floor where the 14 segmented pieces resolve to make a series of five columns supporting the interior and back edge. It is a highly interdependent set of elements that gently push on each other to maintain stability.

This interdependency is multiplied at the level of the tessellation where the individual petals work together to form the larger vaults. For the system to work as a whole, each individual petal must perform structurally. We again used geometry to maximize the material's structural performance. The three-dimensional petals formed by folding thin wood laminate along curved seams develop stiffness and stability from otherwise flexible material. The curve also produces a dished petal form that uses the internal surface tension of the wood and folded geometry of the flanges to hold its shape. At the same time, the flanges want to bulge out along the curved fold. This curvature ultimately afforded a way to attach the petals together using the surface area of the flanges for bearing (Figures 2.7–2.8). Unlike a triangulated pattern where modules would meet at a single end point, this bearing surface allows the modules to press upon each other and therefore work in compression. The bulging petal edge is also what affords the vaulted structure porosity; the curvature is only possible if there is an adjacent void.

As mentioned above, the formation of the petals developed along a separate trajectory. After the initial paper models, the ensuing design process focused on calibrating the relationship of physical prototype to digital corollary through iterative empirical testing. It was first necessary to determine the appropriate construction of the curved fold-line in plan. We began with the constraint that in order to bear upon each other, each petal must meet tangent to its neighbor at the vertices. The plan curvature at each petal edge became defined at its end points as a set of tangents based on the centroid of the adjacent void. The remainder of the curve's center

- - - - - - - - - - - - - - - - - - -

was developed within this limitation. We tested a number of curvature degrees both digitally and physically to determine the ideal arc. Too acute resulted in an uneven and kinked dimple, too obtuse a flattened sectional profile (Figure 2.9). Our goal was to achieve a smooth but noticeable dish so that each petal remained visually distinct yet integral to the overall surface.

The next and most challenging step was deciphering and digitally scripting the proportional relationships between the curved fold-line in plan and the resulting sectional deformation. From the models we could establish that the sectional deformation of the petal is related to the plan curvature and degree of bend, but by what amount exactly? It was also clear from the physical models that we could create the three-dimensional dished module with a non-doubly curved surface, but this proved difficult to digitally define. We were fortunate to discover a conference paper, "Folded Developables," from which we could discern key geometric principles.[1] One key determinant was that if the flanges of the petal are perpendicular to the original cell surface, the maximum curve offset, or delta, from the original triangular cell in plan is the same as the maximum delta in section.

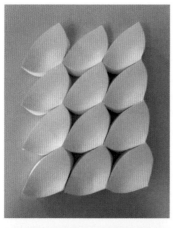

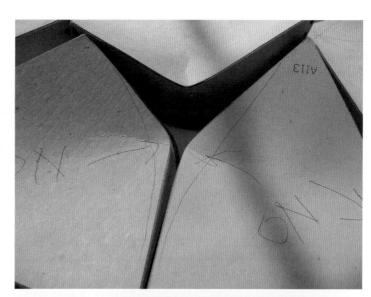

Figures 2.7–2.8 Early material prototype examining aggregative relationships

Figure 2.9a–b Flat assembly paper mock-up showing successful delta values between plan and section

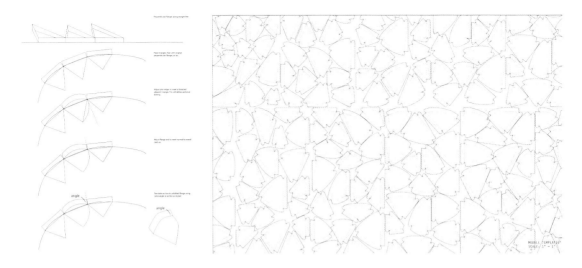

Figure 2.10 Illustrated process to determine flange angles
Figure 2.11 Unfolded petals for laser cutting templates

In order to evaluate this, we moved once again to small paper models. If each cell was an equilateral triangle as in a geodesic dome, this would be a relatively simple exercise. In our case, however, the form of the vaults and desired tessellation pattern demanded that each triangle be asymmetrical on all three sides. Therefore, the curve offset on every side was most likely different, and we needed to establish their combined effect on the petal's sectional deformation. We determined that if a set of aggregated modules remained flat and did not distort with the fold at 90 degrees, then the relationship of the three plan curves was good. We first tested equal length offsets on the three sides which did not result in a flat assembly. It was a trial and error process to discover how best to assign values to the three curves based on the tangents and side-length that would give us a predicted sectional dish. Knowing this set of values would ensure that the unfolded petal would form what we were expecting in three dimensions.

We also gleaned from "Folded Developables" that at any other flange angle than 90 degrees, the amount of sectional dish in section varies with the plan curvature according to a logarithmic function. This

Figure 2.12a–c Single petal variations showing appropriate direction of wood grain

was important because the sectional change affects the final plan dimensions; the more the sectional dish, the smaller the petal size in plan – which again affects the accuracy of how they fit together. In the case of *Voussoir Cloud*, none of the flange angles are at 90 degrees. They are dictated by the normals of the vaults rather than the cell itself, so the amount of petal dish, and therefore its size, has a unique geometry that needs to be calibrated to fit into the overall arched form (Figure 2.10). Though mathematically, the relationship of flange angle to sectional height is non-linear, we felt confident in simplifying it to a simple percentage based on our physical tests. Here, we relied on the forgiveness of the material to accommodate the small imperfections of final petal size to the original plan triangle.

From the proportional and geometric data we were able to develop a computational Rhinoscript that managed the petal edge plan curvature and instantiated the three-dimensional modules into our tessellated surface. A second scripted batch process was also developed to unfold, label, score, and add holes for fasteners (Figure 2.11). The only manual pre-assembly activity was nesting the modules on the 4 x 8 sheets for laser cutting. While we sought material economy here, it was also critical that the unfolded petals align properly with the grain of the wood. Wood is a non-isotropic material, more flexible along the grain and resistant to bending against. Though there was only a micro-thin layer of wood on our wood/paper laminate, the grain had a dramatic effect on the ability of the petals to dish. The grain had to be aligned to the long direction of the petal or longest side, or perpendicular to the short side in order for the petal to form properly (Figure 2.12). Ultimately, each petal behaves in a slightly different manner based on its size, edge conditions, and position relative to the overall form; it is here that the two scales of exploration – module and form – merge.

Combining the structural and modular geometries was largely a packing problem. We sought to organize the petals for the greatest functional and perceptual performance. Each vault was tessellated using Delaunay triangulation. We chose this pattern because it is at once visually informal and can capitalize on structural logistics. There is greater cell density where smaller more connective petals gang together at the

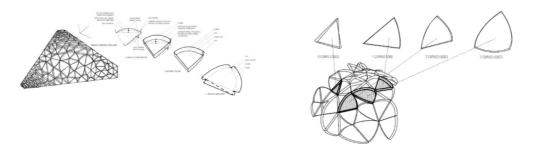

Figure 2.13 Tesselation pattern of unfolded vault

Figure 2.14 Petal types

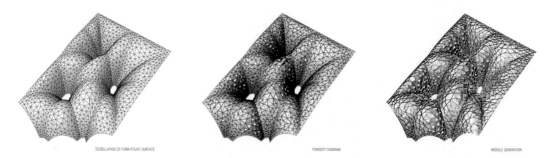

Figure 2.15a–c Rhinoscripting process

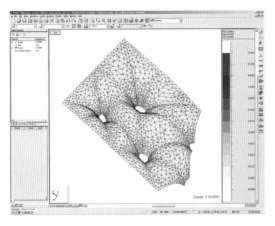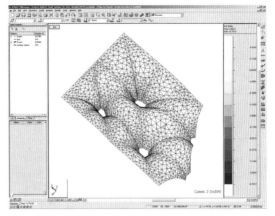

Figure 2.16a–b Structural analysis of axial and shear force

column bases and at the vault edges to form strengthened ribs, while the upper vault shell loosens and gains porosity (Figure 2.13). In the end, there are four petal types in *Voussoir Cloud* dependent on whether the petal edge is next to a voided cell. As there can only be a curved edge when there is a void, the petals have zero, one, two, or three curved edges (Figure 2.14). In the design, the petals are more closely packed, defined with less offset, and therefore flatter towards the base and edges where they connect to straight triangulated cells. The petals have greater offset and more curvature at the top where there is more porosity, creating the dimpled effect on the interior. Our Rhinoscript calculated and instantiated each of the 2300 petals according to these criteria (Figure 2.15).

Once the petals were instantiated, Buro Happold conducted a set of analyses from which we refined the tessellation pattern. They again employed ROBOT to conduct a finite element analysis of the tessellated structure to test its performance and ensure that the load values and the load path were as predicted (Figure 2.16). In some instances, the seams needed to be strengthened, sponsoring us to create a vertical load path by having the petals weave back and forth across every continuous seam. As a part of refining the petal organization, our office also built several full-scale mock-ups of a single vault. These were used to affirm structural viability and develop connection methods for the petals.

Figure 2.17a–b Chipboard vault mock-up

Figure 2.18 Chipboard vault mock-up structural failure

Figure 2.19a–b Assembly process at SCI-Arc

We evaluated the entire process of modeling, laser cutting, assembling, and connecting the petals for the vault (Figure 2.17). Additional tabs for gluing the individual modules and the connectors developed at this stage. For the connectors, an inexpensive solution developed, moving from an original idea of pop-rivets to lacing the petals together with simple 1/16" zip-ties. This posed a new issue for the mock-ups, however. The mock-ups were made out of chipboard which ultimately proved far inferior to the wood. Though the petal geometries could be replicated accurately, the resistance to pull-out was far lower, resulting in the vaults tearing apart at the connection points within a few moments of standing (Figure 2.18). After some improvisational testing with Buro Happold on pull-out resistance at the connection holes of the wood laminate, we collectively determined that it would bear the force if the petals were arrayed with enough density. The size, density and porosity of the final petals were thus a direct response to such digital and physical analyses.

Once the overall geometry, structure, tessellation, and material system were aligned, the actual fabrication and final assembly at SCI-Arc were an exercise in scheduling and material management. The 2300 petals were cut off site in Michigan near the material manufacturer due to cost and equipment considerations; the laser cutter could handle 4 x 8 sheets yet power down sufficiently so as not to burn the material while scoring. The pieces arrived in batches which the SCI-Arc students sorted, folded and glued (Figure 2.19). As with many experimental installation projects, students and volunteers made the construction possible.

Our only construction document was an installation diagram specifying the order of assembly (Figure 2.20). One limitation we had was very limited physical access, particularly above the vaults when they were complete. We were also not using any centering or scaffolding typical in traditional in vault construction. Therefore, the vaults had to be somewhat self-supporting during the construction process. To deal with these issues, our strategy was to build the column bases first, followed by the "ribs" where the vaults come together, and then finally filling in the remaining centers beginning with the least accessible vaults near the entry first (Figure 2.21). This proved to be an adequate sequence though we encountered the typical unanticipated difficulties. One such issue was that without centering, the vaults flexed and shifted considerably until fully closed. In some instances, adjacent petals were as much as several feet apart leaving large gaps in the surface. By pushing on the vaults in a trial and error manner to better approach the funicular shape, the pieces eventually fell effortlessly into place. Hence, the construction process again revealed the specificity and criticality of the vault geometries relative to petal aggregation.

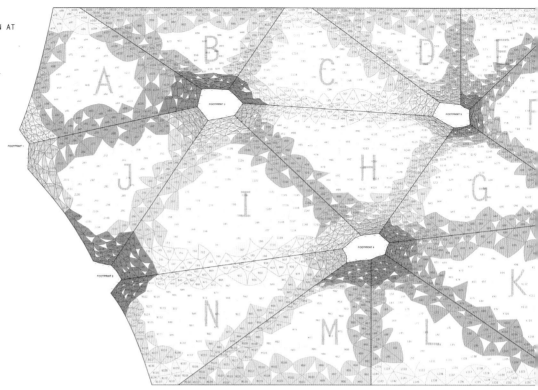

NOTE VIEW LOOKING DOWN AT
CONVEX SIDE

ORDER OF INSTALLATION
(DIFFERENTIATION OF
COLORS INDICATES DIVI-
SION OF PARTS)

1 COLUMN FEET

2 RIBS

3 TOP EDGES

Figure 2.20 Construction drawing
Figure 2.21a–d Gallery installation

In the end, *Voussoir Cloud* attempts to reform both structure and material to create new readings of a traditional architectural typology and construction method. Vaults are modulated and adapted to new plan and material configurations. These inflections are made possible by computational methods that are able to model, structurally analyze, and organize large quantities of non-uniform elements. It is not without considerable effort in the physical realm, however, that the conceptual and experiential goals of the project are made manifest. Our material exploration was essential in the derivation of the architectural idea. The petals – our reconstituted "voussoirs" – are light, paper-thin surfaces made into compressive elements. And their fluctuating visual quality from solid wood block to thin luminous surface as material affect drove the atmospheric intentions of the project (Figures 2.22–2.24). It is here, in the perceptual performance of *Voussoir Cloud* that seeks to be at once visceral and immediate, and instigate more considered speculation that our goals for the project ultimately lay.

Note

1   J. P. Duncan and J. L. Duncan, "Folded Developables," *Proceedings of the Royal Society of London*, Series A, Mathematical and Physical Sciences, Vol. 383, No. 1784, September 8, 1982: 191–205.

Figure 2.22a–b View of final installation at different times of day

Figure 2.23 Detail photograph

Figure 2.24 (overleaf) View of final installation during opening

Chapter 3
Light Frames
Matters of material in making

Gail Peter Borden

Borden Partnership

- -

This is a project founded in material. Begun with the fundamentals of its capabilities; engaged with a distinct process for generating components; developing systems out of these components; deploying media and representation to confront, challenge and experiment with the formal capabilities; and ultimately deriving form, experience and effect from the collaboration of all of these systems, the methodology comes from an intrinsic dialog with making.

This project is an engagement of material geometry, and the deployment of these tectonics to generate a light space experience. One not destined to be left at form, though this is an interesting point of arrival, here the descriptive geometry is laden with historical reference, spatial implication and when combined with the materials of which it is fabricated, the space and effect dominate all else.

Transcending scale, the material quality becomes unnoticed and enigmatic in form. The reference is left, leaving only a density of visual complexity. The geometry becomes latent. What is left is the experience of space through light and the mapping of the body into the world around it. A sequence of shadow to light and projected to projection, the layers of this project derive from the experience.

History and thinking

The work of Claude-Nicolas Ledoux (March 21, 1736–November 18, 1806) is materially founded. Enigmatic in its development of a hybridization of style and tectonic, his work emerges from a combination of traditional systems of French Neo-Classicism, with a desire to engage materiality and meaning. The combination of style and function embedded with a social and experiential agenda, all through the matter of material, combine to develop an "architecture parlant" but more explicitly a "material parlant."

Release of material | form

The release of a material into form comes from an essentialism of understanding the matter with which you work. The series of figural sculptures done by Michelangelo for the tomb of Pope Julius II (1513–1516), including the rebellious slave, the bound slave and the dying slave (Figure 21.1), each represent the frozen motion of the writhing human figure pulling against itself and the material from which it is made. These arguably unfinished, raw, and vibrant statues emerge from the overall figure of the raw stone, riding an edge between the material and the anthropomorphic representation. Derived from the quarried figure of the stone block and collaborating with the natural cleaving of the raw rock, the boundary is blurred between the natural and choreographed. Bathed in process, the three-pronged chisel and the method of emergence, revealing, and removing the material to expose the figure trapped inside establish the ideal translation of matter to form.

Michelangelo wrote that a pure and true sculpture should "retain so much of the original form of the stone block and should so avoid projections and separation of parts that it would roll downhill of its own

- - - - - - - - - - - - - - - - - - - -

Figure 3.1 Helicopter view of light frames

weight." This relation of the found form to the figure of the original quarried marble requires a reverence to the material. Michelangelo maintained an intense and exhibited devotion to the integrity of the original material. The stone block was the foundation upon which his form was derived. His engagement with the material led to a personal responsibility and connection to the rock itself. This conviction brought him repeatedly to Carrara, Italy, a Tuscan region of Italy renowned for its marbles from Roman to contemporary times, for the white marble to self-select the material origins of the works and forms, revealing his connection to the dialog with the material.

In a letter from 1549, Michelangelo defined sculpture as the art of "taking away" not that of "adding on" (the process of modeling in clay), which he deemed akin to painting. This subtractive association of technique to material allowed for a method that focused on freeing the figure born in his mind but visualized in the material from the confines of the marble block.

This attitude is picked up by Ledoux at the scale of architecture in the Royal Saltworks at Arc-et-Senans (1774–1779), but heightened to engage not simply the material translation to the figural and formal potential of material, but to engage meaning. Meaning emerges from a pictorially representational intention that has an abstract legibility that engages simulation, reference, and material experience.

Ledoux: brief history – two movements

Ledoux's work contains a series of moves that are anterior in their neo-classical agenda. This deference to style, when met with the heroic scales and sensibilities of his contemporaries Etienne-Louis Boullée (1729–1799) and Jean-Jacques Lequeu (1757–1826), allowed for a localized innovation: first, of the utopian sense of the piece and the second the heroic overview scale of the collective composition. He was able to most impressively implement both through the Saltworks at Arc-et-Senans.

At the Saltworks (Figures 3.2–3.4), Ledoux developed two major design moves that engaged the translation of material process into form. The architectural vehicles by which he accomplished these moves were:

- The development of a representational salt mine at the Entry Pavilion to the Royal Saltworks at Arc-et-Senans. The portico developed the minimal power of the over-riding figural geometry allowing a contrast with the internal grotto.
- Invention of a new column formed from a singular architectonic order of alternating cylindrical and cubic stones superimposed for their plastic effect; these are evident in several projects but most prominent in the House of the Director at the Royal Saltworks at Arc-et-Senans.

Figure 3.2 Ledoux Saltworks: Entry Pavilion

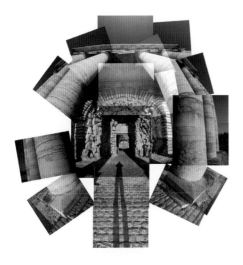

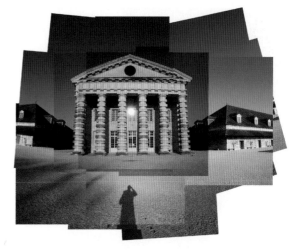

Figure 3.3 Ledoux Saltworks: grotto

Figure 3.4 Ledoux Saltworks: House of the Director

Fabricated experience: material and expression

Set on the north–south axis, where the line of approach intersects the semi-circular perimeter, the entrance to the Saltworks at Arc-et-Senans is the culmination of the complete planning of the complex. The entry pavilion holds a place of honor both within the complex and as the only architectural expression of the exterior, the rest of the exterior being defined by a 4-meter-high protective wall. Due to the value of the salt produced within, (known commonly as white gold during this era), the careful control and measure of the salt were essential. The entry building served as a threshold of comings and goings. Housing a guard post and their quarters, the surveillance and oversight (both physical and numerical), of this portal were essential.

The power of this threshold is announced through the dominant position in the landscape. The approach is dramatic and axial. One crosses the natural river and is immediately oriented to the axis of the complex and the entry. Several kilometers in length, the dramatic line, choreographed and tree-lined, leads to a massive Doric portico.

The power and sterility of this six-columned face, with Doric order and an eliminated base, likely taken from the Temple at Paestum which had recently been published, the rhythm and figure of these elements establish an austere, yet archetypical motif of Neo-Classicism. This powerful streamlined, but normative condition innate to contemporary architecture of its time, follows the rules so that attention for innovation may be paid elsewhere. Making simple overall massing moves with regulated and minimal ornamentation, the emphasis is on the clarity of the portico to establish a foil and contrast for that found within. Masked behind this colonnade is the simulation of an organic grotto intended to depict the entry to the salt mine. The rough stone and the vessels spilling forth with the liquid brine create a material change that transposed from the highly rationalized and controlled material deployment of the neo-classical surround to a morphology directed by a seemingly natural condition. The juxtaposition of this exterior with the interior cavernous hall that simulates the entrance to an actual salt mine, translates the traditional to the actual with the concrete decoration and ornamentation founded in the rawness and amorphous formalism of nature. The power of the natural world and the influence of the sublime as the organic forces, greater than the organizational systems of man, provide a physical and metaphorical threshold. Materially, there is an expression of form and intention through the method of making. The transitions from the smooth and subordinated stone masonry to the rough figuration of the "mine-like" rock rely upon a usage of technique to provide intention. Juxtaposing raw with refined, natural with man-made, high with low material, the ambiguity comes from the questioning of which is of greater significance, dominance, and importance. The power of the composition comes through the understanding of a method of material expression and the resulting formal manifestation.

Interlaced column: material and form

In this period, taste was returning to the antique, to the distinction and the examination, of the taste for the "rustic" style. Ledoux presented an alternative. Focused on primal geometries and the bold simplicity of the circle and square, he developed an interlaced column (Figures 3.5–3.6). Formed of discontinuous figures, the layered composition stacked segments of alternating shapes. The result is a dramatic double façade: a visual interlock of two geometric methods. The rigidity of the orthogonal square block and the suppleness of the circular round segments provided for both readings simultaneously. The orthogonal representing the purity of the material and the geometry form which it came. Revealed beneath the remnants of this boundary, the circular columnar figures emerge from the partially stripped sections to reveal their refined and referential iconography.

The bay

The bay of the House of the Director represents the essential hierarchy of the system. The banded columns, illustrating their conceptual as well as physical material method of making, reveal an honesty in their expression. Illustrating both the geometric systems governing their formal composition and the material process by which they are made, the neo-functionalism of their composition in the removal of detail invents a new order and produces an architecture of abstraction. Concerned more with the geometric purities of systemization and mathematics, the removal of ornament and stylized details, so popular at the time, present an experiential legibility to the architecture. Further, the forms require an honesty in the methods of construction and the translation of the idea into form, engaging the view and requiring them to interact and collaborate actively with the austerity of the composition to impose themselves into the reading of the building. No longer was the passive viewer, engulfed by ornament relevant. This architecture required an active engagement with the mind, the body and the material.

The column

The column holds the essence of the material expression. Defined by both geometries of circle and square, refined and primitive, the alternating forms intertwine to produce a grain and expression to the coursing. Intrinsic to all temple fronts, but no longer denying the practicalities of the segmented coursing, here the masonry coursing is engaged and celebrated. The differentiation between layers allows for alternating geometries and legibilities. The equality of the alternating figure removes the hierarchy and dominance of either one of the figures. The result is the simultaneous implication of two façades: one with cylindrical columns, traditional and referential to Greek and Roman architecture and foundational to the Neo-Classicism of the era, while the other is square and massive, with pure geometries robustly referencing something else. Its forms imply the geometric solids from which the cylinder was removed, the figure in a "pre-" made state, allowing the mind to translate through the process, both of the geometric description, but also through the hand tooling. The translations from the original figure to intended effectual figure engrain the stone block or the platonic rectilinear volume as equal participants in the final refined form. The reading of the two actively engage the viewer and bring geometry, the process of both design and fabrication, and material into the necessary reading and understanding of the building. The result is abstraction, a compositional requirement of engaging the viewer to actively participate in the interpretation and completion of the composition. As a result, this is the first modern building, the first building to be materially expressive.

Man as unit

The anthropomorphic dimension defines the relationship of material to man. In dimensional terms of fabrication, installation, construction, and ultimately experience, the scale of the unit and the component are essential. Intrinsically segmented, the joint is the expression of craft. The method of making and assembly emerges from the approach and articulation of aggregation. Here the dimension of the material and the dimension of the human body create a dialog between production and experience. The mastery of this systemization is the expression of craft through assembly.

Focus

Ledoux's engagement with abstraction through geometric expression and material celebration is evident through his interlaced elevation and the entry pavilion grotto. The two conditions riding between natural and man-made are both founded in their material expression and method of construction. Collectively they present a new view of architecture, one engaging the abstraction of composition, one celebrating and embracing the material, and one skirting between locally legible and super-structural. This systemization of process, material engagement for derivation of form, and the bridge between meaning and composition through material, make Ledoux the first modern architect.

The self in its dual natures between high and low, sacred and profane, biological and cognitive, is perhaps the most base of interlaced dialectics. The balance, interlock, and interdependence of both these worlds simultaneously require attention yet equality to both. Architecture is a service to both. Responding to the dimensional and perceptual limitations and abilities of our physical selves, yet appealing, engaging, and challenging the experiential qualities of the mind. Material and experience are thus *Doppelgängers*. Their balance and inter-relation are illusive yet essential. The impregnation of their methods into process allows for the unification and collaboration of matter with space. Architecture is born of their union.

Figure 3.7 Material and process

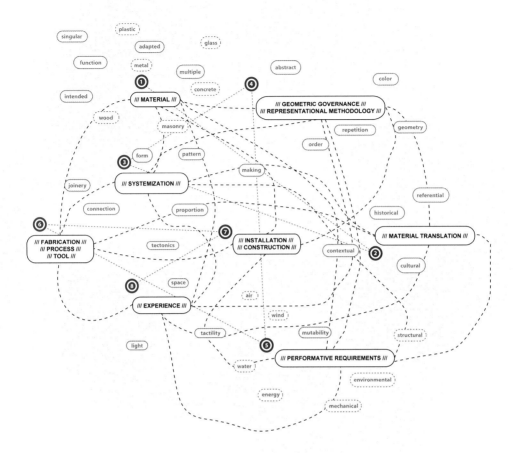

Points: methodological stages

Though the discussion here is specific to this project, its localized context and material, scale, and budget and the precision of these methods of fabrication, construction, and tectonics, it represents a broader belief in a larger methodology – one that commences with the material from which a project is made, experimentation with its capabilities, understanding of its history and tectonic and developing a system, with associated geometries defined by scale and site to determine an overt form. The method, though dangerous to follow in any formulaic manner, is as follows (Figure 3.7):

1. *Material*: The nobility or opportunity for effect is not in the material, but rather the relationship of process and tactic. The choice of a material can come from foresight into seeing how one can engage it. Costs, availability, workability, performance and durability are all elements in selecting the material, but the ultimate potential comes from the ability for the material to be engaged. This is where the variation and celebration, denial and test can begin to transcend. All materials hold nobility.

2. *Material translation*: The importance of translation is to generate the dialog with the material to find a collaborative method. Inserting control into the process of manipulation, melting points, derived modules, ductility, etc. – this is the engagement with process that allows for control, mastery, and collaboration. This can only come from the thoughtful address of the material itself.

3. *Systemization*: The systemization of the material translation comes from the material process as applied to the architectural questions. Translating from the independence of the translation, the system now requires the responsibilities of architecture – engaging structure, form, space, lighting, ventilation – all of the performative requirements of architectural discourse. This systemization is both functional and formal. It defines the system and method by which the material is engaged.

4. *Geometric governance + representational methodology*: The mediation of these techniques emerges from the engagement with technology – representative methods and parametric methods allow for complexities, efficiencies and predictabilities previously impossible. The media, in conjunction with new fabrication, allow for a translation of virtual to physical. The mastery of geometry to allow for relation and optimization to calibrate the significance of intention and to deploy the complexity of part to whole to allow a bridge from individual component to the collective whole.

5. *Performative requirements*: Performative requirements are defined by the translation of object into architecture through the impregnation of form. Making the materials and systems responsible for functional aspects of architecture, to mediate climate, information, site, use or any practical need; the performative aspect of the building brings function to the forefront to collaborate with material, fabrication, geometry and systemization to determine morphological decisions. These performative requirements, either passive or active, are points of instigation and engagement to challenge the future of architecture.

6. *Fabrication – process – tool*: Fabrication is the physical engagement of process with material. The method of manipulation, of engaging the physical and environmental practicalities: hardness, malleability, material, molecular organization (fibrous, crystalline, etc.), specific gravity, weathering, thermal properties … these all determine the way in which one engages matter. The method of material engagement is the foundation of fabrication, relating the material to the form intrinsically. Every object has latent in it surfaces, mass and tactility, the way in which it was made. The decision to cut, the method by which the cutting happens, the way a material cuts, this establishes the inter-relationship indelible in materiality of process. This functional practicality requires great savvy of not just the matter (the material) that one is engaging, but the history, technology and capability of the tools and technologies to operate upon it.

7. *Installation – construction*: Installation, or construction, refers not simply to the physical construction of aggregated pieces, to assembly to make a larger construct, but similarly the design of the assembly: the systemization of the units to assemble to define architecture. The geometric convergence of performative practicalities through materials and fabrication processes unify to define assemblies as systems. Systems of enclosure, systems of ventilation, systems of structure and systems of effectual experience, to name a few; all become facilitators for the generation of form and architecture. The stage of their assembly allows for the unified field effect. Building upon the material effect, heightened by its process of refinement and manipulation, is now addressed through the larger geometric and performative systems of the building as a whole. The unitization, collaborating with the material demands originating in production, drawn out through fabrication process, is ultimately engaged with the overall systemization. The part to whole relationship through unitization (necessary at variable scales in every building material) establish modules of their systems allowing for differential methods of unitization, variability in familial systemization of the units, methodized articulation allowing levels of variability, and their combined iteration of both unit assembly and tectonic assembly system(s) to produce field effect(s). The resulting system of assembly defines the super-structural architectural reading.

8. *Experience*: Experience refers to the final intent, reading and experience of the building. Defined by architectural agendas beyond materiality, it is a reading grounded in intellect and emotion. The experience of the totality is the legibility of the piece, the process, the reading of the total form, and the ultimate legibility of space. This fundamental engagement with form, light, material simultaneously – each perceived through the experience of the building.

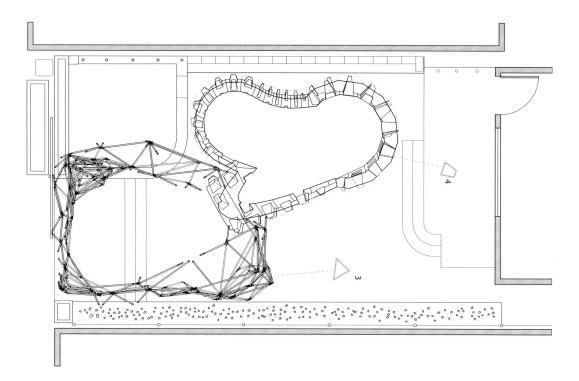

Figure 3.8 Plan

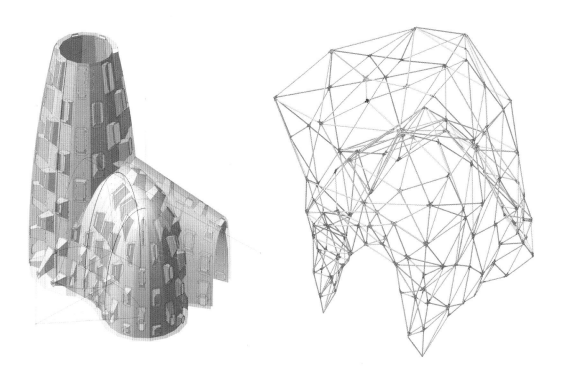

Figure 3.9 PVC inflatable chapel

Figure 3.10 Conduit double dome

Specific thinking

To describe how these principles apply here, a current and most recently executed project installation at Materials & Applications Gallery is described. The specifics of its manifestation emerge from a material methodology. The result is intensely effectual, though one that emerges from the evolution from material, to tectonic to form. Its serves as one iterative example of the following:

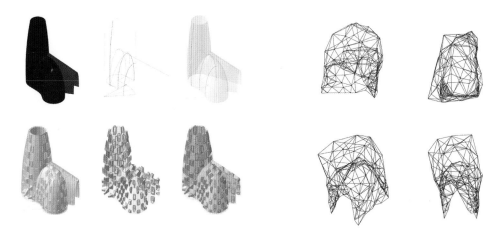

Figure 3.11a–e Descriptive geometry   **Figure 3.12a–d** Structural form-finding

Material: The doubling of the material arose from the individually desired expression of each pavilion piece as well as the interrelationship of the two. Chosen for their cultural identities as well as their effectual qualities, their existence in the realm between transparent and opaque began the conversation about their optical potential and light effects with an ambiguity between the two worlds and their ability to create even further ambiguity with their effectual results (Figure 3.8).

The mode of plastic and conduit each deal with the idea of density. A density of the material that is neither solid nor void, but rides the edge between. Hiding in the realm of translucency and multiplicity, the intrinsically enigmatic nature of their material properties established them as fertile ground to accelerate these properties effectually and test their other formal, structural, and functional capabilities.

Plastic as a continuous surface material with translucent capabilities forms as a planar material and engages temperature-based forming that lends itself to panelization (Figure 3.9). Conduit as a linear material woven into field configurations allows for the mesh effect of the line within the confines of the surface (Figure 3.10).

One with translucency intrinsic, the other with a translucency through the moiré effect of the density of the field, the two meet to produce a dialog through their light effects of emissivity, transmission, and shadow. They compose the spaces bound within and refract and reflect to impact the spaces around.

Material translation: The action of fabrication and development of tectonic. From the intrinsic material properties, plastic as sheet and conduit as extruded section, the material properties introduce themselves to define the derivation of form.

Plastic, used here as a laminated PVC fabric, is available in a modular two-dimensional sheet material and, when welded under heat and pressure, provides specific formal opportunities (Figure 3.11). As a futuristic material, glossy and reflective, formally flexible and able to be a self-supporting skin, the potential of plastic challenges the idea of two-dimensional surface. The limitation of a factory-dictated flat dimension with the organicism of an air-inflated structure allows for the framework of the formal system to engage with

Figure 3.13 Flat sheet templates   **Figure 3.14** Prefabricated chunks

the flexibility of a natural system. Embracing the capability of introducing depth to the material through pressure, as a weldable fabric, it provided an opportunity for a panelized, but choreographed depth and form to the surface.

The galvanized conduit (EMT) evolved from the ubiquitous fencing material and the legacy of its use in Los Angeles architecture (Figure 3.12). Seen as a vertical liner surface, the dense figure produced through its implied surfaces allowed for an opportunity to engage the density of field, the associated moiré effect of dynamically layered and performatively figuratively formed surfaces. The translation comes through the method of deployment and the density of its overlap.

Systemization: The organization of the material comes through its panelization and effect. In the light cones chapel, the four-sided truncated pyramid defines the individual units (Figure 3.13). Projecting out of the inner opaque surface, they act as accumulated variably figured forms that produce aggregated effects through their unitization as well as structural bridges. Modular in their construction and gradient effect, they link to generate the overarching forms: conical entry, taper conical open-topped drum, and a bending barrel vault culminating in an apse.

In the conduit tower, the panelization relies upon a triangulated three-sided unit (Figure 3.14). A combination of structural requirements combined with the double domes (one shallow and one highly arced) produce the collective figuration of the whole. The localized composition is determined by the combination of the structural requirements and the tectonic regulation of the joint.

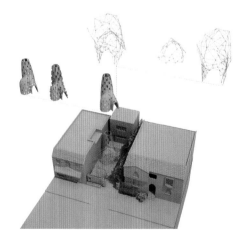

Figure 3.15 Exploded axonometric of primary elements   **Figure 3.16** Exploded axonometric of prefabricated chunks

Geometric governance + representational methodology: The PVC light cone chapel was designed and fabricated through parametric models in CATIA (Figure 3.15). Using a regimented system to allow for diversity of form with a simplicity of fabrication, the system starts with a four-sided flat sheet (Figure 3.19). Maintaining planarity with the inner and outer surface, the depth of each cone is determined by the structural taper of the wall and the overlap of descriptive geometries determining the overarching form. The variability of the cone angle and size gradients vertically from more to less wall, allowing a visual evaporation of the wall, and from more to less away from the structural overlaps of the primal geometric forms. To allow simultaneous flexibility built into the system of formal investigation, a flexibility of allowing a formal variation without losing the standardization of the units and the template production, parametric digital control permitted the simultaneous maintenance of the two.

Similarly, on the conduit tower, the regulation of the three-sided faceted system occurs at the joint (Figure 3.16). This detail moment requires an engagement of the overall system to prevent an over-complexity of any one connection. Defined by economy of fabrication and to minimize complexity, all joints were limited to crimped and bolted connections. Thus, the gradient length density of the individual members illustrates the structural forces (Figure 3.18).

Figure 3.17 Formal derivations   **Figure 3.18** Structural analysis

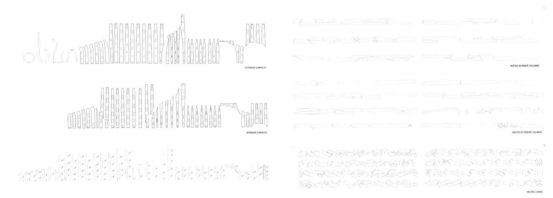

Figure 3.19a Templates   **Figure 3.19b** Nested templates

Performative requirements: The variable cones of the PVC chapel are governed by light. Creating a scalar dimension as they ascend, each of the panels varies in depth and perimeter frame size (Figure 3.17). The composition is based on the experience of light.

The conduit tower similarly works with light, but as opposed to framing, funneling and projecting, it works in the opposite direction, with the projection of shadow. The density of the frame and the pattern of the infill serve to project shadows. The effect is not generated from an emphasis on the form, but from the projected figure resulting from its presence.

Fabrication – process – tool: Using standard controls and geometries derived from the CATIA model, the formal structure is derived from the varying wall thickness and the relative position of the cone in the field effect of the surface. Upon removal from the form, they now have both the shape of their individuated conical body and flat skirt perimeters for welding. Each piece is cut from the fabric and then heat-welded into place to develop the volume (Figure 3.20). The parabolic section creates vertical and lateral thrusts that are internally resolved by the cones linking the two faces. The lattice of the inner and outer surfaces with their varied wall thickness allows the production of the final form and light effect.

The conduit tower uses simple fabrication techniques: crimping, bending and bolting (Figure 3.21). The system is calibrated digitally, fabricated in individual units, chunked for prefabrication, then grouped for final installation. Based on a triangulated module, the structure generates its density through the double-domed canopy.

  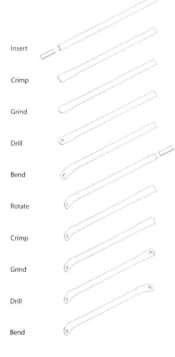

Figure 3.20a–b Prototypes

Insert

Crimp

Grind

Drill

Bend

Rotate

Crimp

Grind

Drill

Bend

Figure 3.21 Crimping sequence

Installation – construction: The installation is the actualization of the units to define their relationship to the collective whole. The precision of the process permitted the translation of the digital model through templates and fabrication models. The accuracy of dimensional pieces is all output to directly and accurately cut the flat sheet material, and collectively weld the figure of the chapel. The conduit tower similarly relies upon the dimensional precision and output to permit the component fabrication that then precisely regiments and allows for the tolerances and cohesion of the whole.

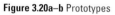

Figure 3.22 View from steps

Figure 3.23 Original study model

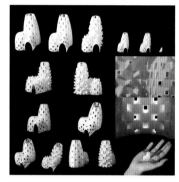

Figure 3.24 STL prototypes

Figure 3.25 View up oculus

Figure 3.26 Shadow effects

Figure 3.27 View towards entry

Experience: The experience of the piece(s) comes through its engagement. The layering of light and shadow, the density of the projected light, funneled light, cast light, patterns of light and dark, and translucency of skin and surface all aggregate to allow for an array of visual effects. The individual effect of each of these systems allows for a transitional chamber. The result is a place that one can engage oneself and the ambient environment around oneself. The experience of light becomes a compositional interplay (Figures 3.22–3.30).

Figure 3.28 View from street

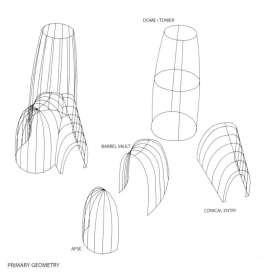

DOME / TOWER

BARREL VAULT

CONICAL ENTRY

APSE

PRIMARY GEOMETRY

Figure 3.29 Geometry and sheet segmentation

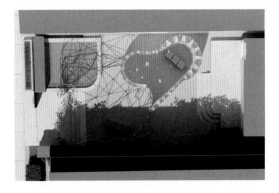

Figure 3.30 Plan with light effect

Project description

The premise of space is light. The effect and experience of the view from the street begin with the modified gate, housing both frames and super-graphic white Plexiglas panels, the composition announces itself to passers-by. Upon entry, one is immediately engulfed. The front figure of the conduit tower holds the urban edge while sitting delicately on the ground. The two nested figures provide the double density moiré effect of the superimposed frames. The galvanized surface allows its presence to play with the light and evaporate, leaving the densities of the shadow field below. The first figure is not about the form or the object but the shadow of its presence (Figures 3.31 and 3.35).

As one ascends the existing steps and slides past the fountain, the pneumatic chapel reaches out its entry to beckon you in. The transparent surface of the outer skin reveals the complexity of the inner figure. Its over-arching figure evolves from a conical entry into a bent barrel vault connecting an apsidal end and a chimney vaulted dome, the forms are figural yet primal. The architectural elements, clad in the new parametrically controlled PVC, reinterpret the shape while providing referential glimpses to historical architectural forms. The compositions of funneled, reflected, and refracted light produce a light room that transitions through the day, and at night inverts the relationship to make the entire structure a glowing projective lantern (Figure 3.32).

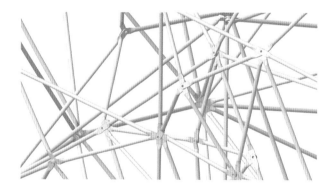

Figure 3.31 Detail of crimped pipes
Figure 3.32 Night: inversion of light

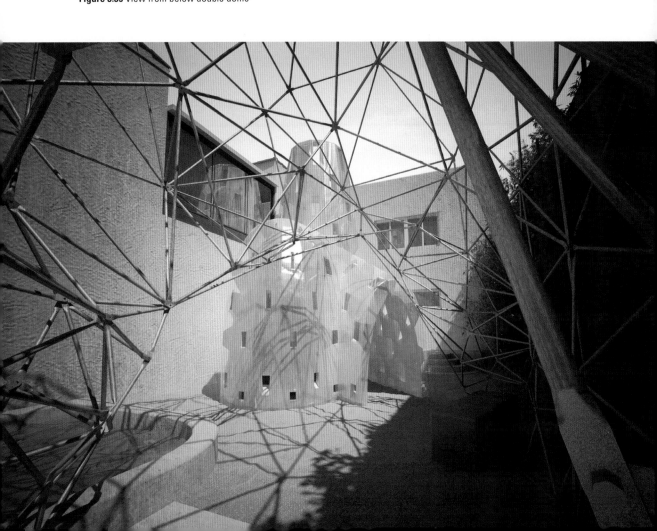

Figure 3.33 Lateral section

Figure 3.35 View from below double dome

Figure 3.34 System elements of double dome

Wireframe

Joints

Pipes

Figure 3.36 View of interior light
Figure 3.37a–c Elements of chapel

Ribs   Geometry   Cones

Material history and reference

Conduit

The use of conduit in the contemporary history of Los Angeles architecture made it a perfect reference. Like the fragmented structure of the early chain link works of Frank Gehry, the material as a ubiquitous, but under-celebrated element is further deployed here.

Similar to the effect of the *Two Running Violet V Forms* by Robert Irwin, building a fence in the canopies of the trees to create a diffused line, here the density is folded back on itself like a crumpled piece of paper to allow the re-layering of the field upon itself. The intricacy of the delicate frame replicates a three-dimensional line drawing in the space.

The common material is refigured into a three-sided fractal element using its overlapping field densities to allow for the concentrated layers to create a visual density. Two elements, one nested inside the other, create an inner figurative shape and an outer structural one. The interlocking of the two creates the double density.

The figure serves as an effectual generator. As an object its intention is to produce a cloud of shadow in its wake. The frame structure projects light on the space below and the objects around provide the urban void of the existing room and the powerful light of Southern California to collaborate.

The galvanized color reflects the evaporative color of the sky as daylight slowly diminishes at sunset.

Figure 3.38 Longitudinal section

The effect of light allows for the multiple readings of the figure as it evolves and changes through the day and under varied light conditions. The result is an immaterial presence.

PVC

The PVC figure is founded in pure descriptive geometries. As an evolutionary element, it is the hybridization of a dome, a vault and an apse. The figure comes from the inter-relationships of each of their forms and the adaptive responses each geometry must make to the other. To provide entry, a truncated cone engages at the knuckle of the vault and the open chimney dome. The resulting figure creates a chapel-like enclosure focused on the spirituality and effects of its light space.

The resolution of the material, through process and its translation into form arrive and collaborate in the generation of the experience. The projected light effects that define the architecture are possible through the systematized and regularized understanding of the material, methods of fabrication, and the effectual experience of the final composition.

Acknowledgements

I would like to thank my collaborators: W. Andrew Atwood for his CATIA support and management of the design fabrication models; Buro Happold Los Angeles (Greg Otto, Kurt Komraus, and Matthew Melnyk) for their structural design of the conduit tower; and my employees: Ahad Basravi, Greg Creech, Isaac Luna, Arsine Mnatsakanyan, Tristan McGuire, Ashley Peng, Alexandre Salice, Danielle Saunders, Martin Schubert, Jason Straight, T.J. Tutay, and Aaron Yip for their belief and persistence.

Figure 3.41 View at night

Figure 3.39 View of inflatable chapel
Figure 3.40 View of interior of chapel

Chapter 4
Nebula Macula

Florian Idenburg
SO – IL

This chapter describes the application of stainless steel, chainmail mesh as an architectural façade in order to create a tactile blur. Traditionally used by various groups including Gallic warriors and Japanese Samurai to mold into protective armor, chainmail mesh is now primarily used in butchers' gloves, fencing gear, and in exotic Goths outfits and belly dancing attire (Figures 4.1–4.2). We are interested in its ability to confuse and mystify rather than to thwart assault, although one might argue that these are in fact just two different survival strategies.

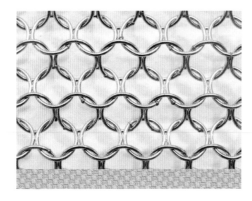

Figure 4.1 Chainmail mesh
Figure 4.2 Chainmail armor

Concept/context

Kukje Gallery – one of the more serious contemporary arts galleries in Korea – engaged us in reimagining its presence in the historic urban fabric of Sogyeok-dong, a low-rise area in the northern part of Seoul. Small alleyways and courtyard houses characterize this neighborhood which is currently being colonized by newly constructed galleries, boutiques and coffee shops. On weekends the fine grain of the city is clogged by herds of artsy adolescents in search of gourmet pudding and a leisurely stroll.

    Kukje Gallery was one of the first galleries to move to this area. Initially a small building, it has been expanded a number of times, and has become a local landmark. Through a combination of strategy and chance, the gallery's owner was able to acquire a number of lots surrounding its original building. In 2006, a second gallery building was completed. Currently we are designing a third building – a project space – and developing ideas to create a sense of unity between these three structures.

    The program is simple. A quintessential gallery box, as large as the zoning envelope allows. The ground floor space is to be used for large installations, performances, and other functions, while the two underground floors house a sales room, a lecture space, and storage areas. Circulation is pushed to the perimeter to maintain the pure geometry of the box (Figures 4.3–4.4). A perimeter skylight admits natural light.

Figure 4.3 Model elevation
Figure 4.4 Model top view

    The outward appearance of the building towards its context is more complex. As the Seoul arts community is increasingly more globalized and professionalized, it is important that *Kukje Gallery* remains influential as a destination. Simultaneously, concerns grow within the local government that oversized and eclectic architectures are destroying the delicate urban fabric. A recent decree requires new construction to blend in within the historic city fabric.

    Our design responds to these ambivalent forces by creating tactile ambiguity. The clear diagrammatic geometry of the white cube would be too rigid in the historic fabric. Our idea was to envelop the building in a permanent nebula by wrapping a soft veil around the box. Taking cues from traditional Korean painting, we explored techniques to create "fogginess." With various intentions, the use of the inexact can be seen throughout the history of cultural expression in the arts, both in Western and Asian traditions. Often as a reaction to hard-edged rationalism, the world of deliberate ambiguity affects naturalism, Eastern poetry, and chiffon lingerie. In two-dimensional art, methods to create ambiguity include blurring, layering, and fading. These techniques can be found in traditional Korean painting, pointillism, Richter, etc. In photography, techniques such as *bokeh*, or soft focus, inform the erotic industry but also the work of Hiroshi Sugimoto or Byung-Hun Min, who deliberately utilize the seductive qualities of the ungraspable (Figures 4.5–4.6).

Figure 4.5 Traditional Korean painting
Figure 4.6 Photo by Byung-Hun Min

In the field of architecture, this ambiguity is more complicated to achieve. Past years have yielded a number of experiments with misters and fog machines. In our case we aim to be less literally and temporally bound. How to create a permanent tactile haze? SANAA, for example, blurs its building edges through transparency, reflection and refraction, but due to the programmatic need for walls to hang art, glass was not an option. The chainmail, through a combination of multidirectional reflection, openness, and the moiré pattern it generates through the interplay of its shadows, has the potential to produce a layer of "fuzz" in front of the actual building mass. An additional characteristic of the chainmail mesh is that it can stretch, thus avoiding creasing. It is strong yet pliable, and can easily wrap around crude geometries. On discovery of this material we decided to explore its potential as a fuzzy wrapper around the hard-edged box.

Material research

To date, the application of chainmail in architectural contexts is limited to two-dimensional drapes, mostly as room dividers in settings like nightclubs and restaurants. We were able to find an incidental exterior application in Europe, which provided us with initial engineering data. The largest stainless steel mesh commercially available consists of 18mm rings, which we deemed too small for our purposes. Through cardboard mock-ups of laser-cut patterns, we felt that a ring diameter of 30mm with a 2.5mm wire thickness would yield the correct level of openness and pliability (Figures 4.7–4.8).

We had samples made in stainless steel (grade 316L, the most corrosion-resistant) from three potential vendors which we identified through www.alibaba.com. The company that has most innovatively used the mesh for a Swarovski showroom is based in Germany, but the centers of manufacturing are in China (the industrial uses) and India (the more ornamental uses). After assessment of these smaller samples, the preferred manufacturer consequently provided a larger sample (6 x 6 feet) for further testing and presentation purposes.

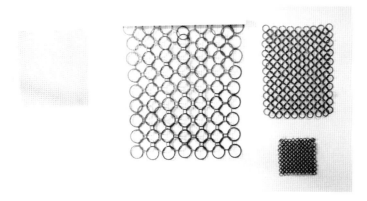

Figure 4.7 L: diameter 95mm, thickness: 7mm; M: diameter 50mm, thickness: 5mm; S: diameter 24mm, thickness: 2mm; next to a 9mm standard (left)

Figure 4.8 Large sample

Material behavior

No meaningful performance data was available from the fabricators. The modest size of the project ruled out large engineering teams, so through modeling in *rhinomembrane*, studying the large sample and physical modeling we developed an initial understanding of the formal behavior of the mesh. One finding was the clear directionality of the weave, which greatly influences the proportions of the mesh (Figure 4.9).

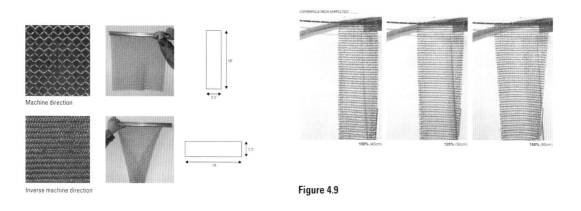

Machine direction

Inverse machine direction

Figure 4.9

By studying the acceptable openness, we could determine the degree of stretchiness, and so define the initial wrapping patterns (Figure 4.10). After establishing the basic geometry and form, we partnered with Min Ra of Front, a façade consultant, to model the exact material behavior and engineer the system.

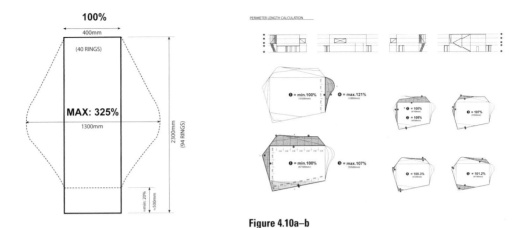

Figure 4.10a–b

The global behavior of the mesh is manifest from the properties of the fundamental behavioral unit of the mesh: the four-ring module. When stretched in one direction, the module contracts in the other, just as, for example, four marbles held in the hand will push out in one direction when squeezed together in the other (Figure 4.11). In this sense, the chainmail mesh is bi-directionally accommodating, but not bi-directionally stretchy (like Spandex). This represents a type of orthotropic behavior, which in case of the chainmail means that a point load will dissipate through four narrow load paths in the material surface, emanating from the loading point. This also means that the mesh is unable to allow high stresses to dissipate broadly and evenly across the global material surface, and the stress distribution tends to be highly concentrated (Figure 4.12). In the architectural application, the phenomenon of uneven stress distribution is addressed through perimeter detailing that permits and restricts movement in very precise ways, allowing the stresses to be redirected around the material surface in order to prevent a problematic over-stress at a single location.

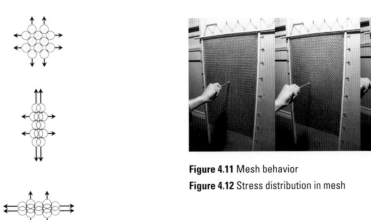

Figure 4.11 Mesh behavior
Figure 4.12 Stress distribution in mesh

Like other tensioned membrane surfaces, the mesh seeks to find a form that represents a resolution of all of the forces acting upon the discrete elements within the skin. However, in tensioned elastic membrane scenarios (again, like Spandex), resolution comes through a minimization in area or stress within a given set of surface bounds. The chainmail surface differs from elastic membranes in that this resolution is not informed by the elasticity of the discreet module, but rather by the self-weight of the discreet module and its resultant tendency to form a type of bi-directional catenary (Figure 4.13). In other words, as the material hangs and is acted on by gravity, interlocking modules will self-tension, eliminating the phenomena of dead-spots and wrinkling, while simultaneously generating the overall surface form. The material behavior as established through the computer will be confirmed through the construction of a 1:10 physical mock-up (Figure 4.14).

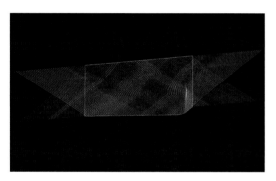

Figure 4.13 Bi-directional catenary
Figure 4.14 Model mock-up

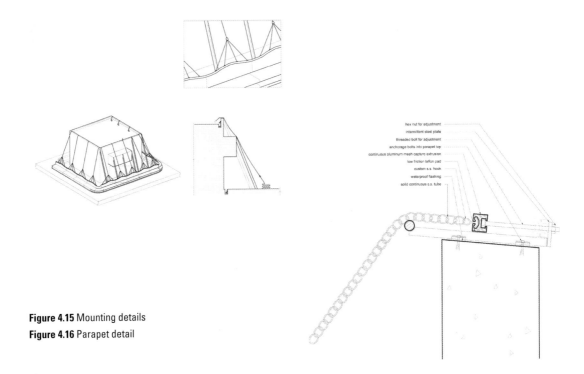

Figure 4.15 Mounting details
Figure 4.16 Parapet detail

Detailing and installation

Limited access to the construction site and the substantial weight of the mesh required us to anticipate an installation method while developing and detailing the system. It is currently stipulated that the mesh will arrive in rolls of about 2000mm width on site. These rolls will be placed around the perimeter of the building, and seamed together locally before being lifted up the façade through pulleys. The mesh will then be mounted on top of the parapet (Figures 4.15–4.16). After removing the support struts, the mesh will be fixed to a bottom anchorage ribbon and pulled tight on both ends.

Conclusions

As this book goes to print, construction will be under way, and the façade will be in production. Since we developed the system to a high degree of detail, we decided to utilize our knowledge to fabricate the façade and oversee the installation ourselves. Through this model of extensive involvement we can better control the budget and final outcome. The building's estimated completion is during the second half of 2011. Only then will we be able to evaluate the strategies described above, and with them the success of our assumptions.

As we continue to develop our research on this project, we discover different readings of the design. The light veil that wraps around the box creates a charged space between city and gallery. This space that can be occupied can be seen as a thickened buffer zone, a dynamic shimmering poché. The multitude of readings will ultimately strengthen the manifestation of the idea of tactile ambiguity.

Acknowledgements
Textual input by Ben Bradley and Jeffrey Kock from Front.

Chapter 5
Parametric Construction of Roof Tile Beach for Instant HERLEV "Suburb Site Environment": *Ukendt Beach*

Oliver Hess and Jenna Didier
Didier Hess

- -

Ukendt Beach is an inclined Danish roof tile deck that descends into a rainwater-reflecting pool in the front yard of an inconspicuous home in suburban Copenhagen, Denmark. The beach is part of an ongoing experiment colliding public and private space, architecture and art, the individual and the community conducted by the artist Anja Franke. The project "deals with the global community with a focus on consumerism, the environment, architecture and residential areas and how these current phenomena have an impact on nature/culture, body/ psyche and social relations."[1] Opening in August 2009, this installation is part of an exhibition comprising of several temporary public art experiments by artists from three different cities – Copenhagen, Los Angeles, and Tijuana – on Franke's property and around her neighborhood, Bakkedraget, that relates to the scale of the neighborhood, garden details, and current boundaries.

Our installation continues an exchange with the Danish artist Anja Franke which started when a London-based curator and friend, Saul Albert, was biking in the Danish countryside in 2004 and upon visiting the first Instant HERLEV realized the similarity to our curated site, Materials & Applications (M&A) in America. He introduced us to her work, she submitted a proposal to us that was suitably absurd yet potentially useful, and we invited Franke to our exhibit space to mount an exhibition in 2007. Franke and a team of volunteers from both Denmark and Los Angeles built an igloo out of industrial felt and bamboo in Silver Lake that summer entitled *Ukendt* (igloo) – see www.emanate.org/ukendt (Figure 5.2). Franke created this iconic symbol of the extreme northern climes with the help of Los Angeles-based architect John Southern and our lead fabricator at the time, Nicholas Blake.

When she reciprocated by inviting us to Denmark to participate in an intervention at her suburban home in the late summer/fall of 2009, we felt that bringing to Denmark a little piece of Southern California – a beach – would be perfect. We planned to flood the grounds outside of the residence at the Instant HERLEV 2 site with rainwater caught off the roof of the residence, then fabricate a synthetic beach using the roof construction materials and technologies of Denmark. The construction process for the "beach" was adapted from traditional Danish roof construction technologies which we spent a month studying during a residency with the Danish Institute of Arts & Crafts in 2008. We envisioned the beach as an undulating surface of ceramic tiles, the "beach", gliding into a gently lapping "sea" (Figure 5.3).

- - - - - - - - - - - - - - - - - - - -

Figure 5.1 Complete installation

Figure 5.2 *Ukendt Beach* at Materials & Applications, in Los Angeles, in the fall of 2007

Ukendt technical

The decision to use locally manufactured ceramic tiles was based on the similarity of the texture and color of ceramic tiles in Denmark to that of the beaches of Southern California. We attempted to use the same materials and to some extent construction methods as would be used to construct a Danish roof to allow for the construction process to engage visitors and the local art students who helped us build it without alienating them (Figure 5.4). One of the briefs for the location was that the neighbors would not necessarily welcome our modification to their community and in an effort to temper their fears, we thought that producing something recognizable might be more humorous and light-hearted than something that appeared overly technical or complex (Figure 5.5). Mid-way through our construction of the undulating decking, a neighbor strolling by stopped dead in their tracks to wonder aloud how the roof of the building had flown off and landed there. We knew we had a hit! Additionally, the choice of the roofing technology allowed us to acquire materials easily when we discovered we needed more wood than initially calculated.

The first approach to creating dunes from tiles was to envision the probable outcome as a dual curvature structure that carefully allowed the maximum angular disparity between tiles. Since we did not know this number when we began, we simply used 7.5 degrees and created a paneled surface in Rhinoceros 3D as our guide (Figure 5.6). It quickly became clear that the shape of the surface would need to be both inviting and mysterious but with only a very subtle variation. A series of harmonic sine waves were used in Grasshopper

Figure 5.3 Initial concept image illustrating how the elements are to come together on site

Figure 5.4 Contemporary Danish roof construction technique. Ceramic tiles hung on wood framing

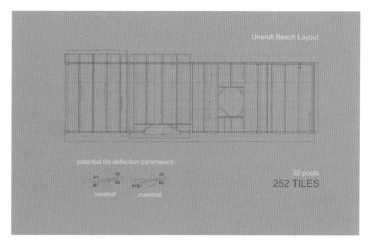

Figure 5.5 Future trends in Danish roof construction: fiber tiles bolted straight into metal framing

Figure 5.6 CAD site analysis with tile layout and angular parameters

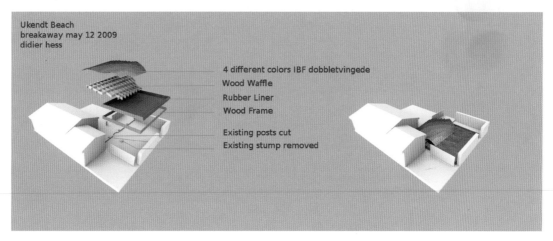

Figure 5.7 Construction breakaway illustrating basic components

to create a parametric surface which granted the tiles their correct angular variation but also created a surface that was pleasing as a shape and bore enough resemblance to a beach dune that it retained its intended identity (Figure 5.7). Once the system existed to create a physically replicable tile surface, the next most important aspect was complexity. In Grasshopper it was simple to alter the periodicy of cuts along curves to create as detailed or as coarse breaks as needed in the support "laegters" or joists (Figure 5.8). Working on the computer allowed us to understand the relationship of tile – to planes – and to frames, but it was not until later that we realized that we needed to build the piece not with the flexibility the computer allowed us but rather with the flexibility the materials allowed us.

It is probably worth digressing here to explain that Scandinavian hand tool mastery and lumber terminology were key to this project as they became integral to the realization of the piece. We worked with a very skilled crew comprising primarily of graduate art students from Tromsø Academy who had extensive woodworking confidence. Lea Basch Opheim, Anna Bak, Geir Backe, awed us with their finesse using simple hand tools like the lowly hand saw. Most times they would eschew the electric saber saw we had purchased for the job, preferring the hand saw to trim down square 100mm by 100mm posts at the odd angles required by the shifting contours of our decking method composed of horizontal "raegters" 135mm long x 27mm x 70mm (the width of three roof tiles laid side-to-side) that held the "peaks" of the tiles interspersed between parallel rows of "laegters" 135mm long x 120mm x 12mm that supported the "dips" in the tiles.

Wood construction layers

Our first act on site was to tear out the existing deck whose surface was badly weathered. This revealed a not-so-regular decking support system that was not too worn, was relatively level and sufficiently sturdy to support the weight of our tiles. Next we began to build prototypes, small 900mm x 900mm tile models of different constructions to find the approach which required the least cutting, the least connections and the maximum stability. It was not enough to build a stable structure. Because we wanted the tile pattern to resemble exaggerated "ripples" that one sees on beach sand, we turned the tiles 90 degrees off the axis upon which they were designed to be mounted. Also, each individual tile had to have a consistent level of support to prevent cracking while people walked, danced and played on them. These performance requirements were very different from those for which they had been designed. We tried the traditional box frame as well as the plywood waffle, but in the end we developed a hybrid scaffold similar to the actual wood framing the Danes used for roofing because it was simple to assemble and extremely adaptable (Figure 5.9). Following our prototype, we subdivided the support grid with joints every three tiles (approximately 135mm) and laid out three sets of tiles, three columns wide creating nine on a single plane that measured 135mm x 112.5mm. This system allowed us to achieve steeper angles without threatening the integrity of the tiles.

Each tile was extremely fragile; particularly the edges were vulnerable due to a typically uneven casting process. They each had a 4mm tab at the front and back edges with stamped grooves that were meant to lock together when lapped. We decided to use this surface primarily as a hinge and allow other edges to butt up against each other, or simply have small gaps that we kept at less than 12mm for safety (Figure 5.10).

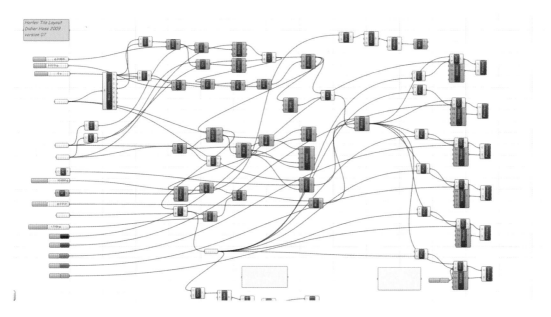

Figure 5.8 Grasshopper script for tile layout; parametric system to analyze flexibility of approaches

Figure 5.9 Selected prototype. This approach was refined significantly but at this point we could already see the flexibility that it offered

Figure 5.10 A flexible construction technique was key to resolving angular decisions which required resolution to iterate into grid. Often we would build and unbuild to optimize relationships. Therefore, we would start with just one screw

Figure 5.11 Techniques were derived with increasing accuracy in predicting measurement offsets to exploit maximal curves in tile assembly

With tiles laid out in modules, it was easier to figure out the maximum angle of displacement for a group of nine that would act the same and therefore allow us to predict the types of angles needed on adjoining modules of the grid. It was at this point that we began to notice that even with a computer model or mathematical prediction, it was faster and more trustworthy to simply assemble each cell with one screw per laegters and then populate it with tiles, and adjusting its position up and down to find where the tiles rested most naturally, while still allowing us to follow the basic form that we anticipated. At the point where we had constructed five modules, we discovered a host of smaller problems related to stability and support so we determined that it was not actually necessary to trouble ourselves with trying to follow a computer simulation which at this point was really just trying to keep up with what we were learning while assembling. As mentioned, the craftspeople we were working with were excellent and confident carpenters skilled with all hand tools and capable of creating whatever structure we felt was appropriate to the limitations that our design presented. So, as such, about one-third of the way into construction we ceased using the computer or diagrams and simply allowed the siting of the tiles to dictate each section as we built it (Figure 5.11).

This process presented a couple of problems which would cause us in the future to retain the hybrid construction approach. First, while we could easily follow the rules of positioning the tiles, we could not predict how quickly or slowly they would reacquire our basic form, so after building two columns of over 60 tiles we discovered that we could not return to our originally prescribed shape and we had to disassemble that section and take a slightly more radical sweep or we would have hit the ground before coming back up again. Additionally we found that while the system seemed to work perfectly, there were certain locations on the surface that would always be off by a fraction of an inch as a result of the height of the ripples in the tile. We accommodated this disparity by trimming the top corner off of the peak from approximately ten tiles where they were crashing into a wall. Most of these problems would probably have existed in any way we had selected to follow a computer-generated assembly of the piece but by working through it organically we were unable to predict how to avoid these angles or position them so that they were in inconspicuous locations (Figure 5.12).

Luckily our two most irresolvable geometric catastrophes, which were located at the front and nearly center of the piece, also made for perfect opportunities for planting living palms which, along with an umbrella, were considered for the design even before we understood how useful they would become (Figure 5.13). At those points the angle of the intersections was more than the 7.5 degrees that we could allow in our stabilizing system and even with additional support it was clear that we would not be able to make it a safe enough surface to walk on, without having some edge or corner raised in the air.

- - - - - - - - - - - - - - - - - -

Figure 5.14 Sample tiles at IBC factory. Wet and dry testing of tile colors and finishes for final selection

Figures 5.12–5.13 Contrasting tiles were used to identify tiles which tended to break most often. A pattern was identified and the issue was resolved as construction went on. The structure where the grid points could not be resolved with a planar tile. Broken tiles were added to reference the tension between nature and geometry

From the beginning we knew that simply laying the tiles on the wood directly would most likely not provide the perfect amount of support. IBC, a Danish brick and tile manufacturer, provided us with samples of all of their tiles so that we could select those that would perform best. The Director of Operations from IBC, Mr. Bentzen, considered it an impossible task for us to build an atypical surface with the tiles mounted the opposite direction from usual. The fact that we intended people to walk and dance on these when they are not generally durable enough for this even in a standard installation made him laugh at us good-humoredly. Nonetheless, he gave us a memorable tour of the tile and brick manufacturing facility just outside Copenhagen and when we had made our decision on which tile to use, IBC delivered to the suburban job-site two pallets of roof tiles. In analysis of our tile choice we had originally been drawn to a glossy black glazed roofing tile that was significantly harder and more stylish (Figure 5.14). However, we found that the tile was much more dangerous with wet feet, much hotter in the sun, and far less like a beach then nearly any other choice in their catalog. In the end an unglazed yellow tile met every need, and while the locals told us that the black tiles were in fashion, those who followed these sorts of things speculated that the unglazed yellow was the up-and-coming trend anyway, due to their higher albedo value.

Although we carefully selected the lumber and even the angle with which it was mounted to complement the shape of the tiles, there was still an asymmetrical lip on the underside to lock onto neighboring tiles and also variations in manufacturing which the lumber could not easily support (Figure 5.15). So we added closed cell polyethylene foam pipe insulation on top of each raegters (Figure 5.16). This material was perfect because it came pre-split, was readily available and inexpensive. We found that by simply wrapping it on top of each board when the tile was placed on top, it was able to rest nearly in contact with the board and ensured that all of the underside surface of the tile's "peak" was supported and cushioned from footfalls. We tested a number of foams before settling on one that made adequate contact when relaxed and when stepped on; the optimum solution for support (Figure 5.17).

During construction we periodically walked and even stomped on the surface to test the strength of our design (Figure 5.18). We found that while it was adequate in most cases, there were still instances in certain acute situations where the joining angle was less than 160 degrees where the pressure from the tiles pushing

Figure 5.15 Inspection of lumber. Commercial lumber was used for prototypes. Once specified, the remainder was primarily salvaged from excess construction materials

Figure 5.16 Foam tests mounted to on-site construction test

Figure 5.17 First application of tiles to selected construction system

edgewise on one another combined with walking would crack the edges or corners off the tiles repeatedly. To fix this, we shaved the tiles or created special shims to add a mere 2–4mm of support to prevent this unique condition from occurring. In those situations it was less a matter of total force and more a question of the force being focused on very specific regions relentlessly. Another problem we found after construction was that in those same acute joints there would be further cracks along the tops and bottoms of the ripples. These cracks were remediated by removing all uphill tiles from the rupture and attaching small tabs on top of the laegters that prevented the tiles from sliding down and multiplying their force on the bottom tiles. It is worth mentioning that all of the final steps in preparing the surface were easily accomplished because the tiles were never attached to the structure, they were simply laid on top in a lapped fashion allowing for easy replacement if one were to be broken in the future (Figure 5.19).

Figure 5.18 Walk-on test of construction. At this point the surface was quite flat so the performance was deceptively good

Figure 5.19 The front edge that descended into the water was constructed and then unconstructed and stored for the final phase of installation

Rainwater capture

In producing the installation, the act of capturing rainwater to create an "ocean" is meant to popularize the idea of this affordable and effective method of using natural resources (Figure 5.20). Rainfall is abundant in Copenhagen, this example should inspire visitors to capture rainwater and recycle it for washing, landscaping and other household uses rather than depending on city drinking water. Luckily, July is the month that gets the most precipitation on average each year (73.7mm) in Copenhagen, so we attempted to capture rainwater for our installation that opened in August 2009. Conveniently, a downspout from the raingutters along one side of the roof emptied directly into the donated rubber roofing underlayment that we spread out to capture the water to create our "sea" (Figure 5.21). Franke's son, Johan, became the rain tsar and unfailingly would set out buckets each time it rained, filling several 50 gallon drums and an inflatable pool in the back via another downspout in anticipation of the completed basin (Figure 5.22). We continue to emphasize this method of water reuse as a viable source of supplemental water in Southern California, using it in our own work and producing storm water workshops developed for the Environmental Affairs Department of Los Angeles in the spring of 2008.

Figure 5.20 The basin membrane being laid out. The ground was flattened, removing twigs and roots and filling any dips with sand, then a layer of polyethylene felt underlayment preceded a thick layer of EPDM liner molecularly bonded along the seam with tape from the manufacturer

Figure 5.21 Completion of basin entering the water. Care was taken walking on the liner. After the opening, kids immediately started to go bananas on this surface and it survived

Figure 5.22 Rainwater pool. Temporary rainwater collection from rooftop prior to final basin completion

Program

Just as M&A began in 2002 as an exhibition space in the front courtyard of Jenna Didier's home in Los Angeles, Instant HERLEV is an exhibit space in and around Anja Franke's home in Denmark. In 2004, her first iteration of Instant HERLEV was in cooperation with a group of architects and fellow artists to create new living zones, routes and viewpoints that transcended traditional infrastructure and property lines with the method of surrounding her Herlev home with temporary constructions. The goal was not so much to render private areas public and accessible but precisely to soften the borders between interior and exterior, between home and municipality, between individual and collective space, to make them more flexible. These goals are similar to our own ongoing experiments in contemporary social-aesthetic architecture and design at M&A (Figure 5.23). Every six months we host a different large-scale site-specific installation selected from concepts submitted by artists, architects, and designers. Each installation positions itself as an effort to utilize new or underused materials and techniques to achieve what many would term an architectural folly. The larger function of each project, however, is achieved in relation to the public who visits and uses the courtyard as a pocket park. A public park on private property where there is no fee for entry and the hours (10am to 10pm) rival even the most liberal public parks maintained by the municipality. Insofar as the organization is volunteer-operated and each project is executed by volunteers, a post-profit business model is in place where the financial reward

Figure 5.24 People found some comfortable positions for lying on the beach during the opening party

Figure 5.25 Installation under snow. Neighborhood children especially enjoy the iced-over "sea" beneath the snow which they shovel clean and skate on

Figure 5.23 *Here There Be Monsters,* a previous installation involving large rainwater pond in publicly accessible residential space at Materials & Applications

for working is non-existent. The compensation that exhibitors and volunteers receive is far more valuable; experience, credit, and frequently, a high degree of visibility on national and international media.

The Danish people are apparently not used to the concept of volunteering and do not like to have the boundaries between public and private blurred. The 2004 Instant HERLEV met with much resistance, mostly due to the Bakkedraget Homeowners Association's discomfort with the use of a private garden and home as a public exhibit space. However, thanks to the notoriety that the county gained from the first Instant HERLEV (national news media attention, the art community of Copenhagen applauding the novel approach to art-making), the community may now have a more positive attitude towards the project (Figures 5.24–5.25), but as added insurance, we anticipated that the placement of the public beach on private land would signal the intent for the beach (and the rest of the grounds) as publicly accessible; after all, in Denmark, as in California, it is illegal to privatize the beach.

Note

1   Malene Valberg, "Introduction," Instant HERLEV exhibition catalog, 2009.

Part III
Matter Processes

Engaging technique to generate and effect the idea of the process produces an individuated effect to the design that is choreographed and controlled through the technical systematization that remains evident in the final outcome. Synthesizing fabrication, technology, and making, the material technologies are the process logic made formal. Derived from the material, but subscribing to a larger effectual agenda, the use of natural or manmade forces feeds the engagement between the physical and resulting experience. Light, wind, energy, economy, etc. become overtly illustrated in the final outcome. The interdependence upon emerging fields of robotics and high technologies to accomplish the iterative nature of the work allows for the systematized to be fabricated and made while retaining the process within the final outcome.

Eric Höweler and J. Meejin Yoon, Höweler + Yoon Architecture
David Benjamin, The Living
Jason Oliver Vollen and Dale Clifford, Binary Design

Chapter 6
Reciprocal Media

Eric Höweler and J. Meejin Yoon
Höweler + Yoon Architecture

Force to form

The classical Greek concept of entasis introduces a calculated geometrical deformation of a column to achieve a particular effect: that of weightiness. The slight bow carved into the marble gives the eye the impression that the column is carrying load – or, according to other theories, compensates for the illusionary concavity that the eye perceives in a perfectly straight column. The use of entasis is perplexing because it falls outside the realm of function. The bowed column does not carry load more efficiently or more effectively. It appears to be an instance of pure rhetoric, an optical device that suggests a physical and material process. It performs its role through a material theatricality. Neither a product of function or rationality, entasis is the imaging of tectonics – or rather the imaging of its *effect*.

With the rise in accessibility of electronic circuitry and a more comprehensive understanding of environmental effects, architecture has lately become more concerned with the intangible – both as producers and transmitters of effects. We can re-describe the question of entasis as an instance in which a tangible (stone) is modified to suggest the presence of an intangible cause (force) or to counteract an intangible transmission (visual perception). To characterize architecture in this way suggests that there is a relationship between two types of things whose distinction is not physical vs. nonphysical but rather lies somewhere on a continuum between fixed and fluid, transmitted and transmitter, or, to borrow from media studies, "medium and content."

Building on McLuhan's mantra, "the medium is the message," where the medium of communication is reprioritized over the content, the four projects below actively work to reconfigure both medium and content, drawing them into a reciprocal relationship, where both are essential, necessary, and codependent. We understand both tangibles and intangibles as materials whose physical properties can be explored, understood, and exploited to varying effects. In the classical Greek column, one half of the equation (the tangible stone) is modified to compensate for the other half (the intangible force or perception). In the example of entasis, material as a medium is enlisted to broadcast its load-bearing function: the content. The four case studies below suggest a more active and reciprocal interaction between medium and content; in these works both sides are open to modification so long as it is understood that any changes made to one will necessarily affect the other.

Materialization

The following body of work utilizes materials to achieve particular spatial, optical, or sensorial effects. The materials are deployed in combination with sensors, lighting, or servo motors to amplify or modify their material effects. Inherent material qualities are not the focus of our practice. Material is a *medium* for manifesting a set of behaviors or effects; reciprocally, behaviors and effects act as media for materials. Material and phenomena are inseparable components of the projects; the materialization of the tangible components simultaneously enhances the possibilities of the intangible components in the production of varied effects.

The projects represented here constitute a material practice which aims at a new material performativity through precise deployments of materials, forces, and effects. *White Noise White Light* is an interactive installation of fiber optic stalks, sensors and speakers to create a responsive field of lighting and sound effects. *Current* produces the animated effects within a thick surface by combining the optical effects of glass, curvature and choreographed lighting. *Wind Screen* harnesses wind power through an array of micro-wind turbines, utilizing the curvature of a surface to create lift, rotation, and ultimately illumination. A kinetic installation, *Entasis* creates a dynamic portal through the computer-controlled manipulation of two columnar polypropylene structures.

In each case, the trajectory from conception to implementation is understood as a model of research and development. A series of tests, prototypes mock-ups, and failures are necessary to arrive at the physical instantiation of the "finished" piece. Each realized project is also understood as part of a larger trajectory of design research, where they are tested within a sited context to engage multiple audiences, subjects, and users. The interplay between the artifacts and the behaviors that they engender is part of the open-ended nature of the work; a project is only complete when it incorporates the interactions and unscripted responses from a user, viewer, or public.

Catalog

The projects are described in the format of a lab report, documenting each material used as well as the applications, qualities and effects that they produced. Some necessary adjustments: hypotheses describe in this case the tangible and intangible components and our proposed engagement of the two, procedures describe the processes of design research, and, in our case, "results" document the momentary materialization of the research as a particular installation. In the conclusion we borrow from lab reports more conventionally by summarizing the data, discussing possible applications of the "experiments," and articulating possible errors (which often suggest further investigations). While we are adopting a common descriptive format, the unequal emphasis given to the various sections of each project reflects their particular histories.

Taken collectively, these projects illustrate a catalog of material applications. Working with material specificities does not necessarily lead to an essentialist understanding of the targeted materials. Unlike practices that aim to showcase the essences of materials, we believe in an unstable and revisionary understanding of materials, with the hope that such explorations will inform new applications, inspire new behaviors, and provoke new reactions.

White Noise White Light
Hypothesis
To produce the effect of a responsive immersive light and sound environment, the use of a microcontroller and passive IR sensor allows the transmission of white noise and white light through the fiber optics and speakers in direct response to the detection of thermal change due to the presence of a human body.

Materials
Fiber optics, outdoor speakers, passive infrared sensors, custom microcontroller, LEDs.

Procedure
The project consists of a field of luminous stalks that are responsive to the occupants. By moving through the field, each occupant triggers individual stalks which emit white light through the fiber optic stalk and white noise through a speaker (Figures 6.1–6.2). The basic behavioral response relies on a hidden passive infrared sensor, a microcontroller, and an outdoor speaker (Figures 6.3–6.5).

Fiber optics exploit the properties of total internal reflection to transmit light from end to end through a glass core. This acts as a means of displacing light, phenomena, or signals, producing a kind of visual displacement. Utilized as a medium for the *White Noise White Light* project, the fiber optic stalks were the primary conduit and medium for the light response behavior of the interactive field.

The fiber optic stalk is a ¼" solid core fiber optic strand housed in a clear PETG sleeve. The sleeve keeps the fiber upright, while allowing for some deflection as people brush through the field. The stalk is capped with a bead of clear silicone which acts as a diffuser for the light displaced at the end emitting fiber.

The assembly below the deck consists of a waterproof housing, a custom microcontroller, a passive IR sensor, an outdoor speaker, and three white LED lights. The assembly was prototyped and tested prior to its fabrication and deployment at the 2004 Olympics in Athens. Testing and development of the electronics included responsiveness of the passive IR sensor, the pattern of light once triggered, and the sound intensity, duration and fade of the white noise.

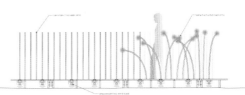

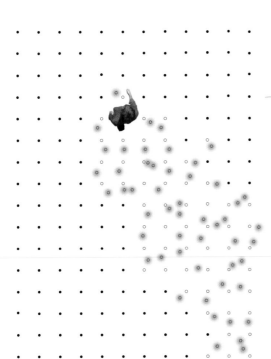

Figure 6.1 Diagram of behavioral response of fiber optic field in response of movement by occupants

Figure 6.2 Speakers on the electronics modules mounted on the underside of the deck reflect sound off the hard plaza surface back up through the open joints of the wood deck

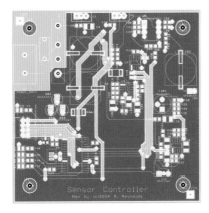

Figure 6.3 Printed circuit board

Figure 6.4 Custom microcontroller, PIR sensor, and outdoor speaker assembly

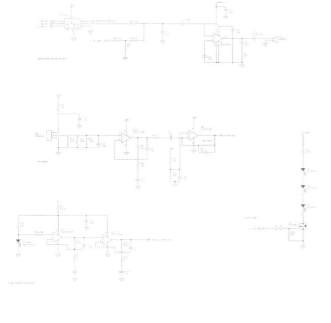

Figure 6.5 Controller diagram

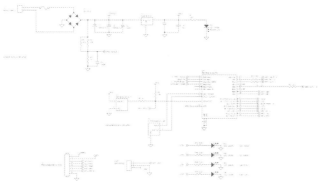

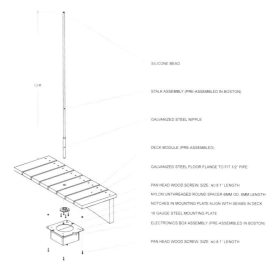

Figure 6.6 Axon of components and assembly of electronics, fiber optic stalk, and raised deck

SILICONE BEAD

STALK ASSEMBLY (PRE-ASSEMBLED IN BOSTON)

GALVANIZED STEEL NIPPLE

DECK MODULE (PRE-ASSEMBLED)

GALVANIZED STEEL FLOOR FLANGE TO FIT 1/2" PIPE

PAN HEAD WOOD SCREW, SIZE: no 8 1" LENGTH
NYLON UNTHREADED ROUND SPACER 6MM OD, 6MM LENGTH
NOTCHES IN MOUNTING PLATE ALIGN WITH SEAMS IN DECK
16 GAUGE STEEL MOUNTING PLATE
ELECTRONICS BOX ASSEMBLY (PRE-ASSEMBLED IN BOSTON)

PAN HEAD WOOD SCREW, SIZE: no 8 1" LENGTH

1.2 M

The deck construction was a prefabricated South American mahogany plank raised 6 inches off the ground. The deck created an artificial ground plane to conceal and protect the electronic components and the light sources. Logistics included the prefabrication and shipping of all parts to be installed in time for the opening ceremonies of the Olympic Games (Figure 6.6).

Results

For this installation, the light source and sensor housing unit were mounted to the underside of a wood deck, while the fiber optic strand projected above the surface. The displacement of light from below the deck through the fiber optic strand-capped silicone resulted in a reflection of the white light back through the stalk, making the end-emitting fiber optic appear to be a side-emitting fiber optic. The displacement of sound from the individual speakers facing downwards on the stone surface, bounced the sound back up through the cracks. The delay in the trigger of light and sound was imperceptible to the occupants moving through the field.

Conclusion

White Noise White Light is a test case in the production of immersive environments, where the visual and audible signals are calibrated to create a responsive spatial field. The space of the project is defined primarily by phenomena, behaviors and signals, yet it is enabled by material: the fiber optic strands and the silicone diffuser. In this case the material presence is minimal and highly transparent, seeming to almost disappear during the day. Furthermore, the nature of the material itself suggests a certain displacement of effect from cause. Fiber optics exploit the properties of total internal reflection to transmit light from end to end through a glass core. At dusk and in the evening, the project is animated by the disembodied flicker of solid state lighting transmitted through the fiber optic cables and the buzz of electrons in the hidden speakers (Figures 6.7–6.9). Seemingly immaterial effects combine with effortless activation (the installation is triggered by an aspect of your presence that you have no control over) to construct a sensorial spatial experience.

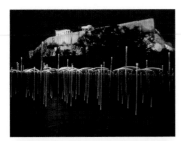

Figure 6.7 View of fiber optic field installed for the Athens 2004 Olympics

Figure 6.8 View of illuminated field receding towards the Acropolis

Figure 6.9 Fiber optics housed in polycarbonate tubes allow for flexibility and bending

Current

Hypothesis

To produce simulated wave patterns, *Current* combines the material properties of flat and curved edge glass with the performative effects of computer-controlled lighting.

Materials

Low-iron float glass, LEDs, computer.

Procedure

Installed in an interior wall, the glass is stacked horizontally, creating a stratified volume of solid glass, with a flat face and contoured back (Figures 6.10–6.11).The CNC water-jet cut contour of the back edges produces an interior topography that is visible through the face, and is highlighted when lit from the edges. The curved glass mass acts like a large lens, focusing and dissipating light, based on its geometry. The low-iron glass, which is optically clearer than regular soda lime float glass, allows better light transmission and more accurate color rendition.

Material research for the project involved the mocking up of blocks of glass in both low-iron and normal soda lime float glass. The stacking and restraining of the glass investigated the possibility of a chemically bonded assembly as well as a dry stack of individual lites of glass clamped from above. The face edges are polished to allow the passage of light, while the back contour remains frosted (a natural side-effect of the CNC waterjet cutting) to encourage its diffusion (Figures 6.12–6.13).

The contoured back surface was designed to form a continuous topography of concave and convex curves. In order to eliminate material wastage, the curves were calibrated to use both sides of a single cut. The curves plotted as a series of points in an Excel spreadsheet; 0, +1, −1, +2, −2, +3, −3. Each series was interpolated by a smooth curve. Since all the curves were produced from the same shared cut lines, a positive curve on the right-hand side corresponds to a negative curve on the left-hand side. This "splitting" of the material also minimized cutting time (as the cost of the material was a function of time on the water-jet bed), as one tool path could produce two curved faces (Figures 6.14–6.17).

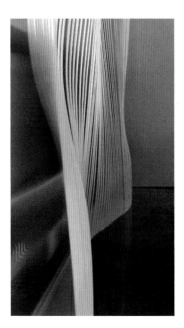
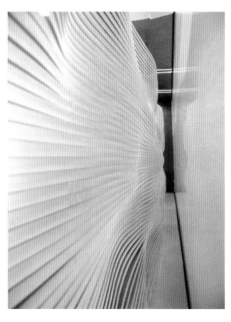

Figure 6.10 Smooth gradient of curved back side of glass

Figure 6.11 Curvature of glass on backside

Figure 6.12 Small mock-up prototype to test the curvature of glass, dry stack technique and custom-controllable LED electronics modules

Figure 6.13 Mock-up to test the throw of light through the length of a 1/2" piece of glass curved on one side and flat on the other

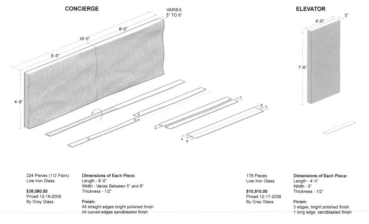

CONCIERGE

VARIES 5" TO 8"

16'-0"

8'-0"

8'-0"

4'-6"

ELEVATOR

4'-0"   5"

7'-6"

224 Pieces (112 Pairs)
Low Iron Glass

$38,080.00
Priced 12-16-2008
By Gray Glass

Dimensions of Each Piece:
Length - 8'-0"
Width - Varies Between 5" and 8"
Thickness - 1/2"

Finish:
All straight edges bright polished finish
All curved edges sandblasted finish

176 Pieces
Low Iron Glass

$10,510.00
Priced 12-17-2008
By Gray Glass

Dimensions of Each Piece:
Length - 4'-0"
Width - 5"
Thickness - 1/2"

Finish:
3 edges, bright polished finish
1 long edge, sandblasted finish

Figure 6.14 Glass is cut to minimize waste, using one curve down the middle to create two mirror image pieces that are then re-organized to create an asymmetrical wave pattern across the installation

Figure 6.15 Diagram to coordinate sequence of cutting, flipping and stacking glass

Figure 6.16 Individual profiles of all the stacked lites of glass

Figure 6.17 Waterjet cutting the 1/2" thick low-iron glass

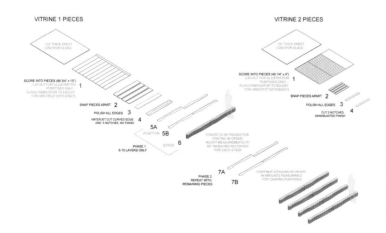

Figure 6.18 LED electronics modules mounted on custom reflector stack to focus LEDs. Blue tape notes where "dimples" are visible that demonstrate that plate glass is not absolutely flat

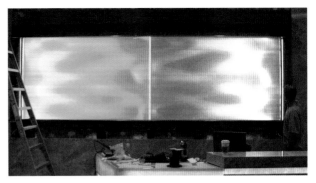

Figure 6.19 The effect of color fades and washes are a result of the controlled by RGB LED modules at each layer of glass in combination with the curvature of the backside of the glass

The edge lighting is achieved through an array of custom RGB LED elements mounted on a sliding armature. The LED matrix allows the mixing of colors and the individual addressing of each lite. With the addressable lighting matrix we were able to control the low-resolution image on the one-dimensional screen, and create a catalog of behaviors based on color, light intensity, and speed (Figures 6.18–6.19).

In order to maximize the light output, we designed the armature to locate the LED elements at the center of each lite of glass. The manufactures stated tolerance for glass thickness allows each piece of glass to be +/– .011 of an inch. Multiplied over 112 layers of glass, we discovered that we could be +/– 3 layers of glass and three LED arrays. In order to accommodate the glass tolerances, we made the LED armature adjustable, and we also used a micrometer to measure each piece of glass as it came off the water jet line.

Glass is extremely strong in compression; however, it is susceptible to point loads and spontaneous breakage due to impurities in the glass, so great care was taken to design and coordinate enough adjustability into the subframe to ensure that it is level and flat.

Results

When stacking glass, we were surprised to discover what appeared to be splotches in between glass lites. These appeared when the glass was compressed by layers of glass above, and disappeared when the glass was removed. Looking more closely into this matter, we discovered that the splotches were the result of two non-planar faces

Figure 6.20 Installation of dry stacked glass with flat side facing front elevation

of glass pressed against each other. Float glass, produced as a suspended liquid which is allowed to solidify, is of course never perfectly flat, though for most extents and purposes, it is flat enough. Loading the float glass revealed slight imperfections that were then found to be minimized by the lighting (Figure 6.20).

Various pattern behaviors were tested to generate a repertoire of effects. The pattern of color mixing between shades of green and blue proved most successful, as the light output of the red LEDs was significantly lower than the green and blues. Further investigations revealed that the wavelength of red light moving through the medium of the glass was causing the red light to taper off abruptly, while the green and blue lights transmitted the full length of the piece (Figures 6.21–6.23).

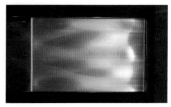

Figure 6.21 View of illuminated stacked glass with shadows and highlights of curved back surface on the oblique

Figure 6.22 Striated wave patterns of light ripple through the edge-lit glass

Figure 6.23 Controllable RGB LED modules at each lite of glass enable color definition to be both precise and dynamic

Conclusion

The research into glass, its optical properties, manufacturing tolerances, and installation requirements informed the design and realization of the piece. The qualities and behaviors of its choreography are a result of the interaction of the material and lighting, as they conspire to produce a complex of effects that simulate wave patterns in a field of water. Trying to use one fluid medium (light) to suggest another (water), we depend on the shared characteristics of the two – in particular, the way the wave behavior of each distorts in response to irregular presences in its path. The demands placed upon the design by the glass itself (which is itself actually a fluid) was a constant reminder of the hidden properties of materials, and the latent particularities which can, intentionally or unintentionally, transform installations foregrounding those materials.

Wind Screen

Hypothesis

To power individual LED lanterns, *Wind Screen* manipulates the geometry of plastic sheets with cuts and folds to transform the kinetic energy of the vertical axis wind turbine into varied patterns of illumination.

Materials

Laser-cut plastic sheet, LEDs, analog circuitry, wind.

Procedure

Wind Screen was conceived as a means of rendering visible the abundance of natural wind energy through the immediate consumption of that energy in LED lighting. The faster the turbines spin, the brighter the LED lighting. The individual turbines consist of a laser-cut sheet of plastic formed into a shell, and a copper coil to translate the rotations into power to illuminate the LEDs (Figures 6.24–6.26).

Existing types of vertical axis wind turbines break down into Darius and Savonius types. The Darius is often referred to as an eggbeater, has narrow blades, and operates at lower wind speeds. The Savonius type

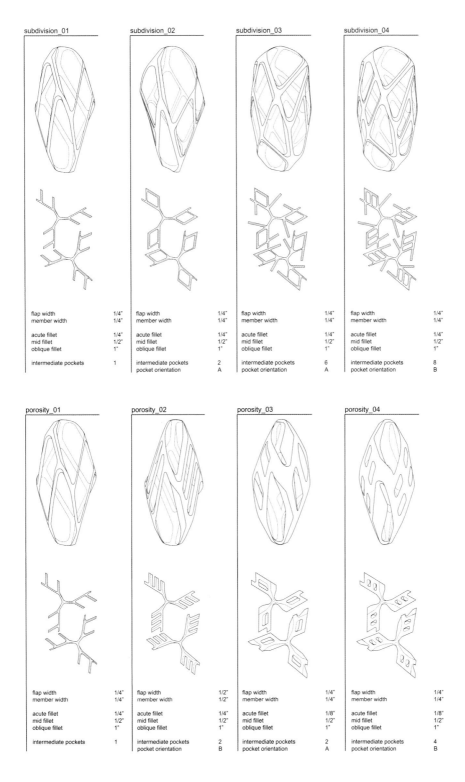

subdivision_01

flap width	1/4"
member width	1/4"
acute fillet	1/4"
mid fillet	1/2"
oblique fillet	1"
intermediate pockets	1

subdivision_02

flap width	1/4"
member width	1/4"
acute fillet	1/4"
mid fillet	1/2"
oblique fillet	1"
intermediate pockets	2
pocket orientation	A

subdivision_03

flap width	1/4"
member width	1/4"
acute fillet	1/4"
mid fillet	1/2"
oblique fillet	1"
intermediate pockets	6
pocket orientation	A

subdivision_04

flap width	1/4"
member width	1/4"
acute fillet	1/4"
mid fillet	1/2"
oblique fillet	1"
intermediate pockets	8
pocket orientation	B

porosity_01

flap width	1/4"
member width	1/4"
acute fillet	1/4"
mid fillet	1/2"
oblique fillet	1"
intermediate pockets	1

porosity_02

flap width	1/2"
member width	1/2"
acute fillet	1/4"
mid fillet	1/2"
oblique fillet	1"
intermediate pockets	2
pocket orientation	B

porosity_03

flap width	1/4"
member width	1/4"
acute fillet	1/8"
mid fillet	1/2"
oblique fillet	1"
intermediate pockets	2
pocket orientation	A

porosity_04

flap width	1/4"
member width	1/4"
acute fillet	1/8"
mid fillet	1/2"
oblique fillet	1"
intermediate pockets	4
pocket orientation	B

Figure 6.24 Flat pack two-dimensional patterns for three-dimensional turbine forms, studying the relationship between surface area and rotational speed

Figure 6.25 Components
Figure 6.26 Individual turbine

typically consists of larger concave-shaped sail-like scoops that capture the wind and produce the lift. Extensive testing of formal variations resulted in a family of forms with varying degrees of porosity and volume. A combination of cutting and scoring of the plastic sheets created the multi-bladed shell. Testing the variations in shell geometry demonstrated that slight changes in curvature, blade width and geometry affect the performance of the turbine. Rather than seeking the "ultimate" model, we chose to develop a family of models whose various efficiencies would be activated by different types of wind, creating an aggregated screen of flickering light and color (Figures 6.27–6.36).

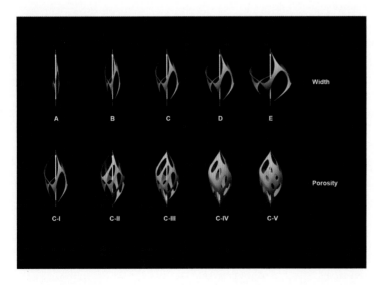

Figure 6.27 Family of forms

Figures 6.28–6.30 Paper study models to study relationship between form and performance of wind turbines

Figures 6.31–6.33 Prototypes

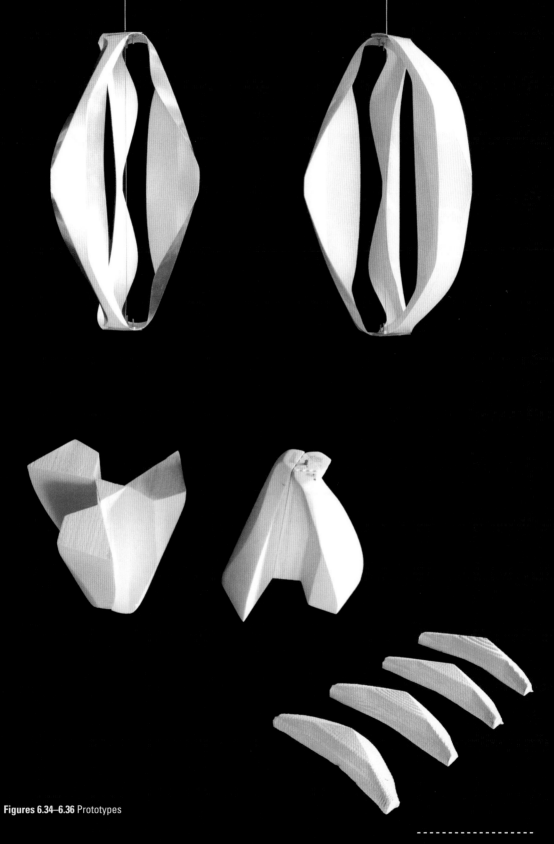

Figures 6.34–6.36 Prototypes

Responsive in real-time to environmental conditions, *Wind Screen* focuses attention on issues of energy consumption and production and raises awareness of these issues through a visual display of forces and intensities. The material medium renders visible the larger atmospheric phenomena through the interaction of material, geometry and electronics. The translation of wind speed into a visual register seeks to transform public opinion and public behavior by foregrounding energy use as well as the means of production and consumption (Figures 6.37–6.40).

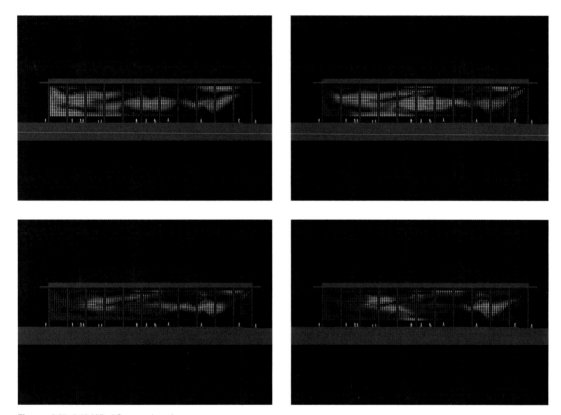

Figures 6.37–6.40 *Wind Screen* elevations

Results/conclusion

This project is still in progress.

Entasis

Hypothesis

To create a variable spatial volume, *Entasis* employs servo-motors to continuously deform a woven structure of polypropylene sheets.

Materials

CNC-milled polypropylene sheet, servo motors, computer.

Procedure

The testing process involved basic simulations in 3D software as well as physical testing with small-scale models. Material deformation under rotation and compression was observed and cataloged as a family of behaviors. These behaviors could be modified depending on the speed of rotation. Even speed alone produces great variation in the quality of the transformation observed – a slow rotation suggests the pulsation of a breathing organism, while a fast rotation produces an aggressive lunge or inflection. A combination of rotation and compression would produce the most varied and expressive behaviors in the polypropylene columns (Figures 6.41–6.43).

Figure 6.41 Study model of twisting weave under various rotations, compression, and torque

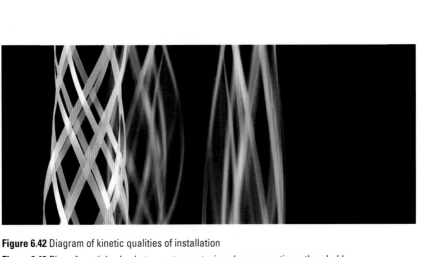

Figure 6.42 Diagram of kinetic qualities of installation

Figure 6.43 Plan of spatial valve between two entasis columns creating a threshold between them

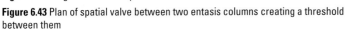

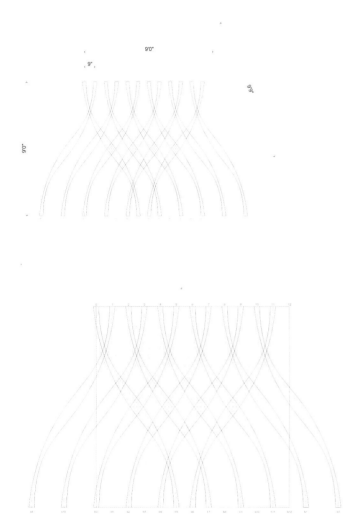

9'0"

9"

9'0"

9'0"

9'6"

Figure 6.44a–b Unfolded geometry of three-dimensional spiral weave

Figure 6.45 Close-up of polypropylene material

Figure 6.46 Installation in Artist Space with large servomotors controlling the rotation, torque, and speed

The ability of the material to deform flexibly allows it to translate the torque forces into an expressive form. A polypropylene sheet is CNC milled into curved strips that are mounted on two aluminum wheels to form a cylindrical volume. A weave pattern of overlapping strips defines the volume of the cylinder and controls the direction of the bulging when the cylinder is twisted. The lower wheel is fixed to the floor, while the upper wheel is attached to an armature and a servomotor, which allows the precise control over the speed and direction of the rotation (Figures 6.44–6.45).

Results

Arranged in the space of a gallery, the two *Entasis* elements form a kind of dynamic portal. As mentioned before, the structural armature to support the servomotors was designed to both rotate and slide up and down to compress the piece. However, the installed piece in the gallery only implemented the rotational movements. As the servomotors slowly wind the cylinders, the polypropylene flexes and bows, pressing against itself and deforming into a bulbous braided figure. The choreography of the two columns appears to breathe, twist, and pulse: as one swells, the other contracts (Figures 6.46–6.48).

Figures 6.47–6.48 Kinetic installation for the Confines Exhibition at the Institute Valencia Art Moderne with servomotors controlled by remote computer

The "personality" of the installed piece was a slow languid curling and unfurling in an aperiodic pattern to produce an evolving spatial composition of concave and convex curvatures. Acting as a spatial valve, the piece cycles through a spectrum of spatial combinations and degrees of aperture; closed to open, opaque to transparent, and solid to diffuse. The space between the two is variable, at moments inviting the viewer to pass between.

Conclusion

The flexibility of the material and the computer-controlled rotations produce a syntax of choreographed behaviors. The forms – while digitally generated, unrolled, and patterned – rely on their material properties to calculate the limits of their deformation and govern the form's behavior, underscoring the *form* in per*form*. As a kinetic sculptural form, *Entasis* amplifies the theatrical potential of the classical principle and utilizes its deformation as a determinant for architectural behavior. As such, the parameters of the form's operation were calibrated to allow occupation and passage. *Entasis* produces an activated figure within the space of the gallery. It has the potential to be an animated architecture, embedded with intelligence and responsive to its environment.

Material media

Let us return to McLuhan's theory of media/content, and specifically his example of the light bulb, in which he argues that the electric light is pure medium without content. For McLuhan, the use or application of the light bulb for surgery or for nighttime baseball is of no consequence; rather, its significance lies in its ability to extend daytime activities, to create social spaces, and to produce environments which otherwise could not exist. Television, by contrast, is a medium capable of delivering high-resolution content. The screen is indifferent to the content that is being broadcast through it.

Architecture as a material medium possesses a far less explicit relationship to its content. The representational capacity of architecture to communicate is filtered through the codified structures of type and tectonics. Our interest in material as a medium focuses on the capacity of material to generate environments that are capable of conveying content. By incorporating new materials, electronic media, sensor technologies, and public participation, the corporeal and sensorial production of space is animated and amplified. Immersive environments become "live" through the deployment of designed material responses and effects.

White Noise White Light, *Current*, *Wind Screen*, and *Entasis* utilize specific techniques and technologies to achieve these effects in highly calibrated ways. In each case the material medium and the communicative content are tailored to suit one another. In *Current*, the length of the glass lite is calibrated for the intensity of the LED lighting and the LED wavelengths utilized to throw the length of the lite; in *Entasis* the cut edges of the polypropylene are curved to accentuate the torque produced by the servomotor and the motor's behavior is calibrated to heighten particular deformations of the polypropylene. Taken together, these projects suggest an expanded palette of materials and effects, where materials must be understood and designed relative to the effects that they sponsor – and vice versa.

Contemporary practices are working in an expanded mode to realize works that engage broader audiences with more diverse means. Accessibility of new fabrication technologies has transformed the process of making. Craft has evolved into digital craft. Mass customization allows every instance to be unique and every component to be custom – and yet – with the new tools come new economies, and a renewed demand for strategic intelligences to direct them towards particular outcomes.

Chapter 7
Open

David Benjamin
The Living

- -

1. The garage

Open the garage.

Look inside and you will find amateurs hunched over the workbench. You will find saws biting measured parts out of supplies. There is the thin metallic smoke of solder.

Forget the car. Its familiar machineries will only be in the way, so it has to go. The garage is for *new* projects, and they require room to breathe.

Matter. No doubt there will be matter and material processes in the garage. Matter in the form of low-grade plywood and duct tape and spools of wire organized in neat rows of drawers. Matter appearing in sketches about assembly.

The work here is raw. It is quick and rough. You may find skill in the garage, but skill is not what really counts. Inventive ideas and breaking down the problem are closer to what is needed.

In the garage, there is urgency, because the territory in question is unknown. There is hunger, there is sacrifice, yet there is freedom because, until you open the garage, no one realizes there is anything going on in here. No one is expecting anything of consequence to emerge.

The garage where Apple Computer began, in Los Altos, California, used to be indecipherable from all the other garages on Crist Drive. But in 1976, Steve Jobs asked his parents to contribute space for his new project. Jobs' father agreed to pack up his car restoration equipment. Jobs and his friend Steve Wozniak moved into the garage and made it center of operations for a mission to steal computing from button-down corporations and give it to the rest of us. The garage became a place for software, circuit boards, and young misfits with long hair. It was a room for combining concepts with physical materials, through a method of experimenting and prototyping.

The garage meant suspicion of conventional thinking. The garage was a place to say f*** you to the way things are usually done.

Open the garage and open the basement, since the basement is basically an underground garage.

In 1986, Fugazi launched a revolution in independent music from a basement in Arlington, Virginia. This band had ideas. The front man, Ian MacKaye, believed normal life was something to fight against. "We despise established ritualistic patterns," he said. MacKaye believed music and music culture could change the status quo.

Fugazi created a new sound that was not exactly punk, or dub, or any other known style. The sound was disorienting, and it challenged typical categories. The band released music on its own Dischord Records, rejecting cash advances from corporate major labels. It booked shows in Elks Lodges, abandoned supermarkets and, of course, in people's basements. Fugazi insisted on all-ages admission and $5 tickets. The band decided it wouldn't do interviews with magazines they wouldn't read themselves.

- - - - - - - - - - - - - - - - - -

When the four members of the band were not rehearsing or recording or touring, they gathered, in the basement, to cut, fold, and glue the covers of their own seven-inch singles. They also photocopied and put up flyers for their own shows. They made D.I.Y. political, and they made it cool.

For creative young people, the garage and the basement were not just practice spaces. They were a state of mind.

2. Flash Research

A few years ago, I developed a D.I.Y. design method, with Soo-in Yang, for our architecture research and practice. We call it Flash Research. Flash Research projects involve targeted, intense explorations of architectural ideas. They involve self-imposed limits of time (three months) and budget ($1,000). They test design possibilities through full-scale, functioning prototypes.

The work from this method is raw. It is quick and rough. It explores unknown territory. Flash Research is something like garage architecture.

While some architectural projects involve design exploration through rendered images, Flash Research involves design exploration through full-scale prototypes. While some architectural projects involve a linear sequence of research, then design, then construction, Flash Research involves all three at once. For this method, research = design = construction. For Flash Research, it doesn't count unless we can make it.

Yet each Flash Research project is a beginning rather than an end. The goal is not to produce a single refined design, but instead to record new experiments and identify paths for future research. We offer documentation through assembly instructions, circuit diagrams, and source code so that others might pick up where we leave off. From the instructions, a thousand distinct projects might emerge like tree branches. Our own is just one possibility, one branch.

In another register, we imagine Flash Research projects to be swappable modules in new and existing buildings. The modules are precise and immediate. They can upgrade old systems without replacing the entire structure. The projects, then, are not stand-alone building designs, but they have their own mass and significance. And they are part of a fluid, open source research endeavor being conducted, loosely and jointly, by us and others.

To put it another way, rapidly changing conditions in our world call for entirely new architectural propositions. New propositions call for testing physical constructions. And testing constructions calls for iterative prototyping.

Prototyping and testing are the heart of Flash Research. Material processes are the meat. Matter, here and now, matters.

3. *Living Glass*

Nitinol is an unusual material. It is sometimes called shape memory alloy (SMA) because it can be deformed and then "remember" its original shape when triggered by a specific activation temperature. Nitinol blends nickel and titanium and it is often manufactured as wire. Since it is small, strong, durable, and easy to trigger, it is used in products like human heart stents and the CD ejection mechanism of laptops. Since it moves silently and organically, it is used in mesmerizing toys like a slow, continually-flapping plastic butterfly.

Our first Flash Research project took Nitinol as a *material premise*. We wanted to start with SMA, explore its material possibilities, and test them in applications of responsive architecture. The terms of the project were as simple and open-ended as that.

At the outset, we were aware of several precedents of kinetic building elements, but none involved SMA. This meant using Nitinol in architecture was unknown territory and was a good subject for Flash Research.

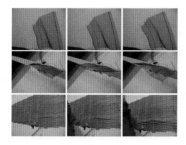

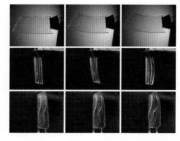

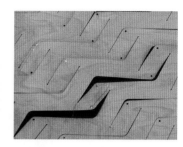

Figure 7.1 **Figure 7.2** **Figure 7.3**

We obtained a sample of the material from university researchers in Indiana (at the time, Nitinol was not readily available) and immediately began experimenting. We produced at least one prototype every week. First we imitated an example from an electrical engineering book, then we mocked up our own unit of movement as a narrow, four-inch-tall triangle. The short side was basswood and the long sides were Nitinol and metal rod. When the Nitinol was connected to a nine-volt battery, it contracted and caused the metal rod to bend over slightly. When it was disconnected, the metal rod stood back up, pulling the Nitinol into its expanded state. The rhythm of movement was eerie and lifelike.

Yet since Nitinol contracts by only 5 percent of its length, we faced a serious material constraint. What effects might we produce with this narrow behavior?

In our experiments, we quickly explored many permutations, varying the geometry of the triangle, the gauge of Nitinol and metal rod, the voltage of electrical signal, and the attachment details. After calibrating the triangle for maximum transformation, we created a simple electrical circuit and programmed a microcontroller to trigger it. We linked together several triangles and re-programmed the microcontroller to produce more complex patterns of movement. With the addition of a low-cost infrared sensor, we established our first fully responsive kinetic system – when an object neared the rods, they morphed in the opposite direction (Figure 7.1).

In our next round of prototypes, we replaced the metal rods with thin flexible materials: model airplane plywood, acrylic, neoprene, and rubber. We discovered that if we cut slits in these surfaces and attached Nitinol wires to them, the slits would open when the Nitinol contracted. The surface would transform from solid to permeable (Figure 7.2).

In one late night experiment, we cast Nitinol in transparent silicone. It was a hack job. We taped together scraps of foamcore to make a rough mold. We used T-pins to hold the Nitinol in tension while the solution cured. With this prototype, as with all of our experiments, we did not know exactly how it would function until we wired it up. The Nitinol might contract and then refuse to expand. It might not move at all. But when we switched on the silicone surface, it curled and flattened, moving gradually, in a repeating rhythm, as if breathing. The surface moved with as much magnitude as previous ones, but it had the benefits of being nearly transparent and insulating the Nitinol from exposure to air and human contact. We decided this new combination of materials – originally a long shot – was the best direction for our remaining prototypes (Figure 7.3).

As we neared the mark of two weeks remaining in our research, we selected a unit of movement with 5-inch-long Nitinol wires cast in a 16th-inch-thick sheet of silicone. There were s-shaped slits running alongside the Nitinol, and when the Nitinol contracted, the flat surface moved into the third dimension and opened its gills.

To establish proof-of-concept, we solved the final issues of casting with uniform thickness, connecting one panel of eight gills to another, and embedding sensors in the surface. After three months and $1,000, we demonstrated *Living Glass*: a thin, transparent building skin that breathed in response to human presence, controlling air flow and displaying information (Figure 7.4).

- - - - - - - - - - - - - - - - - -

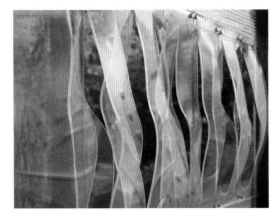

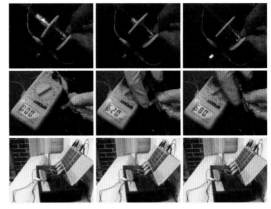

Figure 7.4 *Living Glass*

Figure 7.5a–i Field-testing TFPVs

4. *River Glow*

In New York City, as in most of the world, there is no on-site public interface to water quality. How can we tell if the water is cleaner this year than last? How do we know if it is safe to swim? Or eat the fish?

In our second Flash Research project, we set out to explore energy self-sufficient architecture, and then quickly expanded the topic to include real-time interfaces to environmental quality. This time we did not start with a single material, but we followed the same design method of prototyping and testing.

Originally we intended to harness energy from the everyday movement of people. Our experiments involved straightforward old technologies (homemade solenoids) and complex new systems (electroactive polymers, or EAPs). But our first several prototypes failed. Each one generated such a small amount of energy that we deemed it unfeasible given our limited time, budget, and technical expertise.

With our research method, material feedback could work in multiple ways. A test could validate promising assemblies, but it could also deflate problematic designs. Yet each prototype, failed or successful, offered important evidence and helped advance the project. In our energy testing, solenoids and EAPs were worth trying, but after encountering difficulties with them, we decided not to force it. We turned to photovoltaics even though this required leaving behind the idea of harnessing energy through movement.

Since we wanted to maintain design flexibility, we chose to work with flexible solar cells rather than larger glass-backed ones. But in a series of tests with thin film photovoltaics (TFPVs), we determined we could harvest only a very small amount of energy. Our field tests produced numbers much lower than the product specifications. Once again we had a serious technical problem (Figure 7.5).

This time, instead of looking for a way to *harness more energy*, we decided to look for a way to *consume less energy*. Based on the test results, we again revised our idea. Now we proposed to create a *micro-economy of* electricity – micro-units of energy harnessed and micro-units of energy consumed, working together in a sustainable cycle.

We thought this system would make sense in an off-the-grid location, rather than in buildings where energy was cheap and unlimited. We thought urban waterways would be good sites because they were within the city but removed from its energy infrastructure. And at this point we decided to charge the project with further politics. We wanted to see if we could make visible environmental conditions that were normally invisible, and expose water quality as an indication of urban health.

For our next round of prototypes, we worked with TFPVs, rechargeable batteries, and low-energy lighting in the form of LEDs and electro-luminescent films and wires (Figure 7.6). We developed additional components for sensing water quality and housing all of the electronics. We tested each technology independently, and then integrated it with the rest of the system (Figures 7.7–7.8).

By the end of three months, we demonstrated *River Glow*: a floating pod that harvested solar energy, detected water quality, and triggered illumination. It was energy self-sufficient and required no on-site wiring. We built and tested only one pod, but we deliberately designed it to be independent, modular, and scalable. Our system could function with one or ten or a hundred. Scaling up only required building more identical pods. If many pods were installed together, they created a public interface to water quality. It was a cloud of light hovering above the river that changed color according to conditions below (Figure 7.9).

Figure 7.6

Figure 7.7

Figure 7.8

Figure 7.9 Integrated systems

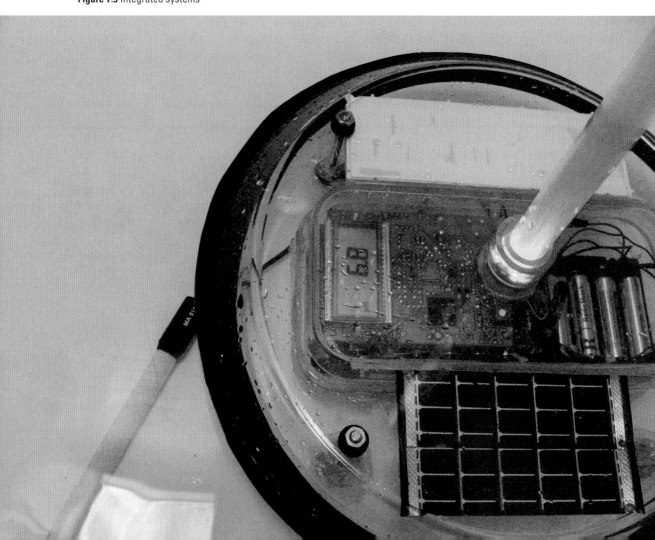

5. *Better, Cheaper, Faster*

Quarter-inch plywood is cheap, common, and weak. In its default state, you can break it with your hands.

But consider an old parable called "The Quarrelling Brothers." In this story, a father interrupts a fight among his children and sits them down for a lesson. He asks the youngest to pick up a stick and break it – no problem. He asks the second child to pick up two sticks and break them – more difficult, but do-able. He asks the eldest to pick up three sticks and break them – the child tries, but it is not possible. Even though each stick alone is weak, the handful is strong. The father tells the brothers to stop quarrelling and acting individually – instead they should work together (Figure 7.10).

Perhaps the same strategy could be used to create a strong structure out of weak plywood. In a third Flash Research project, we began with a material (quarter-inch plywood), a technique (CNC routing), and a hypothesis (digital fabrication might be able to bridge the gap between "experimental architects" and "bottom-line real estate developers"). Again matter drove the research, but again we looked for opportunities beyond the technical aspects of material processes.

The question was how exactly all of this might come together, and of course we buried ourselves in prototypes. This time we worked at three scales simultaneously. Prototypes at 1:96 – created by laser-cutting two-ply chipboard – allowed us to explore massing, stability, and extendability. Prototypes at 1:12 – created by laser-cutting model airplane plywood – allowed us to explore joints, rhythm, and system strength. And full-scale prototypes – created by CNC routing quarter-inch plywood – allowed us to explore joints, rhythm, system strength, material strength, stability, and detailing.

In our initial tests, at all three scales, we investigated the sizes and shapes of individual pieces and the system for connecting them. The first three problems we addressed were how to handle sufficient load, how to extend vertically, and how to make a collapsible system that starts flat and expands on site into its full shape. Based on several prototypes of a wall region about 3 feet wide and 9 feet tall, we discovered that the best system was alternating between one and two layers of 4-inch-wide plywood slats, in an endless M configuration. We used bolts to pin each layer of slats to the next. The joints also involved a jigsaw-puzzle shape to lock together two elements in a single layer (Figure 7.11).

One of the issues that required most testing was how to connect vertical elements with horizontal elements, and here we built on our configuration for extending vertically. At 1:12 scale, we explored dozens of permutations, varying the seam trajectory, the position of the bolts, and the shape, size, and number of puzzle-piece arcs. We designed and mocked up one round of permutations, evaluated their performance, identified areas of strength and weakness, and repeated the process (Figure 7.12). After additional studies at full scale, we settled on a horizontal seam with four bolts and a double puzzle-piece configuration. The top and bottom layers shared the seam trajectory and the bolt holes, but their puzzle-piece arcs were mirror images of each other. This allowed for easy assembly but it minimized overlapping in the seam, which minimized weakness in the connection (Figure 7.13).

For the overall framing geometry, we created a U-shaped portal which was rigid in one axis but swayed in the other axis. To address the swaying, we overlapped two separate portals so that each one would compensate for the weakness of the other. We then solved local issues such as how to lock the two portals together, how to keep the module expanded, and how to attach an envelope to the frame.

As with each Flash Research project, we kept a working list of the unique characteristics of our system. This served as a guide at every stage of prototyping. It reminded us of the most important qualities of our matter and material processes. It also reminded us of precedent projects and our potential contribution to a larger body of research.

When specifying our final full-scale demonstration, we referred to our list of unique characteristics. We designed a frame for a 10-foot cube that included just enough of the system to prove all our essential issues. It had a floor, four walls, and a roof. It was lightweight and collapsible. It was strong despite being made of a weak material. It was easy to transport and quick to assemble. Non-experts were able to build it with only a few

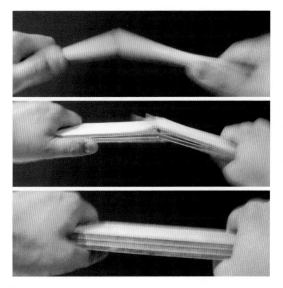

Figure 7.10a–c

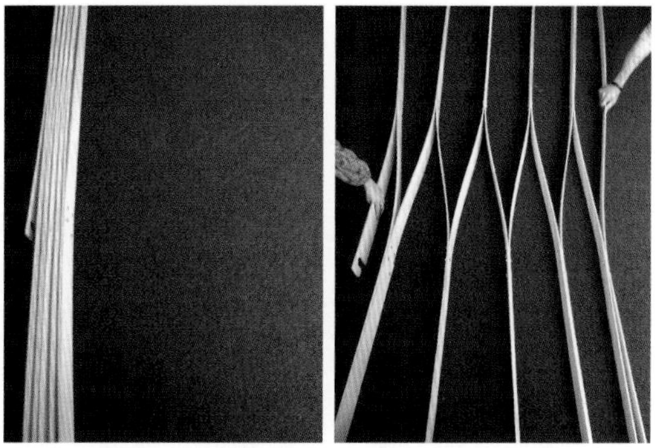

Figure 7.11a–b

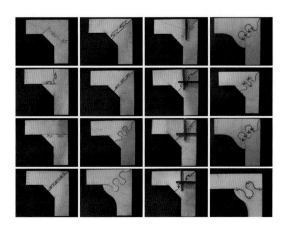

Figure 7.12a–f

Figure 7.13

standard tools. Since it was low-cost, and since it used CNC technology for economic efficiency and structural efficiency rather than formal expression, it might appeal to some of the general desires of both architects and developers. We called it *Better, Cheaper, Faster* (Figures 7.14–7.16).

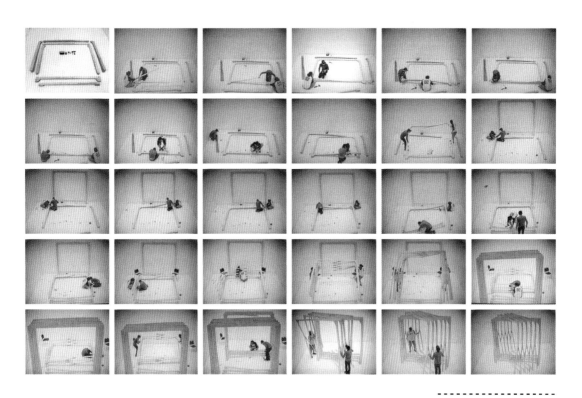

Figure 7.15 Parts

Figure 7.14 Detail

Figure 7.16a–dd Assembly sequence

6. Open

Three months in the garage pass quickly. But the limited duration of Flash Research – along with the constraints of budget and material performance – energize the projects. Our discoveries and our designs would not be the same without them. And our research would not be the same without the garage. The garage is a place to start addressing today's urgent problems with today's available technologies. The garage, low-fi and under the radar, is an ideal incubator.

But what comes after incubation?

For Flash Research, each project might be judged by whether its prototypes are promising enough and open-ended enough to be re-usable after the three-month development cycle. This may not happen immediately, or even ever, but within the past year or so, we found ourselves re-using each of these three Flash Research projects as components in new constructions. We picked up where the original research left off and transformed the prototypes for new applications. We moved them from the workbench to small structures, and from the garage to urban public spaces.

We used an enhanced version of *Living Glass* for a project called *Living City,* which explored the intersection of public space, the environment, and interactive architecture. It created a platform for buildings to talk to one another, with a building envelope that breathed in response to local and remote air quality (Figure 7.17).

River Glow led naturally to *Amphibious Architecture*, a floating installation in the East River at the Manhattan Bridge, developed in collaboration with artist Natalie Jeremijenko. Building on our final Flash Research prototype, we added sensors for presence of fish and an interface for exchanging text messages. We improved the design of our single pod and created a large array of them in a highly visible public space (Figure 7.18).

We used the general system of *Better, Cheaper, Faster* – but not its specific materials or geometry – for the frame of *Living Light*, a pavilion in a public park in Seoul that glows and blinks according to air quality and public interest in the environment (Figures 7.19–7.20). This project also re-used aspects of *Living Glass* (it was a building envelope responding to human engagement) and *River Glow* (it was an architectural interface displaying real-time pollution levels).

In each case, the quick and rough research fed naturally into a more comprehensive and refined project.

But there is no magic formula or perfect location for design.

Flash Research explores ideas and material processes, but it does not guarantee re-usable prototypes.

The garage is a physical space for experimenting, but it is also a myth. Its power is intertwined with the

Figure 7.17 *Living City*

myths of American individualism and American suburban homes. It conspires with the story that anyone with a good idea and some hard work can become infinitely successful.

But what if you don't have a garage? And if you do have one, as well as a good idea and a strong work ethic and some luck, what exactly does your success in there mean? Who does it serve? Is it private or public, closed or open?

In 1977, Apple Computer moved out of the garage. Its incubation was complete. The company was blowing up and it needed more space. The project that started quietly in the garage was mushrooming. People were gaping.

In its new rented office in Cupertino, and later in its own building and campus, the company still waved a pirate flag, and it still aimed at giant corporations. Its product breakthroughs were still dazzling. Steve Jobs still possessed a genius that others could not match.

But as the company peaked and declined and staged its comeback, it grew more and more distant from the garage state of mind. Apple became a giant itself. It was closed and secret.

Fugazi never moved out of the basement. It evolved, but it maintained this underground base.

Over the years, the band shared its D.I.Y. processes, and others used them as launching points. The band's garage politics were an open call.

The Fugazi story was not about rags to riches or about David and Goliath. It was not about a garage culture of the solitary genius inventor. Instead, the Fugazi story was about a multitude of bands and politically-active kids. It was about an open and inclusive community. You too could be Fugazi.

Here, the band believed, was the way to challenge the status quo. Here was the real revolution.

So open the garage.

Let others in. Share the experiments. Release the innovations.

Matter is not your lackey. Material processes have their own lives to live. Open the garage, Young Turk, and set them free.

Figure 7.18 *River Glow*

Figure 7.19 *Living Light*
Figure 7.20 Connection detail

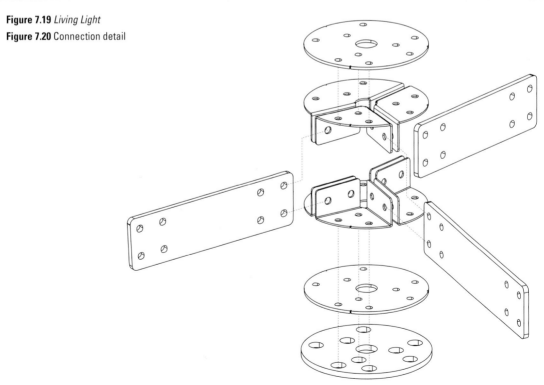

Chapter 8
Porous Boundaries

Material transitions from territories to maps

Jason Oliver Vollen and Dale Clifford

Binary Design

- -

> The pedagogy of modeling must not operate by giving precepts, but by the culture of experimentation making an appeal to the imagination in its transactions with reason, eliciting aesthetic and rational judgment, and giving to precise criticism the positive force that advances the sense of the proposition.
>
> (Álvaro Malo)[1]

> The map is not the territory.
>
> (Alfred Korzybski)[2]

Up up and away!

Stochastic modeling can be traced to nineteenth-century scientific efforts to better understand the nature of fluid mechanics. As mathematical models they evolved to reveal not a singular answer but a territory of behaviors for statistical probability. These models provide a glimpse that events, mathematic or empiric, are not discreet but combinatorial and transformational. Each new "game of chance" contributed to the structured territory of observable occurrences and experiences in the natural world. These models of flows, where one state of matter passes by another, were maps of the territory that the experiment sought to recreate. Fast forward one hundred years and multiple disciplines, not the least of which is architecture, now rely on many of the same mathematical models, or at least their principled underpinnings as the platform to proceed with the development and implementation of new technologies. The effect that this trend has had on architecture is that modern architectural thinking may have replaced modeling with simulation, which, from one point of view, the goal is the same, to recreate a likeness and organize information. We might consider that the map has collapsed over the territory where information and simulation illicit rules for design, and in this sandbox there lies the opportunity for the material culture of architecture to make a significant leap forward.

The benefit of the collapse of the map and the territory[3] is the return to judgment over interpretation – and the Wright brothers exercised theirs by launching paradigmatic technology; the effect of which was transformational change to the modern world, where accelerated transport literally collapsed both map and territory.

At the turn of the twentieth century, the Wright brothers' transition from two wheels to winged flight embodies the itinerant relationship between material knowledge, emerging fabrication processes and the human imagination (Figure 8.1). The Wrights knew both how things were made – and how to make things. Their ideas, rigorously developed and tested, were supported by first-hand knowledge of tools and material; in their workshop there was no separation between manual and intellectual modes of production. Aerodynamic performance was critical for their breakthrough of controlled flight and performative values were critical to their process of design.[4]

- -

Figure 8.1 Quasi-experimental theory/experiment that led the Wright brothers to both validate their understanding of aerodynamics and debunk years of scientific theories, leading directly to the first manned flights of heavier than air vehicles

The Wrights ushered in a fundamental world change based on a quasi-experimental mode of technological development that bridged two previously distinct forms of modeling: mathematical simulation and physical testing. Without the benefit of empiric testing, the Wrights would have continued to work from incomplete or erroneous mathematical assumptions; the empiric refined the theoretical. Two important discoveries provided a platform from which the Wrights could leap: the development of the model wind tunnel in 1871 in London by Wenham and the development of the Reynolds number which disproved Newton's drag theory and characterized the relationship of turbulent and laminar flow laying the foundation for modern aerodynamics (Figure 8.2). As Wilbur Wright would later claim, that although they had become famous for the "Flyer," the instrument that led to radical thinking was the use of the wind tunnel: a model which actively engaged the map–territory relation.

Figure 8.2 The transitional patent drawing that followed the experiments in Figure 8.1 and preceded the first powered flight

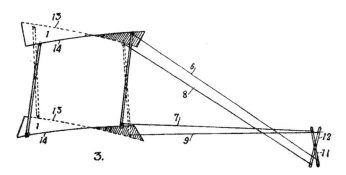

While most of the early inventors of flying machines concerned themselves with building highly stable aircraft, the Wright's intentionally built unstable aircraft that exhibited a high degree of control. Controlled flight at this time was a tenuous prospect; it might more effectively be termed "balanced" or "interactive" flight where body and mind were responding to an unpredictable and fluctuating environment. Their methods brought *a posteriori* knowledge of mathematics, stochastic modeling, and *a priori* knowledge of materials and processes to define a method of performative discovery that challenged the well-established scientific method. It is through this lens that our work has sought to reconsider this map–territory relationship, and to reconsider what is matter in architecture (Figure 8.3).

Figure 8.3 The first moment of the twentieth-century space–time collapse, folding the map over the territory at Kittyhawk where the first manned and powered heavier-than-air vehicle sustained flight

Material thinking

The Wrights' material was the model, a combination of mathematical speculation, physical simulation and observation of aerodynamic responsiveness. In this sense the material was not what could be handled or seen, rather it was the effect that the material could make – the Wrights systematically uncovered the materials potentiality. The quasi-experimental method is part discovery, part validation and part falsification – an inventor's method. The Wrights joined development and verification as a near simultaneous iterative with the combination of simulation, as wind tunnels, and full-scale physical models, as kites. Keenly observing the behavior of their handiwork, they translated physical observance into useful information: thinking advanced making and making advanced thinking. This realignment of the principle, so dear to architects, that form follows force to form follows flow represents a fundamental shift in thinking about materials.

Homeostasis as a model

To understand material technology today, we can emulate the Wrights' quasi-experimental modes of discovery. In our work, we find creative and practical prospects in the redefinition of material through the lens of emerging material technologies and their traditional and contemporary forming logics. This view is characterized by Henri Bergson's conception of matter which consists of "modifications, perturbations, changes in tension or of energy – and nothing else"[5]; it is the performative displacement of material that gives architecture new operative potentials – in the case of Kittyhawk, the reality of controlled flight. The new paradigm shift in material technologies for the built environment today was defined by the Wrights a century ago: the more we look at materials, the more we see the natural world as a system of non-deterministic interactivity and energy exchange.

Paradigms

Correalism and the similar Equipoise are perhaps the first sustained theoretical movements towards a homeostatic paradigm of ecology and technology in architecture, and both deal with dynamic balance and technology conceptually.[6] The former in terms of expression, and the latter in terms of reaction, yet both promote a holistic approach to building. Developed immediately subsequent to the Wrights' work on manned flight, these ideas emerged by rethinking our philosophical and technical relationship with the natural world and by reexamining accepted building practices. These movements posited that social change, or behavioral modification was the goal of creative production, and this change would come through an unscripted response with our environment.

There has been a strong contingent of innovators calling for a fundamental change in the way we conceived buildings in the first half of the twentieth century.[7,8] And to fully understand the problem, we must rethink technology holistically, rethink building holistically and re-engage in a new material relationship. We have attempted to engage this dialog by re-examining material as a synthesis of abiotic and biotic principles, to develop material controls for homeostatic conditions in the built environment.

Prospects for self-regulation: energy

In terms of materials' distribution and performance, our thinking is directly influenced by the topological systems of Henri Poincaré and his description of singularities and instances, which while at the same time are part of a larger system, each singularity affects each other. The emergence of complexity is resurgent in our work, always an effect of combinatorial relationships between environmental, tool and material. According to Sanford Kwinter, form is an instance of structural stability in a system as it seeks homeostasis, thus all form is the result of growth and resistance, it is the convergence of material and force (Figure 8.4).[9]

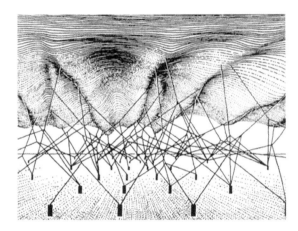

Figure 8.4 Conrad Hal Waddington's *Epigenic Landscapes* discussed by Sanford Kwinter as the illustration of the moment of singularity of a topological system

Our approach draws from the intrinsic nature of nature, as an adaptive technology, and we apply a collaborative systems approach to correlate the shape, variability and kinetic distribution of material at the interface of the built and natural ecologies: the building envelope. The work concerns the development of building technologies that operate in accordance with the biologic condition of homeostasis: the ability of an organism to maintain equilibrium in response to fluctuating environmental conditions. The building envelope becomes a selective filter, a three-dimensional porous topography that, through active or passive means, advances the building envelope's interactivity.

Quasi-experimental inquiry

In this spirit, we explore the processes of advancing an architectural proposition by thinking directly through the material: the process of empiric data derived from observation of the principal nature of material and flow, rather than the initial statement of a fully working hypothesis. Through inquisitive material exploration, patterns are recognized, relationships are uncovered and one can characterize events to pragmatically extend the range of perceived possibility – architecturally and experientially. Each project detailed for this chapter proceeded inductively and correlated materiality, fabrication processes, and system performance. Each example operates at a spectrum of scales and draws from a range of disciplines in an effort to step towards the boundaries of our field. Material investigations include advancing the architectural potential of ceramics, the oldest of construction materials to experimental applications of shape memory alloys and polymers for responsive façade systems to patterning titanium sheets for spinal implants. It is these points, attuned to the peculiarities of locality that lead to a built aesthetic.[10]

Molecular Geodesics, Inc.

After working with mechanical engineers, programmers and mathematicians to design novel structural scaffolds, devices and materials from a biologically inspired perspective, we are now compelled to reach beyond the perceived boundaries of disciplines.[11] In this context, a common language can be developed to articulate appropriate questions to solve multidisciplinary problems.

The motivation for working with research-based companies is the development and application of new knowledge. This experience was pivotal in developing the contribution of an architect to knowledge frontiers in diverse fields. Operating as a multidisciplinary "think tank," our groups' competitive edge was the ability to draw from multiple viewpoints and knowledge bases in real time – as we were all at the same table with a strong drive to solve the problem at hand. A palpable sense of confidence emanated from the team; this was simply the result. The team approached leading companies involved in the design and manufacture of surgical implants and instruments, high-performance wing design, and Space Shuttle tiles (Figure 8.5) – and worked with them to advance materials and fabrication technologies from our collective ability. We have endeavored to continue this approach, synthesizing expertise from diverse disciplines to advance the environmental and experiential prospect of a project.

Figure 8.5a–c Enlarged view of a marrow scaffold to support artificial bone growth. Complex aluminum casting proposed for a heat-dissipating Space Shuttle tile. Spinal implant with improved resiliency for greater spinal flexibility. Constructed from stamped, rolled and welded titanium sheet

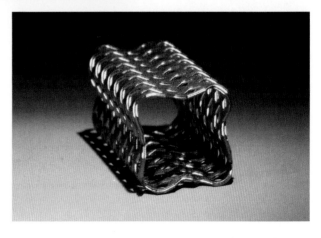

Sonic Membrane

Our goal for this project is to produce an acoustic band gap material system that provides significant noise abatement when compared to current acoustic materials. The hypothesis is to characterize the relationship between material placement and acoustic performance.

The mathematical contribution for this work is attributed to UA Materials Science Professor Pierre Deymier, whose work has advanced the field of acoustics by researching the relationship between sound propagation and geometric arrays of materials of different densities. Properly aligned, this new class of material can produce a band gap in the audible range. For example, if lead spheres were suspended in air, in a regular cubic array seven rows deep, and sound waves entered one side of the array – there would be a gap in the wavelengths transmitted through the far side. The frequency range of the acoustic band gap is dependent on the array proximity and the difference in density between the two media, in the case above, lead and air.

There is something about the synergy between the skill sets of architects and material scientists. The samples were filled with water to serve as a high-density medium – the sterolithography resin serves as the low-density medium. Acoustically, the models provided a band gap and therefore noise abatement within the audible range. They also had unforeseen visual properties in responses to light. Further research is moving towards less expensive means of fabrication to produce an acoustic/visual block for sound-sensitive building applications.

In *Sonic Membrane*, the map is the soundscape, and the territory is the phenomenological interrelationship of frequency and material density (Figure 8.6). Through this lens, the spectrum of density that we call material (all material) can be understood as local variations in frequency.[12]

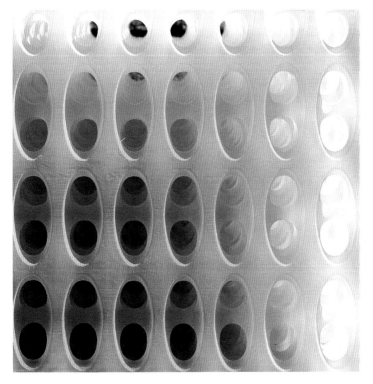
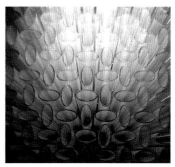
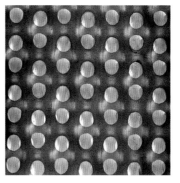

Figure 8.6a–c Material/geometry sonic band gap models used for testing frequency cancellation

EcoCeramic Phase I: metabolic building membranes

In the age of green anything, new envelope systems for the building industry must be energy-efficient, utilize abundant or recyclable materials, and encourage local economic development. Terracotta meets these requirements, yet in order to reintroduce architectural ceramics to the construction industry, traditional terracotta must take on the added thermodynamic criteria of twenty-first-century high-performance construction systems.

The EcoCeramic envelope system is designed to perform in arid climates by producing habitable thermal ranges through passive cooling strategies. The approach is derived from an understanding of regional climatic conditions and study of the evolutionary thermodynamic characteristics of natural precedents: barrel cacti and termite mounds. In the upper Sonoran Desert, the barrel cacti, in response to transpiration losses, have lost their leaves and transferred their photosynthetic organ to their trunk. The cacti have developed self-shading highly articulate surfaces that mitigate intense desert sun and extreme diurnal temperatures – a passive strategy that lowers the trunk surface by as much as 30°F on a hot summer day.

Based on the passive strategies of the termite mound and the barrel cactus, in combination with local solar incidence, a preliminary profile was established. The profile was further developed through simulation, physical experimentation, established material properties, and measured radiant thermal gains, leading to an idealized thermal section. The tile is shaped to perform on an annual basis, the winter condition accepts solar radiation into the concavity of the tile, the summer condition provides shade and the high surface area re-radiates energy to the environment, decreasing thermal gain (Figure 8.7).

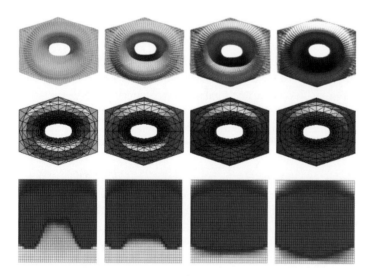

Figure 8.7a–l Face tile at solstice and equinox conditions, Ecotect solar insolation simulations, Ecotect solar penetration section simulation

The fundamental strategy for thermal performance between the EcoCeramic wall system and the typical concrete masonry unit (CMU) is the management of energy: the CMU is conceived as a unit independent of direct thermal transmission and requires additional insulation to perform effectively in hot and arid climates. The EcoCeramic system advances the design and performative logic that an established system can be enhanced via the informed and precise placement of material.

Design principles

To design a thermally responsive wall system capable of passively tempering the Sonoran Desert climate to habitable temperatures, the application of first principles, specifically surface area ratios, material thickness, self-shading and ventilation were applied to the series of ceramic modules. Design principles, or second principles guide thermal control through form, color and texture.

Based on empiric thermal experimentation, the following principles apply:

1. Smooth surfaces minimize thermal gain/loss and increased surface area reduces thermal transmission and increases dissipation in the direction of the heat source.
2. The tile surface can be shaped according to solar angles to maximize shading in the summer months and increase solar gain during the winter months.
3. The increased surface area facing the wall on the interior surface directs gains back into the wall cavity.
4. The cone, which receives only winter sunlight, absorbs, stores and transmits solar insulation.
5. The tile is thinnest in regions most affected by summer sun and thickest in regions most affected by winter sunlight, similar to principles found in cathedral and dome termite mounds.

Research objectives

The aim of this research was to demonstrate that surface geometries articulated by localized climatic criteria and developed through intrinsic material properties will impact the thermal performance (thermal transfer) of building envelopes while remaining adaptable to existing low-tech and ubiquitous streamlined manufacturing techniques.

Methods

The development protocol followed a parametric feedback loop derived from climate analysis, digital simulations and physical material properties optimized for a small production run. The initial phase included the fabrication of several molds for Ram pressing the ceramic structural modules, producing multiple iterations of ceramic composite test panels, development of face tiles with multidimensional complexity, and performing initial strength and performance analysis to gather data for use as the building product.

Parametric criteria

The primary method for performative design research was the inclusion and exploitation of indexical data applied as parametric constraints in a digital environment. By constraining multiple points on a reference plane and tagging them to climatic and indexing feedback loop criteria, we developed an initial 3-D polygon surface. The model was then tested with pre-design simulation software Ecotect and Flow Wizard for insulation and thermal assessment.

Emerging process/fabrication

Molds were designed with parametric modeling software Maya, Rhinoceros and MasterCAM, and fabricated using a Techno LC 4848 Series CNC router. With the numerically controlled computer fabrication equipment, the design and fabrication process was significantly streamlined over the traditional Ram press mold-making process and produced a more precise ceramic profile. Once the press molds were fabricated, the structural units and face tiles were rapidly produced (Figure 8.8). After pressing, the modules were air-dried, then fired in a kiln to cone 4 for the face tiles and cone 6 for the structural modules, 2142F and 223F respectively, removing any trace amount of moisture and sintering the ceramic. The firing process molecularly alters the clay body to achieve the durable properties required for weathering. Once cooled, the fired structural modules were bonded using woven glass fiber reinforcement. This process takes advantage of the porous property of the ceramic molecular matrix to form a strong mechanical bond.

Figure 8.8a–c Tile/module fabrication process

Strength-testing protocols

Recombinant samples were tested in compression, tension and three-point bending using an industry standard Instron 3369. Material test samples and scaled prototype modules underwent micro-inspection using a Leica SP8 APO stereo microscope. The inspection checked the ceramic samples for the degree of sintering, fracture patterning, and surface variability. The visual check was followed by the American Society for Testing and Materials (ASTM) tests C-134 bulk density and C-20 porosity and absorption.

Material properties

Although largely considered historically a traditional material, terracotta is making a small resurgence onto the construction palette as a rainscreen and sunscreen system. However, the ceramics building industry has produced little in the area of performance-related products. The complexity of molds and dies, latent associations to non-structural and non-performative applications (ornamentation), and material failure when exposed to water for long periods of time all contribute to a negative perception; coupled with the trend in modern building for steel and glass façades, an opaque wall made of dirt might stand little chance of making any significant impact. However, we hope this research shows that via the precise control of raw materials, specialized additives, sintering temperatures, and when combined with woven glass fiber composites, a product can be formulated to be structural, performative, easily formed, and exhibit high moisture resistance.

The researchers began investigating the clay recipe by taking the traditional terracotta formula and altering the raw ingredients for property augmentation or retardation. A series of test samples provided an empiric guide for developing the desired performative qualities for the finished ceramic. The researchers found that the clay body expanded rather than contracted at temperatures above 1166°C. The expansion was caused by a chemical reaction with talc. Previous research had determined that to handle water, the clay body needed to shrink approximately 12 percent, and have a porosity of at least 7 percent to achieve water retention for the desired evaporative cooling effect. Through an iterative process of revising the ceramic recipe, the researchers were able to optimize the ingredient ratios in the clay body.

After moving through several clay bodies, the researchers arrived at a formula which exhibited the desired material properties. Laguna Clay Products Inc. was approached about producing a limited quantity small batch for production.

The addition of glass fiber composite reinforcement significantly increased both the tensile and the compressive strength of the clay body. Using an Instron 3369 material tester, the researchers found that tensile strength increased by approximately 100 percent and compression strength by approximately 300

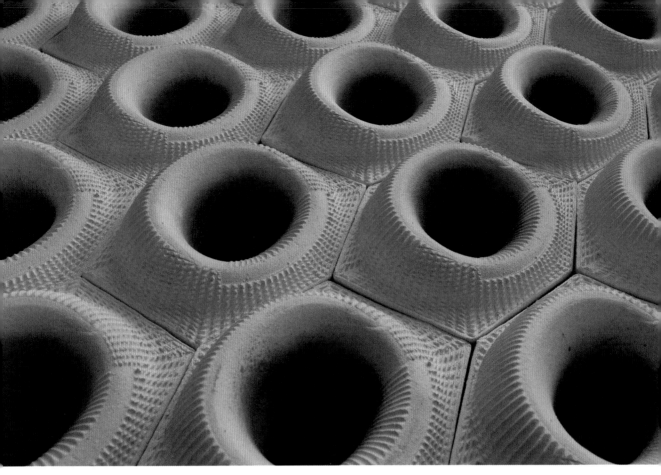

Figure 8.9 Face tile in field condition showing three distinct toolpath patterns and color variation tuned to collection/redirection at different times of year

percent. Further tests conducted by setting the maximum force to 2000 lb/ft found that the sample could withstand up to five repeated loading tests before failure, validating the initial hypothesis that a composite ceramic system could resist catastrophic failure and be viable for use in seismic zones. The increase in strength is posited to come from the interconnected matrix of glass-lined tubes left after the glass fibers are absorbed by the surrounding clay body during the firing process in addition to the added silicon content.

A limiting factor in ceramic building assemblies is the lack of tensile strength of the ceramic material. In the traditional brick or CMU wall assembly, the masonry unit is in compression. For lateral stability, steel reinforcement is required. EcoCeramic blocks incorporate fiberglass and composite materials, replacing steel reinforcing, for localized post-tensioning between each block.

These composite materials are used for the joining of the individual units. Due to the method of fabrication, each structural ceramic unit (SCU) is one half of a complete SCU. Traditional modes of joining ceramics include slip joining, the same method most commonly used to attach a coffee mug to its handle. A second, traditional and higher performing joining method uses a high fired-glaze slip. This method resists tension, but uses cone 11 firing temperatures, adding extra time and energy expenditure, and excessive vitrification of the clay body, whereas the SCU EcoCeramic clay is fired to cone 6. By applying composite bonding with woven glass fiber and high-strength epoxy, the fired SCU halves are easily joined and resist compressive, shear and tensile forces.

Fabrication logistics

The EcoCeramic module is tileable as aperiodic, semi-periodic and periodic Penrose patterns. All sides of the base module geometry are of equal length with two distinct angles of adjacency. The formal dimensional extents of the SCU module are defined by sun angles and limited by the platen dimensions of the 30 ton Ram press. Taking advantage of established production bowl-making technology, the shape of the SCU was developed, in part, to increase the finished depth while facilitating production with the press dimensions.

Production molds require a pinch point that creates back pressure under load, forcing the clay into every corner of the die. The clay charge follows the path of least resistance and without the "pinch point" would fail to fill the mold where even back pressure is particularly important for asymmetrical and complicated shapes. The centers of both the structural module and some of the face tiles have openings; material left in the center of the modules must be easily removable. Using the logic of the "pinch point" the modules are templated to facilitate material removal with a traditional sheet metal clay punch.

The metal die box, which both contains and restrains the Cerami-Cal mold, is fabricated from $^5/_8$" steel bar stock. The corners are joined with a double-bevel groove weld and then ground smooth creating a continuous structural seam that under load resists outward pressure and deformation which would result in the cracking on the finished mold. Connection tabs are ¼" steel angle stock fillet welded to the metal die. Handles are double fillet welded through machined holes in the die box. The welding resulted in a $^1/_{16}$"–$^1/_{32}$" deformation in the die box that was adjusted for in the master molds. Medium Density Fiberboard (MDF) master molds were cut on the Techno NC router and sealed with polyurethane allowing for multiple castings of the Cerami-Cal production molds. Wire mesh is used as reinforcement and to suspend Moldduct tubing 1" away from the master mold surface. The master mold is removed just after the Cerami-Cal sets and air pressure is applied through the Molduct, purging the production mold of moisture. The air pressure creates a matrix of capillary tubules leaving a permeable plaster mold that is purged during production, facilitating in the release of the clay modules.

Expectations

The thermal testing was conducted during the winter solar cycle, at which time the entire system receives greater solar exposure than summer months, maximizing potential winter radiant thermal gains (Figure 8.9). The researchers expected the interior cone of the face tile to absorb solar radiation during the day and retain heat into the night, delaying the cooling of the wall. In order to limit horizontal air movement and conduction, expandable insulating foam was added to the interior half of the SCU. Continuous vertical ventilation between the face tile and the SCU would act as a convective thermal barrier. With these strategies, the researchers hoped to offset the cool winter nights and to retain thermal swings to within 23–30ºC.

The American Society for Testing and Materials International (ASTM) does not have a standard radiation thermal gain test procedure. Therefore the researchers adapted ASTM C1363 (Guarded Hot Box) by exposing the test surface to solar radiation. Unlike other standard tests, which wait for thermal equilibrium, this experiment requires a three-day cycle, similar to field experimentation. In order to reduce weather-related errors, the researchers alternated the test series between wall surface assemblies.

The testing chamber was 1 cubic meter in volume, or 35.3 cubic feet. Floor dimensions are 1.3 meters wide by 1 meter deep. Five of the six sides are sheathed in 7.62 cm of homogenous polystyrene insulation with an R-value of 12. The combined material R-value is 13.4 on five sides of the cube, with a wall thickness of 12 cm. Nine thermocouple data loggers record environmental, wall, and interior temperatures.

Thermogenic findings

The EcoCeramic external surface consistently warmed above ambient temperatures, with the highest recorded temperatures on the surfaces perpendicular to the solar path. The articulations allowed the surface to quickly cool to below ambient temperatures with the loss of direct solar exposure. The EcoCeramic wall system reduced thermal swings by up to 5ºC, while the CMU wall mitigated thermal swings by 2.2ºC. Variations in solar exposure due to the articulations delayed conduction through the wall system.

The surface articulations appeared to delay conductive thermal transfer through the wall section. If the cavity were completely filled with insulation, a reduction in thermal transfer and a greater retention of heat would be expected. A vertical ventilation system that is operable (open for summer and closed in the winter) would further help retain and release thermal gains. The CMU wall system had the same internal temperature as the external ambient temperature. The EcoCeramic internal temperature is significantly lower (7°C) than the ambient temperature and remains cooler despite humidity, number of cloudy days and rainfall.

Expected summer results

After observing the thermal performance of the EcoCeramic wall system in the winter months, the research team proposed a revised summer performance hypothesis: The wall system should perform better than expected when evaporative cooling is utilized during the early morning through the afternoon. As the degree of heating is directly linked to solar exposure, self-shading will eliminate radiant thermal gains throughout the summer months.

Throughout May and June, the wall system should be able to cool wall conditions up to 15°C. The termite mound-inspired ventilation strategy will carry away built-up heat, allowing the skin to radiate thermal gains back into the environment and not towards the interior side of the wall. Traditional wall systems (flat planes, non-articulated) allow an even build-up of heat that moves through conduction to the internal surface. The EcoCeramic wall system, which creates variations in thermal gains across the surface, will enable conduction to travel laterally (as opposed to directly) towards the interior.

Material porosity was maximized to capitalize on the cooling effects of evaporation in the extreme arid climate and, when combined with the self-shading surface, the face tile will mitigate the intense summer heat of the Sonoran Desert. At the mezzo-scale, surface tile sections and texture were tuned to minimize heat gain. For humid or cold climates, a different material and geometrical response would be necessary.

Contrary to widely accepted practices, where the surface area of building skins is reduced in an effort to control thermal gains and losses, we significantly increased the surface area in the meso and micro scales and minimized exposed surfaces to incident solar heat gain. The wrinkled surface has the added effect of re-radiation back towards the heat source. The high surface area exchanges heat rapidly, while the smooth backside of the tile exchanges heat much more slowly, encouraging heat to flow from smooth to rough. Further, the thermal storage capacity of tile varies in proportion to the sectional thickness. The energy flows of the system are the functional material and the ceramic is the result of a thermogenic ecosystem system seeking balance. The territory is the topological system of energy flows around the built ecology while the map is the remnant object whose conflict and strife are forged by the struggle for homeostasis.

EcoCeramic Phase II: climate camouflage

Biotic systems have evolved a myriad of strategies to take advantage of the same forces with which we continue to struggle: the constant flux of light, humidity and temperature. While nature takes advantage of local climatic conditions to diversify and thrive, we have tended towards mitigating these same conditions, often framing phenomena as the antagonist to our discipline.

Climate camouflage harnesses bioclimatic energy flows through a modular ceramic curtain wall system in order to seek a more effective thermal balance through the conspiracy of multiscalar color, texture, and morphology that play to tune the façade towards ever changing localized environmental conditions, effectively creating the built ecology (Figure 8.10). Strategized again on principles from bioanalytics and the experience of Phase I, energy that flows through the building envelope is harnessed to offload excess thermal loads and passively cool internal load dominated structures (Figure 8.11).[13]

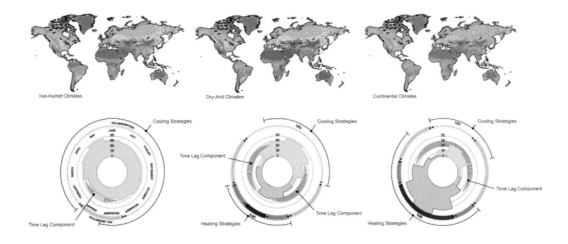

Figure 8.10a–c Climate camouflage clocks for determining material and texture distribution across façades in different climate types

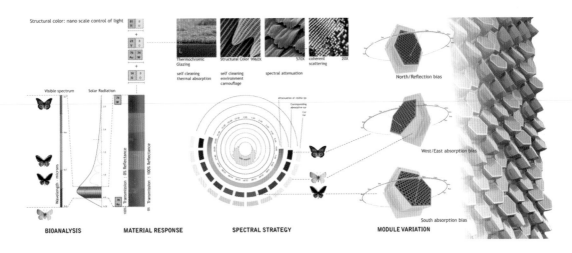

Figure 8.11 Phase II integrates both material science and biology in a curtain wall system. Initial energy simulations show performance significantly better than current state-of-the-art curtain wall and rainscreen systems

Paradigm shift: how do we know?

Technology transfer from the disciplines of biology and materials science to architecture enables new and relevant avenues of inquiry that operate via the soft and pliant mechanisms found in nature. In this way, architecture is an instrument that invokes the experience of nature – without mimicry – one that is calibrated to amplify natural conditions, to generate awareness, and potentially serve to extend the range of our perceptive spectrum. We see the passive and active flows as a gradient rather than supplemental or complementary strategy whereas both rely on the distribution of material to enable architecture to gain a competitive environmental edge by micro or macro scale response to site conditions. To bring architecture into the next phase of technological development we must, as the Wrights did for flight, accept the interactivity of flows, and enable architecture to serve as a porous and selective filter between the built and natural world.

The paradigm shift for architecture will be an attitude adjustment towards compliance and exchange between the natural and built environment through increased capacity for building self-regulation, and an increased ability for architecture to manage the complexity of a constantly fluctuating relationship of resource and demand. If complexity is an emergent property based on simple rule sets, then oscillations in complexity are simply different modalities that adjust for form; form is an instance of structural stability in a system as it seeks homeostasis, thus all form is the result of growth and resistance, it is the convergence of force.[14] As clusters of stomata control the porosity of a leaf in response to varying levels of heat, light and CO_2, we view the building envelope as a filter that can be metered and tuned to better accept the flow of matter and light.

The quasi-experimental viewpoint suggests that all life is essentially problem solving. And problem solving has a fundamentally different goal than the established traditions of justification through the scientific method; problem solving needs to be understood through failure.[15] We now understand the nature of paradigm shifts in scientific thought through revolutions, whereby there exists the ultimate evidence as fundamental world change.[16] And fundamental world change is the only true verification of the quasi-experimental mode of technological evolution.

Theories must compete through the experimental process for Darwinian fitness, the fitter, the stronger the evolutionary traits and larger the impact upon the world that particular set of theory/experiments will have.[17] The quasi-experimental modality is fundamentally a process of theory/experimental fitness and, while wholly understood to be scientific, it lacks the random sampling necessary to be characterized as the widely accepted scientific method.[18] However, that which it lacks, it gains as accelerated discovery, and as the world evolves, then so must scientific thought and on these terms one might consider that the territory *is* the map. Or perhaps we might consider the evolutionary model of our technological paradigm shift is where the material model is *flow* as territory and map is material, manifested as built ecologies.

The evidence of the paradigm shift forged by the Wrights is shown in the fundamental change in the world, understood to be that of a collapsed global map where time and space as understood one century ago have all but evaporated into a real/time/world/space approximation, a collapse of the map and the territory. The predicament of contemporary architectural thought, and the opportunity, is the seductiveness of the map: if those who build the environment are to respond accordingly, architectural theories must be falsifiable, lest the map *replace* the territory. The opportunity of the collapse of the map and the territory for architecture is to develop the built ecology, where the remnants of the struggle to find homeostasis, energetic and programmatic, define a new material ecology and where purpose is paramount whether that be structural, thermodynamic, spiritual or poetic.

Notes

1   Álvaro Malo, "Syllabus for ARC 561j; Materials: Modelling," Emerging Material Technologies graduate program, University of Arizona.

2   Alfred Korzybski, "A Non-Aristotelian System and its Necessity for Rigour in Mathematics and Physics," a paper presented before the American Mathematical Society at the New Orleans, Louisiana, meeting of the American Association for the Advancement of Science, December 28, 1931. Reprinted in *Science and Sanity* (1933), pp. 747–61.

3   Gregory Bateson defines information as "a difference which makes a difference." For Bateson, information mediated Alfred Korzybski's map–territory relation, where the map is by no means the territory.

4   Dr. Fred Culick, Chief Engineer for the AIAA Wright Flyer Project states: 'The science of aerodynamics, the physics as described by mathematical equations, had been codified centuries earlier by men such as Newton, Bernoulli, Euler, Navier, and Stokes; men whose names are attached to some of the fundamental equations of fluid dynamics. However, not until the Wright brothers had anyone successfully conquered the engineering – turning the science into an airplane of practical use.' In this way, the engineer may be said to privilege applied over general and perhaps be more apt at methods that are considered quasi-experimental.

5   As described in Sanford Kwinter's seminal essay "Landscapes of Change," in *Assemblage* 19 (1993).

6   The idea that homeostasis should be a central tenet of architecture, with some theoretical clarity, goes back at least to Frederick Kiesler, publishing in 1939, "Correalism and Biotechnique: A Definition and Test of a New Approach to Building Design," *Architectural Record* 86, no. 9 (September 1939), 60–75.

7   Well characterized by William Braham and Jonathan Hale eds. in *Rethinking Technology: A Reader in Architectural Theory* (London: Routledge, 2006).

8   The populous appeal of Janine Banyus and the Biomimicry Institute has contributed to the view that nature embodies a wellspring of design research and now, and perhaps again, terms such as biotechnique, biomimicry and biological analog have firmly planted roots in design thinking. The call of Braham and Banyus, and Fuller and Kiesler 60 years prior, are essentially the same.

9   As described in Sanford Kwinter's seminal essay "Landscapes of Change: Boccioni's 'Stati d'animo' as a General Theory of Models" in *Assemblage* 19 (1993).

10   These points resonate with Giuseppe Zambonini's thesis that the nature of form is inlaid in the process of making, detailed in "Notes for a Theory of Making in a Time of Necessity," *Perspecta* 24 (1988), 2–23.

11   Collaboration with Molecular Geodesics, Inc., led by Dr. Don Ingber, Director of the Wyss Institute for Biologically Inspired Engineering, has helped to shape our view of multidisciplinary research.

12   Conducted in collaboration with Materials Scientist Meredith Aronson at the University of Arizona.

13   Phase II received a citation in the New York Center for Architecture's 2010 Façade Competition.

14   According to Kwinter.

15   As professed by the philosopher Karl Popper.

16   Thomas Kuhn framed the criteria for paradigm shifting in *The Structure of Scientific Revolutions* (Chicago: University of Chicago Press, 1962).

17   Popper's simple equation describes the feedback loop of evolutionary fitness of technology: $PS_1 \rightarrow TT_1 \rightarrow EE_1 \rightarrow PS_2$ whereas PS is the problem situation, TT is the tentative theories, all processed under EE, error elimination, to give us the new problem situation.

18   On this point, Kuhn and Popper might agree.

Part IV
Matter Precedent

Looking at history as a generative mechanism, the work in this section is driven by the engagement of a reading of precedent to be materially applied. By deploying case studies in material application and conceptual detailing of design as points of generative departure, the engagement of the reference and the history of the material and technology and its limitations and perceptions become the point of departure. Indirectly addressing architecture in its sources, diverse natural and engineered systems serve as inspiration. The instigation of the effect to engage material and a way of making or thinking address the principles of the precedent, but evolve them into a new ideal of individuated application. These architects, rooted in history engage with the systems to advance them through reinterpreting their material function, cultural interpretation, and architectural potential.

Laura Garófalo and David Hill
Kentaro Tsubaki
W. Andrew Atwood, ATWOOD
Michael Carroll, atelier BUILD
Heather Roberge, murmur

Chapter 9
Fixing the Drape
Textile composite walls

Laura Garófalo and David Hill

In the course of designing disaster-relief housing for the "What if New York City ..."[1] international design competition, we were interested in the possibilities offered by lightweight, homogeneous material assemblies for building prefabricated housing. The benefit of material "lightness" was in direct response to the special transportation and assembly needs of disaster relief housing. Such construction allows for expediency in deployment as well as lowered cost in transportation and erection. Our proposal illustrated a systematic consideration of these affordances and sought examples outside of architecture such as the transportation, textile, and marine industries to explore potential manufacturing processes and delivery methods for panelized textile composites.

As sponsors of the competition, the New York City Office of Emergency Management (OEM) recognized that dense urban neighborhoods would face severe consequences from catastrophic storms and they sought "innovative ideas for providing provisional housing" for displaced residents.[2] More significantly, the OEM called for designs that would offer alternatives to the typical FEMA trailer and establish a "new paradigm"[3] that would allow residents to quickly return to their neighborhoods and be active participants in the recovery effort. Our entry, *Threading Water* (Figure 9.1), proposed ways in which disaster-relief housing could play a role in remediating the Hudson and East River estuarine ecosystems while also providing disaster victims with safe, proximate inhabitation that created communal identity and provided a positive understanding of living within an ecologically sensitive architecture. The scheme deployed the housing along pier-like infrastructural "threads" that extended from the shoreline. Pre-assembled housing would be delivered on barges and attached to the threads to form patches of dense urban communities. The "threads" themselves provided remediation services, including water filtration, which revitalized the shoreline ecology. The challenge for the housing would be its inhabitation and environmental performance over this period of remediation. How well could a fiber composite building system, designed for easy deployment, respond to the shifting needs of human comfort? How adaptable was it to radical environmental shifts like temperature? Could it be adaptable for other climates and hence become a universal disaster housing prototype? Could the choice of fiber composites and the technical constraints of disaster relief housing provide some basis for formal and aesthetic experimentation?

Figure 9.1a–c *Threading Water* proposed housing and landscape regeneration systems

---

Textile enclosures

Gottfried Semper theorized that clothing developed over time into forms of large-scale enclosure.[4] Textile's potential transition from garments to built enclosures has longstanding precedent. From the tent structures of nomadic cultures to textiles that embellish walls and floors of religious, civic and private buildings, the allusion to garments are both metaphoric and performative. Textile's potential as an adaptable weather boundary remains its most notable characteristic. *Architectural Graphic Standards* long promoted canvas for roof waterproofing. Albert Frey experimented with marine grade canvas as an external wrapper in his *Canvas Weekend House* (1934).[5] The textile was used as an all-weather envelope for the entire wooden exterior, creating a watertight composite with the assistance of paint. Frei Otto's research and work explored the formal and structural potential of textiles. His cable structures – based on the physics of homogeneous membranes – find their form through the tensile forces applied across the material. They suggest an economy of means and material lightness that is driven to reduce energy in both their production and deployment. By the 1940s, the invention of fiber reinforced resin matrix materials had initiated a new use of textiles as part of composites. This opened new formal and structural opportunities where textiles could now take on self-structuring shapes. Books like Albert Dietz's *Plastics for Architects and Builders* (1969)[6] and *Composite Materials* (1965)[7] examined the malleability, weathering, durability, and strength of fabric-reinforced composites. This resulted in a variety of experimental constructions like the *Monsanto House of the Future* (1957) and the *Moscow Pavilions* (1959) that demonstrated the architectural potential of the material.

In post-disaster housing, the need to quickly shelter fleeing refugees and reach hard to access places has made tarps and tents the default temporary housing. The United Nations Office of the High Commissioner for Refugees (UNHCR) has used them extensively because they are portable and can be erected rapidly. Their Lightweight Emergency Tent provides basic shelter and works best for warm climates such as Chad (Sudanese refugees) and West Sumatra (Indian Ocean Tsunami in 2004). However, tents are problematic particularly in relation to insulation, durability and security, which mitigate their use as long-term inhabitations. Extended and at times permanent residence in post-disaster housing is unfortunately a reality where return to normalcy is improbable or at the least lengthy. As such with all emergency relief housing, designers have to address issues of privacy, security, and longevity of materials, but these goals are often at odds with the portability that tent-type enclosures provide. However, fiber-reinforced composites may offer a useful compromise.

Textile composites

The US textile industry has been confronted with a downturn in domestic production.[8] As a consequence, textile research has broadened to investigate possibilities beyond wearable goods and has realized considerable advances in developing high-strength composite materials suitable for use in automotive, military, and marine applications.

Composite materials are typically composed of a reinforcement material (particulate, flake, laminar, or fiber) and a thermoset or thermoplastic bonding matrix.[9] Fiber composites are classified according to four basic reinforcement types that include: (a) continuous fibers; (b) woven fibers; (c) chopped fibers; and (d) hybrids. Glass fibers are the most commonly used, and recent advances in three-dimensional weaving have produced fabrics composed of intertwined X-fibers (warp), Y-fibers (weft) and Z-fibers. This weaving process can be used to produce thick fabrics with deep-draw molding capabilities, as well as hybrid fabrics that optimize structural capacity and moldability.[10] There are numerous methods of applying resin matrix to woven reinforcements. Hand lay-up and spray-on application are the simplest and most inexpensive procedures, but other techniques such as injection, compression, resin transfer, and preform molding offer alternatives.[11]

Certain drawbacks, including high production costs and limited material availability, have challenged the viability of textile composite use on a large scale in architecture. Critics also point out that the manufacturing processes of composite materials are not eco-friendly. However, researchers have been studying renewable material sources such as hemp (for use as reinforcement) and cashew nut shell liquid (CNSL, for use as resin).[12] Though textile composites present significant economic, ecological, and manufacturing challenges, they offer promising possibilities for architecture, particularly in mass-produced, panelized applications. They have high strength-to-weight ratios that make them suitable for structural applications, and their lightness significantly reduces shipping costs and accelerates on-site construction. Textile composites can also be used to produce panels that combine structure with enclosure.

Component-based systems: Jean Prouvé's *Maison Tropicale*

The component-based housing of French designer and craftsman, Jean Prouvé, provides a useful precedent for understanding the relationship between design thinking, material experimentation, and construction technologies. Prouvé's innovative pragmatism developed unique construction techniques to build prefabricated housing that addressed the needs of transportation and the specific climatic conditions where it was to be installed. The Second World War and the French colonial presence in Africa provided an opportunity for Prouvé and his production facilities. His simple steel and wood portal frame barracks for soldiers display a preoccupation with elemental housing and the virtues of portability and rapid construction techniques. This essentialist approach led to more sophisticated designs for prototype housing that would address local climate conditions, specifically the arid Sahara and tropical West Africa. The houses employed air-delivery and component-based rapid construction methodologies, and each pioneered new material processes and uses.

Prouvé's most famous housing prototype is the 1951 *Maison Tropicale* (Figure 9.2) that he designed for Niamey, Nigeria, and Brazzaville, Congo – both hot and humid equatorial locations. In this scheme, Prouvé employed his signature tilt-prop structure, layered façades, double-skin roof, and ventilated aluminum wall panels. The whole kit was flat-packed in a Bristol aircraft and flown from Paris to the Congo where it was erected in a few days.

Figure 9.2 Jean Prouvé's *Maison Tropicale,* 1951

The *Maison Tropicale* increased thermal comfort by emulating traditional bungalow housing types found across this biome. This promoted the thickening of the exterior thermal boundary by creating a shaded zone around the living unit with an enclosure layer to control rain and maintain security.[13] The house was never mass-produced as intended, but it inspired a series of individual building components that would be used to construct over 600 prefabricated schools and administrative offices in Cameroon and Guinea.[14] These components focused on the climate-responsive performance of wall panels using materials that could provide appropriate form, enclosure, and structural stability. The *Onde* (wave) wall is scalloped in section to shed water while admitting cooling breezes through adjustable ventilator perforations (Figure 9.3). In other ventilated wall applications, Prouvé arranged large, adjustable aluminum louvers across entire façades to protect interiors while allowing views and air movement (Figure 9.4).[15] Such "breathing walls"[16] or screens provide greater enclosure, however, the space most open to ventilation is either distanced or buffered from the living space by an enclosure layer.

Figures 9.3–9.4 Jean Prouvé's *Onde* (wave) wall and aluminum louvered "breathing" walls

A louver system's reliance on repetition of a standardized unit and its highly functional nature make it an ideal item to be appropriated by Prouvé's factory. The translation of this staple of vernacular bungalow architecture into a highly engineered component merges interests in industrial innovation with the logics of thermal comfort. Combining shading and ventilation into one building system is an inspiring overlap of functions. This model informed our intent to collapse the positive environmental aspects of the bungalow's extended envelope into a lightweight self-shading, ventilated and water-repelling skin. Such combination of functions into a single building component is important for rapid assembly and minimizing extraneous built space in the temporary housing.

Prouvé continued to engage new materials later in his career with the St. Gobain Company where he used plastic to compose novel monocoque structures that combined skin, insulation, and structure into a single stressed-skin panel. His all-plastic house of 1965 provides an example of Prouvé's expectation that these self-structuring panels could be used in a fully-integrated residential application. Other than integral ribbing in the overhanging roof components, the 2.6 x 1.2 meter panels were nearly identical, and efficiently configured edge to edge in both wall and roof conditions. The panels proved effective as components of a rigid enclosure system, but plastic cruciform columns were added to carry primary structural loads.[17]

Environmental challenge and the opportunity of an illusive material

Composites are illusive materials because their properties cannot be ascertained from the individual performance of their constituent parts. Their behavior results from either the sum of their constituents' properties or the interaction of its parts which yields new properties. While designing our panelized enclosures for the disaster housing, we focused on manipulating the composite's underlying woven textile reinforcement. This allowed us to explore the composite's formal, structural and architectural possibilities. We used a series of strategies, including faceting (*TW-1*), pleating (*TW-2*), and patterning (*TW-3*) the weave of the fiber reinforcement. Initially these strategies were implemented in the pursuit of a self-structuring panel (see *TW-1*). However, as the project progressed, the three became perforation strategies to guide the design of the panels in response

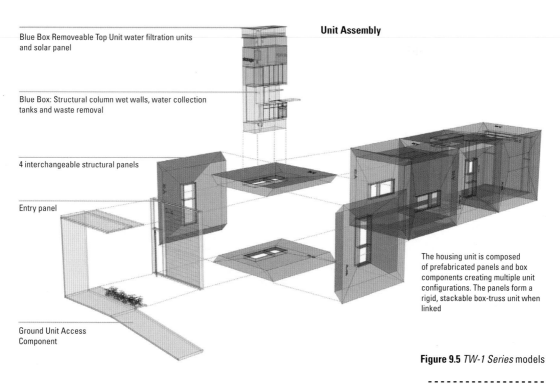

Unit Assembly

Blue Box Removeable Top Unit water filtration units and solar panel

Blue Box: Structural column wet walls, water collection tanks and waste removal

4 interchangeable structural panels

Entry panel

Ground Unit Access Component

The housing unit is composed of prefabricated panels and box components creating multiple unit configurations. The panels form a rigid, stackable box-truss unit when linked

Figure 9.5 *TW-1 Series* models

to specific climate conditions. These included their ability to filter, absorb, or repel light, heat and water respectively, depending on their beneficial or adverse impact on inhabitant comfort.

When working on our original set of panels (*TW-1 Series*) (Figure 9.5), we established external environmental performance constraints in order to focus our explorations. We used digital modeling and analysis software, rapid prototyping, and physical mock-ups to develop alternative schemes that could meet our performance requirements. Each iteration that we explored through these methods revealed limitations and new potentials relative to the panel's environmental performance, aggregation, and manufacture.

Digital models were useful for developing initial panel forms, tiling strategies, and performance speculations based on simulations. The 3D printed models allowed us to carefully evaluate aesthetic qualities and analyze viable packing and delivery arrangements. These methods, however, were limited in their ability

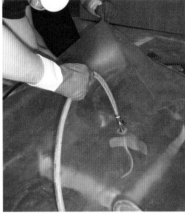

Figure 9.6a–c *TW-1 Series* vacuum-molded panel experiments

to simulate the textile composite's material characteristics. Once we began to work with the fiber and resin, we became intrigued by the formal and structural qualities of the woven fiber substrate at a macro (sheet) and micro (weave) level. For panels in the *TW-2* and *TW-3 Series*, the fabric rather than the resin becomes the driver for both form finding and environmental interaction strategies. The panels are designed to channel water, admit natural ventilation, and avoid or permit insolation to achieve thermal comfort.

TW-1 Series

The *TW-1 Series* is based on fabric lamination and vacuum-molding techniques to produce faceted panels (Figure 9.6). These are composed of multiple laminations of uni-directional and woven fabrics that are layered and oriented to counteract specific structural stresses.

The fabric component is made with an innovative three-dimensional weaving technique that incorporates closed-cell foam rods into the reinforcement fabric, resulting in a hybrid that synthesizes structure,

Figure 9.7a–c Three-dimensionally woven fabric and cured panels
Figure 9.8 *TW-1 Series* panel wall system for *Threading Water* temporary housing

- - - - - - - - - - - - - - - - - - -

insulation, and finished surface. This fabric is suitable for use in high-strength, moldable composite panels (Figure 9.7). When a resin matrix is added, the composite material is molded into rigid, self-structuring, lightweight, and waterproof panels with apertures that allow natural ventilation and views (Figure 9.8).

The panels' structural capabilities are derived from creasing, faceting, and pleating the fabric prior to setting the mold. In the *TW-1 Series*, the perimeter is folded to a depth of 2'–0" and the center facets to 6". This ribbed structure allows each panel to be self-supporting while creating cavities that can accept removable rigid insulation. Alternatively, water can also be used as an insulator in cavities. The water – added on site – would not add weight to the panels during transportation, but it would aid in stabilizing the lightweight units after full assembly. Once structural stability is achieved, passive ventilation and precipitation control are the main drivers in the panel's form. The 15' x 15' panels are composed of four trapezoidal components, and are designed with a 3' x 9' aperture placed in such a way that rotating the square panel will produce four distinct window configurations. Apertures can be formed as positives in the panel's mold before resin casting, or they can be cut out of the rigid panel after the resin has cured. Subsequent panels in the *TW-1 Series* are designed with apertures of various forms and scales, and the openings provide a porous skin that allows daylight in addition to natural ventilation (Figure 9.9). The apertures are formed on the panels to intake air in directions parallel and perpendicular to predominant winds.

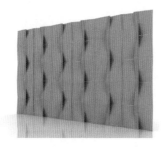

Figure 9.9a–c *TW-1 Series* of ventilated panel variations

TW-2 Series

In this series, we overlap traditional sewing techniques with the three-dimensionally woven fabrics. We limited the *TW-2* panels to single sheets of three-dimensionally-woven glass fabric, and used pleating and smocking techniques to create their form (Figure 9.10).

By drawing the fabric taut and fastening it at specified points along fold lines, the sheet gains depth and contours that channel water away from ventilation and view apertures. The folds also produce lateral stability

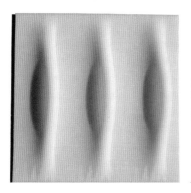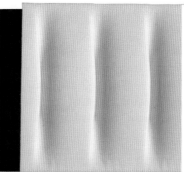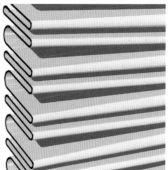

Figure 9.10a–c *TW-2 Series* of ventilated panel variations

Figure 9.11a–c *TW-2B Series* panel fold patterns

and the resultant depth allows them to support their own weight. In addition, the fold patterns create elliptical forms on the panel's exterior face but its orthogonal edges facilitate panel repetition when constructing an entire wall (Figure 9.11).

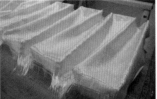

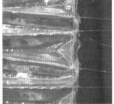

Figure 9.12 Jig configuration. Diagram depicting the patterned textile and its pleated condition for *TW-2D* panels

Figure 9.13a–e *TW-2D Series* panel experiment on the reconfigurable jig

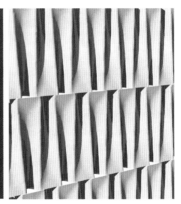

In further studies, we combined pleating and smocking techniques with gravity-based jigs. A simple wire-strung apparatus suspends the draped textile within a frame (Figure 9.12), stretching and bunching the fabric into a new form. Grids of wires running through the textile act as control lines along which the fabric is distorted and shaped into three-dimensional forms that merge catenary curves with elliptical ridges (Figure 9.13). This fabrication process allows an intuitive and iterative design sequence that offers immediate feedback on formal capabilities and limitations.

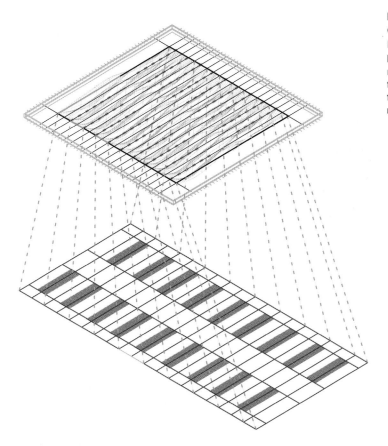

Figure 9.14 Jig configuration. Diagram depicting the patterned textile and its pleated condition for *TW-3* panels

Figure 9.15a–d Detail of the reorganization of the weave pattern of the textile, and the patterned textile on the jig, and patterned weave production mechanisms and pattern cards

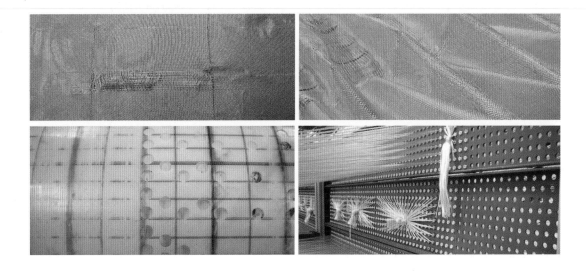

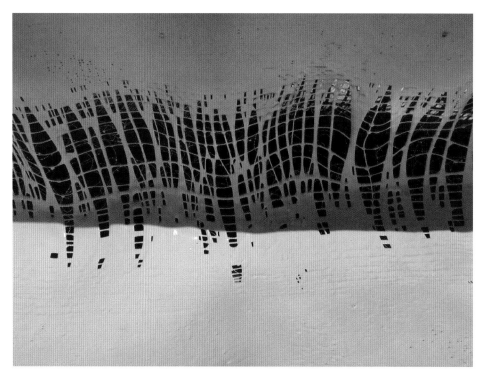

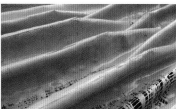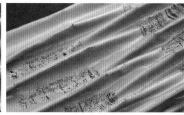

Figure 9.16 *TW-3 Series* composite panel micro perforations for consistent ventilation
Figure 9.17a–c *TW-3 Series* panel type A configured on the jig

TW-3 Series

TW-3 Series panels are porous panels fabricated from the interaction between the weave pattern of the textile and the controlling forces and regulating lines imposed by a gravity-based jig (Figure 9.14). This series reorganizes the weave of the textile to create strategic gaps in the weft (Figure 9.15).

In an industrial setting, the weaving pattern would be programmed into the machine but was manually done for the experiments. The separation of the threads creates gaps between the fibers which are augmented once the epoxy is applied and the fibers are fused together. Portions of continuous weave create impermeable areas on the same surface (Figure 9.16). A woven pattern of open and closed modules is then aligned with the gravity jig to create a pattern of ridges, valleys, and scoops that repel rainwater (full weave) and permit constant airflow (warp only) (Figure 9.17). *TW-3 Series* results in a flexible breathing skin conditioned for hot and humid environments.

The *TW-1 Series* seeks to adapt a textile composite panel system to a *temperate* climate by providing mass and insulation to a material that does not commonly have either. In temperate climate zones, thermal comfort-seeking strategies must accommodate variation in diurnal temperature shifts through a boundary layer that insulates, provides thermal mass, and controls ventilation and precipitation. In response, we found multiple means of adding the needed insulation either by weaving it into the fabric or by injecting it into the voids created by the pleated fabric. Insulation providing low heat transfer values ensures fewer pollutants are released to the environment because less energy is consumed heating and cooling the housing unit. Through the thermal insulation both within the panel fabric and in the panel cavities, the system could achieve an R-value well over 19, greatly reducing the energy required to heat and cool the units.

In the *TW-2* and *TW-3 Series,* we responded to performance parameters for *hot/humid* climates by capitalizing on the textile composite's lack of mass and its potential to exploit air flow (Figure 9.18). In tropical and sub-tropical regions, the temperature is relatively hot, humidity is high, and precipitation is abundant. The primary means of achieving a thermo-stable – though not altogether comfortable – condition through passive means involves maximizing ventilation and avoiding insolation. While the temperature and relative humidity are not radically reduced, the increased air movement promotes evaporative cooling. A hot humid environment is qualified by nominal diurnal temperature variation, and textile composites are beneficial in these zones because they minimize solar radiation absorption. In combination with the water-repelling resin, the textile component of woven fiber-reinforced composites can offer new opportunities by making a membrane that is both watertight and open to air flow. Reflective surface treatments (gel coats) can assist in lowering heat gain as well, and the fold patterns are designed to channel water, self-shade the wall, and provide insulating air pockets within a single membrane.

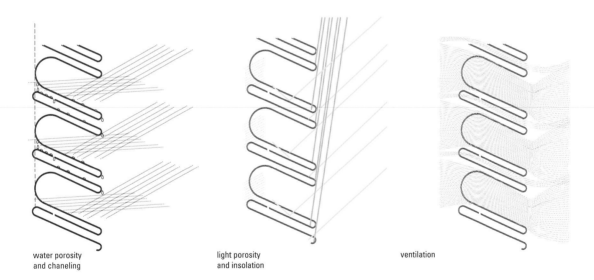

water porosity
and chaneling

light porosity
and insolation

ventilation

Figure 9.18a–c *TW-3 Series* panels A and B environmental performance diagrams

Aggregation patterns and structural frames

We have studied panel forms that can be aggregated to enable structural expansion (Figure 9.19). The resulting configurations form larger-scaled surfaces requiring fasteners that are compatible with the panel layout, composite reinforcement type, and material cross-section.

Both mechanical and adhesive connection methods are under consideration. In a demountable system, mechanical compression fasteners such as rivets draw the edges of panels together and a layer of neoprene is compressed between the panels to form a watertight seal. In a full unit deployment system, an adhesive joint used in the assembly will join the panels and provide the weather seal simultaneously. The choice is based on the delivery method most appropriate to the situation. If the components are flat packed and assembled on site in inland areas, the mechanical system is desirable. If they are to be barged pre-assembled into coastal regions, then they could be adhered (Figure 9.20). As shown by Dietz in the US Pavilion in Moscow,[18] a structural frame of fiber-reinforced composite can be constructed for these units. Not only will it use the same bonding systems mentioned above, but it will also comply with the system's transportation and deployment needs.

Most current architectural materials research concentrates on one of two extremes: either the research focuses on the chemical/molecular properties of advanced materials, or it is preoccupied with finding new applications for existing materials. Innovation within these approaches is often challenged by the costs of testing or the risk of material failure in full-scale application. But regardless of performance characteristics, architects continue to debate appropriate material applications, at various times invoking "what-a-brick-wants-to-be" idealism against subversive material "misuse" tactics.[19]

Throughout the development of this project, we have engaged the mutually-informative processes of design, research and prototyping, and the textile composite material itself has enabled us to vacillate between high- and low-tech methodologies.[20] At times, we have tried to be "honest" in our use of the material, but at other times we have questioned its salient properties to achieve new formal or performance characteristics. Because we are working with two materials – glass fiber cloth and resin matrix – that could be deployed independent of each other, we have considered many permutations that affect the hybrid nature of the composite.

As the basic substance of architecture, materials impart meaning while achieving functional and performative requirements. We have embedded our material research within the confines of a larger design project, and as such our experiments have opened questions of material appropriateness that we have considered relative to multiple parameters including lightness and durability – often mutually exclusive characteristics. The examination uncovered – sometimes through transgressive methods – latent material qualities that make textile composites suitable for disaster-relief housing, while also challenging to implement for this purpose. This research has allowed us to frame the question of material appropriateness through a larger frame than the aesthetics and performance of the houses, by including alternative manufacturing processes, delivery procedures, and assembly methods.

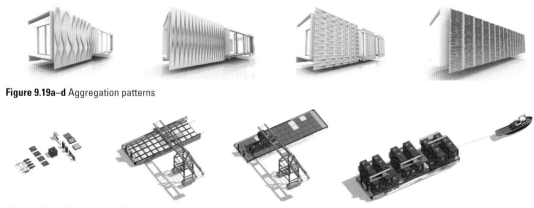

Figure 9.19a–d Aggregation patterns

Figure 9.20a–d Deployment diagrams

Notes

1   Our competition entry was one of ten winners. Team leaders include: Laura Garófalo, David Hill, and Nelson Tang. Team members include: Megan Casanega, Davis Hammer, Will Lambeth, and Henry Newell. "What if New York City ...," available at: http://www.whatifnyc.net/detailsUpdate.aspx?r=254&homeTab=0 (accessed March 10, 2010).

2   "What if New York City ...," http://www.nyc.gov/html/whatifnyc/html/home/home.shtml (accessed March 10, 2010).

3   Ibid.

4   Kenneth Frampton, *Studies in Tectonic Culture: The Poetics of Construction in Nineteenth and Twentieth Century Architecture* (Cambridge, MA: The MIT Press, 1995), p. 95.

5   Joseph Rosa, *Albert Frey, Architect* (New York: Princeton Architectural Press, 1999), pp. 42–47.

6   Albert G. H. Dietz, *Plastics for Architects and Builders* (Cambridge, MA: The MIT Press, 1969).

7   Albert G. H. Dietz, *Composite Materials* (American Society for Testing and Materials, 1965).

8   In the 2002 Economic Census, the US Census Bureau shows that the number of Broadwoven Fabric companies in the US fell from 743 in 1997 to 639 in 2002. Similarly, the number of production workers dropped from 115,792 in 1997 to 69,957 in 2002.

9   Thermosets: cross-linked polymer chains that are rigid upon curing. Thermoplastics: non-cross-linked polymer chains that remain remoldable.

10   North Carolina-based 3Tex is a leading manufacturer of three-dimensional fabrics. See www.3tex.com.

11   For a detailed technical description of composite materials, refer to Jack R. Vinson and Robert L. Sierakowski, *The Behavior of Structures Composed of Composite Material* (Dordrecht: Kluwer Academic Publishers, 2002).

12   Caroline Baillie, ed., *Green Composites: Polymer Composites and the Environment* (Cambridge: Woodhead Publishing Limited, 2004), p. 154.

13   Peter Sulzer, *Jean Prouvé: Œuvre Complète/Complete Works*, Vol. 3 (Basel: Birkhäuser Publishing, 2005), pp. 124–131. Also Jean Prouvé, *Prefabrication: Structures and Elements* (London: Pall Mall Press, 1971), pp. 131–132.

14   Alexander von Vegesack, ed., *Jean Prouvé: The Poetics of the Technical Object* (Weil am Rhein: Vitra Design Stiftung GmbH, 2005), pp. 214–223.

15   Peter Sulzer, *Jean Prouvé: Œuvre Complète/Complete Works*, vol. 4 (Basel: Birkhäuser Publishing, 2005), pp. 293–294.

16   Olufikayo Otitoola, "Breathing Wall: a modernist architectural heritage," in *ArchiAfrika Conference Proceedings: Modern Architecture in East Africa around Independence* (Dar es Salaam, Tanzania, July 27–29, 2005), pp. 67–70.

17   Alexander von Vegesack, ed., *Jean Prouvé*, pp. 280–283.

18   Albert G. H. Dietz, *Plastics for Architects and Builders*, pp. 18, 104.

19   This term is taken from Christoph Grunenberg and Sheila Kennedy, *Material Misuse: Kennedy and Violich Architecture* (London: AA Publications, 2004).

20   Toshiko Mori suggests that architects should "adopt a scavenger mentality" toward materials, and that they should familiarize themselves with "various modes of fabrication, both low- and high-tech." See "Materiality and Culture," in Bernard Tschumi and Irene Cheng, *The State of Architecture at the Beginning of the 21st Century* (New York: The Monacelli Press, 2003), p. 31.

Chapter 10
Tumbling Units
Tectonics of indeterminate extension

Kentaro Tsubaki

Determinacy/indeterminacy

Figure 10.1 *The Forge,* Joseph Wright

From Garrard to Turner, the path is very simple. It is the same path that runs from Lagrange to Carnot, from simple machines to steam engines, from mechanics to thermodynamics – by way of the Industrial Revolution. Wind and water were tamed in diagrams. One simply needed to know geometry or to know how to draw. Matter was dominated by form. With fire, everything changes, even water and wind. Look at *The Forge*, painted by Joseph Wright in 1772 [Figure 10.1]. Water, the paddlewheel, the hammer, weights, strictly and geometrically drawn, still triumph over the ingot in fusion. But the time approaches when victory changes camps. Turner no longer looks from the outside; he enters into Wright's ingot, he enters into the boiler, the furnace, the firebox. He sees matter transformed by fire. This is the new matter of the world at work, where geometry is limited. Everything is overturned. Matter and color triumph over line, geometry, and form.[1]

Magnesium oxide, a white powder-like substance commonly used as anti-acids, embodies a simple face-centered cubic crystalline structure resulting in a beautiful rectilinear form observed in a molecular level. I have once witnessed a perfect MgO crystal degrade and disappear in real time battered in a beam of electrons. It was in the Spring of 1989, first day of the basic training in electron microscopy. A spartan metal microscope I was introduced to was the first practical and versatile hi-voltage transmission microscope custom built for Kyoto University Institute for Chemical Research by Shimadzu Seisakusho Ltd. in 1962.[2]

Devoid of any extraneous optical accessories and video enhancements, refracted electron beam through the matter is magnified and projected directly on to a fluorescent screen as shade and shadow to be observed. This is as direct and unfiltered observation experience as one can possibly expect. The irony is, the agent allowing one to observe the matter is simultaneously destroying it from being observed. I turn the dial to focus. As soon as the rectilinear shape of the MgO crystal appears on the screen, it begins to fade and dissolve completely within a mere few seconds. This is the precise moment in which I have realized the complex nature of the physical reality. That the world consisting of matter we observe daily is not stationary. It is profoundly temporal, tenuous and imperfect so that an action as basic as observing will change the state of the matter irreversibly:

> It is true classically that if we knew the position and the velocity of every particle in the world, or in a box of gas, we could predict exactly what would happen. And therefore the classical world is deterministic.[3]

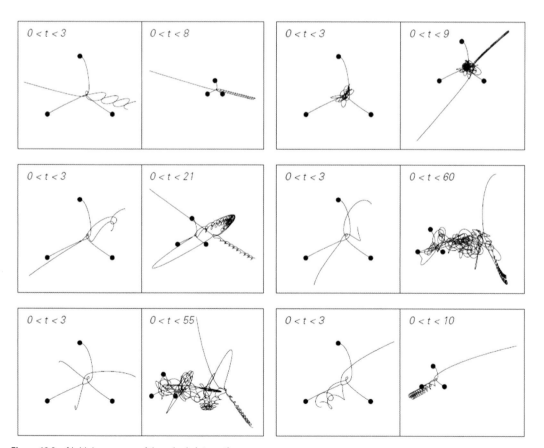

Figure 10.2a–f Initial sequence of three body interaction

Classical mechanics are known to be a simple and beautiful way to describe the relative motion of macroscopic objects. In principle, any problem in mechanics can be solved based on Newton's second Law of Motion. This is indeed true when dealing with one or two bodies in motion. However, it becomes exponentially difficult when the number of bodies involved is greater than two. The famous three-body problem, two planet bodies rotating around a sun, for example, challenged the power of human analysis for ages (Figure 10.2).[4] Such problems cannot be solved in elegant, analytical mathematics with the deterministic accuracy. It is necessary to resort in approximations through heavy numerical calculations.

One of many Joseph-Louis Lagrange's contributions to the field of physics was resolving the three-body problem for a special simplified condition based on the hypothesis: The trajectory of an object is determined by finding a path that minimizes the action over time. The significance of this assumption is that it allowed the physical motion of an object tracked in time in Newton mechanics to be treated as a field, a topographic condition over time through the emerging concept of "energy" and a new mathematical tool, "calculus of variations." Trajectory is implicated as field of potentials, no longer described in a strict form of discrete geometry. Newton mechanics is now reduced to a solution of variable calculus under particular conditions, in Lagrangian mechanics. The results just happened to be geometric. From this perspective, Lagrange was already beyond "simple machines" and "geometry" in the territory of the pre-Impressionist painters such as Turner (Figure 10.3):

> Everyone knows that heat can produce motion. That it possesses vast motive-power no one can doubt, in these days when the steam-engine is everywhere so well known ... Nature, in providing us with combustibles on all sides, has given us with the power to produce, at all times and in all places, heat and impelling power which is the result of it. To develop this power, appropriate to our uses, is the object of heat-engines.[5]

Figure 10.3
The Burning of the Houses of Parliament, Joseph Mallord William Turner

On the other hand, contrary to Serres' remarks, Nicolas Léonard Sadi Carnot may still be well within the Newtonian mode of deterministic thinking. He is often noted as the father of thermal dynamics due to his pioneering work on the relationship among temperature (heat), work (motive-power) and matter in an idealized form of steam engine, the Carnot cycle.[6] The implication: the interchangeability of thermal energy and kinetic energy (first law of thermal dynamics) and reversibility/irreversibility (second law of thermal dynamics – introduction of entropy) were major factors in triggering the fundamental paradigm shift in the world of physics. However, he was very much concerned with quantifying the efficiency of the steam engine in exactitude using standard analytical tools of its time parallel to Garrard's and Wright's paintings (Figures 10.1 and 10.4).

Figure 10.4 The Carnot cycle

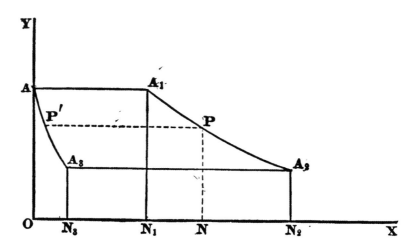

In order to truly appreciate the radical departure, the spatial and material nature depicted in Turner's painting, we must look at the works of Maxwell and Boltzmann. As discussed earlier, classical physics dealing with more than three bodies in motion already posed an insurmountable obstacle to the nineteenth-century scientists. Thus, dealing with a molecular level description of the behavior of gas, the task of numerical calculation for every single molecule was technically impossible without massive computational power at their disposal. Instead, they discovered an ingenious work-around in the form of "probability," giving birth to statistical mechanics. The Maxwell–Boltzmann distribution describes the probability distribution of gas molecules' speed in relation to the temperature of the system. Through the introduction of statistics, the individual motion of particles described in classical mechanics can now be treated as an aggregate behavior of molecules over time. The development finally bridges the conceptual gap between Newton mechanics and thermal dynamics, paving the way to the development of quantum mechanics by such giants as Einstein, Heisenberg and Bohr in the early twentieth century. The equation, $S = k \log W$, carved into Boltzman's tombstone, describing the logarithmic relationship between Entropy (S) and Probability (W), the number of possible micro-states corresponding to the macroscopic state of a system, says it all. It demarcates the clear departure from the deterministic thinking in classical mechanics to accepting indeterminacy as part of the fact in nature.

Complexity/precision/extension

> The properties of shear-tie are fully embedded within the solid representation. Any dimension can be derived completely and accurately from the solid model, rendering the once necessary dimensional drawings now obsolete.[7]

The shear-tie mentioned above fastens the exterior skin to the frame of a Boeing 777. In the book *Refabricating Architecture*, Kieran and Timberlake discuss how every component of this airplane is precisely modeled in the virtual environment. In addition to the full description of geometric information, each virtual part is embedded with other design controlling factors such as the physical properties and its lifecycle records. A Boeing 777 consists of over one million parts, an object the size of a small building with enormous complexity. Kieran and Timberlake argue that without the technology to predetermine the data in pinpoint accuracy beyond the simple dimensional tolerances, it would not be economically feasible to build such a complex object. They make a convincing case for architecture and construction industries to adopt the technology already fully embraced in automobile and aerospace industries.

Frank Gehry was one of the earliest to do so. In the Foreword to the book *Iron: Erecting the Walt Disney Concert Hall*, Gehry writes:

> CATIA also allowed extremely complicated steel to go together on the site without the kind of problems that happen on similar sized buildings. Due to the consistency of information and the precision of the calculations, every element tied back to an origin. When an Ironworker was on the scaffolding, he could get someone to survey him a point and know he was within an eighth of an inch.[8]

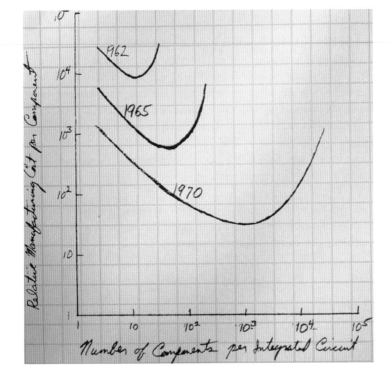

Figure 10.5 Cost vs. component – Moore's original graph

For Gehry, it was an absolute necessity to adopt the technology in order to realize his complex sculptural forms. He goes on to speculate that if it was not for CATIA, the three-dimensional surface modeling program developed for the aerospace industry, it would have taken him decades to meet the computational requirements alone for the design of the Walt Disney Concert Hall.

A building system is literally and metaphorically an extension of a vast number of similar elements. In general, the more complex the building, the more accuracy is expected in extending the elements both in design and in execution to make them economically feasible. The construction of an exceedingly complex building such as the Walt Disney Concert Hall is testament to the recent technological advances in the field, namely the precision and the speed made possible by the new digital tools. If the future of architecture is dependent upon these new digital tools, what makes these tools possible?

Computational muscles

> The complexity for minimum component costs has increased at a rate of roughly a factor of two per year. Certainly over the short term this rate can be expected to continue, if not to increase. Over the longer term, the rate of increase is a bit more uncertain, although there is no reason to believe it will not remain nearly constant for at least 10 years. That means by 1975, the number of components per integrated circuit for minimum cost will be 65,000. I believe that such a large circuit can be built on a single wafer.[9]

In 1965, Gordon Moore, the future co-founder of Intel Corporation, published the now famous article, "Cramming more components onto integrated circuits," in an obscure electronic trade magazine, *Electronics*. He predicted that the number of transistors economically placed on an integrated circuit would increase exponentially, doubling approximately every two years as mentioned in the above quote. This notion has since been widely embraced by the industry as "Moore's Law." The key in reading the article is his careful attention to the impact of such rapid technological advance in the context of economy. If we assume that the computational power is proportional to the number of transistors on the single chip, we will see exponential growth in the power for the same price year by year (Figure 10.5).

Gordon writes, "Computers will be more powerful, and will be organized in completely different ways. Machines similar to those in existence today will be built at lower costs and with faster turn-around." Many future products he mentioned in the article did come to fruition – electronic wristwatches, home computers, automatic controls for automobiles, personal portable communications equipment, to name but a few. The availability of the ubiquitous, increasingly powerful computing and its effect on the way of life seem to echo the technological optimism of the era.

Patrick P. Gelsinger, the current Intel Corp. Senior President, confirmed that the performance/dollar ratio of computers has increased by a factor of over one million in the past 30 years, in line with Moore's Law.[10]

We are surrounded by computers. Our future advancement seems to rely ever more on the continuation of this trend, the exponential increase of the affordable computational muscles. This is precisely what makes these new digital tools possible and increasingly viable in the field of architecture.

Tumbling Units

In the field of computational physics, there is a resurgent interest in resolving previously unattainable classical mechanics problems through sheer computational power. We are now tantalizingly close to predicting exactly what would happen in the box of gas, molecule by molecule. The affordability of the computational muscles has also impacted the field of architecture. It is evident from the overwhelming trend in the profession as well as in education. However, has the digital revolution really contributed to a significant shift in the way we think and produce building systems, analogous to the way the Industrial Revolution triggered a paradigm shift in the world of physics and ultimately changed the way we see the world?

The current technological obsession in architecture is rather simplistic. As is evident in Gehry's earlier remarks, the advances are measured in terms of speed, accuracy and, in turn, economy. With the deterministic precision made possible by inexpensive computational power, we can design and build a complex building cheaper in a much shorter time. Kieran and Timberlake merely reaffirm this point through the idea of prefabrication and mass customization. I often wonder what would have happened if the massive computational power we have now had been available to the nineteenth-century scientists. Would it have facilitated the paradigm shift? Or would it have hindered the game-altering development in thermal dynamics and statistical mechanics since they did not have to confront the kind of resistance they had to contend with?

My work approaches this question from the opposite end. How can we introduce an architectural idea equivalent to "probability" in nineteenth-century science? Can we conceive a building method that does not rely on precision in an ordinary sense? Is it possible to form a building system with an indeterminate system? What will be the tectonic implications (Figures 10.6–10.7)?

Tumbling Units were conceived in an attempt to address these questions. The friction-bound ceramic structural units were designed and fabricated as a possible building system with indeterminate internal extensions.

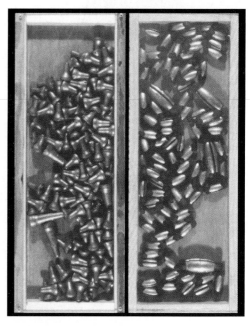

Figure 10.6 Tangling tree branches
Figure 10.7a–b Lead fishing weights under gravity

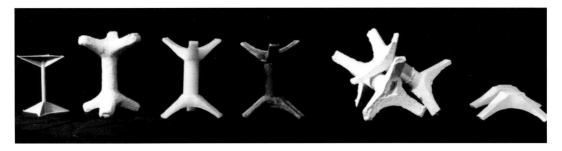

Figure 10.8 Various fabrication attempts of the positive mold and the result of the hydro-cal casts

Figure 10.9 Fabrication method via sheet goods

Figure 10.10 Masonite/plywood *Tumbling Units*

Basic geometry

The basic geometry of the unit is conceived as a hybrid of two tetrahedrons attached at a vertex with 30 degrees offset rotation, composing a dumbbell shape. The prongs at both ends of the main axis function as an indeterminate joint condition to cling and/or stack to one another. The member connecting the tetrahedrons gives the capacity to span.

The actual form of the units depends on the material and the production methods. Several alternative designs were investigated and evaluated based on the ease of production, rigidity, density (scale/weight) and esthetic concerns (form/materiality) (Figures 10.8–10.10). This design based on ceramic stoneware proved to be the most desirable, allowing the rigid continuous forming of complex geometry with substantial material quality.[11]

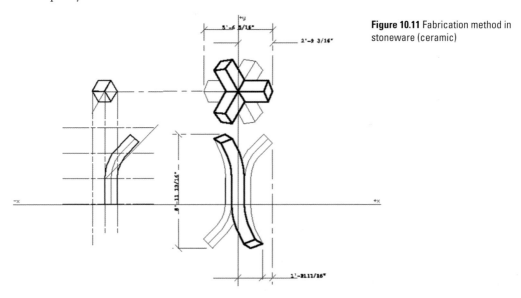

Figure 10.11 Fabrication method in stoneware (ceramic)

Fabrication

There are a number of resistance factors to contend with in fabricating elements of multiplicity. The design parameters were established so that it is feasible for one person to economically produce (1000) units in (30) days using a single 5 c.f. electric kiln.

The property of wet clay is typically characterized as plastic. However, this is not necessarily an accurate description. Clay exhibits an elastic property when the moisture content is relatively low. Its property swings from plastic to elastic depending on the moisture content. The fabrication method exploits this subtle variation of stoneware to the fullest extent.

The pre-mixed stoneware was extruded through a custom-fabricated hexagonal die in approximately 3' length and left to dry for about 45 minutes to the desired stiffness. The strand of extruded clay was then cut to length. Subsequently, both ends were manually split into three prongs and spread into the approximate shape.

The weight and the size of each unit were the critical controlling factors in the production tolerance. It was necessary to carefully balance the drying time required to meet the production schedule against the changing elasticity of the clay prior to firing. The spread of the prong depended on the weight of the unit and the elasticity of the clay. The units were air-dried for approximately two hours at room temperature in an upright position, the sides flipped and dried for an additional three hours to three and a half hours (Figure 10.12). The timing of flipping was also crucial to balance the top and bottom spreads since the unrestricted prongs on top began to close in as the clay dries.

Figure 10.12 Air-drying *Tumbling Units*

Note how the tolerance of form depends on the material's internal response to the gravitational forces, not through a direct artificial manipulation. The external controls imposed are the initial condition and the duration. The material tendencies will take care of the rest. The air-dried units were then loaded in the kiln, fired at cone 2 and left to cool overnight. At the end, over 600 units were produced. One of the unexpected formal outcomes was the unique inflecting surface observed in the unit.

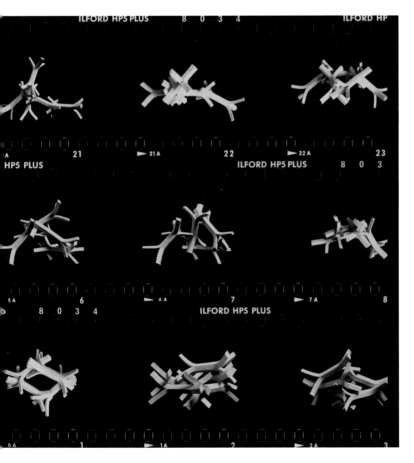

Figure 10.13 Tectonics of four

Figure 10.14 Tectonics studies with multiple units

Figure 10.15 Tectonics of nodes

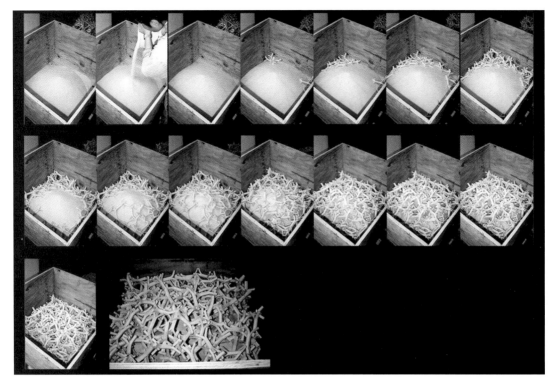

Figure 10.16 Silica sand formwork experiment

Tectonics of an aggregate system

As the production progressed, the behaviors of a small number of units were systemically cataloged. Simultaneously, a larger number of units were employed to explore the range of tectonic possibilities as an aggregate (Figures 10.13–10.14).

Based on observation, a simple extension offers three distinct directional freedoms without considering the specificity of the exact angle in a pair of units. Assume the average number of units consisting of an extension node is three units for an aggregate of 100 units total.

Possible extension combination per node: 3^3 = 27.
Possible node combination in an aggregate of (100): $_{100}C_3$ x $(1+1/3+1/3+1/3)$ = 323400[12]

Then, the possible combination (state) of the aggregate reflecting the directional freedom at the nodes: 323400 x 3^3 = 8731800, a rather large sum. The number tells us the magnitude of the possible configuration of the whole aggregate, a step towards quantifying the tectonic characteristics using statistics.

Let us consider what can be quantified as tectonic characteristics of this aggregate. One of the obvious parameters is the number of units composing each extension node. In the previous analysis, we simply assumed the average condition. The further observations reveal that the number can vary somewhere between two and five. It is also clear that these are not randomly assigned numbers. It is the result of an equilibrium reached against the conglomeration of various geometrical, gravitational and contextual influences that can be held constant in the macro scale. Thus, by conducting a large number of empirical experiments, it is possible to statistically establish a distribution pattern against the overall state of the aggregate system. In turn, through the numerically established distribution pattern, it is possible to predict the probability of observing (x) number of extension nodes constituted by (y) number of units in an aggregate system with (z)

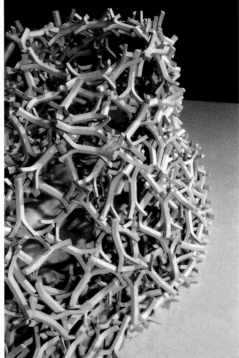

Figure 10.17 *Tumbling Units*: canopy

Figure 10.18 *Tumbling Units*: canopy (detail)

number of total units, and so on (Figure 10.15). A role equivalent of the Maxwell–Boltzmann's distribution in statistical mechanics.

Through the introduction of statistics, it is conceivable to establish a "most probable" tectonic characteristic of an indeterminately complex system.

Construction sequence of an indeterminate system

Human judgment involved in the extension of the units is one of the controlling, yet less consistent, macroscopic factors in the earlier tectonic studies. The sensory and motor skill level of the human hand depends on the individual's talent and training. Further, it is impossible to replicate the kind of delicate balancing act human hands are capable of in the scale of building construction.

The skilled labor/judgment issue is a common topic in building construction. In fact, this is one of the reasons why this kind of precision, the ability to virtually map every building component with accuracy, is sought after by such architects as Kieran and Timberlake and Frank Gehry as discussed in the earlier examples. It is an attempt to eliminate the discrepancy between the design and execution by identifying every building part and correlating them one-to-one in the model. The thinking is that by minimizing the unknown, little skilled on-site judgments will be required. The ultimate goal of such a system is for the components to fit together in a predetermined, singular manner.

An alternative approach in deploying the units is speculated and tested in the following example. A mound of silica sand is formed inside an elevated 3' x 3' plywood box. The bottom of the box is designed to evenly drain the sand, sloping to the 1" x 1" center opening. The units were first placed along the edge of the box in higher density to accommodate the anticipated lateral and vertical force transferring into the box. Then the remaining area is loosely filled in with layers. General attention was paid only to the direction of the units to lie evenly distributed against the slope of the sand. As it was drained, the units fell into place and locked into each other seeking a gravitational equilibrium without any external interventions. This resulted in a formation of a shallow dome, spanning across the plywood box (Figure 10.16).

In actual building scale construction, slightly different tactics may be employed substituting the mound of sand with inflatable formwork. Once the elements are roughly placed in position by crane, the formwork is deflated slowly, inducing a similar effect to draining the sand. In this scenario, the skilled on-site judgments are also reduced, however, without relying on computational muscles and the precision necessary for a predetermined system.

Installations

Over and above the basic human need for shelter, architecture aims to evoke an emotional and intellectual response. Acrobatic forms are often justified as one of the elements of the surprise. However, there are other phenomenal qualities such as materiality, texture, light, shade, time, sequence, scale, proportion and spatial, structural order. Various aforementioned experiments have culminated in temporary installations for two exhibitions exploring these qualities beyond the acrobatic form. All (600 +/−) units were used for both occasions.

In the first exhibition, the Graduate Degree Exhibition at Cranbrook Art Museum, Bloomfield Hills, Michigan, the units were configured into a self-supporting oblong dome in the size of 3' x 4' x 3'. Exploring the tectonics of spatial/structural order was of prime interest. Attention was paid to the gradual transition from the more ordered configuration at the foundation to more random configurations at the top. A layer

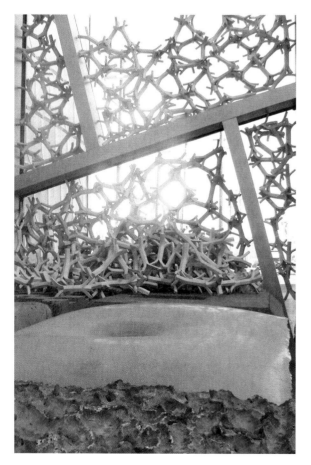

Figure 10.19 *Tumbling Units*: light filter
Figure 10.20 *Tumbling Units*: disassembled

of silica sand stabilized the foundation by filling in the gap, increasing the friction against the platform for lateral support. The viewers were fascinated by the contrasting qualities of the dome; the surprising stability as an assembly despite the delicate qualities of the ceramic units in friction-bound. The museum guards have informed me that there were numerous attempts to touch and to dislodge the units during the two weeks of exhibition in May 1997 (Figures 10.17–10.18).

In the second exhibition, the CoA Faculty Exhibition at Louise Hopkins Underwood Center for the Arts in Lubbock, Texas, the units were stacked against a large storefront window to take advantage of the given context. Exploring the phenomenal qualities of light/shade and scale/proportion were of the prime interest (Figure 10.19).

Conclusion

I have often marveled at the dunescape of the American West: White Sands National Monument in New Mexico, Great Sand Dunes National Park and Preserve in Colorado to name but a few. Standing on the top of the dune crest reminds me of the realization I had under the electron microscope some years ago as a student of physics – that the world consisting of matter we observe daily is not stationary. It is profoundly temporal, tenuous, and imperfect. The amazingly rich phenomenal environment is a result of simple principles governing the interaction of matters, a dynamic equilibrium reached among wind, gravity, and sand particles. Airflow shapes the sand surface. Simultaneously, the surface changes the direction of the airflow and then the modified flow changes the shape of the sand surface. This goes on until computational tendencies of nature works its way out to a temporal stationary condition. How can we imagine a way of shaping matter in this manner for architectural purposes? The reality of current building practice is to execute a complex building efficiently with minimum risks. The technology and its computational muscles are almost exclusively used for this purpose. The *Tumbling Units*, the exploration of indeterminate extensions, aims to raise a fundamental question about the way current architectural practice engages the matter and the act of making.

Acknowledgements

Tumbling Units were designed and fabricated as part of the author's MArch II thesis at Cranbrook Academy of Art in 1996–1997. Thesis advisors were Dan Hoffman and Peter Lynch (Architect in Residence, Architecture Department). I have also sought advice from Tony Hepburn (Artist in Residence, Ceramic Department) on various occasions. The article is largely based on a paper of the same title published in ACSA West Conference 2008 Proceedings[13] as well as in ACSA Annual Meeting 2009 Proceedings.[14]

Notes

1   Michel Serres, "Turner translates Carnot," in Josue Harari and David Bell, eds., *Hermes: Literature, Science, Philosophy* (Baltimore, MD: The Johns Hopkins University Press, 1982), pp. 56–57.

2   Kobayashi, Keinosuke, Eiji Suito, Shinichi Shimadzu, and Masaya Iwanaga, "Construction of 300 kV Electron Microscope," *Bulletin of the Institute for Chemical Research*, Kyoto University, 42(6). 1965, 425–438. KURENAI: Kyoto University Research Information Repository. Available at: http://hdl. handle.net/2433/76045.

3   Richard P. Feynman, Robert B. Leighton, and Matthew Sands, eds., *The Feynman Lectures on Physics*, Vol. 1 (Reading, MA: Addison-Wesley Publishing Company Inc., 1970), pp. 38–39.

4   Stephen, Wolfram, *A New Kind of Science* (Champaign, IL: Wolfram Media, Inc., 2002), p. 973.

5   N.L.S. Carnot, "Reflections on the motive power of heat," ed. R.H. Thurston (New York: John Wiley & Sons, 1897), pp. 37–38.

6   Ibid., p. 147.

7   Stephan Kieran and James Timberlake, *Refabricating Architecture* (New York: McGraw-Hill, 2004), p. 61.

8   Gil Garcetti, Foreword by Frank O. Gehry, *Iron: Erecting the Walt Disney Concert Hall* (Los Angeles: Balcony Press, 2002), p. 8.

9   Gordon E. Moore, "Cramming more components onto integrated circuits," *Electronics*, 38, 1965.

10 P.P. Gelsinger, P.A. Gargini, G.H. Parker, and A.Y.C. Yu, "Microprocessors circa 2000," *IEEE Spectrum*, 26(10), October 1989, 43–47.

11 Due to the complexity of its geometry, it requires at least eight part molds to cast a rigid continuous unit. The author has fabricated a few units in this method with marginal success. See Figure 10.8.

12 "nCk" stands for combination: n is the number of objects from which you can choose and k is the number to be chosen.

13 K. Tsubaki, "TUMBLING UNITS: Tectonics of indeterminate extension," in Gail Peter Borden and Michael Meredith, eds., *Material Matters: Making Architecture* (Washington, DC: ACSA Press, 2008), pp. 284–291.

14 K. Tsubaki, "TUMBLING UNITS: Tectonics of indeterminate extension," in Phoebe Crisman and Mark Gillem, *The Value of Design: Design Is at the Core of What We Teach and Practice* (Washington, DC: ACSA Press, 2009), pp. 292–298.

Chapter 11
Monolithic Representations

W. Andrew Atwood
ATWOOD

"Discovered" by an English-born explorer in 1873, "Ayers Rock" in central Australia is the known world's largest natural monolith. Geologists claim that the "island mountain" – which stands 2831 feet above sea level and is composed primarily of sandstone – was formed through a combination of forces spanning at least 550 million years. Water draining from a once-massive mountain range carried sand into a large basin and, over time, the basin flooded and the sand deposits hardened into stone. Once the waters receded, new rock formations were revealed in the evolving landscape. Wind, weather, and sand slowly eroded the smaller formations and left only a single large rock. Aboriginal culture has a different story. Per Pitjantjatjara legend, "Uluru" owes its origin to two boys and a mud puddle: as the children played, they piled the mud into a mound that amassed at a rapid rate. As the burgeoning formation hardened and thrust toward the sky, the boys fell sliding down its sides while dragging their fingers through the clay, thereby defining Uluru's iconic shape and forming the gullies on its southern face. To this day, Uluru holds significant cultural and spiritual meaning for the indigenous locals who discourage climbing their sacred mount.

Like its natural-born counterparts, contemporary architectural monolithicity is not immune to morphological contradiction and mythological corruption. Seemingly an issue of purity of mass and object, more recent discussions of the architectural monolith have evolved towards issues of surface, material effect, and human perception. In 1995, Rodolfo Machado and Rodolphe El-Khoury published *Monolithic Architecture*,[1] wherein they defined monolithic architecture's "paradoxical representation"; that of a single materiality belies a necessary aggregation of material parts. Through an examination of a series of projects completed in the late 1980s and early 1990s, Machado and El-Khoury examine the transition of the monolith's central issue – singularity of mass – into a previously-unidentified problem of surface integrity. By introducing the term "epidermal monolith," they reposition monolithic architecture as a problem of negotiation between the interior and exterior, solved within the thickness of the building envelope. In this context we can begin to view the monolith in architecture as a discrete problem, resolved within the context of a single material system and isolated within an architectural object's exterior surface depth. The problem of the monolith, then, is no longer a question of a singular material object but rather a singular material system working towards a singular affect.

More recently, as the formal excesses of the past decade have come to a close and the limitations and ecological excesses of high formalism continue to reveal themselves, systems of formal restraint studied within the context of increased technological dexterity and material advances seem relatively under-explored. It is from this vantage point that my interests with the *monolith* have emerged. For my purposes, the term "monolithic" describes something that can be read as a singular, unified whole. In this way, it functions as a metaphorical diagram that drives both a desire for formal restraint as well as a singular surface affect. In addition, it is viewed as a diagram that is inherently non-indexical and stands in opposition to contemporary issues of complexity which are often understood through an examination of the aggregations of (many) parts.

All material systems are, by definition, networks of assemblies whose scales range from molecular to urban. But due to its metaphorical boundaries, the architectural monolith requires a unique repression of its aggregate systems. Issues of surface discretization and material precision are uniquely important. The monolith, rather than allowing an expression or indexing of its part-to-whole relationship as an alibi for technical ineptitude, or a desire to express its "complexity," must suppress it. What emerges is a material system that must be precisely calibrated to mitigate the tensions between a smooth, uniform surface and a faceted, fragmented surface. Rather than solely quantitative decisions, made by material or geometrical determinism (which are still important), material and tectonic decisions must also be made within the scales of human experience. In this case, issues of resolution and perspective are of increasing importance. Evidence supporting the monolith's experiential subjectivity in nature lies in the geologists' tendency to avoid the term "monolithic," based on its nebulous boundaries, even within the realm of science. Certain rock formations may appear "monolithic" from one side to one observer, for example, while an opposing face of the same structure may appear distinctly "un-monolithic" to another. This inconsistency in perspective makes the integrity of the monolith's abstract form even murkier because it highlights the fact that geometric rationalization is only one aspect of an object's corruption.

In addition to issues related to human perception, the application of narrative and meaning onto architecture is an unavoidable consequence – magnified in the case of the monolith. Because the monolith is tectonically inscrutable, its workings hidden and unknowable, it deflects and defies contemporary architectural readings and analyses (see above) and represents (for me) a forced redirection of current architectural issues. Instead of a discourse on parts and performance, the monolith's indexical void allows a broader range of architectural readings and analysis. Of particular interest to me is the way myth and narrative often fill this void. The Pitjantjatjara interpretation of Uluru is one of many examples of creation narratives attached to monoliths. The application of narrative to architectural monoliths is well documented; one of the most interesting cases is the churches of Lalibela, Ethiopia.[2] Formed through a process of extraction and subtraction, the Lalibela churches are pure in their material smoothness. The part-to-whole relationship is non-existent. Even the process of their construction imbues the structures with ambiguity. Due to a technique of extraction, the original form of these structures can never be known. Is their current form the first iteration? Or the last in a series of alterations? Questions such as these, left unanswered even by archaeologists, have only helped perpetuate the mysteries and mythologies surrounding this complex of structures.

I offer these mythological antidotes, not because I am interested in architecture as a purveyor of myth, *per se*, only because they acknowledge the possibilities of an object's corruptions, when architecture allows for readings outside of those that currently dominate architectural discourse.

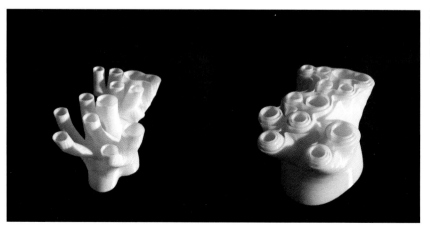

Figure 11.1
Stereolithography prints of weighted offset surfaces

Monolithic processes

It is within this context that the *monolith* as a process metaphor has inspired a series of our own investigations. In this case, the studies exist more as provocations and studies of the corruptions that necessarily occur as singular objects navigate the boundaries of architecture and the constraints of monolithicity. They are part of a larger body of research that focuses on issues of form and representation in architecture and the necessary compromises and corruptions that occur as abstract design concepts mitigate architecture's roles, ambitions and ambiguities via an ever expanding list of available mediums.

The studies were conducted based on a calibration of material control, fabrication precision and process fidelity through a formal technique of offsetting and material process of layering. The material used was acrylonitrile butadiene styrene (ABS) plastic. It was chosen because it is widely available and widely used as a representational medium but often overlooked as materials in and of itself. Various studies were conducted at the beginning of the project to test the limits of the material when matched with the fabrication process. In the case of ABS, we built a modified DIY (Do It Yourself) 3D printer, based on a hybrid of the MakerBot, RepRap 3D Printer and our own design. Geometric and physics engines were used to develop project specific digital modeling tools (Figure 11.1). In a similar vein to the DIY ethos of the 3D printer, the studies were used as the means to develop and explore the creation of unique digital modeling tools with custom graphic user interfaces. Using open source, and widely available libraries, the tools were able to simulate and predict material successes and failures within an acceptable tolerance given the scope of the project. The software and hardware are not meant to replace existing technologies but rather are extensions of the concept of monolithicity in contemporary process. By developing and building our own tools we hope to achieve something closer to what we termed a "monolithic" (or singular) process. One interested in issues of control, precision and fidelity.

The study's morphology is based on a series of weighted offset surfaces (Figures 11.2–11.3).

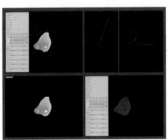

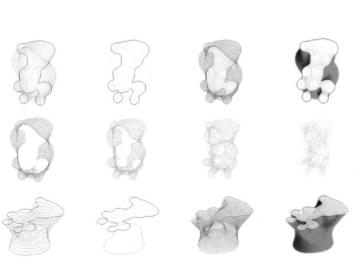

Figure 11.2 Software interface

Figure 11.3a–l Plan and axonometric drawings of weighted offset surfaces

Using isocurves, we developed a technique of offsetting which generated the GCode to communicate with the 3D printer. Rather than a process of post-rationalization where the model is created via one technique and then carved, combed, clipped, and filled by a separate (and often unrelated) tool to create a representation of the process, in this case, the process of form generation is the same as the process which creates the fabrication script. By linking the techniques of digital modeling and fabrication output, we were able to quickly link the software to the 3D printer, creating a more streamlined, singular process. We quickly discovered a series of glitches (or corruptions) in the fabrication process and we began to study all of the ways that we could gain control of these occurrences and then subvert and exploit the oddities of the process (Figure 11.4).

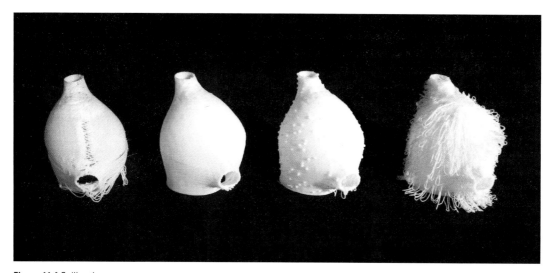

Figure 11.4 Calibration

We identified three different outputs that routinely occurred during the research phase, titling them: *Gap*, *Pause*, and *Loop* (Figure 11.5).

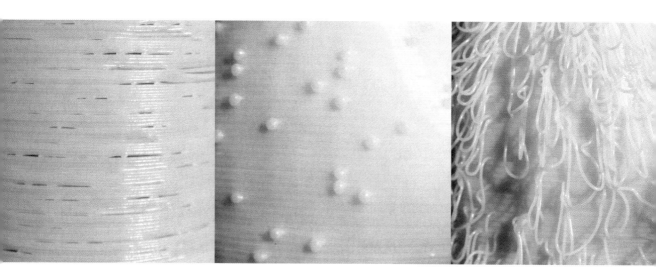

Figure 11.5a–c *Gap, Pause,* and *Loop*

Because we controlled access to all phases of the design process, we then did a series of calibration studies to extract the necessary parameters and control points of each of these occurrences. In the case of *Gap*, we discovered that pausing the extrusion of the plastic not only led to a small gap but also resulted in a scalloping as the ABS continued to build in subsequent layers (Figure 11.6).

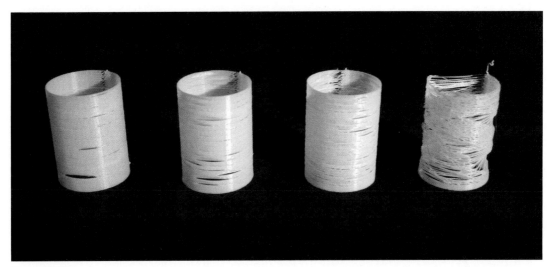

Figure 11.6 *Gap*

Pause stopped the extruder from moving but not the extrusion of the plastic, creating bumps on the surface; the size of the bump was linked to the length of the pause (Figure 11.7).

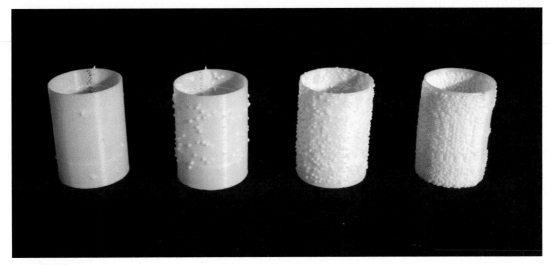

Figure 11.7 *Pause*

By controlling the placement and location of the extruder tip we were able to control the placement of the dots, allowing us to explore varying densities and patterns. *Loop* was created by extending the extruder tip beyond the boundaries of the initial isocurves, resulting in a strand of material which succumbed to gravity and created a kind of "furry" appearance (Figure 11.8).

Figure 11.8 *Loop*
Figure 11.9 Form and GCode generation

Acknowledgements

The design assistant was Nicholas Murao and editorial assistance was provided by Brendan Muha.

Notes

1   Rodolfo Machado and Rodolphe El-Khoury, *Monolithic Architecture* (London: Prestel, 1995).

2   The prevailing story dates back to the late twelfth century, when the current town of Lalibela was known as "Roha." It was then that the youngest son was born into the royal line of the ruling Zagwe Dynasty. They named him Lalibela. Although he had many older brothers before him, his kingly destiny was foreshadowed from a very early age. According to Ethiopian legend, one day when Lalibela was an infant, his mother found him lying in his crib, surrounded by a swarm of bees (a symbol of great significance in Ethiopian culture at the time). She quickly proclaimed that even the bees knew he was fit to rule the land. However, this challenge to the throne angered the current king, who poisoned the boy. The child's spirit then journeyed through the first three levels of heaven, where God – supplying Lalibela with the complete design and construction details – instructed him to return to Roha and build a series of awe-inspiring churches. When the boy returned to Earth, he was crowned king, and he immediately began assembling large crews of masons, sculptors, and other craftsmen. As a result of the mandate from God, the churches of Lalibela were constructed with incredible speed by the king's laborers by day and a team of angels at night.

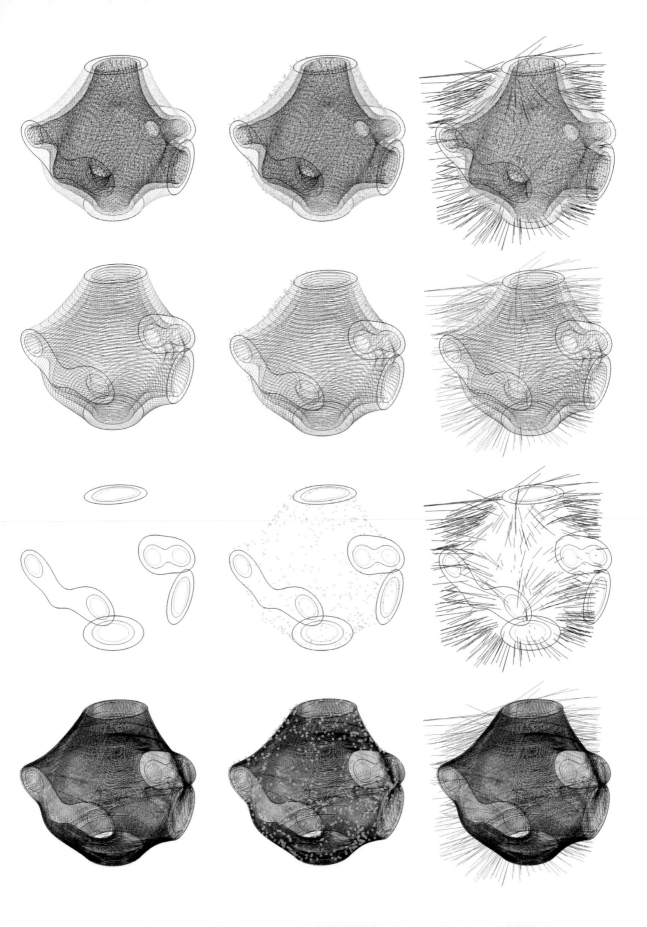

Chapter 12
Materiality of the Infrathin

Michael Carroll
atelier BUILD

"Infrathin," a concept invented by Marcel Duchamp, characterizes a thickness, a separation, and a difference between two things. In basic terms, infrathin describes something very, very thin – as Duchamp asks, will a sheet of copper always be opaque?[1] As Hector Obalk, a philosopher at the College Art Association in Boston, has stated, infrathin has three possible trajectories:

> At first step, "infrathin" means "very, very, very thin." It could be "1/10e mm = 100 μ = minceur des papiers" as Marcel Duchamp says in note MAT 11.[2] But at this level, the concept means "infinitesimal" ... At a second step, "infrathin" characterizes any difference that you easily imagine but doesn't exist, like the thickness of a shadow: the shadow has no thickness ... At a third step ... "infrathin" qualifies a distance or a difference you cannot perceive, but that you can only imagine.[3]

The word "infrathin," like Duchamp himself, is slippery and aloof, its definition(s) scattered among the 46 scraps of paper (Figure 12.1) that he scribbled upon in the late 1930s while he was repairing the *Large Glass* after it had been shattered. What is the meaning of infrathin? Duchamp's response is: "*On ne peut guère en donner que des exemples. C'est quelque chose qui échappe encore à nos définitions scientifiques.*" ("One can hardly give examples [of infrathin]. It's something that escapes even scientific definition.")[4]

Figure 12.1 Duchamp *Notes*, Vitrine @ Philadelphia Museum

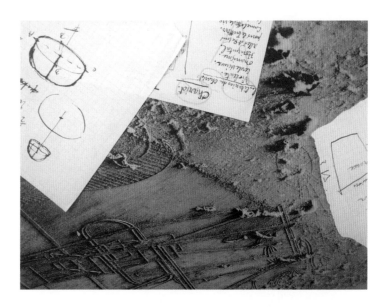

Duchamp's twentieth-century notion of the infrathin is an intriguing concept in the early part of the twenty-first century, given the recent advances in material engineering and the emerging field of nanotechnology. Materials of infinitesimal thickness are now possible. Given this, an interesting question emerges, how will materials and architecture itself appear in the future? How thin is thin? Given the current array of technologies from organic light emitting diodes (OLED) flat screens to ink-printed photovoltaics, will the hardware of architecture itself become increasingly thin and lean? How will an architecture of disappearance appear?

In the expanded field of architectural production, architects and designers today not only make material research and development a priority but also address issues of fabrication and building performance. In their book *Refabricating Architecture*[5] Stephen Kieran and James Timberlake contemplate the future of architecture, as digital technologies allow mass customization, and architects begin to incorporate within their design thinking the processes that underlie building production, including the exponential growth in the research and the development of materials.

SmartWrap™, conceptualized by Kieran and Timberlake, is composed of thin film silicon solar cells, flexible organic light emitting diodes (OLEDs), microcapsules of phase change materials and batteries (networked with conductive ink) (Figures 12.2–12.3). All these components are printed on a polyethylene terephthalate (PET) substrate to create a super-thin film. Kieran and Timberlake worked with DuPont and ILC Dover to create a working prototype that was incorporated into a multi-colored facsimile of the *SmartWrap*™ system exhibited at the Cooper-Hewitt National Design Triennial in 2003.

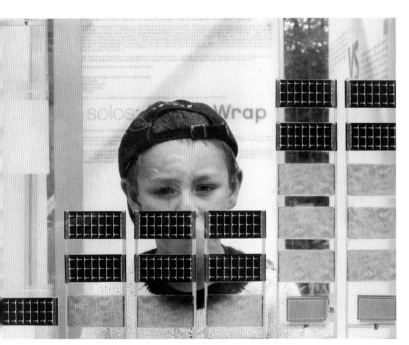

Figures 12.2–12.3 *SmartWrap™ Pavilion* detail

In 2008, Kieran and Timberlake's subsequent vision of a thin, transparent and performative skin was demonstrated in their *Cellophane House*, exhibited in MoMA's *Home Delivery: Fabricating the Modern Dwelling* (Figures 12.4–12.5). The project introduced *NextGen SmartWrap*™, a prototype for a wall assembly of the future in which the mass of the wall and its overall thickness are drastically reduced. The outer layer comprised transparent PET, with thin-film photovoltaic cells adhered to its surface. An inner layer of a solar heat and UV blocking film allowed daylight in, while it deflected solar gain. Between these two layers, a vented cavity was introduced to trap heat in the winter and vent it in the summer. Given the recent advances in photovoltaic technology, one can imagine the next release of *NextGen SmartWrap*™ in which elements such as the thin film solar cells are upgraded arrays of 3D nanopillar photovoltaics that promise to be more flexible, thinner and more efficient.

Figures 12.4–12.5 Cellophane House, MoMA

Nanoarchitecture explores materials in terms of a nanometer (nm), i.e. one billionth of a meter. Architecture, rather than being an assembly of parts from the top-down, is an approach that is directed from the "bottom-up," at the atomic or even sub-atomic level. Materials and devices are built from molecular components that assemble themselves chemically by principles of molecular recognition. Marcel Duchamp surely would have been intrigued.

Buckypaper, first developed in the 1990s, is made from carbon nanotubes that measure about 1/50,000th the diameter of a human hair. Buckypaper is named in reference to Buckminsterfullerene, or Carbon 60 – a type of carbon molecule whose powerful atomic bonds make it twice as hard as a diamond. The discovery of "Buckyballs" (named in honor of R. Buckminster Fuller) earned Sir Harold Kroto, currently at Florida

State University, Robert F. Curl Jr. and Richard E. Smalley, both of Rice University, the1996 Nobel Prize in Chemistry. Their discovery has led to a revolution in the fields of chemistry and materials science – and directly contributed to the development of buckypaper (Figure 12.6). Carbon nanotubes (CNTs), in terms of strength-to-weight ratio, are significantly stronger in tension than an equal mass of steel. As some kind of supermaterial, it has the potential to effectively conduct both heat and electricity, and filter particles. Applications are diverse and include the creation of more robust military body armor, the next wave of computer screens, artificial muscles, and more effective fire-protection.

Figure 12.6 Buckypaper wafer

Although nanotechnology is normally the territory of scientists and engineers who investigate its applications in electronics, medicine, and the military, architects have begun to also see its potential within the realm of our built environment. One studio that is part of this growing movement is Decker Yeadon, a research-based professional practice based in New York. Peter Yeadon is an Associate Professor at Rhode Island School of Design where his research and teaching focus on smart materials and nanoarchitecture. In early 2010, Decker Yeadon's research in the field of nanotechnology became a material reality as they became one of the first architecture firms to synthesize a thin wafer of single-walled carbon nanotubes (SWNTs). The outcome of this experiment was a super-black, superthin, flexible sheet of buckypaper that measures 70 microns thick (Figures 12.7–12.9).

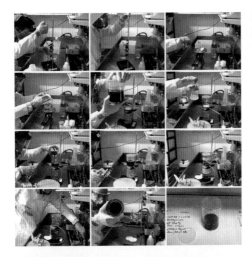

Figure 12.7a–l Video stills of buckypaper procedure
Figure 12.8 Microfiltration unit
Figure 12.9 Buckypaper disk

Decker Yeadon has disclosed their procedure for the production of buckypaper in the following 12 steps:[6]

1. Prepare a measured amount of deionized water (DI-H$_2$O).
2. Add sodium dodecyl sulfate (SDS) to the DI-H$_2$O at 1 percent concentration. This will serve as a surfactant for the nanotubes, which are hydrophobic and normally do not disperse well in water.
3. Prepare an amount of single-walled carbon nanotubes (SWNTs) that measure 1nm to 2nm in diameter and are 90 percent pure.
4. Add the SWNTs to the DI-H$_2$O and SDS solution.
5. After sonication, the nanotubes are well dispersed in solution.
6. Prepare a wash of methanol or ethanol (MeOH/EtOH) and DI-H$_2$O.
7. Introduce the nanotube solution into a vacuum microfiltration system.
8. Set the vacuum pressure of the filtration system to 35 kPa.
9. Draw the solution down into the bottom chamber of the filtration system, leaving the SWNTs on the microfiltration membrane.
10. Add the MeOH/EtOH and DI-H$_2$O wash, and pass it through the filtration system.
11. The SWNTs form a buckypaper sheet due to intermolecular non-covalent bonds (van der Waals attraction).
12. Slowly dry the buckypaper and remove it from the microfiltration membrane.

- - - - - - - - - - - - - - - - - -

As an application of buckypaper, Decker Yeadon have designed a kinetic brise-soleil system that, when installed on the exterior face of a façade, can be activated to either direct or shield the interior from the sunlight. The buckypaper mounted on a gel/foam substrate acts as a flexible nanotube electrode that conducts electricity to produce a nano-enabled artificial muscle that can change shape depending on the polarity of the charge (Figures 12.10–12.12).

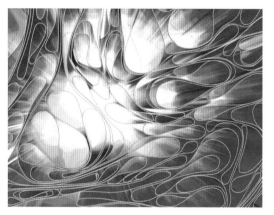

Figure 12.11 Kinetic brise-soleil system

Figure 12.10 Kinetic brise-soleil system

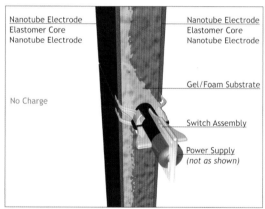

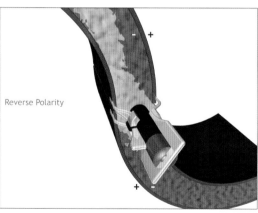

Figure 12.12a–d Detail, buckypaper on gel form substrate

The Rrose Glass Project is a photographic work on glass, an installation that essentially disappears – its very appearance dependent on atmospheric conditions. In our age of high-resolution imagery and quick distraction, the installation demands the astuteness of the casual observer as s/he looks through the *Large Glass* to see the ghosted image of Rrose Sélavy and the definite glimmer in the eyes of Duchamp himself. Maybe *The Rrose Glass Project* is a partial response to one of Duchamp's instructions for the construction an infrathin: "... one can draw or perhaps re-condense at will a picture which would appear by the application of water vapor (or other)."[7]

The Rrose Glass Project, designed by atelier BUILD, is an attempt to bring nanotechnology and Marcel Duchamp face-to-face in a proposal for a temporary installation for the Marion Boulton Stroud Gallery (aka Galerie Rrose Sélavy) at the Philadelphia Museum of Art (Figures 12.13–12.14). The site for the installation is the window/door opening directly opposite Duchamp's seminal work, *La mariée mise à nu par ses célibataires, même* (the *Large Glass*, Figure 12.15), installed at the museum in 1969.[8] The existing fixed glass window, which appears to have replaced a balcony door, measures approximately 33" x 77" and is flush with the floor. From the exterior, the window is located directly below the pediment of the north-east wing of the museum that features polychrome figures of Greek mythology associated with profane and sacred love – Zeus, Aphrodite, Aurora, Cupid, and Adonis.

Figure 12.13 Marion Boulton Stroud Gallery, Philadelphia Museum

Figure 12.15 The *Large Glass*, Marcel Duchamp (with West Light)

Figure 12.14 Marion Boulton Stroud Gallery, Philadelphia Museum

The proposal, which involves minimal disturbance to the existing building, is actually outside the museum's walls and is an exterior application mounted in front of the existing south-west-facing opening of the Duchamp Room. The installation is a series of laminations comprised of sheets of glass, a two-tone photochromatic film and a hydrophobic photographic frit.[9] *The Rrose Glass Project* is an installation that will react to changes in the weather (Figures 12.16–12.18). When it is sunny, the two-tone, rose-tinted glass will darken, this will be especially dramatic in the late afternoon, given the window's south-west orientation. With fog, mist or rain, areas of the glass treated with the hydrophobic photographic frit will repel water droplets and reduce residues. In contrast, water that will be deposited on the untreated areas of glass will create accumulations of dirt and grime. As the main objective of *The Rrose Glass Project*, both the photochromatic film and the hydrophobic frit will reveal, in different ways, a subtle yet compelling new image for both the Marion Boulton Stroud Gallery and the façade of the Philadelphia Museum of Art – that of Duchamp's feminine alter ego, Rrose Sélavy (a pun on *"eros, c'est la vie"*), who was captured in a photograph taken by Man Ray in the early 1920s.

Figures 12.16–12.18 Concept image, *The Rrose Glass Project*

Figure 12.19 *40 Bond*, New York, Herzog & de Meuron

From the interior, as one peers downward through the *Rrose Glass*, another component of the project will come into view, a 33" x 12" sheet of glass installed at the threshold of the window/door's exterior opening. Again depending on the weather, the hydrophobic frit on the horizontal surface of the glass will reveal, with the beading of water droplets, the signature of Rrose Sélavy, a fitting complement to the Man Ray's photograph of her.

It is assumed that the hydrophobic frit will be applied in a similar fashion to commercially available applications developed by companies such as Diamon-Fusion International. The process encompasses a two-stage manufacturing process in which the glass is smoothed and then the hydrophobic layer is applied to repel dirt. A recent application of DFIs technology is the glass façade of the condominium project, *40 Bond*, designed by Herzog & de Meuron in New York (Figure 12.19).[10] As an offshoot of their research in nanotechnology, DFI has also developed a process in which images and text are imbedded in glass and remain invisible until mist, fog or steam is applied to the glass.[11]

As a kind of double entendre, the notion of the infrathin is evident not only in the laminations of the photochromatic film and the hydrophobic frit but also in the image itself – the obvious and yet subtle differences between Marcel Duchamp and Rrose Sélavy. While appearances may differ, the eyes are the same, visible from both the interior/exterior, peering through the narrow aperture of the window/door frame. The image of Rrose Sélavy is revealed through the performative nature of the glass and its response to the weather

Figures 12.20–12.21 Photo montage, *The Rrose Glass Project*

Figure 12.22 Water droplet on hydrophobic glass and Duchamp's *The Bride Stripped Bare by her Bachelors, Even*

(Figure 12.20). The visibility, definition and resolution of the image are dependent on the difference between the two-tone rose-tinted glass, as well as the self-cleaning glass (with the frit of hydrophobic film) and the regular untreated glass (Figures 12.21–12.22).

The Rrose Glass Project attempts to bring technology into the realm of artful speculation, within the context of the museum, in order to create an installation that augments the reading of Duchamp's work. The work of Kieran and Timberlake and Decker Yeadon also demonstrates the importance of experimentation, in order to create architectural skins with embedded technologies that will not only lead to better performance in the field, but also change the way we think about the architecture from the macro to the nano-scale and vice versa.

Notes

1   Marcel Duchamp, Note 11a, from Paul Matisse, *Marcel Duchamp: Notes*, 1980. Duchamp's notes were discovered after his death. It was from this collection of notations, dated from 1912 to 1968, that Duchamp had chosen the notes that he published in the "Green Box" of 1934 and the "White Box" of 1966. This collection of notes was translated into English by Paul Matisse (grandson of Henri Matisse) and published in a bilingual edition by the Musée National d'Art Moderne, Centre Georges Pompidou, Paris, in 1980. G.K. Hall & Co. of Boston reproduced this publication in 1983.

2   Marcel Duchamp, Note 11a, from Paul Matisse, *Marcel Duchamp: Notes*.

3   "The Unfindable Readymade," by Hector Obalk, posted on *tout-fait: The Marcel Duchamp Studies Online Journal*, Vol. 1, Issue 2, May 2000. Available at: http://www.toutfait.com/issues/issue_2/Articles/obalk.html.

4   Interview with D. de Rougemont: "Marcel Duchamp mine de rien" (Lake George, New York, 3–9 August 1945), *Preuves*, Paris, No. 204 (February 1968): 43–47; reprinted in *Journal d'une Époque, 1926–1946* (Paris: Gallimard, 1968).

5   Stephen Kieran and James Timberlake, *Refabricating Architecture: How Manufacturing Methodologies Are Poised to Transform Building Construction* (New York: McGraw-Hill, 2003).

6   See http://www.deckeryeadon.com/projects/Buckypaper1.html.

7   Marcel Duchamp, Note 36, from Paul Matisse, *Marcel Duchamp: Notes*, 1980.

8   Previously the *Large Glass* was exhibited at the Brooklyn Museum before it was accidentally broken and carefully repaired by Duchamp.

9   *The Rrose Glass Project* was partially inspired by Hydrophobic Nanotiles, a concept developed by Decker Yeadon in which, "specific zones of a surface are treated with a hydrophobic nanocoating that repels water molecules and forces them to form spherical pixels. The remainder of the surface is treated with a hydrophilic treatment that does not allow the water to bead." Images and text appear on the surface as water pixels form when it beads within the hydrophobic region of the tiles. See http://www.deckeryeadon.com/projects/Nanotiles.html.

10   Peter Yeadon, "Nanotechnology: Small but Mighty," *Canadian Architect*, November 2007.

11   See http://www.diamonfusion.com/en/products.

Chapter 13
Sheet Logics

Speculations on the organizational and cosmetic potential of sheets

Heather Roberge

murmur

In order to generate a feedback loop between matter and force, a generation of digital designers (those typically described as proponents of technique) have become expert at distributing linework as a medium for speculations on structure, surface and ornament. While not the central subject of this text, this area of research was the first to coalesce around the power of digital representation to condition the architectural atmosphere with its materiality. This design approach was a reaction to the immaterial effects of early digital experiments. In the early to mid-1990s, digital renderings depicted highly reflective, slightly transparent surfaces set against black backgrounds and without additional material or tectonic articulation. Space was rendered ethereal, surfaces intangible, and both projected an atmosphere absent of material, weight, or force. The designers of these surfaces, however, saw other representations of these surfaces and the spaces they defined. The digital environment within which they took shape was full of materiality in the form of linework used to make visible the mathematical description of the surfaces. This representational material became increasingly tangible as matter to be organized and sensed.

As these experiments evolved and interest in digital fabrication grew, designers turned to surface as the primary site of their research. By the late 1990s, an interest in surface had firmly taken hold in professional practices both as an organizational and cosmetic device. Rather than view these as separate devices, this chapter attempts to draw the organizational and the cosmetic together by defining the design framework of sheet logics. The term surface is replaced by sheet because it refers both to topology and substance, to geometry and material. Surface, on the other hand, refers to the exterior boundary of an object. It is defined as part of a whole. Sheets contain parts but can expand and respond to contingency without losing their organizational coherence. The following speculations argue for the use value of sheet logics in opening up disciplinary research that is at once organizational and cosmetic.

Figure 13.1a–d OMA, *Jussieu-Two Libraries* (competition entry), Paris, France, 1992. Program is distributed using the logic of sheets and is distributed along a continuous ramping floor plate. The edge of the floor plate is provisional. What matters is the sequence of spaces and events that unroll along it rather than its boundary edges

----

Figure 13.2 OMA, *Très Grande Bibliothèque* (competition entry), Paris, France, 1989. Program is distributed using the logic of solids. Repetitive floors of stacks define a rectangular block in which figural voids float

Sheets avoid the solid logics typically associated with descriptions of mass. Unlike surfaces, sheets need not conform to the organizational constraints of a geometric solid. Solid logics align spatial boundaries with geometric boundaries and space is conceived as mass or as its absence. Figure/ground relationships emerge from solid logics. Sheets distribute events across a field rather than adjacent to or across a threshold (Figures 13.1–13.2).

Sheet logics unseat figure/ground as the chief organizing principle of planning and massing strategies. Figuration emerges across a field and at scales both small and large. Figure/figure or ground/ground relationships are possible (Figure 13.3).

Figure 13.3 Zaha Hadid Architects, *Dubai Opera House*, Dubai, UAE, 2006. Sheet logics are applied to building massing and landscape, producing a figure/figure relationship

The fundamental design concerns of massing are part of early sheet production rather than emerging from the conventions of material assembly. The formal questions associated with massing using sheet logics require novel approaches. This is necessary because architectural tropes developed for solids provide insufficient solutions to questions of how a sheet meets the ground (formerly a question of figure/ground) or how a sheet meets the sky (now a question of silhouette.) Other questions of sheet description at apertures, at changes in orientation or at changes in material are also left unanswered by convention. Distributions of program and enclosure require new scrutiny as these are not necessarily defined by the sheet logic (Figures 13.4–13.5).

Figure 13.4 SANAA, *Rolex Learning Center,* Lausanne, Switzerland, 2010. Here the sheets repeatedly depart from the ground plane to define space beneath the building volume and alter the silhouette drawn by the roof plane

Figure 13.5 Herzog & de Meuron, Prada store *Aoyama* (*Epicenter*), Tokyo, Japan, 2003. The base of this crystalline solid remains planar and the adjacent, sloped ground plane is manipulated to meet it

With sheets, there is no hierarchy of relationships between master plan, building organization, ornament, and detail. These formerly distinct phases of design dissolve. Building organization and ornament can be generated simultaneously. Ornament is freely distributed across the sheet as intensities within it (Figure 13.6).

Sheets are featureless, boundless and scale-less until operated upon and deployed. Sheets develop features as the result of careful geometric operations. Boundaries may emerge as the registration of internal relationships or may be drawn in response to context, program, or intent. Scale emerges from contextual and programmatic feedback when sheets are deployed in relation to site (Figure 13.7).

Figure 13.6 Frank O. Gehry and Associates, *Experience Music Project*, Seattle, USA, 2000. Sheet manipulations occur at the master plan scale to accommodate the arrival of rail transportation, connect the museum to the park, and respond to vehicular flows. Other modulations occur between building and ornament scale to define areas of pedestrian intensity

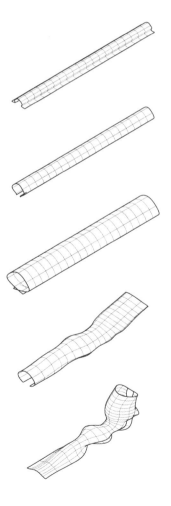

Figure 13.7 Greg Lynn FORM, *Ark of the World Museum and Visitors Center* proposal, Tarcoles River, Costa Rica, 2003. Sheets are rolled, bent and bundled to transform an axial canopy into a fully three-dimensional building volume

Minor operations have major formal repercussions. The ease with which operations produce sheet behavior allows the study of versions. Versions are related families of design work that allow the differences and similarities of each operation to be evaluated and built upon (Figure 13.1).

Sheets require tectonic inventiveness. Sheets require tectonic solutions that respond to local differences without compromising overall coherence. Cartesian systems produce abstract, ordered fields of geometry that downplay materiality in favor of spatial measure. Sheets provide form-active tectonic performance without being reduced to a single, idealized structural profile. This allows secondary systems to step in as sheets require them (Figure 13.8).

Figure 13.8 Gnuform, *Queens Museum of Art Expansion Strategy* (competition entry), New York City, USA, 2001. The project's suspended interior basin is supported by a secondary system of compressive struts and a cable suspension net. The depth of the secondary system increases as the span capacity of the basin decreases resulting in a rhythmic, cloud-like field of material above

Figure 13.9 Gehry Partners, LLP, *IAC Headquarters*, New York City, USA, 2007. The qualities of this mylar study model are revealed in the surface distension and translucency still present in its architectural translation. Gehry expertly confounds material expectations by mixing the qualities of architectural materials with those of modeling materials

Sheets confound material expectations. Sheets imbue surfaces with material qualities rarely associated with architectural production. Surfaces are rendered material rather than abstract. Sheets exhibit posture that results from its material behaviors. Sheets may drape, recline or billow depending on their weight and material properties.

Sheets encourage the co-mingling of the representational and the material. Sheets are the primary site of digital description. They operate as the backgrounds of drawings, are the principal topology of spline-based digital modelers and are the main product of numerically controlled machines. When sheets are produced physically, the actual material from which they are made becomes a medium for the dissemination of qualities produced through digital means. In the most captivating mixtures, the real and the virtual become so intertwined that one perceives a new, synthetic materiality. These synthetic materialities are immediately sensate and exhibit qualities not typically associated with architectural components or the materials from which they are conventionally made (Figure 13.10).

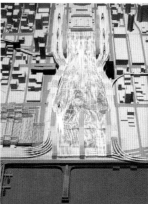

Figure 13.10 Gehry Partners, LLP, *IAC Headquarters*, New York City, USA, 2007. The building's exterior surfaces are articulated by information that is both representational and material. Its subdivisions correspond to those of the physical model as well as those required by its curtain wall assembly

Figure 13.11 Reiser + Umemoto, *West Side Convergence* (competition proposal), New York City, USA, 1999. Cutting operations work across scales to produce material, spatial and urban effects

Sheets move beyond the single surface problem. A sheet is not defined by its capacity to be unrolled onto a plane without tearing or overlap. This definition is overly narrow and ignores promising techniques from other disciplines. In garment construction, for example, complex three-dimensional figures are produced using two-dimensional surfaces embedded with particular qualities or material properties. In this case, the sheet is a textile with specific properties of stretch, transparency, weight, and thread directionality. In knitting, mathematical manipulations of stitches are called gauge and their character produces topological surfaces with unique graphic and material qualities.

Scissors can have their way with sheets. Other geometric sensibilities are readily accommodated by sheets. Sheets can be manipulated using cutting operations at a variety of scales. At fine scales, cutting alters sheet materiality using techniques like perforation. At medium scales, cutting manipulates profile and silhouette. At large scales, cutting produces particular sheet boundaries that relate to urban or local site conditions (Figure 13.11).

Figure 13.12 Future Systems, *Czech National Library* (competition entry), Prague, Czech Republic, 2007. The two-sided sheet used here is emphasized by the application of contrasting colors. The project's drawings and renderings are cut away to heighten the legibility of the sheet

Sheets are sided. Unlike solids that are conceptualized as of the same medium throughout, sheets have sides. This sidedness may be exploited to condition different atmospheres around the sheet. This is often choreographed by the application of graphic material (Figure 13.12).

Graphic material readily adheres to sheets. Cosmetic effects are possible when deploying sheet logics. Graphic material including color, texture, pattern and imagery is easily introduced to sheets using a variety of technologies. This graphic information may be directly printed or applied with films, ceramics or paints. Its application may also result from technologies such as laser cutting, thermoforming or CNC milling (Figure 13.13).

Sheets expand the expressive and performative capacity of seams. Rather than reluctantly accept seams as a byproduct of assembly constraints, sheets foreground the capacity of seams to perform at larger scales. Seams can radically alter the silhouette using techniques borrowed from garment construction. Seams can tightly tailor sheets with careful pattern-making techniques or expand them with sheet inserts. Seams therefore manage and distribute sheet surface area in highly particular and controlled ways (Figure 13.14).

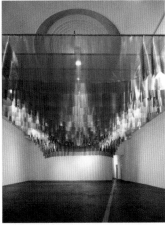

Figure 13.13 Enric Miralles/Benedetta Tagliabue, *Santa Caterina Market Renovation*, Barcelona, Spain, 2005
Figure 13.14 murmur, *Ultra Marine* (gallery installation), Los Angeles, USA, 2010

Part V
Matter Detail

Focusing on the detail allows for an architecture that emerges out of the connection. Engaging the relationship of pieces and their tectonic dialog establishes the premise of design and instigates the compositional intention of the collective. Part to part, and part to whole become the linguistic attitude that produces a genre of thinking. The syntax of the execution and collective envisioning of the localized system lead to architectures that are genetically engaged with their own way of making. The integrity of the system establishes the opportunity for the whole. The tectonics of the assembly and its system is emphasized as equal to material and process.

Axel Prichard-Schmitzberger
Phillip Anzalone and Stephanie Bayard, Atelier Architecture 64
John Enright and Margaret Griffin, Griffin Enright Architects
Dwayne Oyler and Jenny Wu, Oyler Wu Collaborative
Blair Satterfield and Marc Swackhamer, HouMinn

Chapter 14
Real Detail – Detail Reality
The dynamicism of fragmentation and "satisfization"

Axel Prichard-Schmitzberger

It is often that a quest for an optimum solution becomes a quest for "satisfization."

While the problem solving through optimization is motivating, it also remains challenging; commonly, architectural problems are of complex nature and require often intricate resolution scenarios, not able to be compacted within single-phrase questions or unique problem formulations. In response and very recently, the culminate results of many architectural experimentations percolate through an adequately contemporary social networking technique into the architectural practice. As a result, the explorations no longer remain hermetic, but instead the body of work becomes homogenized and evolves through a referencing and crowd-sourcing technique.[1] This new method of solution refinement relies heavily on the public distribution and input from a solicited population with similar interests. With this, the resources are becoming less diversified than specific, freeing up new areas of research and increasingly more detailed investigations; and it does so without an obligation for the architect to establish a built oeuvre. One critical aspect of this technique is the possibility of refining a problem itself; it enables the long-desired ability to review instances of failure and success extent in advance of the actual fabrication process.

The late 1990s brought process-oriented thinking to the representational area of architecture, which created a never before seen transparency in the display and making of architecture, whether a proposal is built or of a hypothetical nature. This transparency is not entirely new; in the early twentieth century, pioneering engineers such as Frei Otto and Konrad Wachsmann had already opened the discourse and offered procedural methodology in line with finite projects. At that time, the architectural experiment had to move beyond the traditional meaning of model, mock-up or graphic representation; architectural forms – often the result of a new shape-finding process with a more complex generative history than the modernist ideology had to offer – had neither representational equivalents nor built predecessors.

Without doubt, today's technology enables and even encourages the increased means of simulation and representation. This enlarged spectrum in return requires a refinement of the questionnaire and material criteria. New categories – or renewed definitions – of established building processes are called into action; the mock-up, for example, is revived as assessment typology, and qualifies as representation for material and geometric explorations. Particularly in the area of algorithmic design practice with a high level of complex element proliferation of differentiated components, where matter is treated frequently on behalf of performative aspects, the mock-up now serves as satisfying proof of success of such explorations (Figure 14.1).

Representational fragmentation: the mock-up

In the past, the mock-up successfully served as a bridging element in the traded representational means; as architectural historian George Bauer demonstrated, a surge in the use of mock-ups in the course of the late sixteenth and seventeenth centuries was partially due to the fact that patrons grew uncomfortable about architects' increased power to represent architecture.[2] Then the production of full-size mock-ups, which could easily be judged by lay people, was considered an assault on architects' monopoly over their representational skills.[3] In contrast, at the turn of the twentieth century, the mock-up became now a measure of the architects' ability to control builders, and of their overall increased authority of professional judgment. Egerton Swartwout, a prominent American architect at the turn of the twentieth century, reported that during the earlier period architects had had little power over the execution of details once drawings and templates had left their office. He noted that two decades later a clause in the standard form of the General Conditions required the contractor to provide full-size molds and, if rejected, to produce new ones until approved by the architect.

Now, at the beginning of the twenty-first century, the mock-up has once again regained significant value in the design and fabrication development process. However, it doesn't only perform as a contracting instance, it is itself a key element in performative and formal material explorations. It further seems to confirm the growing fragmentation process in the architectural design sequences; the increased honesty and necessary display of development in the creative process, augmented by highly precise tools is paired with enhanced representation techniques; clearly, intricate, generative and polymorphic designs may not be satisfyingly represented through conventional tools such as plan, section, elevation. The resulting, impacting increase of information in architectural presentation seems to stand in strong contrast to the acute narrow specifics of contemporary architectural investigation, and while the visual input seek conveyance of completion, physical proof concentrates on the fragmentary building aspect of mock-ups, prototypes and installations.

Completeness and representational fragmentation are, however, not to be seen as contradictory; the complex level of investigation and the pursuit of an optimized solution within such intricacy limits the perceptional clarification and in consequence the ability to evaluate success or failure of the exploration. Building is transformed into a building science, with the architect reclaiming the position of the controlling entity. Therefore, the staging of the experiment with limited sets of criteria, such as testing for specific performative and material optimization, becomes necessary; the experiment requires a hermetic state for the time being and the optimization turns respectively into a process of "satisfization." This specialized process of contained optimization necessitates, however, a reevaluation of the claimed 1:1 relationship of ideation to physical building.[4] Moreover, building itself becomes an oscillatory mergence of "satisfized" conditions in all its parts (Figure 14.2).

Figure 14.1 *Flockwall* installation, Coachella, 2009

Figure 14.2a–b Assembly of installation

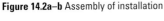

Relativity and oscillation: detailing as procedure

When Dutch architect Kas Oosterhuis calls for a single structure with respectively only one detail,[5] it seems to be following the contemporary trend of full parametric involvement. Expanding his statement, we can identify the building as an input–output machine, an industrial product, in complete exchange with its environment and its contributing and attributing factors. The building shapes itself under the acknowledgement of parametric conditions. Respectively, the building has no need for standardization; as a matter of fact, standardization would contradict the given premise of a responding and responsive building body. Instead, a building design requires a more appropriate reductionism of parts and emphasis on rule-based feedback between such simplified components. This simplification constitutes an aggregate conditioning, where the whole represents much more than the sum of the involved elements.

However, the desire to simplify the interaction of parts and elements in a building and in the design process can be viewed as reactionary to the increase of complexity. The urge for reduction is not novel and may not be entirely realistic. In the process of detailing we frequently encounter a complex interplay of intrinsically interacting elements; the term "detail" itself underwent in the past many changes in meaning and identity, and has obvious practicalities attached, so that such claims need to be carefully considered. According to Marco Frascari, details can be much more than units on the lower end in the building hierarchy.[6] The term "detail" includes more than representations of – either on a graphic or physical level – a producing environment of craftsmen and industry integrated in or adjacent to the realm of architecture. While the process of an oscillating design technique asks for a proliferation of instantiations routed from parametric components, we are relying on a concept that involves causality. In this case, we establish operating systems specified through properties, though none of the properties are properties of any component of that system but features of the system as a whole.[7] It is then, when following Hartmann's identification of different strata and categories, we allow the development of hierarchies within a fluid and oscillating structure.

Though none of the attributing elements are independent, a different range of attributory or influencing factors is relevant for each stratum and category. This relationship reveals the intermingling of recurrent categories and their coherence. Furthermore, it suggests a deep interpenetration of the strata, hence the use of the term oscillation.[8] Allowing this oscillation to take place within the architectural design process, the detail once again is redefined in its meaning – to view it as mere connecting device is as unsatisfying as it is inappropriate; it negates its role in the material development of a project; the detail and the procedural aspects of detailing are highly interlinked with matter, and it necessitates that this matter, materiality and design permeate each other in a constant feedback, creating a percolated design process with constant refinement.

Foregrounding the fragment: the reality of detailing

Through the introduction of material-emulating digital software applications we seem to acknowledge a higher matter consciousness; however, the high level of resolution and tight connection to the field of fabrication create a dilemma in the establishment of continuous oscillation; true 4D applicability, involving an economy of assembly routed in the tradition of making, happens to frequently challenge the parametric, adaptive detailing process. Apparently, design engineering pioneers Wachsmann and Otto dealt with related conflicts in their time; they presented detail solutions that all follow a very clear material and economic consciousness, yet the building as a whole is often pushed back into the background, frequently not even articulated. Wachsmann's detail solutions deliver a high material sensitivity and attempt to optimize production and effectiveness. Form–matter correspondence is brought to the foreground and is put in close relationship to workmanship and professional trades (Figure 14.3).[9]

Otto depends frequently on the physical model in his pursuit of empirical and generative form-finding methods. He is therefore often confined to a top-down strategy and needs to adopt the expression of the detail at a late stage in the form-finding process. In his 1972 essay on tent roofs, he regrets the necessity to simplify details in the lack of adequate representational methods but also recognizes the future potential of automated production of building documentation and model building refinement.[10] A conditional breakthrough can be seen in the details of a temporary grid-shell structure in Mannheim, Germany, an indication of his quest for reduction: a single bolt-connection solution serves as the main, typical detail for this temporary structure with a free span of over 180 feet. Ultimately, oscillating procedures appear paramount in the material-oriented practice; even self-organizing principles can only be successful if the feedback conditions are fully realized in the material realm; detailing becomes integral to the generation of formations in architecture; fragmentation and "satisfization" are as a result again subservient to the clarification and transparency of sought investigations (Figure 14.4).

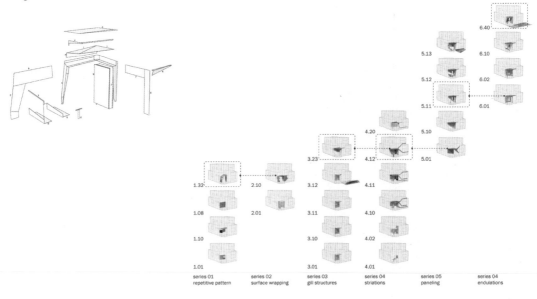

Figure 14.3 *BEC Canopy*, West Hollywood, derivative design procedure, reflecting in its built state the acknowledgement of a hierarchy of parts with emphasis on trade-oriented detailing

Figure 14.4a–b Frei Otto, *Multihalle*, Mannheim, 1975, detail

Realized tessellation: agglomerate detailing

The *Flockwall* project represents a portion of my research from the past five years in the area of digitally enhanced fabrication, often in collaboration with various colleagues at California State Polytechnic University, Pomona. It offered a particular opportunity for an investigation of the economy in design and detail development; as this prototype constitutes a 1:1 built object, it had to compensate for physical, time and budgetary constraints, therefore design criteria were conservatively narrow. Contrary to contemporary design proposals, where diverse generative processes are involved in the articulation of geometry and matter synchronization – a morphogenesis that emulates natural, evolutionary development, often paralleled with an algorithmic input companion – this project positions itself as a hybrid between a cellular, agglomerative method and the largely materially inconsiderate top-down design methods employed in common building practice (Figure 14.5).

Figure 14.5 *Flockwall* installation, Coachella, 2009

The limitation of investigative criteria is not contradictory to the complex material characteristics that are embedded in the logic of geometric behavior and assembly sequences and cumulatively insist on emphasizing the intrinsic performance of a suggested and tested system. Moreover, the compaction of benchmarks allows a more specific analysis of success and failure of a tested system; additionally, the constraining envelope reveals opportunities to invest into optimizing the assembly logic and the apparent material, tectonic, and geometric synthesis. While polymorphic systems are desired, the reality of such is frequently exposed to a dilemma between computational analysis, optimizing progression and a manually driven component fabrication, dictating a regression of assembly techniques (Figure 14.6).

The project is the result of a collaboration between Michael Fox, myself and students at California State Polytechnic University, conducted within two paralleled ten-week elective courses for graduate and undergraduate students. The interactive swarm-behavior installation developed by Michael Fox and students required a supportive structure that enabled the suspension and operation of illuminated interactive agents; the nature of the projected installation also asked the support structure to retreat on a material level; the resulting

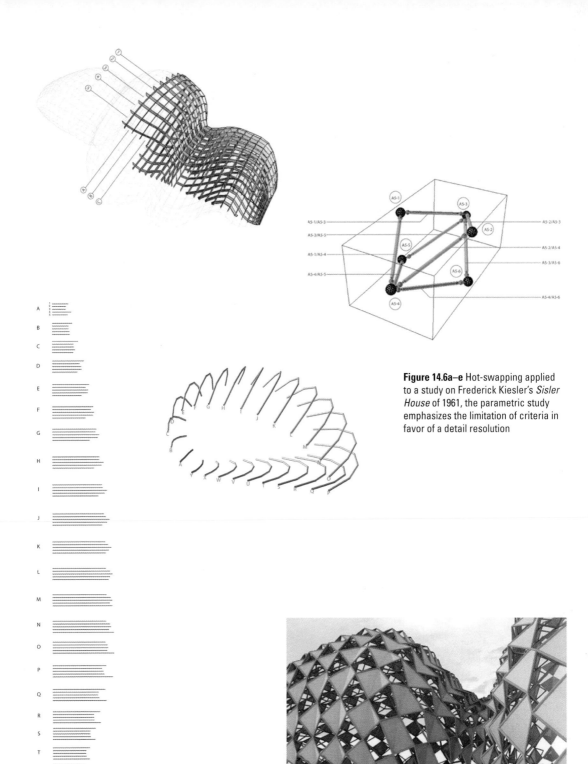

Figure 14.6a–e Hot-swapping applied to a study on Frederick Kiesler's *Sisler House* of 1961, the parametric study emphasizes the limitation of criteria in favor of a detail resolution

Figure 14.7 Assembly of the installation, layout of different parts

accessible shell-like structure became the shape of reference for the beginning investigation of hot-swapping tessellation techniques and material-oriented system speculations (Figure 14.7).

Dome-shape geometries, commonly identified as grid-shells, evoke a particular interest, as they constitute, on one hand, a tectonic optimization through form-finding and, on the other, exhibit non-standardizable nodal connections or forming methods instigated by the double-curved conditioning of the shape. The general shape was exposed to hot-swapping, which in architecture is a means of transgressing from linear, design development with singular, individual input and feedback scenarios, into one that is populated by a multiplicity of instant or even simultaneous solutions and feedbacks; the outcome is the result of a distributed design procedure, taking advantage of the nature of crowd-sourcing systems. This model engages in an economy of selection, with a high and fast throughput of potential, detailed solutions. On a practical level it allows, on one hand, the quick development of a base architecture with enough flexibility and accuracy for future manipulation and, on the other, a fluid oscillation between construction methods until a late stage of design and production (Figure 14.8).

Initial studies of the tessellated shell showed that parameterization of the detail would require an adjustable nodal joint, which in consequence would indicate a complex sequence of interacting and interlocking custom elements; subsequently, this stipulates a hierarchy of parts in the assembly, a typical complexity and necessity in the common and also current architectural investigation. While the traditional understanding of detailing is that of some kind of joint, it itself is frequently an assembly, a nested condition within a series of categorized instances of building and fabrication. With the understanding of a hierarchical nesting, the development shifted towards reductionism and respectively optimization of parameters, speculating that the reduction of elements within a mechanism leads to higher flexibility of the parts and to a better material economy. The studies by Wolfram Graubner on the comparative differences between vernacular wood-joinery in medieval Europe and Japan served as predecessor to this investigation.[11] Seemingly unrelated to the issue of complex geometry and tessellated proliferation of tectonically operating matter, the juxtaposition reveals an applied methodology of material reductionism, taking advantage of physical properties of the material – in his case study, wood – itself. In consequence, our detailing process became a material process, projecting an ideal adoption of the material properties and the assembly method. This subsumes material treatment and manufacturing (Figures 14.9–14.10).

The development commended the shift from a nodal joint to a shear joint, taking full advantage of the material – metal – and its production process. Metal possesses high tensile strength; strategically relocating the active joint to the sides that act in compression and doubling up the cross-section, transforms the detail into

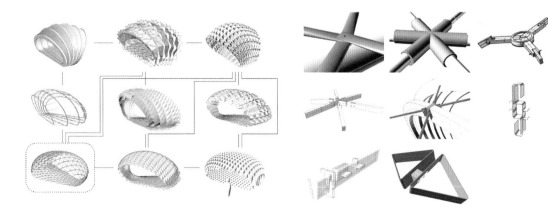

Figure 14.8 Diagram of hot-swapping tessellation methods (samples) for the initial shell system

Figure 14.9a–h Various detail solutions employing a nodal connection and a hierarchy of elements

a bundled connection, which increases the compression strength in turn. The configuration now increased the capacity to act as parametric detail with minimal material diversity; the connections were resolved within the material constraints and taking advantage of a traditional water-jet sheet-cutting method, the current resolution allowed all parts to be taken from the same material sheets, instead of adding typical bolt connections, all parts were cut from the same sheet, maximizing the material economy while minimizing the labor through reduction of manufacturing parties and components. Through sizing and positioning slits for a wedging system and through adjusting the length of the bent strips the system received its necessary parametric variation in one detailing technique (Figures 14.11–14.13).

Following the premise of "one building – one detail," a call for parameterized intelligent systems that can be disseminated over a whole system, our "satisfization" criteria were extended to one building – one detail – one material. The structure, a result of over 4000 different pieces, which form all discrete triangulated

Figure 14.10 Exploded diagram of the bolt-less parametric connection, detail mock-up in steel of one unit

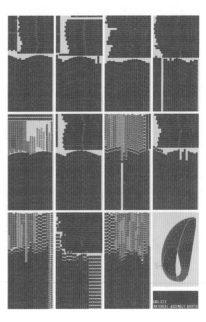

Figure 14.11 Full digital shell-model with all elements in place

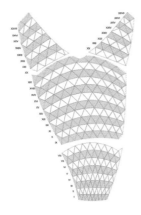

Figure 14.12 Cut sheets for fabrication

Figure 14.13 Unrolled system template

aggregates, which only consist of eight pieces, of which four are different, was erected in two weeks of manual labor. The labor intensity is in contrast to the simplicity of the detail solution. From a detail and material aspect, though, the project indicates that with a selective set of rules a direct link between structure, material and detail can be established to the built environment as a whole. While the installation represents a fragmentary aspect of architectural design, it also moves beyond the form-oriented material sensations; the applied logic, derived from assembly method, material and generative method itself, allows the project and detailing, respectively, to be viewed outside the typical context of the detail as mere connecting device (Figure 14.14).

Figure 14.14 *Flockwall* installation at night, detail close-up

Notes

1   The term "crowd-sourcing" was coined in 2006 by Jeff Howe and refers to a refined diversification and outsourcing practice involving the public, accessible via the internet. Jeff Howe, "The Rise of Crowd-sourcing", *Wired*, issue 14.06 (2006).

2   Architectural historian George Bauer reports on a full-size complete mock-up of the Arc de Triomphe requested by Napoleon, and about Hitler's requests to build mock-ups of large portions of Albert Speer's projects. See George Bauer, "Arguing Authority in Late Renaissance Architecture," *Art History*, 19(3) (September 1996): 428–433.

3   Ibid., p. 424.

4   The Platonic 1:1 ratio of ideation to physical manifestation was criticized by Bernard Cache and Patrick Beaucé, in their article, "Towards a Non-Standard Mode of Production," *Objectile: Fast Wood: A Brouillon Project* (New York: Springer, 2006), p. 30.

5   According to Kas Oosterhuis: "Suppose the building body knows only one detail. In order to intelligently deal with a variety of situations, that single detail must be parametric" (Kas Oosterhuis, *Hyperbodies: Towards an E-motive Architecture*, Basel: Birkhäuser, 2003, p. 27).

6   According to Marco Frascari: "Details are much more than subordinate elements; they can be regarded as the minimal unit of signification in the architectural production of meanings" (Marco Frascari, "The Tell-the-Tale Detail", *VIA* 7 (1984): 23–37).

7   Werkmeister specifies in his commentary work on Nicolai Hartmann's "Vom Aufbau der Realen Welt (*Construction of the Real World*)", that recurrence is essential to consciousness and Being; Causal sequences are part of the Law of modification, which assumes a continuation of dependencies through various realms. He states:

> Because of the recurrence, every higher category is, as far as content is concerned, composed of a manifoldness of lower categories but is not merely the sum of them. The higher category is always something more. It contains a categorical novum that is specific for the higher stratum and relative to which lower categories are variously modified.
>
> (William H. Werkmeister, *Nicolai Hartmann's New Ontology*, Tallahassee, FL: Florida State University Press, 1990, pp. 60–62)

8   Dirk Baecker specifies:

> Das bedeutet jedoch, vom Teil, vom Element und von der Operation immer so zu reden, dass die andere Seite der Oszillation, das Ganze, die Relation und die Schliessung mitgeführt werden, obwohl sie, wenn sie bezeichnet werden, wieder nur an einem Teil, einem Element, einer Operation zu erkennen sind. [It therefore means, that when talking about the Part, the Element and the Operation, the other side of the oscillation – relation and the closure are brought along, though they are only recognized, if determined, through a part, an element and an operation.]
>
> (Dirk Bäcker, *Wozu Systeme?*, Bonn: Kadmos Kulturverlag, 2002, p. 8)

9   Wachsmann states:

> Da es eine der grossen Tugenden der Industrialisierung ist, nur Spitzenleistungen von immer gleicher Qualität zu produzieren, die zweckmässigsten Materialien in der bestmöglichen Form und dem höchsten Leistungsstand in der ökonomischsten Weise den berechtigten Ansprüchen aller Menschen gleichermassen nutzbar zu machen, wird diese nur in einem System umfassendster Ordnung und Standardisierung wirksam sein. [It is one of the highest aspirations of the industrialization to produce consistently at the level of highest quality to provide the most appropriate materials in the best possible form at the highest performance with the highest economy to satisfy the justified claims of mankind; therefore it can only be effective within a system of complete order and standardization.]
>
> (Konrad Wachsmann, *Wendepunkt im Bauen* [Turning Point in Building], Stuttgart: Deutsche Verlagsanstalt, 1989, p. 10)

10   Frei Otto, "Das Zeltdach" [the Tent-Roof], in *Schriften und Reden* [Papers and Talks] (Braunschweig/ Wiesbaden: Friedrich Vieweg & Sohn Verlagsgesellschaft, 1984), p. 99ff.

11   Wolfram Graubner, *Gegenüberstellung Europäischer und japanischer Holzverbindungen*, (Munich: DVA, 1994), pp. 47–167.

Chapter 15
Detailing Articulation

Phillip Anzalone and Stephanie Bayard
Atelier Architecture 64

Conceptual framework

The turn of the century saw the emergence of a new way of thinking about digital production that one decade later is ready for a change. Developments in techniques and discourse on digital design from the late 1990s reaching to the current date centered on a number of concepts and methodologies borrowed from associated fields such as philosophy, mathematics and biology, and then translated and transformed into architectural ideas that inform the academic and professional practice of the production of the built environment. With this translation comes a new language that must engage not only the avant-garde of architectural theory and experimentation, but also the rich tradition of the academy and practice that provides the basis for cultural and practical production. In this chapter, we seek to explore two tendencies involved in the transition from digital design to digital production in the lens of the application of research into built projects and materiality: the concept of continuity and the method of operative uniformity.

One of the initial concepts intertwined with digital design was that of continuity, developed from philosophical reflections on calculus as well as the new capabilities of computer software to readily develop curvature in three dimensions. Continuity in form engages the immediate problem of the boundary condition, which has plagued digital projects with issues of where and how to terminate systems or projects (Figure 15.1). What began as a celebration of potentials in computational geometry has encountered the difficulties that

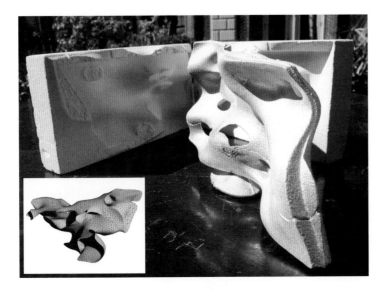

Figure 15.1 Continuous form

abstraction has always dealt with in resolving materiality. The single form of the computer model must engage the reality of building components, shipping sizes, material form availability, joinery and the host of discrete component details.

The new abilities of the computer when developed into physical reality took on an operative language: folding, sectioning, tessellating, and other operations became form generators. This vocabulary was considered a direct physical extension of the computational operations embedded in the software and simulation techniques. New methods of constructing were developed to engage this process, resulting in novel forms and assemblies. However, the relentless uniformity of the operative technique has become normative in that a construction (be it building, pavilion, installation or model) often relies on one sole operative assembly type, defeating the material purpose of detailing and variety (Figure 15.2).

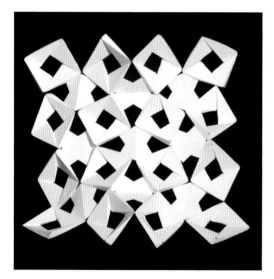

Figure 15.3 Sliced brick

Figure 15.2 Operative technique

We propose that our work approaches a detailed articulation as a critique of some of the normative principles in digital design and fabrication that fall short when resolved into material reality. Our interest in the exploration of new material types and production methods requires us to engage the difficulty of resolving what has become a standard operating procedure, with the requirements of clients, site, structural integrity, manufacturing, cost, and so on; in other words, the reality of physical construction (Figure 15.3). Only through embracing the potentials of materiality at full-scale can we develop a new theory of digitally based design and production.

The work of Atelier Architecture 64 (aa64) focuses on a constructed study of architectural design linked to advanced material and assembly research, put into practice in the academic environment as well as the professional realm. The firm's intention is to expand the theoretical capabilities of our design work by participating in the construction using our expertise in research, advanced computation, digital fabrication and complex assembly procedures. To realize these goals, aa64 is intricately involved in the physical production of work ranging from the scope of complex components to an entire assembly or installation. The projects incorporate innovative materials, fabrication processes, and construction techniques allowing for experimentation with theoretical and applied building components and systems. The design processes and designs themselves are driven by applying experimental methods of fabrication and assembly to traditional building materials and systems. This exploration is then used as a pedagogical tool to teach abstract concepts of performative detailing to our students at Columbia University and Pratt Institute, as we believe that the act of constructing is an excellent means of teaching.

This chapter explores the connection between computational design techniques and craft-based production by examining the material aspect of two recent projects as a critique of continuity and operative uniformity. Processes associated with the linear progression from digital design to physical production including parametric exploration, performative design, solid modeling, computer-numerically controlled (CNC) fabrication, and material studies, are used to generate a full-scale prototype and constructions as part of the research development. The craft of understanding and controlling a material has traditionally been reserved as an act of individual expression designated but not limited to the design process. The near ubiquity of computer-aided design programs and three-dimensional simulations have enabled the designers to engage their creations in totality; however, dependence on these tools has simultaneously produced a synthetic environment where gravity, scale and sequence are irrelevant. While liberating the process of design, these seemingly realistic simulations have gradually begun to erode the physicality of craft. Using contemporary applications of CNC and parametric techniques, aa64 has endeavored to activate the potential of the designer to become more involved in the process of fabrication, while simultaneously bridging the growing rift between the designer and craftsman. This unification of design and construction is the overarching intent that frames the conceptual exploration of this collaborative.

The work has a shared objective: the pedagogical and tectonic investigation of structural and design possibilities seeking to explore the relationship between contemporary methods of architectural construction and craft, a term evocative of Ruskinian notions of tradition as well as the unification of aesthetics and fabrication. By iteratively exploring the parameters of material properties, ornamentation, and assembly details and function, the work engages simultaneously the sensorial and the cerebral through optical, corporeal and conceptual qualities, revealing the possibilities inherent in the juxtaposition of the conventional and the contemporary. The projects are used as a means to explore new ways of integrating engineering into architecture and design; a dynamic dialog between traditional and innovative methods of construction and material use, as well as an alternative mode of professional creativity. Research into materiality, assembly, expression, and other modes of constructive interaction plays a central role in how one develops architectural detail, in the methods of manufacture, environmental performance, connection of the elements, and a host of other parameters that now carry as much importance in the digital process as in "traditional" methods of architecture. One goal is exploring how to use material as a means for understanding the new tools and the allied role in architecture of working with non-computational methods of design, fabrication, and assembly. The desire to build, exploring craft and material through digital and analog methods, is a prime mover for architects and students alike, assuring an exciting environment for exploration and thought.

Structured materiality

In the project *Framing Space*, we sought to question the future of material and fabrication methods emerging from traditional methods of design and construction of wall systems. The perceived continuity of a wall belies a wide range of porosity; from obvious transparencies such as glazing to the intricate hidden pathways that air and water may migrate through in a high-performance curtain wall system. The fact is, a wall is not continuous, but is a highly articulated surface composed of various elements in complex relationships acting individually and in concert simultaneously. We sought to reveal this through the detailing of the structural and panel systems, the relationships between elements and the reference to established modes of construction while utilizing new materials and methods of fabrication.

Framing Space consists of two repetitive structural components: stainless steel nodes and extruded aluminum struts, both of which vary in configuration or length according to their position in the system, combining parametric computer modeling, intelligently programmed analytic and algorithmic software

Figure 15.4 Node
Figure 15.5 *Framing Space* installation

Figure 15.6 Panels

processing, and a patented fabrication and assembly method (Figures 15.4 – 15.5). The use of multiple materials engages the notion of articulating structure through discrete elements programmed into the parametric model as it directly effects fabrication as well as design. The materials are cut with simple CNC machinery such as a two-axis laser cutter, and assembled through methods that can be implemented with semi-skilled labor. The design integrates spanning panels of varying materials: translucent foamed aluminum, composite polycarbonate, shaped high-density polyurethane foam, and incised stainless steel finished sheet (Figure 15.6). The type and placement of the panels are based on the concept of rethinking the fabrication and detailing of the materials as contemporary versions of traditional pre-computational wall system components (siding, glazing, insulation and cladding).

Theoretical and historic trends and implications of this exploration, as it involves wall systems that become lighter, utilize CAD/CAM and CNC manufacturing techniques and develop into complex forms. Notions of lightness and translucency apparent in the cladding materials are made possible by the confluence of novel design processes and traditional material use. The respective geometry and proportions of the three wall systems trace the evolution of building construction from the stability and modular scale of a brick masonry wall to the integrity of infill construction, ultimately terminating with the paradoxical ethereality and monumentality inherent in most modern-day curtain wall systems. This is reflected in the material choices where forces flow through the system in rigid and fluid materials. The installation explores this lineage of building practices while simultaneously challenging traditional characteristics of all three standard construction

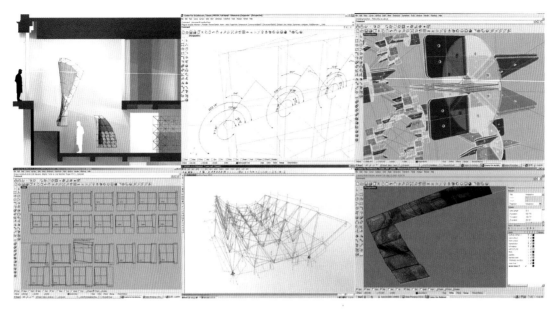

Figure 15.7a–f CNC shots

types through translucency, digital fabrication and programmatic application. The *Framing Space* installation incorporates a number of innovative materials, fabrication processes, and construction techniques that allowed experimentation into theoretical and applied building components and systems. The design process and design itself were driven by the concept of applying innovative methods of fabrication and assembly to traditional building materials. This exploration also revealed abstract concepts of performative detailing as the act of constructing is an excellent means of exploring articulation (Figure 15.7).

One type of panel used in *Framing Space* is made of 0.5" foamed aluminum, a material condition achieved when gas is injected into molten aluminum, creating open or closed cells similar to other foams. The process creates a lightweight and rigid three-dimensional substructure that is used to support thin-shelled constructions and extrusions. In this installation we are exploring the use of foamed aluminum as a critique and reinterpretation of traditional aluminum siding, often a ubiquitous application of aluminum in domestic building construction that superficially embraces the material for its aesthetic value and resistance. Aluminum siding is traditionally homogeneous, continuous and operative (i.e. raised, folded, shingled, etc.) in its application. Rather than simply cladding the structure, we are using the rigidity of the aluminum to provide external bracing to the system, taking advantage of the structural qualities and ductility to act as a diaphragm. Given that the foamed aluminum panels could not be bent or mitered, they were attached at two diagonally opposing edges, allowing for a scale-like overlap and an exposed edge condition, while triangulating the rectilinear units (Figures 15.8–15.9).

Typically a decorative material, in this installation, we are exploring the structural potential of stainless steel as a self-supporting panel system. Traditionally rigid panels would need to be triangularly folded at a specific angle in order to span the warped rectilinear surface of a differential space-truss. Through the use of precisely executed cuts, however, manipulations of the truss masterfully exploit the ductility of steel, resulting in the non-coplanar aggregation of flat panels (Figures 15.10–15.11).

Figure 15.8 Transparent foam
Figure 15.9 Foamed aluminum close-up

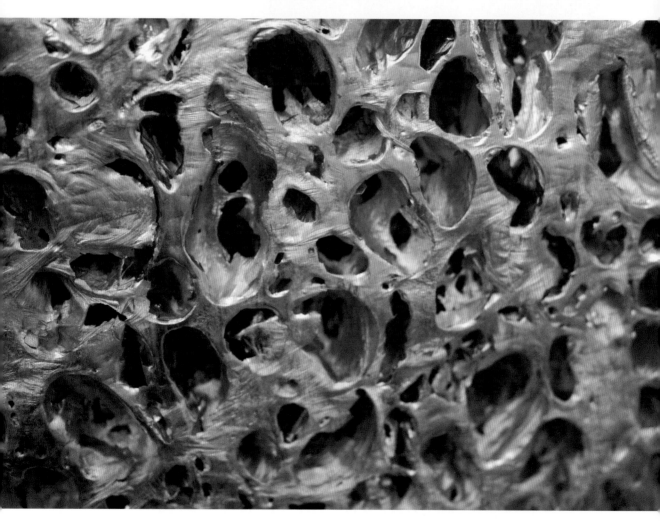

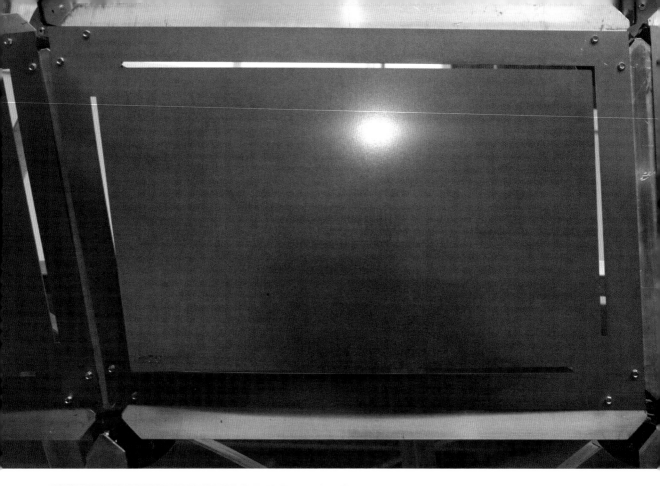

Figure 15.10 Sliced metal, front
Figure 15.11 Sliced metal, side

Deco-performative hybrid materials

The exploration of deco-performative hybrid materials, where the form is not based on strictly aesthetic or functional principles, but by the nature of the properties of the structure as well as the method in architectural use, shows how the detailing of components takes on a polyvalent expression. Discrete detailing embraces ideas about the fact that materials are more interesting when non-continuous (such as reinforced concrete or foamed aluminum) and can be more programmatically performative through material geometries and properties combined. Articulated continuity of historic precedent or the continuity of the matrix within a material as well as the systemic continuity of parametric and material based intelligence in design develops the aesthetic as well as the functional (Figure 15.12).

A research direction during the *Framing Space* project involved self-reinforcing high-density polyurethane foam, allowing the simultaneous expression of its structural properties as well as the potential for decorative application, merging the two aspects into one material. The panels were flip-milled to create a rigid double curved surface with a connection detail incorporated into the milling process at the reinforced "structural" rear face. The front of the panels were CNC milled with a decorative pattern, while material was removed from the back of the panels in a process similar to coffering to reduce mass and provide rigidity. Both patterns can be controlled by finite element analysis and CNC production methods to be completely customizable according to site conditions and design intent, transforming the isotropic nature of the raw material (Figure 15.13).

Precedent studies of the idea of a material process that is simultaneously performative and decorative on multiple scales include leading a research team in the production of an installation called *Amphorae* at the GSAPP. *Amphorae* block units were made from Ductal®, an innovative concrete product engineered by Lafarge. Ductal® is a revolutionary ultra-high-performance engineered concrete that possesses a unique combination of superior properties, including strength, ductility, durability and enhanced aesthetics. The *Amphorae* blocks are as much a process as they are a material. A huge amount of the production effort was put into the fabrication of the molds that the concrete was poured into. The *Amphorae* blocks or units are made entirely of concrete and small organic fibers, not traditional steel reinforcement. This allowed for the thinness of the panels, the smoothness of the surface, and a simultaneously structural and aesthetic curvature. As a means to construct the molds required for casting concrete, CNC-milled light-weight medium-density fiberboard (MDF) was shaped to create the desired forms. Pieces of MDF were coated with polyurethane and finished to be used as both a positive and a negative offset, where urethane rubber was poured between to create a flexible and reusable mold.

Figure 15.12 Foamed aluminum connection

Figure 15.13a–b High density foam, front and back

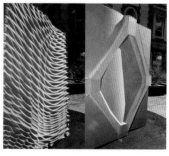

Figure 15.14 *Amphorae* spanning
Figure 15.15 Reinforcing hairs

Once the rubber was set, the MDF positive was removed, producing the mold required to create the concrete casts (Figures 15.14–15.15).

The *Fabre Library* project, designed and constructed by aa64 in France, used the three-axis router to prototype and fabricate a set of high-density foam positives from which tin-silicone molds were made. The molds were used to cast polycarbonate panels with embedded hardware to engage the supporting structure. Conceiving of the wall as kind of field, interrupted and inflected by the boxed shelves, a series of patterns were modeled. We used a script to output a dense parallel array of curves whose control points, while coinciding with a field grid of vector arrows, could be inflected manually or automatically by special attractive/repulsive points and lines. The resultant lines were transformed through another script to translate alternating control points in the curve array producing sinusoidal curves along the full curve. A further finer grain of interference emerged when these lines were used as tool paths on the three-axis router with a round end-mill. The final result was an abundantly varied system of pattern production, which would cover the panels with unique marks. By drawing the path which the three-axis router was to carve, we leveraged the precision and fidelity of the router while claiming it as kind of medium or drawing machine that could produce effects beyond the mere reproduction of, for example, a NURBS surface. This substantially reduced the mill time as well. Finally, by leveraging the trace of the tool to produce the pattern, the geometry of the tool itself became a generator of the pattern. This is opposed to the norm of having the three-axis router erase its own artifacts. This concept of the tool as the extension of the hand returns to the idea of craft as it involves new fabrication processes (Figure 15.16).

As small test molds were milled, various mold and casting materials were tried, we noted the need for both simulation of the milling and full material tests using different resins and tints. The optical performance of the cast resin was, *a priori*, placed beyond the power of our digital tools to simulate. Only material tests would suffice. As we refined the design, we found that the cost of producing 21 unique panels, either by directly carving acrylic panels or casting, would be prohibitive. In addition, the cost of shipping 21 finished panels further compounded the problem. A resolution was reached by producing a reduced set of molds that, through repetition and rotation could still produce the field or, at least, a close approximation. Thus, we were able to reduce the set of 21 panels to a set of four molds. This allowed us to have a simultaneous merging of the decorative pattern in its continuity of surface effect across the wall system with the discontinuity of the fabrication and design process in the ability to cast panels of a discrete size for assembly. The nature of casting also compelled us to face the need for repetition, looking for a solution that satisfied both desires of economy and variety. Casting was able to do things that the three-axis router could not. Casting the negative of our milled panel revealed a surface that is practically impossible for the mill to make on its own – end-mills simply will not fit into such small, nearly asymptotic, spaces between curved volumes. More generally, the means of technical reproduction can have a dialog with each other: their combinations can produce unexpected efficiencies and effects. The medium of casting was affected by addressing the problem of the pattern through iterations of computation and simulation. In addition, we milled armatures to hold the panel attachment hardware at the correct depth and location. The armatures, unique for each formwork, were built from the full wall digital model in order to assure a high degree of precision between the bolt, resin panels and the metal structure (Figure 15.17).

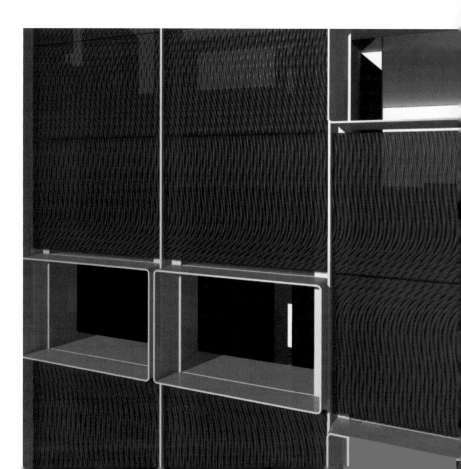

Figure 15.16 *Fabre Library* project render

Figure 15.17a–j *Fabre Library* project molds

The future

With our projects we are looking for a radically new concept of architectural research and design. Recent conventional ideology regards digitally based design as a market commodity produced en masse and therefore as semi-disposable. Currently this outdated dogma is being challenged by a more humanized approach to design. Ultimately the designers would collaborate with builders at every phase from conception to construction in the synthesis of a new environment. Originally the construction of full-scale mock-ups and prototypes had been reserved for only the most advanced projects dealing with the design of connection details and wall sections. With the focus on design and construction of full-scale prototypes and operational assemblies, this full-scale production of experiments has dramatically altered the landscape of design potentials by discovering new means of material expression through digitally based detailing.

The current study of Atelier Architecture 64 looks to further decompose the concepts of continuity and therefore requires operative articulation that engages increased performative detailing. We are currently researching a tensegrity structure incorporating wood as a panel system. Tensegrity takes the articulation of force exhibited in a space-truss structure to further limits by disengaging the tension and compression forces into separate elements. This forces the element to closely engage the material properties in order to achieve equilibrium between the continuous tensile element and the discontinuous compression elements. The play between system and part is further elaborated and yet integrated in the tensegrity systems that we have been designing. The interest in the use of wood stems from its inherent unpredictability, discrete yet continuous nature at the cellular level, and the close connection between material composition and performative variation (Figure 15.18).

We have found that there is a productive middle ground in the hybridization of different fabrication techniques, mixing old and new crafts with normative and non-normative materials and material geometries. Another recent area of exploration is in CNC shot-peening. Shot-peening is an ancient process of mechanically impacting materials to create decorative effects. Through the use of CNC shot-peening equipment, and the concept of strategically laser-cutting metal places, we can begin to control the curvature resulting from the expansion of the surface of the peened material. This forms a structural rigidity through a double curvature while simultaneously giving the material a decorative finish and a complex and non-deterministic global form. The blurring of the functional and the aesthetic allows us to develop detailing which articulates the performative, historic and cultural power of the use of metal in building systems (Figures 15.19–15.20).

The work presented constitutes an exploration through a form of experimentation that is simultaneously research and practice; we feel that theory and application cannot happen independently in constructed work without a disjunction in pedagogical consistency. However, the path along both parallel roads in architectural concept and practice is neither continuous nor mono-operative in its trajectory. We see our work not as a scientific research program, but as a series of demonstrative creations that attempt in a variety of ways to address performative and aesthetic criteria embedded in the context of reality. Just as Foucault's Pendulum does not prove, but demonstrates the rotation of the earth, our work does not seek to definitively solve all problems as in an optimization search, but rather to explore avenues and provide the basis for further architectural expeditions.

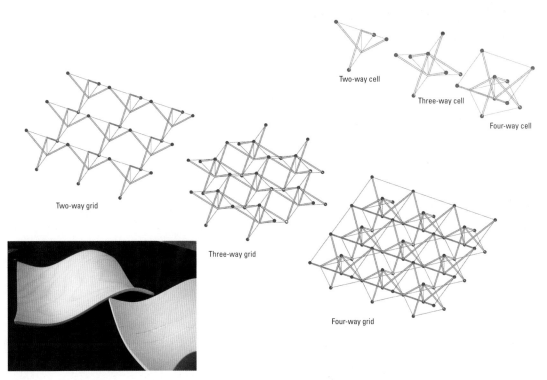

Figure 15.18a–c Tensegrity grid variations

Figure 15.19 Shot-peening, close-up
Figure 15.20a–l Shot-peening, array

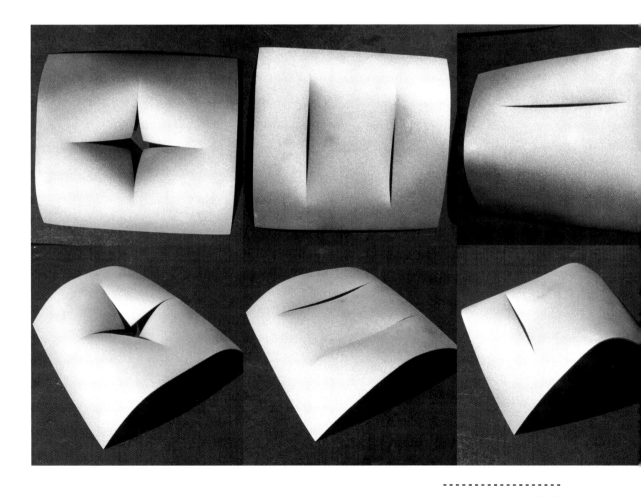

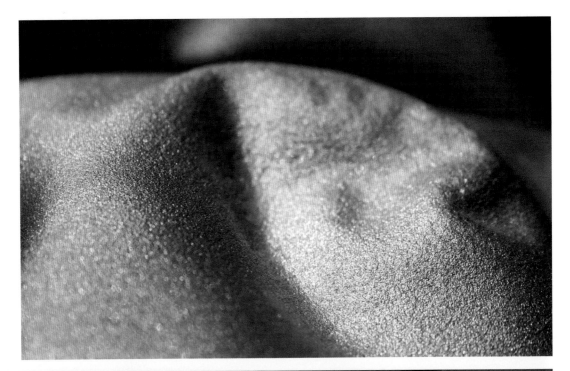

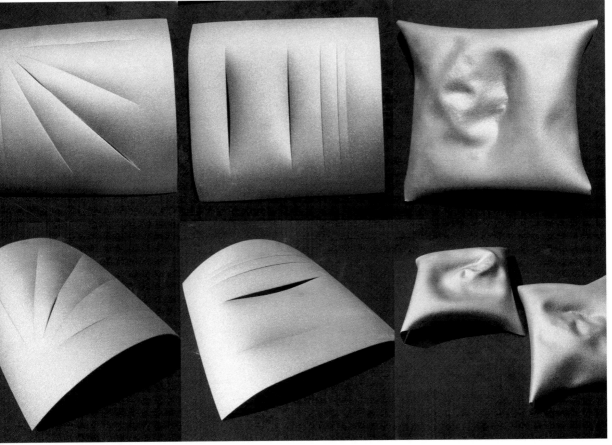

Chapter 16
Lightness

John Enright and Margaret Griffin
Griffin Enright Architects

The idea that material can be at the forefront of an architectural project is an interesting proposition and one that is not always the case within the process of design. How can one begin with material before one has set the conceptual terms of an architectural proposition? More often, materiality is born from the larger parameters of an architectural idea, and gradually material and its effects are introduced, tested, and options considered. This somewhat traditional and linear approach, from the general to the specific, or from form to detail, is challenged in our work through the two projects that we will discuss. Both projects are examples of the use of material as a conceptual demarcation point for the projects, examining the inherent effects of the material first, followed by developing specific spatial and tectonic details that are subservient to, and supportive of, the nature of the specific material.

When one begins with material as a conceptual approach, the effects that are related to its physical composition become the data upon which the project must develop. In our work there are two different ways in which material has been explored. The first is through enhancement or the hyper-effect of the inherent characteristics of the material itself, where the effect is heightened, embraced, and allowed to manifest as the primary form generator of the project. This kind of examination involves identifying the material effects that interest us, then finding manners and techniques that formally relate to the phenomenological relationships of form and material. The second approach we have taken regarding material exploration is to invert the traditional notion of a material's effect in order to make apparent an aspect of the material not previously seen, or that is not obvious. While this process also involves identifying the material effects first, it inverts the traditional notion of the material in order to see an aspect of the material that is underlying and hidden. The common thread through both projects is an interest in "lightness" as it pertains to two distinct materials. While the two materials are completely different in their physical state, the commonality of lightness is explored through two avenues. The first is a visual effect of light and translucency of a surface material and the ability of this material to create a luminous effect. The second is an inversion of an earthbound organic material to one of floating and levitation.

The examination of material effect, whether it be enhanced or inverted, is conditional upon the purposeful tectonic manipulation and connection of the various assemblages of parts and pieces that make up the physical construct. Our interests in material effect have required a close and careful attention to the "detail" of the physical components of the project at hand. In these cases, "detail" is seen as subservient to the phenomenological aims of the project. That is to say, the manner in which material is manipulated through connection, surface treatment, joinery, and spatial relationships is completely contingent upon the desired effect, specifically luminosity and levitation.

(WIDE)Band Nomadic Café

We were asked to create a temporary showroom to display and advertise materials to be viewed over a three-day period in a windowless mall-like location in Los Angeles, CA. We chose to experiment with a composite translucent panel material called PEP made by the 3form company. The inherent nature of the composite translucent panel offered an exceptional strength-to-weight ratio and an intriguing aspect of luminosity that became the impetus of the project. The material's attenuated nature, combined with its orange and yellow translucent qualities, led us to consider a kind of lounge-like reinterpretation of the program of the venue. Our concept was to resist the consumer-oriented premise of the shopping atmosphere, and to instead provide a free WiFi environment that would act as a place of respite for the typical "buyers" journeying through the hermetic hallways of the mall. This created a space where visitors could meet, sit, engage and take refuge from the consumerist venue. We also questioned the waste of materials of such a temporary use and designed the exhibit so that it could be dismantled, rebuilt and reused at another location.

Drawn from the planar aspect of the panels, the project became a continuous surface of transforming materials (Figures 16.1–16.2). The structural capabilities of the materials were explored through the spanning and folding of the skin into a loop that formed floors, walls and ceilings which ultimately manifested in a long counter-like plane where seating was provided. The majority of the surfaces were made of two types of translucent composite panels which were back-lit to create a glowing lighting effect. This luminosity, expressed uniformly along the folds, created the effect of a floating room of light. Portions of the surfaces were more opaque and made up of tactile tiles. The center opening of the spiral space was terminated with panels of slumped glass which helped create a peripheral circulation to the room. The floor platforms allowed for two varying heights of counters, which were accommodated by stools of comparable differing heights (Figures 16.3–16.8).

Figure 16.1 Axon of the installation

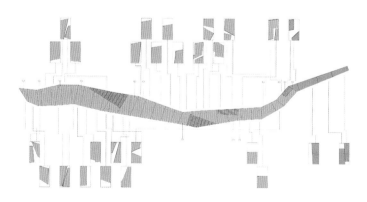

Figure 16.2 Unfolded drawing of the panel surfaces

Figure 16.3 Entry view

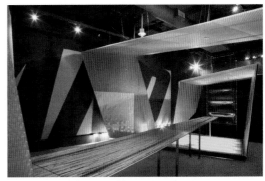

Figure 16.4 View of the interior

Figure 16.5 View of the table area

Figure 16.6 Interior view

Figure 16.7 View of floor detail
Figure 16.8 View during opening

The detailing of the composite translucent panel material was geared towards a minimal expression of support, taking advantage of both the lightness and the structural strength of the materials. The composite panels offered the ability to be attached at discrete points along the surface of the walls and ceilings, thus enabling the material to be used as flooring. Strategic placement of the screw attachments and steel angle supports were positioned to enhance the maximum amount of light transmittance of the material. Hidden light fixtures located around the graphically blacked-out periphery and below the slightly elevated floor were critical to the luminous effect of the project. All connections were made to be easily dismantled so the project could be rebuilt at another venue (Figure 16.9).

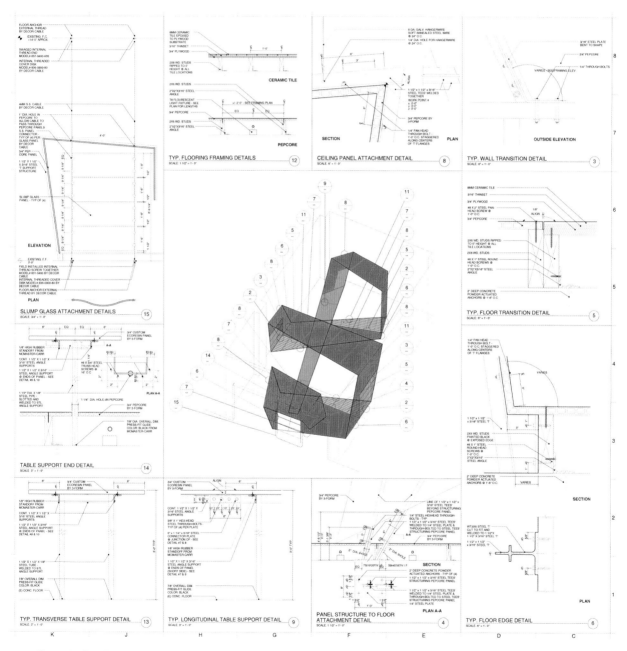

Figure 16.9 Details of the installation

Keep Off the Grass!: planar landscape phenomena

This project was an installation at the SCI-Arc Gallery (Southern California Institute of Architecture). Since there was no real program or pedagogical agenda related to the gallery program, we were able to investigate work in an installation form that was free from the constraints placed on typical projects.

We began with an interest in the paradoxical nature of sod as a material. While sod is bound to the ground plane as a topographical surface, it is also a highly manufactured product. Sod is grown on large farms throughout the United States, then literally sheared off the land in rolls and cut into 2 ft by 4 ft sections that are stacked and delivered to their various destinations. Installed like carpeting, sod is returned to the earth and becomes the ubiquitous suburban lawn that is so prevalent in our environment. We became interested in the notion of exploiting and inverting the heavy earthbound nature of this material, and exposing its hidden but inherent manufactured characteristics. The site of the installation, in the downtown area of Los Angeles, devoid of landscape and green space, added to the paradoxical notion of using a literal green material in an area where little existed.

Over 1,000 square feet of hydroponic sod grass was treated as a floating surface and formed into an undulating, hovering carpet suspended over the floor of the gallery, nearly filling the space. To underscore the plane as a levitated piece, the entire structure was hung from steel cables attached to the gallery ceiling, leaving the ground beneath it free. Two parallel 12-inch-deep CNC-milled plywood beams provided the primary support for some seventy 1-inch steel pipes placed a foot apart (Figures 16.10–16.11). The attachment of the pipes to the plywood beams was purposely separated so the plywood appeared to be floating slightly beneath the underside of the sod. Diagonal cables weaved between the pipes and the plywood beams to provide lateral stability and limit buckling of the members (Figures 16.12–16.13). In one area the sod was omitted and the structure of one beam exposed, allowing an unobstructed view of the support system. The undulating form is derived from obvious notions of rolling bucolic hills, at the same time engaging the visitor by requiring movement around the piece to understand its totality. Thus the undulations required the viewer to move around, under, and finally above the form to the gallery balcony to fully read the piece. The curvilinear plane was lowered at the entrance to invite the viewer into the space. Further deformations arched toward the back of the gallery where a larger volume was created by the underside of the roots and supporting structure (Figures 16.14–16.18).

Figure 16.10 3D view of the installation

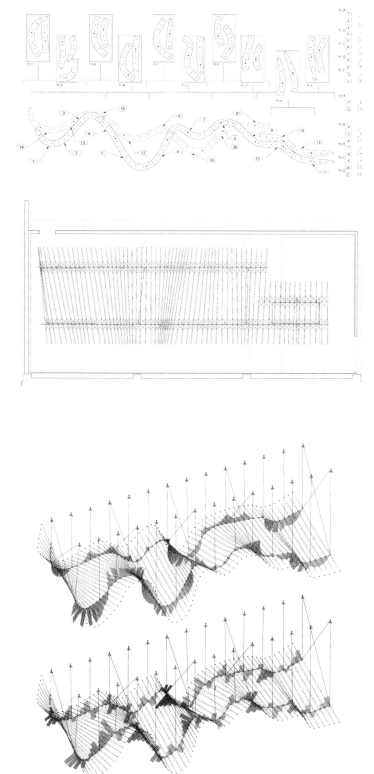

Figure 16.11a–b Plan and section

Figure 16.12a–b Shear and moment stress diagrams

Figure 16.13 Attachment detail

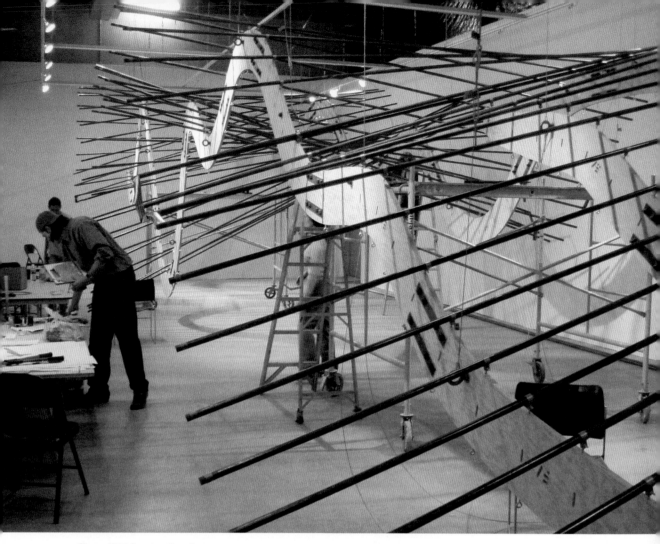

Figure 16.14 Construction photo

The installation acted as a critique on the environmental impact of Southern Californians' devotion to their perfectly manicured lawns. Our challenge was to expose the hidden environmental and societal costs of using this seemingly inexpensive, hybrid material – at once organic and manufactured – within the constraints imposed by an extremely lean budget that necessitated the actual building of the installation by our office. This exercise developed into research on the effects of sod on the environment, while simultaneously formally relating to other projects we were investigating regarding conoid and ruled surfaces as they relate to curvature. We revealed our research through a heuristic exercise, listing sobering statistics on the walls that critiqued the pervasive use of grass in an arid environment. A long, horizontal strip of light was placed against the wall 3½ ft above the floor, as a visual record of the volume of water needed to maintain the sod for one year. Pools of water placed beneath the grass, but beyond its reach, reflected light aimed at perforations in the sod. The installation was both a digitally designed form and a material investigation that required hands-on solutions to the physical realities of the space, budget and technologies available to us. Of particular difficulty was the connection between the inherently two-dimensional CNC plywood beams and the dynamically angled pipe supports. The solution involved the dynamic structural analysis of the inevitable buckling forces on the beams with the use of cable bracing and off-the-shelf tensioning couplers.

Figure 16.15 Entry view

Figure 16.16 View during opening

Figure 16.17 View from mezzanine

Figure 16.18 Detail view of supports

The entropic nature of the organic material enabled a transformation of the installation over the course of eight weeks. By deliberately not watering the grass, we triggered a deteriorating process, causing it to slowly decay, dry and shrink (Figures 16.19–16.20). The scent that resulted could be detected throughout the building, extending well beyond the gallery space. As the material diminished, the porosity increased, altering the quality of light coming through the perforations. The deterioration underscored our precarious relationship to landscape while reminding us of the disproportionate need even a small amount of sod has for water. The project spurred interest for us in how surfaces can perform to a given effect. While this project was admittedly non-utilitarian and existed within an artistic realm, we began to look at applications of other manufactured environmental material that also contained qualities of thinness and light.

Comparative conclusions

The two projects we have discussed are completely divergent in their actual material state. The composite translucent panel of the *(WIDE)Band Nomadic Café* project could not be further from the manufactured grass sod of *Keep Off the Grass!* in appearance, weight, texture, and composition. One is petroleum-based and a product of a series of chemical and mechanical processes giving it a high value of strength and translucence, while the other is organic, high in moisture content and inherently unstable as a structural material. A commonality in the two projects, however, is our interest in the exploitation of the materials' attributes to a maximum desired effect. The definition of lightness, as both a term pertaining to the quality of illumination and the state of being light in weight, is purposefully explored with both projects to create dynamic relationships between the materials and the spatial constructs of the installations. The use of "detail," as a tectonic device to enhance the material effect and to be subservient to this effect, is also an aspect both projects share. Material as a demarcation point within a critical architectural project inherently requires the questioning of the material itself either through enhancement or inversion. In either case, the nature of the material must be exposed in a new manner. Our aim has been to examine materiality critically through thoughtful analysis and delicate detail and hopefully to illuminate new spatial possibilities.

Figure 16.19 View from below prior to de-installation

Figure 16.20 View from above prior to de-installation

Chapter 17
Cumulative Processes and Intimate Understandings

Dwayne Oyler and Jenny Wu

Oyler Wu Collaborative

In this period of extraordinary technological advancement and material innovation, the architectural profession has witnessed an exponential number of practices dedicated to the exploration of new materials and processes. The resulting excitement (and perhaps an effort for architecture to keep pace with its related fields) has placed increased pressure on designers to innovate with each new project. Unfortunately, as these shifts have occurred, so too has the tendency for designers to lose sight of architecture's overwhelming complexity, often confusing the novelty of new materials and processes with the kind of true architectural advancement that comes through the synthesis of a diverse set of ideas. It's understandable that as the creation of buildings have become more complicated, architects have begun to turn to more focused and expertise-based approaches to practice in order to have the most profound impact. However, this conflict between the need for focused expertise and the production of robust and synthetic work presents an enormous challenge for architects today.

As a way of dealing with this conflict, there needs to be a fundamental shift in the way we think about architectural expertise and research. Architecture has always been a field at its best when the *synthesis* of a variety of ideas and issues is of paramount concern. The ability of architecture to bundle and process material, program, structural, and mechanical issues (just to name a few) while maintaining and relating artistic and poetic intentions has been a defining character trait. In contrast to more traditional notions of expertise gained through focused and specific research, architects have an obligation toward synthesis. The production of a body of work should provide a means of slowly accumulating and incorporating a greater range of issues and applications that might not be possible using a more insular and disconnected approach. Additionally, and in order for that to happen, the criterion for evaluating the work must expand alongside the growing expertise. In the field of architecture, focused research should rely on iterative practices over multiple works to connect and bundle ideas; it should acquire new knowledge that expands its scientific realm of influence, and it should be conscious not to leave behind the issues that allow its viability. The ability to deploy the expanded knowledge base is, in fact, what would constitute *architectural research,* as opposed to the kind of insular research that might traditionally occur in a related technical field. Only then can we make meaningful contributions through expertise while maintaining a role with the robustness and breadth of meaningful implementation.

Consumed by our desire for constant innovation, it's easy to forget that the profound level of expertise required to produce truly creative ideas, even at the most basic level, no longer follows traditional models of focused predictability. Contemporary innovation in most fields, perhaps most notably in the sciences, is rarely the product of a singular endeavor; rather, it tends to be the result of expansive thinking, relentless testing, trial and error, iterative processes, and methods that slowly chip away at the hermetic nature of the problem. Ideas need time and research in order to grow, to fail along the way, and to eventually blossom in unexpected ways. We believe that the most creative architectural practices dedicate themselves to constant evolution and growth while recognizing that growth and evolution result from constant and iterative experimentation with a single technique, material, or process. In other words, they do something again and again – not because they know how to do it, but because they know it well enough for it to constantly produce new and untested applications.

At the same time, one needs to be wary of the downsides of expertise-based practice. While this approach is essential to the advancement of architecture, the tendency has often been to reduce the scope of its impact, largely because the issues tend to be addressed through single projects aimed at minute but insular advancement that is disconnected from so many issues essential to the full scope of architectural investigation. The architectural ethics involved in fulfilling client needs, programmatic requirements, and contextual concerns all too often steer projects toward the implementation of tried and true strategies; while tired and worn-out, these tend to be safe strategies nonetheless. In stark contrast to this methodology is the practice of taking an entirely new approach to every new project that comes through the door. Untested and ripe with potential pitfalls, even the most successful of these strategies often fall short, particularly in areas of technical experimentation. Without a relentless questioning of the productive value of any process or technique, a level of comfort leads to simply repeating the same trick, or worse, settling into a stylistic *modus operandi*. This comfort zone is often perpetuated by the market appeal generated by having "gotten it right" at some earlier stage. It's vital that we be conscious of the moment that a strand of investigation fails to yield ideas worthy of additional pursuit.

In order to use a material creatively, one must develop an intimate understanding of it, beginning with its technical characteristics. Its limits are of critical importance and the processes involved in its shaping and connective potential are essential. As easy as these concepts seem to be in the case of basic materials (such as wood, metal, and plastics), a theoretical or "text book" understanding generally pales in comparison to the expertise obtained through an intense hands-on approach. This is especially true when considering the techniques involved in its production and application, rather than just the physical properties of the material itself. But these points alone suggest little more than what might be considered an advanced form of technical knowledge. What sets the architect apart is his or her ability to acquire knowledge outside the technical realm and to find common ground between seemingly disparate fields. Tactility that leads to different forms of human engagement, spatial characteristics that compel a certain type of bodily occupation, and associative qualities that evoke a range of human responses and behaviors are all examples of qualities that fall within blurred zones of professional expertise. An understanding of these qualities is a nuanced, but nevertheless, vital form of knowledge that, when considered collectively, belongs within the territory of the architect and one that can come only from intimate engagement with the material.

Our recent work has been a way of grappling with these issues, through what might best be thought of as an effort to think big about seemingly small issues. While the project presented below is focused primarily on an installation entitled *Live Wire*, the argument relies on a cumulative set of ideas, acquired over a period involving several related projects. In keeping with this idea, the projects must be seen not as a clear end point, but rather as a work in progress – one continually in search of more significant application but ever cautious of its limitations.

The projects

In 2007, we began a series of projects made primarily of aluminum that constitute an important strand of investigation within the office. The projects, entitled *Density Fields*, *Pendulum Plane*, and *Live Wire* (Figures 17.1–17.7) were small-scale installations built in a relatively short time frame of 16 months and for similarly low budgets. While we were somewhat experienced in basic construction techniques, our level of expertise with metal fabrication going into the first project was close to nothing. The short time span afforded little time for second guessing and reflection, but it did immerse us in a field of possibilities that came directly from an up close and personal understanding of the material and necessary processes. The newly acquired knowledge that

Figure 17.1 *Density Fields*, Silver Lake, CA, October 2007

Figure 17.2 *Pendulum Plane*, Hollywood, CA, August 2008

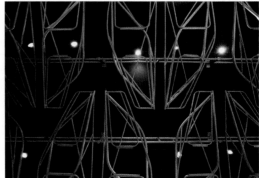

Figure 17.3 Plan view of *Pendulum Plane*

Figure 17.4 *Live Wire*, Los Angeles, CA, October 2008

Figure 17.5 Elevation view of *Live Wire*

Figure 17.6 *Live Wire*, opening in the SCI-Arc Gallery, October 2008

Figure 17.7 *Live Wire*, the final stages of fabrication

came with the projects (and notably, an interest in building on unanswered questions) helped to shape each successive project. Even more importantly, as our expertise grew, the ideas driving the work turned to a more robust intertwining of the tectonic, atmospheric, material, and even programmatic issues at play.

Live Wire, the (provisional) culmination of the work, was an installation in the gallery at the Southern California Institute of Architecture (SCI-Arc). The installation proposed a vertical circulation system, a.k.a. a stair, linking the floor level of the gallery to the catwalk above. Often relegated to pure functional use, the fundamental architectural element was a testing ground for weaving together a multitude of architectural ideas, ranging from the manipulation of light, geometry, and structure to, of course, vertical circulation. In its early conception, the installation was motivated by the desire to occupy the SCI-Arc Gallery in a way that exploits the spatial potential of the existing venue. Conceived of partially as a way of manipulating light, each architectural element required a progressive manipulation in order to negotiate the required performance criteria. With the length of the gallery and the size of the treads providing a scale on one side of the intervention, the opposite side extended up toward the clerestory windows at a dramatically different scale. As the stair moved upward, the geometry took on a transformative quality that pushed the structural limits of the material, relying on the built-up density to carry the load. As much as this density of material was meant to provide structural support, our intention was that it was within these areas that their performance be most easily forgotten, giving way to the spaces they defined. It was at this conceptual intersection that the installation was intended to provide a more expanded definition of architectural elements, one that blurred the boundaries between the simple functions they performed, and the more intangible results that they evoked.

The installation was as equally concerned with function, use, and performance as it was with its visual and experiential qualities, arguing for an expanded relationship between tectonic expression and functional performance. Programmatically, the stair established a new form of movement through the space that challenged the closed nature of the gallery as a hermetic space for objects, effectively integrating it into the daily operations of the school. With the intention of bridging multiple architectural ideas within a single architectural element, the stair exploited a tectonic language appropriate to that objective. In conventional systems of vertical circulation, numerous components are assembled together, with each performing a specific function, for example, guardrails provided along the perimeter, handrail attached to adjacent walls or guardrails, tread and risers for stair surfaces, and a stringer for structural support. Furthermore, these individual components often act independently of systems meant to shape architectural experience. This segregated tectonic formula leaves little room for consideration of the kind of fluid spatial and tectonic implications that might result from a more collective consideration of the parts. Constructed of approximately 2400 linear feet of aluminum tubing and rods, the stair employed a combination of complex loops that performed a variety of tasks as they merged together to form the necessary stair elements. Similarly, the stair incorporated faceted perforated aluminum panels of two different thicknesses to create a continuous, semi-transparent surface from stair tread to guardrail to canopy.

Intimate understandings

In order to provide a more in-depth understanding of the project, it is important to know what led to this point in the design process, both conceptually and technically. As with most new endeavors, the more we learned, the more we realized we didn't know. Nevertheless, a basic knowledge of bending and the welding process was enough to get the ball rolling. There were a few simple factors that guided our initial steps. While they may seem tedious and trivial on the surface, these issues were vital to the development of each project.

First, while aluminum is approximately $1/3$ the weight of steel, its stiffness is less than that of steel by a similar proportion.[1] Given the significant cantilevers proposed in *Density Fields* and *Live Wire*, the decreased stiffness was offset by the lack of weight, effectively making them equal in their structural characteristics (at least for what we needed them to do). The decision to use aluminum hinged on the much more basic principle of workability. Aluminum is soft and easy to work with; it can be drilled with ease, bent and manipulated more easily than steel, quickly tapped by hand for fastening, and cut with an inexpensive chop saw. And while it is more expensive than steel, the finish prevented the need for painting or galvanizing. Experimenting with a number of finishes (including sandblasting, and anodizing), we settled on the labor-intensive, but aesthetically forgiving method of random orbital sanding. While not as clean or durable as anodizing, the intense light on the piece, both from nearby windows during the day and from artificial lighting at night, resulted in a constant glimmer of the material from almost every angle.

One downside to the aluminum, however, is the difficulty in welding it. The challenges include controlling the heat in order to prevent unintentional distortion of the surface, and preventing burn-through.[2] In the case of welding aluminum tube joints at an angle, one needs to also consider how beginning a weld on one side of a tube will change the angle before you are able to move around to the opposite side of the tube. This is best controlled by "tacking" the tube at multiple points before welding the entire circumference – a rule that also applies to lengthy welds at any location. Continuous welds produce exorbitant amounts of heat, so the more the metal can be fixed in place using a tacking method, the more stable it will be while creating the continuous weld.

In the case of *Density Fields*, there were approximately one hundred joints, so it made cutting and welding the joints feasible. Using paper templates created by "unrolling" the digital model (Figure 17.8), the tubes were cut to shape, and then set in a wooden jig for welding. In subsequent projects, the number of joints increased dramatically, so it became necessary to rethink the process. Rather than welding every joint, we experimented with bending the tubes with a hydraulic bender. This move changed the tectonic considerably, as we were no longer creating sharp corners. What were once sharp joints at each corner now became bends that could be made much more quickly and efficiently. It did, however, present a few limitations. Aluminum tubing, depending on both the diameter of the tube, the wall thickness, and the bending method, cannot be bent beyond a certain radius without a buckling of the wall surface. Complicating matters, we found that most standard dies for a hydraulic bender are made to accommodate a radius that is slightly bigger than what the actual material will tolerate. So, knowing that we could create a tighter radius than the standard dye would allow for, we machined a die for a simple hydraulic bender that could bend the 1" diameter aluminum with ⅛" wall to a radius of 2 ¼" inches without the use of a mandrel[3] (Figures 17.9–17.10). This was important in the case of *Live Wire*, as it meant we could make tighter bends over a relatively short distance.

In creating all the projects, we quickly learned that we needed to create techniques that would allow for the inevitable lack of precision inherent in almost any assembly process. Unexpected warping, imperceptible to the eye, caused huge problems when geometries needed to be resolved. The idea that we begin at the base of each piece and expect the final piece to snap into place was far from reality. One essential technique that has been key to the realization of the projects has been the construction of wood jigs (Figures 17.11–17.14). In the case of *Live Wire*, the production of the wood jig required twice as many drawings as the piece itself (Figures 17.15–17.16). Although its fabrication required precision, it did not need to be neat and clean; errors could be patched and filled, and modifications could be made up to the last minute. And as long as the precision of the jig was maintained, the level of supervision could be greatly reduced because mistakes and misalignments became obvious and unforgiving. If a bend was incorrect, or a length was off, it simply wouldn't fit in the jig.

Each of the projects presents a significant challenge in creating (what appears to be) continuous lengths of aluminum. This was accomplished by sleeving the tubes over a smaller interior tube or rod. It turns out, most aluminum is sold in sizes that do not allow for this seemingly obvious technique, and often the inner tube or rod requires significant grinding to fit inside the larger sleeve. Honing the larger tube is also possible but generally more tedious, as most honing tools move less material. In the earlier projects, our method of attachment for the sleeving method relied on set screws that needed to be tapped. We later learned that by creating a full penetration groove weld,[4] we were able to lock the internal pipe in place without the need for set screws.

The geometry of the work also presented a difficult challenge. Today CNC benders[5] are able to take a single tube and create multiple bends resulting in a three-dimensional geometry. This is a method commonly

Figure 17.8a–b *Density Fields.*
By unrolling the digital 3D
Rhinoceros model, paper
templates were made for each
joint. The templates were used
to transfer the precise shape of
the cut to each tube ensuring
accurate assembly of the
geometry prior to welding

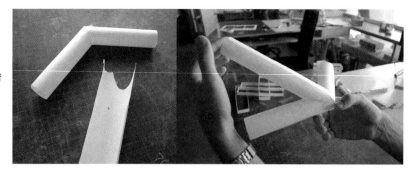

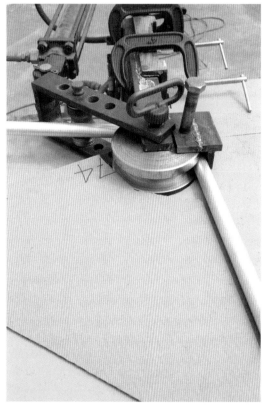

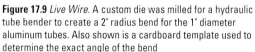

Figure 17.9 *Live Wire.* A custom die was milled for a hydraulic
tube bender to create a 2" radius bend for the 1" diameter
aluminum tubes. Also shown is a cardboard template used to
determine the exact angle of the bend

Figure 17.10 *Live Wire,* detail, Los Angeles, CA, October 2008

used for products such as gymnastics equipment and within the automotive industry, but can be cost-prohibitive
for one-off applications. Without the use of this technology at our disposal, we had to rely on a simplified
method of arriving at the three-dimensional shapes. Before setting out to create the full range of bends that
our schematic design proposal suggested, we worked to reduce the overall number of bends in the piece. Using
CATIA, we were able to optimize the system by effectively creating as many typical bends as possible. For
example, we could identify several bends that were around 110 degrees. We would then adjust all of them to
be 110 degrees and every other angle in the system would adjust accordingly. While this did tweak many of
the angles to fall outside of the established parameters, none of the adjustments were visually perceptible. The
angles were then transferred to a set of cardboard angle templates that could be used as a guide for bending each

Figure 17.11 *Live Wire.* A wood jig was constructed to support the individual tubes prior to being welded together. Because the system of fabrication involved creating a joint between each bend in the tubes, the jig was an essential in ensuring the overall three-dimensional geometry

Figure 17.12 *Live Wire.* Wood jig used for the fabrication of *Live Wire*

Figure 17.13 *Pendulum Plane.* A wood jig ensured accurate overall geometry of each piece during assembly. The jig held each piece in place to aid in welding each of the 16 units together. The design required the fabrication of two jigs, one a mirrored version of the other

Figure 17.14 *Pendulum Plane.* An armature was constructed to test the movement of each unit and to ensure accurate operation. Once the units were placed in the armature, the pivoting flaps were then welded on

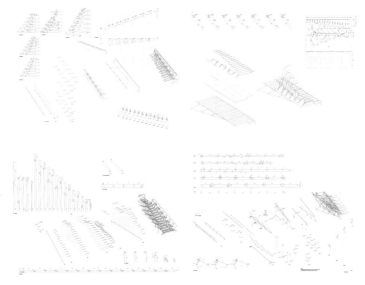

Figure 17.15 *Live Wire.* Drawing of the wood jig used for the fabrication of *Live Wire*

Figure 17.16a–d *Live Wire.* Shop drawings for the fabrication of the wood jig

tube. The three-dimensionality of the overall structure was accomplished by providing a break between each bend and the sleeving system mentioned above. The two bends could simply be connected together and turned until they found a comfortable angle resting in the jig (Figures 17.17–17.20).

Our work with Buro Happold on *Live Wire* was a fruitful experiment in collaboration. The collaboration was constantly alternating between low-tech experiments and digital processes. Beginning with a series of physical models (Figure 17.21), the structural integrity was first evaluated based on nothing more than pushing on pieces to understand the connectivity between individual bars within the three-dimensional mesh. As could be expected, the system was found to be disproportionately flexible in some areas and rigid in others. Geometry was then added or subtracted from the physical model to address problem areas. In a parallel effort, a parametric CATIA model was constructed and updated to match the evolution of the physical model. The CATIA model was eventually linked to software for structural analysis. Unlike most engineering processes where the structural analysis is used to immediately provide a design that will work, in our case the analysis results were used primarily as a way of identifying what *didn't* work. The fabrication process began before a fully stable virtual model was established, largely in the hopes that we would acquire stability with less support than the software suggested. The engineers were comfortable with this approach provided strategic alterations could be made during fabrication and assembly should the need arise. It order to do that, a detail was developed that allowed ³/₄" solid aluminum rods to be added as required to address problem areas while still being integral to the geometric principles of the stair. The final stages of the fabrication process involved testing the system at full scale for acceptable amounts of movement. Those areas were then addressed by adding the rods throughout the system (in keeping with the repetitive nature of the overall structure).

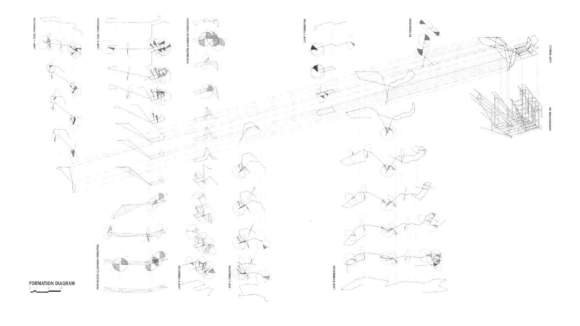

FORMATION DIAGRAM

Figure 17.17 *Live Wire.* Aluminum tubes were first assembled on the ground in the flat orientation. Loops of aluminum tubes were then placed into the wood jig and joints were rotated to the proper orientation in order to fit perfectly into the jig. Once all of the adjacent loops were in position, they were welded in place. After all of the loops of the entire assembly were set in place, the perforated metal screen was attached to the loops

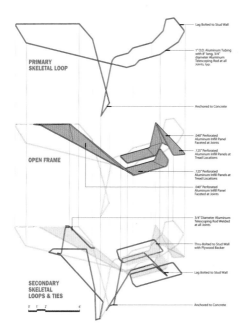

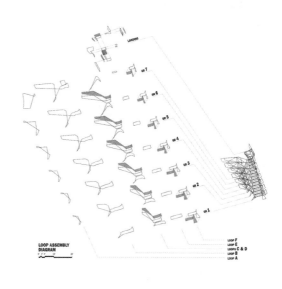

Figure 17.18 *Live Wire*. Diagram showing the breakdown of the loops within the overall assembly. Each tread/handrail/wing assembly is made up of 5–6 distinct loops

Figure 17.19 *Live Wire*. Diagram showing how six loops and perforated screens come together to form one tread/handrail/wing assembly

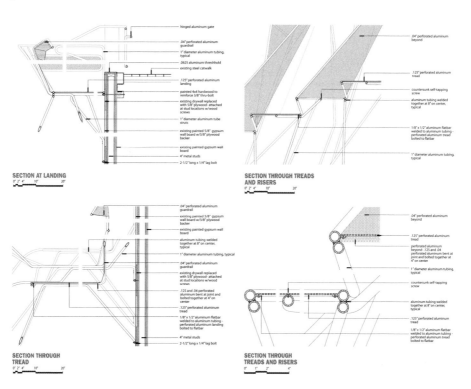

Figure 17.20a–d *Live Wire*. Connection details of the stair assembly

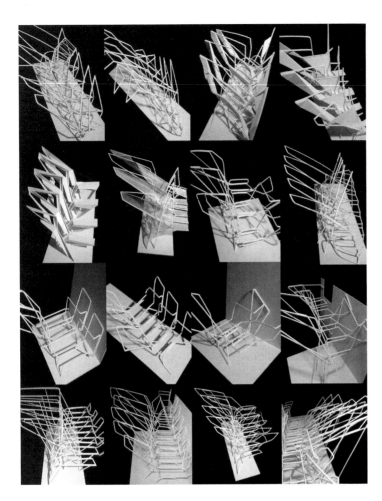

Figure 17.21a–p *Live Wire.* Study models created during the design process for *Live Wire* were typically intended to study a specific design issue, for example, the perforated metal system used for treads and risers, the stair landing, or the "looping" system

Going forward

The advancement and, in fact, the survival, of our field rely on our ability to develop an expertise of our own, one that goes well beyond that of mere coordination – a frequently suggested alternative to expertise. The role of coordinator undoubtedly lies within the obligatory realm of the architect, but it ultimately risks a shift in professional focus to an area with less creative and artistic influence (as architects are left assembling a tapestry consisting of the expertise of others). We are not suggesting that the expertise is gained solely through fabrication, but rather that we strive to better understand a material application or process as a means towards developing expertise, not as the end result but as an instructive step in the synthesis of the array of architectural concerns. None of the techniques mentioned above are especially groundbreaking within the metal industry, and, in fact, they have all most certainly been used individually at some point architecturally. That isn't exactly the point; we're more concerned with suggesting a way of working that could yield meaningful results as a cumulative set of knowledge in order to influence architectural decisions. This is a tall order without a relentlessly iterative and intimate understanding of the limits and possibilities of one's medium. This period of unprecedented material development and interest offers an incredible opportunity to reconsider how we build, design, and define ourselves as a profession, ultimately allowing architects to play a more pivotal role in that development. But in order to do that, we must reconsider both how we acquire expertise and the means of deploying it. It is through this depth of investigation that we believe architecture obtains and maintains its most significant breadth of influence.

Acknowledgements

Principal Architects: Dwayne Oyler, Jenny Wu. Project Leaders: Ming Jian Huang, Matt Evans. Design Team: Fayez Ahdab, Phillip Cameron, Ming Jian Huang, Huy Le, Erik Mathiesen, Dwayne Oyler, Jenny Wu. Engineering: Buro Happold Los Angeles; Project Team: Matthew Melnyk, Ian Carter, Yukie Hirashima, Steven Boak.

Notes

1   This is based on the comparison of the elastic modulus of a typical grade of aluminum to high-strength steel, E = 10,100ksi for 3003-H14 Aluminum vs. 29,000ksi for A572-50 Grade Steel. Essentially, while aluminum is lighter than steel, it is also more flexible and will more easily bow and buckle under load. Interestingly, the strength – a measure of the amount of stress a material can resist before yielding or fracturing – of aluminum alloy can vary depending on its particular metallurgy and for some alloys can nearly equal that of high-strength steel (comparing the yield strength of the two, fy = 45ksi for 6066-T6 Aluminum Alloy vs. 50ksi for A572-50 Grade Steel). See *Aluminum Design Manual: Specifications and Guidelines for Aluminum Structures*, 8th edn (New York: The Aluminum Association, 2005).

2   Distortion occurs as a result of contraction of the base material caused by excessive heat during the welding process. Prevention of distortion can also be prevented by lowering the voltage (when possible without compromising penetration), increasing travel speed, or by welding small segments and allowing each segment to cool between welds. Burn-through refers to the weld metal melting completely through the base metal, resulting in holes in the material. This is typically caused by a voltage setting that is too high, a "travel speed" that is too slow, or a material that has an insufficient thickness for the desired weld type. See *Millermatic Passport Plus Owner's Manual* (Appleton, WI: Miller Electric Mfg. Co., 2007).

3   Mandrel, short for mandrel assembly, is the tooling component that provides support to the inside of the tube. Its primary function is to prevent the tube from buckling and necking. Many different variations of mandrels exist. The required style and material depend on the outside diameter (OD) and wall thickness (WT) of the tube being bent. The simplest design style is the plug mandrel and the most complex design style is the ball mandrel. The ball mandrel is designed to internally support the tube beyond tangent and depending on the number of ball segments, throughout the entire bend. See *Hines Bending Systems: Basic Tube Bending Guide* (product literature), Hines Bending Systems, Fort Myers, Florida.

4   Drawings of this type of weld and others can be found in 10th edition of *Architectural Graphic Standards*, John Ray Hoke, Jr. FAIA, Editor in Chief (New York: John Wiley & Sons, Inc., 2000), pp. 264–265.

5   CNC tube benders are produced by a large number of companies; additional information on these technologies can be obtained from manufacturers such as Horn Machine Tools (Unison Electric Tube Benders), Hines Bending Systems, Inc., and Pines Technology.

Chapter 18
Built to Change
A case for disintegration and obsolescence

Blair Satterfield and Marc Swackhamer

HouMinn

Introduction

> When your house contains such a complex of piping flues, ducts, wires, lights, inlets, outlets, ovens, sinks, refuse disposers, hi-fi reverberators, antennae, conduits, freezers, heaters – when it contains so many services that the hardware could stand up by itself without any assistance from the house, why have a house to hold it up?
>
> (Banham, 1969)

In traditional stick-built homes, occupants are, at best, marginally aware of the complex systems that allow them to live comfortably. We perceive the single-family house as a static commodity, too big and too expensive to constantly change. Except for minor modifications and the occasional full-scale renovation, the house is rarely amended. Instead, we change our environments with furniture, appliances, and paint. These modifications might be motivated by evolving technologies or maturing tastes. The stuff within our homes is in play, but rarely, if ever, is the house itself conceived of as a modifiable, customizable platform (Figure 18.1).

Contrast this with our disposition towards computers and smart phones. With these devices we expect to continuously update both "operating systems" and hardware. The operating system evolves to accommodate increasingly sophisticated applications and programs. The hardware in turn evolves to support improving operating systems. This cycle, predicated on a fluid system that does not recognize either software or hardware

Figure 18.1 "Suburbia Winter Sunrise." The suburban house is a lifestyle accessory, a storage unit, and a commodity. It is only recently that the buildings we live in are seen as high-performance objects capable of both housing our stuff and lessening our impact on our surroundings. Winter in suburban Calgary, Alberta, Canada

Figure 18.2 Human skin – a flexible and responsive exterior

Figure 18.3 The Rally Fighter is a crowd-sourced or "co-created" design offered by American automobile company Local Motors[1]

as a static condition, results in rapid change, improved performance, and greater flexibility. The same logic that drives the technology forward also allows for customization. The same family of parts (hardware and software) can provide unique functionality according to need, profession, lifestyle, technological sophistication, intensity of use, and personality.

With *OSWall* (*Open Source Wall*), and its precedent research projects, *Drape Wall* and *Cloak Wall*, we endeavor to do for the single-family home what the Apple "App Store" or the Google Android "Marketplace" has done for the smart phone. *OSWall* is an experimental wall system that challenges conventional home construction through an open, collaborative approach to material selection, fabrication, and installation methods. It proposes an "open source" construction platform in which third-party designers, engineers, scientists, or creative "do-it-yourselfers" can design, produce, market, and sell wall "applications" that are plugged into a standardized structural armature. Our strategy for *OSWall* is predicated on the notion that the house is an assembly of parts that will continuously evolve. Think human skin (Figure 18.2): we continuously slough off old skin and grow new skin cells. The epidermis layer of our skin is in effect replaced every 35 days. Similarly, *OSWall* components are designed to be replaced, reused, and relocated. The house is as modifiable as furniture arrangements, paint colors, or photos on the wall. Where skin stretches and folds to accommodate movement, the house might change according to lifestyle and program. *OSWall* can adapt to season or climate just as skin senses environmental fluctuation and regulates body heat and moisture content. The system will continually draw on current technological innovations (Figure 18.3).

This chapter will argue for a new residential construction platform in three parts. First, it will briefly review the history of stick-frame construction, identifying both its current advantages and disadvantages from a practical perspective. Second, it will outline the systemic, material, and performative advancements explored through three full-scale construction prototypes by HouMinn Practice. Finally, it will critically position the work, especially *OSWall*, in an historical context, through a mini-manifesto called "A case for disintegration and obsolescence."

What's the big problem with stick-frame construction?

In 1795, Jacob Perkins patented a nail-making machine that could cut nails from sheets of iron. This resulted in considerable increases in production efficiency when compared to forging nails in a blacksmith shop. Over the next few decades, nail prices dropped steadily. Improved lumber production created other possibilities. In addition, improvements in transportation made it feasible to transport wood economically from greater distances. The solution to the housing problem was within reach and simply required the right touch of inspirational genius.

(Armstrong, 2010)

Light-frame construction has been around for a long time, and for good reason. Many of the reasons for its widespread adoption and appeal are the same as they were over 200 years ago. Let us briefly review the history of this uniquely American technology.

In colonial America, houses were typically constructed with heavy timbers, often resulting in what we recognize as log cabins. Around 1830, home building made a radical shift as the population increased, resources declined, and several technological advancements were introduced (Armstrong, 2010). Two characteristics in particular made the development of stick-frame construction different in the United States when compared to European countries. The first was a continent full of virgin forest. There was an abundance of wood. The second was a lack of skilled craftsmen. Labor was precious. "[Americans] had to be Jacks-of-all-trades" (Leinhard, 1988–1997).

The first recorded example of a stick-frame building occurred in 1833 when a man by the name of Augustine Taylor built St. Mary's Church in Fort Dearborn, Illinois (in what is now Chicago). He constructed a 36- by 24-ft church for the incredibly low price of $400, using no skilled laborers. He eliminated mortised beams and fittings, replacing them with light two-by-fours and two-by-sixes set in a tightly spaced arrangement. The entire building was comprised of studs and cross-members held together with nails. Experienced carpenters swore it would blow away in a high wind and gave it the derogatory name "balloon construction." The structure didn't blow away, but the term stuck (ibid.). "These buildings were like balloons, or maybe more like woven baskets. They were light, flexible, and tough. Stresses were taken up throughout the structure" (ibid.).

Light framing offered several key advantages over timber-frame construction. It was easier to transport materials to the marketplace. The lumber could be dried at a sawmill, rendering it light, easy to handle, and simple to package (Armstrong, 2010). Once the lumber became a commodity, creative marketing further

Figure 18.4 Stud wall. Default construction methodology for single family housing

bolstered the innovation of its construction. Companies like Sears and Roebuck, from 1908–1940, sold pre-cut house "kits." Sears sold about 100,000 houses over this period. By 1854, a light-frame housing industry had taken shape as specialized companies began to fabricate high-quality doors, windows, and staircases as "off-the-shelf" products (ibid.).

Note the dates along light framing's timeline. The industry as we know it today has changed little (with a few exceptions) since it took hold in the mid-nineteenth century. What are the reasons for its longevity?

Advantages of stick-frame construction: why has it stuck around for so long?

There are numerous practical, systemic, and logical reasons for the continued longevity of stick-frame construction (Figure 18.4). First, a stick-framed building is relatively fast to construct. It is flexible and can be easily edited on the fly. It is possible to create a variety of geometries and volumes using a stick-frame system (within certain limits). Stick-frame construction is deeply embedded in the residential construction industry. The system is well-known, well-documented, and predictable. Both contractors and architects know it and accept it as a default approach. Our entire economic system for housing in this country, including material production, delivery, and assembly, is based on this model of construction. And while the industry has been working to reduce costs and improve the system's ecological footprint, it has done so within the constraints of a two-hundred-year-old craft. Improvement has been strategically built around commodity and control, while reinvention and performance have been secondary considerations.

Disadvantages of stick-frame construction: is it time for it to go?

While stick-frame construction is relatively inexpensive, it can be costly in terms of its relative ecological footprint – the materials it uses as well as the fabrication and construction methodologies necessary to erect a typical house. As evidence of the sheer volume of wood used in a typical residential house, consider the following:

> More than 33 percent of the lumber and structural wood panels and more than 25 percent of the nonstructural wood panels consumed annually in the United States are used in building housing units. More than 75 percent of wood products used for all residential construction were used in single-family houses.
>
> (McKeever and Phelps, 1994)

Additionally, between 1950 and the present day, according to the National Association of Home Builders, the average size of houses in the United States climbed from about 1,000 sq. ft to about 2,300 sq. ft (Infoplease, n.d.). The overall use of raw lumber has decreased over the past 50+ years, while the use of plywood, MDF (medium-density fiberboard), and other manufactured wood products has increased. These composite materials take more energy to produce and often use harmful glues, solvents, and binding agents to hold themselves together (although this is changing a bit, it is still standard practice) (McKeever and Phelps, 1994).

From our experience working with both wood construction and other construction technologies, we have observed a few other shortcomings in stick-frame construction (or, more precisely, advancements in other technologies that highlight stick-frame's shortcomings).

For example, we believe homes could be produced with far less waste than is currently produced by stick-frame construction. According to the National Association of Home Builders, 8,000 pounds of waste are produced from the construction of a 2,000-sq. ft house. Additionally, the Environmental Protection Agency estimates that waste from construction accounts for up to 40 percent of the nation's solid waste (Bittle, 2009).

We believe homes could be produced using less embodied energy than a typical stick-frame house ("'Embodied energy,' or 'embedded energy,' is an assessment that includes the energy required to extract raw materials from nature, plus the energy used in primary and secondary manufacturing activities to provide a finished product", Mumma, 1995). According to the Canadian Mortgage and Housing Corporation, a typical house will exist and operate for about ten years before the total operating cost starts to outstrip the embodied energy contained in the building components of that house (Mumma, 1995).

We also believe houses could be constructed to better accommodate chases, wiring, and other necessary systemic technology in a typical home. Currently the problem with chases in stick and platform construction lies in the fact that plumbers and electricians tend to compromise the structure in order to accommodate their work. Often, all of these systems are coincidental and require the removal of material. This can significantly weaken and compromise a structure. The result? We over-structure houses to accommodate the removal of material. Said another way, we add more material so that we can take material away and place it in a landfill.

Finally, we believe that the use of conventional HVAC systems needs reexamination. This is not necessarily an indictment of light-frame construction as a system, but is nonetheless central to our overall critique of conventional home construction. We suspect that there could be a reduction in energy use through the replacement of centralized HVAC systems with cellular, distributed systems. Our argument for this approach is expanded upon and substantiated later in this chapter under "A case for disintegration and obsolescence."

Drape Wall, Cloak Wall, and *OSWall*

Over the past five years, our wall prototype research has taken up the cause of interrogating the clear shortcomings of light-frame construction and proposing alternatives to it. The research has culminated in three projects: *Drape Wall, Cloak Wall,* and *Open Source Wall* or *OSWall* (with many sub-explorations under each).

In broad terms, the research proposes three shifts in how we approach residential construction. First, it suggests that we consider building performance as an issue of resolution. This is an argument for technological decentralization. Instead of a single building brain, like a furnace/duct/thermostat system, it promotes a system of many simple components operating responsively, like an adaptive ventilation system that opens one zone of a house while closing another. Second, the research examines how we might specifically tune a building based on local climate, program difference, or advancements in technology. It allows and even encourages a homeowner to change, replace, and recycle the components of a house. Finally, the research explores the idea of a universal structural system for erecting a basic house quickly, efficiently, and inexpensively, with very few tools and little waste. It promotes a system that is light, can be densely packed, and strategically uses local materials. Into this system can be plugged interior and exterior wall components with varying degrees of technological sophistication, at varying price points, with varying compositional/esthetic characteristics.

The relative successes and failures (failure is not a pejorative term for us, but an essential reality of this type of explorative research) of each have served as a road map for guiding the direction of subsequent exploration. A brief summary of each project follows.

Drape Wall

Drape Wall explores energy conservation, pre-fabrication, and modular-component assembly (Figures 18.5–18.6). The project was initially inspired by advancements in high-performance, layered clothing systems – specifically a running shirt developed by Nike. This shirt is digitally woven to create areas that are thinner where the body tends to sweat more and thicker where shirts tend to wear thin from repeated abrasion (Nike ACG Seamless NAROPA, 2004). The result is a garment that specifically responds to the performance requirements of the person wearing it. We thought a house envelope could do the same. In *Drape Wall*, interplay between a structural shell and a soft fabric liner enables the homeowner to customize the interior environment. In a way analogous to adding or removing layers of clothing, the wall can be made thicker, thinner, more open, or more weather-tight according to climate and personal comfort.

The wall is assembled by vertically stacking high-strength, low-weight exterior bricks, and then holding them in place with smaller, interlocking interior bricks. A pattern of small, clear apertures controls levels of daylight. Porosity is determined during fabrication by adjusting the aperture size, its pattern density, and the surface angle of the panel on which the pattern occurs. During installation, the bricks are rotated to face towards or away from the sun. This ability to fine-tune light infiltration reduces the need for electric lighting while minimizing heat gain in a warm climate or maximizing it in a cold climate. Holes between the bricks allow for natural ventilation, reducing cooling costs. Additionally portions of the wall provide storage, reducing the floor area needed for that function and thus shrinking the house's overall footprint and cost.

A quilt-like fabric on the interior surface of the wall makes use of innovative materials to create an interactive weather seal. Through a dialog between the hard outer shell and the soft inner fabric, the homeowner can control the interior environment in response to outside conditions, such as temperature, humidity, weather, light levels, and desired views. The quilt is comprised of multiple layers of materials. One layer serves as waterproofing, another as insulation, and a third as a soft, acoustically absorptive surface that the homeowner can customize. The fabric system utilizes waterproof zippers from the tent industry for delivering simple, user-operated control of the environment. Some zippered openings allow air to circulate through the wall, while others keep air out but allow for additional light infiltration. Other zippers access storage space created in the empty zone between the quilt and shell.

Figure 18.5 *Drape Wall*. Exterior

Figure 18.6 *Drape Wall*. Interior

There are several technologies not included in the built prototype of *Drape Wall* that would, nonetheless, be pivotal to its future development. For example, the interior surface of the quilt would incorporate luminescent fabric to supply light at night. This lighting would be powered passively by photovoltaic paint and thin film batteries printed directly on the exterior modular bricks. Sandwiched inside the quilt would be a layer of "aerogel" which would provide thin, highly efficient insulation. Finally, the quilt would include sewn-in, flexible tubes containing radiant heating and cooling liquid as well as an integrated electrical system. This would allow the quilt to be intelligently pre-networked with services that currently require expensive on-site trades.

Cloak Wall

Cloak Wall represents numerous advancements over *Drape Wall*. First, *Drape Wall* required a cumbersome aluminum frame for support; *Cloak Wall* is self-supported, aided by post-tensioned cables (Figures 18.7–18.8). Second, *Drape Wall's* openings were uniform in size and fixed; *Cloak Wall's* have a bias. As blocks slide, they create adjustable openings that respond to orientation or view. Third, *Drape Wall's* blocks were monochromatic; *Cloak Wall* utilizes a new and dynamic type of paint. Small metallic flecks in this paint can be oriented to receive light in very specific ways. This advancement was the result of collaboration with University of Minnesota Computer Science Associate Professor Gary Meyer. We proposed a color pattern using color prediction software developed by Professor Meyer. Wall panel colors were parametrically linked to site colors (viewer's perception of color) and seasonal sun angles (capture or reflect radiant heat). The resulting paint pattern has both a perceptual and performance impact on the wall.

The color-shifting qualities of the paint on *Cloak Wall* were initially explored as a way to visually "cloak" the house under certain conditions. Photographs of the project's hypothetical site were mined to establish a color pallet for its exterior skin. Greens and yellows, informed by the foliage on the site, form the wall's base. These give way to dark browns and grays, matching the site's horizon line, along the beltline of the wall. Colors gradually transform into blues and purples, from the site's sky, at the top of the wall. During certain times of the year, the house would phenomenally disappear, minimizing its visual impact on its surrounding, picturesque landscape. Like grass moving in the wind or clouds moving across the sky, the perceived composition of the wall would fluctuate as one moved around and towards the house.

Ultimately, however, the color-shifting paint had an unexpected, but more performance-driven application. A coordinated "flop" color in the paint makes the house more responsive to the sun's changing position in the sky (Figure 18.9). This means that the house "appears" different to the sun during different seasons: dark during the winter, when the sun is low in the sky and light during the summer, when the sun is high. The house tunes itself, absorbing more radiant energy in winter or less during hot summer months. This recognition of a situational shift in performance could reduce reliance on energy-intensive cooling and heating systems, even in relatively harsh climatic conditions.

Another advancement of *Cloak Wall* over *Drape Wall* lies in its treatment of the interior quilt surface. Rather than sandwiching all of its layers together, *Cloak Wall's* quilt is organized so that the soft interior felt surface is separate from the weather barrier. This way, the quilt can more easily accommodate storage, power, light and data. Once the quilt is pulled apart, the functions of insulation, waterproofing, and light infiltration are accommodated by an air-filled ETFE (ethylene tetrafluoroethylene) surface. ETFE is a highly transparent polymer that can be heat-welded with a pattern of air bladders to form an effective insulation and waterproof surface. In *Cloak Wall,* specific zones of the ETFE skin can be inflated or deflated to increase or reduce the insulation in the wall. Consider how we change from a heavy parka in the winter to a light jacket in the spring. We change our clothing to respond to subtle variations in our environments. Similarly, *Cloak Wall* can respond seasonally to temperature and humidity fluctuation.

Figure 18.7 *Cloak Wall.* Exterior
Figure 18.8 *Cloak Wall.* Interior

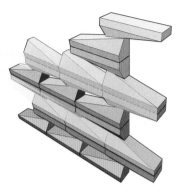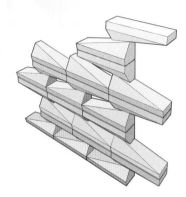

Figure 18.9a–b Diagrams illustrating the relationship between the position of the sun and *Cloak Wall's* painted exterior. Efficiencies would be accomplished by specifically orienting a flop color within the paint. In the winter, when the sun is low, the paint would absorb radiant energy. In the summer, when the sun is high and collecting heat is not desirable, the exterior of the house would reflect radiant energy. A coat of paint applied across a neighborhood could decrease energy use

OSWall

Our most recent wall project, *OSWall* (*Open Source Wall*) (Figure 18.10) was inspired by the rampant popularity of "apps" (or applications) for the iPhone. If a wall system could employ this open-source model for quickly delivering technological innovations to the user, we believe the house would become a constantly evolving, continually improving organism. In our investigation, we are working with an open structural armature (a thin net-like structure) and relatively inexpensive modular panels ("apps") that can be easily replaced when a newer, more advanced version is developed (Figure 18.11). For an exhibition of the system in *Envelop{e}s*, a show at the Pratt Manhattan Gallery,[2] specifications for these panels were posted online. We solicited design ideas from anyone (architects, designers, engineers, inventors) who wanted to develop a new "app." By leveraging the intelligence and creativity of the internet community, our hope was to rapidly identify new and unanticipated technological innovations – panel systems that would harness the energy of the sun, automatically adjust for ventilation, or collect and re-use rainwater as examples. We selected three ideas as winners of our *OSWall* "app" competition. We then funded these three projects for fabrication and installation at the *Envelop{e}s* exhibition.

Through the exhibition and fabrication of *OSWall* at Pratt, we developed a new, more sophisticated structural system for the wall. The key component of this system is a universal connector. To understand why this is significant, consider a precedent from biology: the common barn swallow (Figure 18.12).[3] The barn swallow is a bird whose nest comprises both universal materials (a matrix of mud and saliva from the barn swallow) and variable local materials (reinforcing material like straw or grass in a rural area, or newspaper and trash in an urban area). Like the barn swallow's nest, *OSWall's* structural frame is made up of both universal connectors and locally procured materials. The universal component is an aluminum laser-cut bracket (Figure 18.13). Multiple copies of this component can be efficiently shipped in a flattened state to the site and then bent into form with a foot-operated bending jig. This connector is then used to hold together locally procured "sticks" that are common to a particular site or region, like two-by-four lumber in North America or bamboo in Asia. The standardized connector allows us to be opportunistic about the types of material we use to construct the wall. Both the frame and its accompanying components or skins (apps) create a system that is intended to liberate the user from pure standardization while maintaining efficiency and cost-effectiveness (Figure 18.14).

In the North American two-by-four version of *OSWall*'s structural armature, spacing of connectors and lengths of members result in a construction system that produces very little waste. Every eight-foot two-by-four is simply cut in half in order to be used as a four-foot diagonal member. Ten-foot two-by-fours form the vertical components. Further, our research has shown that the two-by-four members are excessive for the required load-carrying capacity of a house. When we reduce member size to one-by-two, the result is a floor/wall/roof framing system with an approximate 30-inch plenum space around its perimeter that uses less material per linear foot and produces less waste than a standard stud wall with a 3-inch plenum space. Our strong suspicion, which we have substantiated empirically, is that the wall system is much stronger in sheer than a standard stud wall and that it will resist sheer forces without the use of bulky sheet materials, like plywood. When combined with thin insulation technology that arrives on site in small rolls, flat-packed exterior panels that acquire their strength from hand-folding on site, and lightweight interior surfaces made of fabric; *OSWall* emerges as an extremely compact, efficient construction system (Figures 18.15–18.18). Our goal with this system is to be able to ship an entire 1500-square-foot house (excluding the locally procured "sticks") in the back of a van. This would include structure, insulation, waterproofing, exterior cladding, and interior finishes. The implications this might have on our own housing stock in the United States are significant (cheaper housing, use of fewer resources for production and delivery, adaptability of housing stock and therefore increased performance and efficiency). We also see this system as one potential way to address pressing global problems like refugee housing, disaster relief, and Third World housing.

Figure 18.10 *OSWall* exterior. A formal skin pattern developed to channel water into storage bladders at the base of the wall construct. The pattern was informed by whale anatomy. Ridges and folds on the whale's body allow the animal to expand its throat when feeding. The same ridges streamline the animal

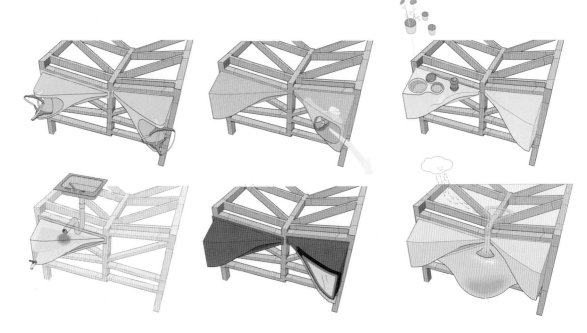

Figure 18.11a–f *OSWall* app ideas. A series of drawings speculating on the performance of individual applications. The ideas range from simple apps like windows to more complex ideas like micro-turbines and hydroponic apps

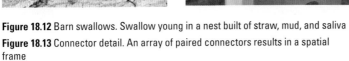

Figure 18.12 Barn swallows. Swallow young in a nest built of straw, mud, and saliva

Figure 18.13 Connector detail. An array of paired connectors results in a spatial frame

Figure 18.14 Frame detail. A frame assembled using two-by-four members and a single repeated connector

Figure 18.15 *OSWall* prototype. The exterior of *OSWall*, as seen at the Pratt Manhattan Gallery, NY. Vacuum formed panels arrayed over a two-by-four timber frame

Figure 18.16 *OSWall* prototype. This is an image of the interior of *OSWall*, as seen at the Pratt Manhattan Gallery, NY. Digitally cut plywood panels allow for storage and access to the frame. Operable skins allow access to transparent "window" apps on the exterior wall

Figure 18.17 *OSWall* prototype detail. The pattern in the wall expands and padding emerges to provide support for the home-owner

Figure 18.18 *OSWall* prototype detail. Here a responsive pattern of holes provides space for storage bags

A case for disintegration and obsolescence

Disintegration and obsolescence are not generally considered to be good things.

Disintegration can be defined as the breaking of a whole into its constituent parts. It is an idea that runs counter to what we do as architects and builders. We are trained to *integrate:* we bring materials and goods *together* to assemble them into a cohesive meaningful whole. Our approaches to the design and construction of buildings typically reflect this understanding. Bricks are assembled into a wall. Walls act as singular spatial barriers, usually represented on plans as coordinated parallel lines. Windows are "cut" into or "punched" out of the unified surface. Houses, while often spatially cellular, are conceived of as a consolidated object. A house possesses an array of systems that heat, cool, plumb, and power. These units are typically installed as a single source with a networked distribution hidden in chases and interstitial spaces – only revealed through individual vents, outlets, or spigots. The typical home has *an* air conditioner, *a* water heater, *a* fuse box ... singular, one. More than that is considered redundant (Figure 18.19).

Obsolescence is generally associated with failure, or at best waning usefulness. When one couples the word "planned" with "obsolescence," the meaning turns more sinister, conjuring images of wantonly wasteful producers designing items to fail. Abusing resources and the marketplace to turn a profit, while common practice, is seen as nefarious. The very idea works against our sensibilities as consumers. We are conditioned to want things that are "built to last" and "here to stay." We don't want to be manipulated into replacing products and goods on an accelerated schedule. While it is a sound financial strategy for our production-driven economy, this practice strikes a negative chord. It is even more off-putting as we become increasingly concerned about the Earth and the overtaxing of its limited resources. "Conservation" is the word of today. Use and reuse is the appropriate practice. Disposability and failure are not options.

Given all this, how can we possibly make an argument for disintegration AND obsolescence?

We see both disintegration and obsolescence as opportunities. Both ideas offer the potential to rethink how we approach our built environments and the systems that allow us to live in them. What if the traditional stand-alone air conditioner/heating unit of the house was disintegrated? Better yet, what if the systems responsible for heating and cooling were reduced to a fraction of their original size, multiplied, and distributed across the entire surface of the house? What if it was embedded in each individual building block? If this were to happen, a wall could use its entire exterior surface to maintain its internal temperature. It could respond with precision to create a series of microclimates throughout the house. With distributed sensors coupled with these miniature mechanisms, the house could sense and respond to changes locally. Similarly, what if a house could inflate when it was cold, or open a series of pores when it needed to cool off? What if it could change color to collect or repel radiant energy? What if it could generate its own power? By disintegrating systems and by reducing and distributing performance, walls could work like skin. The structural systems of the house are handled in a similar way. The reduction in scale and repetition of parts would increase efficiencies in performance, fabrication, and distribution, while dramatically reducing the energy and resources required to produce, deliver, and operate a house.

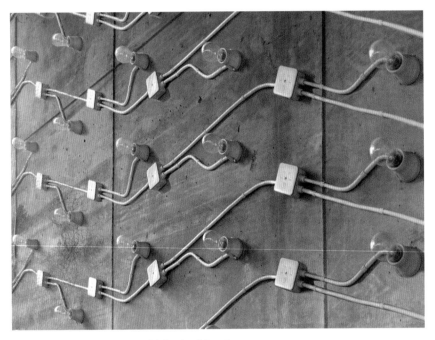

Figure 18.19a Sigurd Lewerentz. Lighting detail from flower kiosk. Completed 1969

Figure 18.19b Local Lewerentz = Transparent Design vs. Global Lewerentz = Transparent System. A more responsive system is possible with redundant parts. Sigurd Lewerentz – Modified Lighting detail from flower kiosk

Conclusion: built to change

When we embrace obsolescence, we are not arguing for designed failure in economic terms. Instead, we are promoting the willingness to consider that each system is always in play. We are arguing that our homes and their systems should be thought of in terms of software, hardware, and operating systems. They should and will be rapidly improved upon. They should and will be replaced, redistributed, and recycled. By introducing an open-source strategy for modifying the parts and systems of the home, we anticipate a rapid evolution.

Temporal or cyclical obsolescence – obsolescence as a local or short-term condition – could imply the changing of a brick during the winter, as a car-owner would switch to snow tires.

In our work, systems are designed and problems are solved in a manner analogous to the construction and composition of a Chuck Close painting (Figure 18.20). The detail reveals logic. Space is metered, and shape, medium, and stroke are relatively consistent from square to square. It isn't until we pull back that we begin to see real variation emerge from a locally consistent marking strategy.

The difference between a conventional architectural approach and the approach we have taken with *OSWall* lies in a comparison to the difference between Mies van der Rohe's *Farnsworth House* (Figure 18.21) and the work of Sigurd Lewerentz (Figures 18.22–18.23). Consider how Mies treats the kitchen in Figure 18.21. He puts it on display in a gallery-like box. It is no longer a hidden necessity. It is part of the architecture. This said, Mies never reveals the actual systems that make the kitchen perform. The revealed systems for Mies are the building's structural components, its program, and its occupants. Lewerentz takes "exposure" further than Mies. For him, the mechanical and electrical systems are as material as the bricks and concrete. The conduit that connects fixtures to the main power source and the pipes that feed and drain a lavatory say as much about the methodology of making, the performance and the occupation of the building, as the surface and space. They ARE occupant and program-exposed. Amazingly, Lewerentz treats windows (Figure 18.23, bottom right) in the same way he treats plumbing and conduit.

Our strategy for *OSWall* learns from Close and Lewerentz. It is predicated on the notion that the house is an assembly of parts that will evolve, and that as designers and occupants, we should create a system that allows the house to do just that. Parts are designed to be replaced, reused, and relocated. Ironically, disintegration and obsolescence are precisely the strategies that render the project economical, efficient, and light.

Acknowledgements: *Drape Wall, Cloak Wall,* and *OSWall*

Project designers: Blair Satterfield, HouMinn Practice/Asst. Professor, Univ. of British Columbia; Marc Swackhamer, HouMinn Practice/Assoc. Professor, Univ. of Minnesota.

Primary contributors: Susanna Hohman, Terrazign, Portland, OR (prototype design/fabrication); Dave Hultman, Univ.of Minnesota (prototype design/fabrication); Rob Tickle, Industrial Art & Design, Minneapolis, MN (prototype design/fabrication); Gary Meyer, Assoc. Professor, Univ. of Minnesota, Dept. of Computer Science (paint research/software development). Design criticism: Marcus Martinez, Patrick McGlothlin, Adam Rouse (Aidlin Darling Design), Karl Wallick (Asst. Prof., Univ. of Cincinnati), David Wulfman (Boston Scientific CRM).

Other contributors: Seth Berrier (University of Minnesota), Carly Mick (Terrazign, Portland, OR), Michael Kisch (RSP Architects, Minneapolis, MN), Alison Rubin de Celis (editing, Jacksonville, IL), UH Green Building Components, Director Joe Meppelink (Houston, TX).

Fabrication: Chris Rizzo (ind. fabricator, Portland, OR), Chad Loukes (Box Lab, Houston, TX), Kevin Groenke (Univ. of Minnesota), PN Products (Scandia, MN) Eric Neuman (CNC Routerworks, Minneapolis, MN), Discount Steel, (Minneapolis, MN), Ameristar (Minneapolis, MN).

Student assistance: Matthew Haller (UMN), Michael Hara (UMN), Kevin Lin (Rice), Jeff Montaque (UMN), Antonio Rodriguez (UMN), Jon Siani (Rice), Don Vu (UMN), Jesse Yang (Rice).

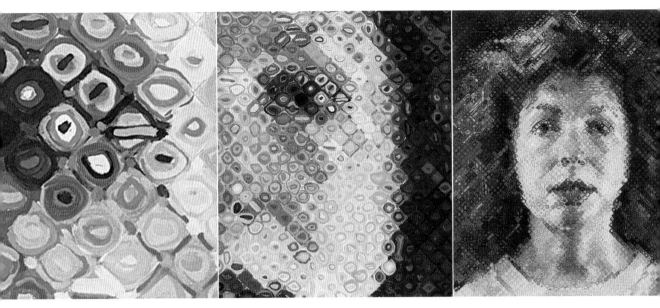

Figure 18.20a–c Idiosyncratic vs. systematized vs. rendered. Chuck Close, *April*, 1990–91, oil on canvas, 100 x 84 inches

Figure 18.21 Mies van der Rohe. Kitchen in the *Farnsworth House*

Figure 18.22 Sigurd Lewerentz. Sink details from St. Peter's Church at Klippan. Completed 1962–66

Figure 18.23 Sigurd Lewerentz. Exterior window details from St. Peter's Church at Klippan. Completed 1962–66

"App" comp. winners: Laurie McGinley, Jeff Abuzzahab, and Andrew Gastineau (Univ. of Minnesota), Jeff Montague (Univ. of Minnesota), and John Steingraeber (Univ. of Minnesota).

Notes

1   Local Motors distinguishes co-creation as a process that allows the community to join the team and exchange ideas. The company seeks to respond directly to customers by innovating throughout the design, fabrication, and retail processes. The strategy includes: "Micro-Factory Retailing" – a distributed fabrication model that would fold dealerships and manufacturing/service centers into a distributed network of small singular units; "Web 2.0 Community" – customers and designers participate directly in the process of designing the vehicles which provides a market-responsive product; "Environmental Efficiency" – through hands-on clientele and an inclusive process, the company strives to achieve best in class efficiency by innovating in both process and material use.
2   Curated by Associate Professor Christopher Hight of Rice University.
3   Brought to light through research conducted by MArch graduate student Michael Kisch in Assistant Professor Swackhamer's "Bio-Inspired Design" coursework at the University of Minnesota.

References

Armstrong, D. J. (2010) *Wood Science 100: The Innovation of Light Frame Construction*, Morgantown, West Virginia: West Virginia University.

Banham, R. (1969) "A home is not a house," *Architectural Design*, vol. 39 no. 1, January, 45–48.

Bittle, J. (2009) *Home Construction's Dirty Secret: 8,000 lbs of Waste Per 2,000 Square Foot House.* January 8. Retrieved April 13, 2010, from Green Building Elements: http://greenbuildingelements.com/2009/01/08/%20home-constructions-dirty-secret-8000-lbs-of-waste-per-2000-square-foot-house/.

Infoplease, E. o. (n.d.) "What is the average home size in the U.S.?" Retrieved April 13, 2010, from Infoplease: http://www.infoplease.com/askeds/us-home-size.html.

Leinhard, J. H. (1988–1997) *No. 779: Balloon Frame Houses.* Retrieved April 13, 2010, from Engines of Our Ingenuity: http://www.uh.edu/engines/epi779.htm.

McKeever, D. and Phelps, R. (1994) "Wood products used in new single-family house construction: 1950 to 1992," *Forest Products Journal*, 4: 11/12, 66–74.

Mumma, T. (1995) "Reducing the embodied energy of buildings," *Home Energy Magazine Online*, January/February.

Nike ACG Seamless NAROPA (2004) *Runner's World*, September, p. 101.

Part VI
Matter Ecology

Engaging the relationship of materiality to energy and site, place and physical perception, matter ecology presents an important aspect of performative and theoretical instigation. Going beyond, but definitively founded in, the interrelationship of material and issues of sustainability, the framing demands a hybrid condition that is both and neither. In dialog with the systems, both natural and manmade, in terms of rituals of use and time, the ecology of the material becomes the foundation of the analysis, approach and process. Here the energy of the system is embodied in the intention and performance of the physical object.

Kiel Moe
Hilary Sample, MOS

Chapter 19
Matter is but Captured Energy

Kiel Moe

Matter and energy are too often understood as distinct systems, agendas, and areas of expertise in architecture. In most curricula, courses on material and construction systems are taught as a distinct topic from energy and environmental systems. Likewise in practice, a building's structural, construction, and energy systems most often have separate systems and consultants. This pedagogical and professional separation of matter and energy has resulted in a design paradigm that views matter as inert fodder – an alibi – for the visual, tectonic, phenomenological, or parametric scenographic cul-de-sacs in recent architectural discourse. In turn, the physically and intellectually rich topic of energy is routinely left as completely latent in a typical design process. This mentality has confined the role of matter in architecture as a primarily visual/semantic enterprise in the past few decades of architectural production and energy as undesigned milieu in architecture.

The separation of matter and energy, however, is a false distinction that obfuscates how building materials and buildings actually behave; for matter is but captured energy. This false distinction strains against reality. As such, it constrains novelty in architecture and amounts to an unimaginative capitulation of disciplinary, professional, and formal possibilities. This chapter argues for an alternative against the persistence of this technological and formal acquiescence: in theoretical and practical terms this chapter points towards practices that collapse the performances of energy and material in a building into a single, more integrated system in the service of more complex and rich performances for architecture. This approach adjusts the scene of complexity in architecture from preoccupations with the intricacies of visual compositions to the more nuanced behavior of material/energy compositions. This ultimately amounts to greater awareness of the relationship between a building and its developmental shape space rather than merely a building's shape. In a context in which energy is increasingly a primary parameter of performances in and outside of architecture, architectural strategies overtly based on matter/energy stand to amend ecological and economic practices while fundamentally altering how buildings are figured; engendering novel relationships among matter, energy, body, construction, and form. Understanding that matter is captured energy stands to transform critical assumptions about the formal, ecological, and economic life of architecture.

Matter and energy

Matter is but captured energy. Any physical thing – a building, landscape, or body, for instance – is a set of vibrating molecular lattices; an accumulation of molecular processes that eventuate in a form that maintains an organization for a certain duration. The bonds of these molecular lattices that compose matter itself are fundamentally energetic. Captured energy is the only thing that maintains or alters matter's bonds. Further, the exchanges between these lattices and their milieu are also entirely energetic. If there is any event, that is, if anything happens at all, it is because energy has been exchanged between the lattices of one piece of matter and another. All matter is continuously sending and receiving forms of energy; some energy is captured and embedded, some is exchanged back into the milieu. Given the deep prevalence of energy in matter's very

----

existence, all matter – all of its properties and behaviors – is really only an expression of the energetic exchanges between molecular lattices and their milieu. The persistence of any physical thing is a function of the energy embedded in, and exchanged with, its matter.

For example, an object, such as a rock formation, is often thought as a fixed, inert object or shape. However, it is actually an expression of dynamic energy systems and processes that range from the molecular to the territorial. Its shape is the result of historical and fundamentally energetic processes; the result of active formation not platonic shaping. D'Arcy Thompson described this process of formation in *On Growth and Form*, "The form of an object is a 'diagram of forces,' in this sense we can deduce the forces that are acting or have acted upon it."[1] Force is energy imbued with direction and pattern. Thompson views the present form of any physical thing in terms of its shaping forces, the pattern of its historical development. Thus, more than matter, what gives any physical thing its shape at a particular moment is ultimately contingent on a certain pattern of energy. As Norbert Wiener emphasized, "One thing at any rate is clear. The physical identity of an individual does not consist in the matter of which it is made."[2] For Weiner, these immaterial but very real systems and processes determined more about a thing's appearance than matter. In short, the physical world does not consist of shapes of matter but rather of ceaseless formations of energy patterning matter. Shape is ultimately a function of energy. As such, it is thus a mistake to think of matter and shape without thinking of energy.

Energy is not only what bonds matter together, but also is the agency that activates matter, connecting it to the world. Ralph S. Lillie, a biologist, saw that "fundamentally the living organism is an integrating center. Materials and energies which previously were isolated and independent come into closer association, under some kind of directive influence or compulsion, to form a characteristically organized unity."[3] Lillie is here focused on living entities. However, this integrating capacity is applicable to living and non-living entities for as Luis Fernandez-Galiano states, "Energy injects life, processes, and transformations into the inanimate world of matter, and thus into the world of Architecture."[4]

When matter becomes material – becomes an artifice of human agency – the role of energy is only amplified. Human agency multiplies the patterning of matter with additional energy inputs and processes. The energy of many processes are embedded or embodied in materials. Energy is what binds matter, what activates matter, what transforms matter, and what organizes matter. Matter is captured energy.

The denial of matter as captured energy in the discourse of architecture, perpetuating the separation of material and energy in architectural systems and expertise, deforms architecture's view of reality and the physical world. In doing so, it also deprives architecture of richer formations of matter and energy. When matter is understood as an expression of a pattern of energy, it can alter the way we think not only of materials but it call also alter the way we think of whole systems and techniques. What would change if architects viewed matter as captured energy?

Appearance

The formations and patterning of matter by energy discussed here have potentially rich visual implications that are not to be denied or underestimated. However, it is much more critical to understand that the energetic formations and patterning role of energy discussed here absolutely transcend visuality as the dominant criteria of architecture's appearance. When this formation and patterning become the focus of design activity, architecture engenders possibilities that are as novel as they are necessary in today's resource-constrained realities. This shifts the presence of complexity in architecture from its excruciating preoccupation with the visual composition of a shape to the actual behavior of a formation. In this context, seemingly simple building shapes may nonetheless perform in complex ways. It may even be the case that truly rich and complex performances can only emerge from such seemingly simple formations in architecture.[5] Thus what is to be composed and formed in architectural design is no longer merely the appearance of building shapes alone but also other criteria that are not immediately legible in a building's shape but only in its shape space.

Not shape but shape space

As in the example of the rock formation above, architects are routinely preoccupied with the appearance of an object's shape. Since matter is captured energy, however, peering into a formation's shape space is far more consequential than its shape alone. Shape spaces are virtual but real multi-dimensional spaces that are used in complexity science to help explain the phenomena of formation. Stuart Kauffman, in a discussion of molecular diversity, describes shape space as follows: "Three of these dimensions would correspond to the three spatial dimensions, length, height, and width, of a molecular binding site. Other dimensions might correspond to physical properties of the binding sites of molecules such as charge, dipole moment, and hydrophobicity."[6] Each variable is another dimension that can mutate a virtual shape. In this way the formation – its variables of processes, matter, and energy – can be modeled, illuminating key developmental moments and possible pathways. Ultimately an understanding of how something appears – how energy patterns the agencies and contingencies of a thing's developmental milieu – matters more than its mere appearance. In architecture, the shape space of a material or of a whole building will inevitably engage an enormous set of variables. What is important to grasp is that a shape space is how energy patterns matter.

The following two examples help illustrate aspects of what can change in architecture when matter is understood as captured energy; how energy patterns matter. At times the agencies and constituencies in a shape space exert force and yield a material in a building. This is the case of the first example: a solid wood zero-operational-energy building in Colorado. At other times, attention to architecture's shape space may yield immaterial but no less real pressure on the development of a whole system. This is certainly the case with a body of research focused on thermally active surfaces in architecture.[7] Any technique or system, such as structure or an energy system, has a particular shape space.

Back to mono: stick vs. stack

A default, and rather unquestioned, assumption of contemporary construction is the convention of the multi-layered wall. In this modality, architects add yet another material or energy system every time another technical requirement or an aesthetic issue emerges in building design; a highly additive approach. Each layer adds another layer of labor, often less and less skilled labor. Each layer drains budgets through extra design, specification, coordination, material, transportation, scheduling and installation. Each layer adds a network of externalities to the building, increasing its ecological footprint. Each layer, it seems, is often less substantive than the last. In short, it is an excessively time- and resource-consumptive approach that engenders a receding horizon of opportunity for architects, drains design fee and building budgets, makes practice unnecessarily more complex, and follows a hubristic model of planned obsolescence; all straining against modes of sustainability.

Departing from this convention of contemporary construction, a recently completed design-build project in Colorado presents a more monolithic approach to construction (Figures 19.1–19.6). This case provides a comparison of a solid, stacked wood wall compared to a conventional stick framed, multi-layered wall. The following description of the assembly and its multivariate performance foregrounds an integrated modality in which building components do multiple jobs that conflate matter and energy. A primary impetus of this project is an assertion that architects can do more, achieve more, by doing less and consuming less; a paradigm of lower-technology, higher-performance buildings.

Figure 19.1 Exterior view

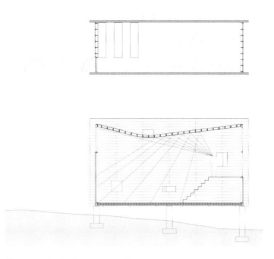

Figure 19.2a–b Plan and section

Figure 19.3 Perspective

Figure 19.4 Site

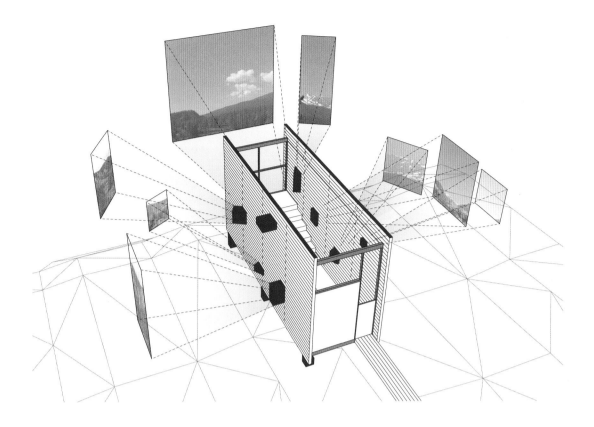

Figure 19.5 Building views

Figure 19.6 Interior view

Stack assembly and structure

The walls of this building are composed as a stack of 6 x 8 spruce timbers either 6, 12 or 18 feet long (Figure 19.7). This single material comprises the structure, enclosure, air/water/vapor barriers, finish system, cladding, as well as the thermal conditioning system of the building. These timbers perform all the functions of a typical multi-layered wall and once a timber is installed, there is no additional labor involved with the assembly of that part of the wall. The timbers are compressed together with a series of threaded rods that pass through the height of the wall along with log screws that are used to install and straighten the timbers along their length during installation. The threaded rods are fixed at the top of the wall and tightened from the bottom of the wall as the wood will collectively shrink in time about 2 inches over its 19½ ft height as the wood dries. This shrinkage requires slip joints at all wood and steel connections. The solid timber walls at times behave as very deep beams spanning from pier to pier (Figure 19.8). At other times, the timbers behave more like a masonry wall in the distribution of their corbelled load paths (Figure 19.9).

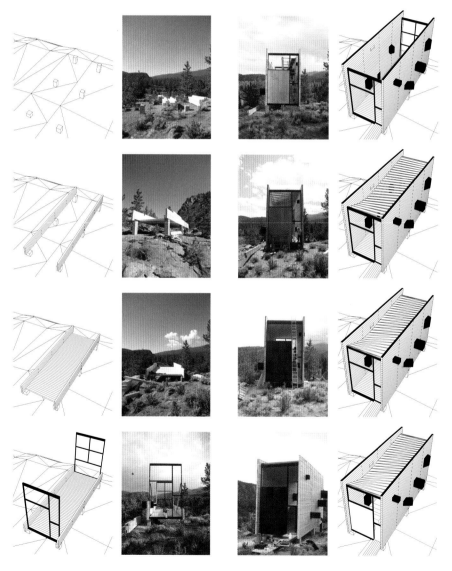

Figure 19.7a–h Assembly

The roof of the building is a ruled surface that pitches rain and snow to an oversized scupper on the east wall (Figure 19.10). This three-dimensional shape of the roof diaphragm helps stiffen the walls and helps resist lateral movement of the walls in the middle section of the building whereas steel moment-window frames brace the building at its ends (Figures 19.11–19.12). Further, the asymmetrically curved belly of the ceiling distributes sonic and luminous energy (Figure 19.13).

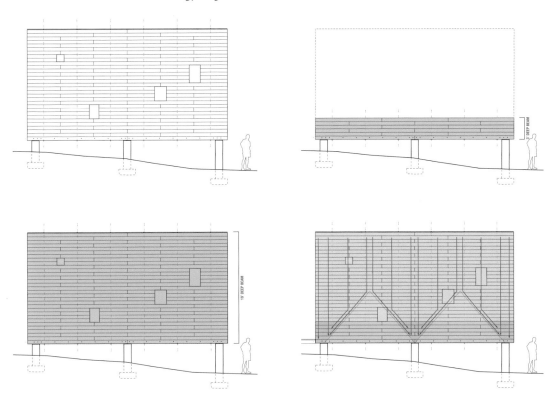

Figure 19.8a–d Structure

Figure 19.9 Exterior view from below

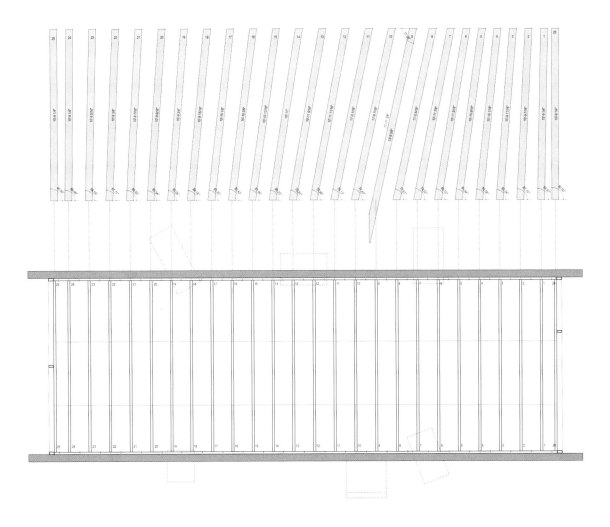

Figure 19.10 Ruled surface framing
Figure 19.11 Roof framing from above

Figure 19.12 Roof framing from below
Figure 19.13 Ceiling view

Externalities of stick and stacks

While the appearance of a stick-framed, rain-screen clad wall would have been more or less satisfactory and well-performing in a limited sense, the shape space of a stick framed wall – the patterning of its externalities or how its materials are extracted, transported, manufactured, transported again and again – is as vulgar as it is destructive. Even if the stick-framed building is pleasant enough, this vulgarity is evident in the plundered landscapes of its extraction, the factories of its manufacture, and the pollution, and risks conflicts associated with its petro-transportation.

In contrast, the spruce wood for the stacked wall comes from the same valley as the project location. Likewise, they were processed into timbers at a mill in the same valley. The result is radically little transportation costs and pollution compared to other approaches. The cut-off remainders of the timbers also proved to be excellent firewood that was used both for cooking and conviviality on the remote mountain site during construction. As the dominant material in the building, the spruce provided dramatically less waste than a typical stick-framed assembly. A major point here is that more budget was spent on material for the building assembly rather than the externalities of a typical wall.

An analysis of the embodied energy provides a more concrete illustration of the shape spaces of these two wall systems (Figure 19.14). As a construction (hopefully) becomes more energy efficient in terms of its operation, the role of its embodied energy becomes increasingly important; it becomes a greater part of the ecological resources required for a building. Certainly as a building team claims to yield a "zero-energy" building (zero-operational energy building), then its embodied energy is all important. This timber structure has no power-operated systems and is thus a zero-operational energy building.

Figure 19.14a–b Stick and stack wall types

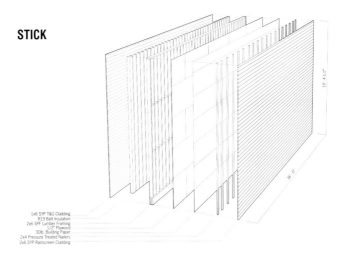

STICK

1x6 SYP T&G Cladding
R19 Batt Insulation
2x6 SPF Lumber Framing
1/2" Plywood
30lb. Building Paper
2x4 Pressure Treated Nailers
2x6 SYP Rainscreen Cladding

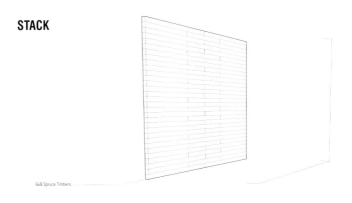

STACK

6x8 Spruce Timbers

The embodied analysis for the stacked and stick approaches to wall construction is revealing (Figures 19.15–19.16). The 6 x 8 spruce timbers for the walls and floor of this building were locally harvested and air-dried in the desert-like climate of the Upper Arkansas River Valley. On account of this the embodied energy value for each wall is 7421 megajoules. The embodied energy value for a stick-framed and clad wall of a kiln-dried lumber of the same dimensions is 42958 megajoules, or nearly six times the embodied energy.

STICK	qty	length	linear feet	volume per	cu feet	cu meter	MJ per unit		MJ
2x6 stud	39	18.2	710	0.05729	40.66444	1.1514888			
2x6 plate	2	36	72	0.05729	4.12488	0.1168036			
blocking	76	0.875	67	0.05729	3.809785	0.1078811			
2x12 beam	3	36	108	0.11458	12.37464	0.3504108			
						1.7265842	4692		8101
Plywood	qty			volume per	cu feet	cu meter			MJ
1/2"	23			1.333	30.659	0.8681662	9440		8195
Batt Insulation	qty	length	sf		lbs	kg	MJ per unit		MJ
R-19 x 12"	36	18	648		162	73.5	150		11025
Interior Finish	qty	length	linear feet	volume per	cu feet	cu meter	MJ per unit		MJ
1x6 SYP #1	39	36	1404	0.01909	26.80236	0.7589583	4692		3561
Rain Screen	qty	length	linear feet	volume per	cu feet	cu meter	MJ per unit		MJ
2x4 nailer	19	19.2	365	0.028645	10.4497	0.2959024			
2x6 cladding	39	36	1404	0.05729	80.43516	2.2776701			
						2.5735725	4692		12075
									42958

STACK	rows	length	linear feet	volume per	cu feet	cu meter	MJ per unit	MJ
6x8 timber	31	36	1116	0.276909	309.0304	8.7507677	848	**7421**

Figure 19.15 Embodied energy analysis 1

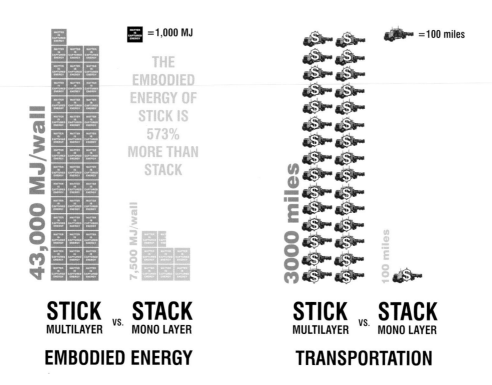

Figure 19.16a–b Embodied energy analysis 2

Related to this topic of embodied energy is durability. Embodied energy at the time of construction is important to consider but it is equally important to consider the life cycle of the assembly in question. For instance, while a massive ancient Roman bridge may have almost twice as much embodied energy as a contemporary concrete and steel bridge, the Roman bridge has served about 90 generations of Romans and the contemporary steel bridge may only serve two or three generations. As such, the durability of the Roman bridge has a radically lower embodied energy per generation served. This amortization of resources is critical to the concept of sustainability. Further, it can be argued that there are also social and cultural dividends to be gained from highly durable construction that become integral to the life of a city.

The solid timber wall that provides for adjustments and tuning engenders durability through mass. In contrast to the increasingly thin layers of materials in contemporary construction, the thickness of the material provides a redundancy of material that points to a longer use life due to a different paradigm of maintenance. In the case of plywood, oriented strand board, and of other engineered wood products, there is no data that establishes their performance or integrity beyond a few decades, especially depending on the quality of their detailing and installation.

While there is an argument about the efficacy of the monolithic wall in terms of its embodied energy, its impetus in the project has as much to do with its effect on the building and those inside the building. The thickness and robustness of the wall are palpable. But there are other, more nuanced effects of the monolithic wall. This wall assembly engenders a radically different thermal perception of the space. Spruce is a softwood and thus not particularly dense so it does not conduct thermal energy as readily as more dense species. This creates a thermal lag: cold exterior surface temperatures conduct more slowly in the winter and likewise warm surface temperature transmission is dampened in the summer. At the same time, the spruce is dense enough to absorb solar energy and its interior surface is thus warmed in the winter, affecting the building interior's mean radiant temperature. The performative result is that the owner can read in the space in a T-shirt, sitting comfortably in a mid-sixties ambient temperature while exterior temperatures are sub-zero in the winter. So there are some subtle, often unconsidered, experiential differences between the stack and stick approaches.

The comparison of stick and stack approaches in respect of their performance as conflated matter/energy systems in this case points to practices that run counter to many assumptions of contemporary construction. It helps illustrate that conflated material/energy strategies have more nuanced and complex performances in a wall assembly and its respective shape space. This is also case of a second example that focuses on more systemic effects of a conflated material/energy strategy: thermally active surfaces.

Thermally active surfaces in architecture

The second example questions a primary determinant in much of contemporary buildings: heating and cooling buildings with air. In a transformation of energy and building practices, with thermally active surfaces, the thermal conditioning of a building is decoupled from the ventilation system by using the mass of the building itself as the thermal system. This method of heat transfer is physiologically and thermodynamically optimal. It also reinvests the fabric of the building itself with a more poignant role: The structural system and other primary material systems are the primary energy system. Here matter is captured energy but also channels energy. As the basis of energy and construction strategies, it yields a cascading set of advantages for the building design and construction industry: radically lower energy consumption, more durable buildings, healthier buildings, and more integrated building systems and design teams. An important aspect of thermally active surfaces is that they are low-tech yet high-performance and are thus equally applicable in the developed and developing worlds. As such, thermally active surfaces are central to multiple, systemic aspects of sustainability.

To adequately address the shape space of a technique that treats matter as energy, the research must address a range of past, current, and future practices but it must also address thermodynamics and physiology, the implications for professional practices, and finally provide a guide for implementation. Accordingly, the research contrasts the parallel histories of thermally active surfaces and air conditioning. These histories explain the material, social, marketing, and technical unfolding of building technology in the twentieth century as a means to explain why we build the way we do and why that will change in the new century. This research also covers the physiological and thermodynamic basis of thermally active surfaces in terms designed for engineers and architects to grasp the logic and advantages of this technique. Inherent in this technique is a de-fragmentation of buildings and design practice. Finally, a major impetus of this matter–energy technique research is formal. In addition to energy, human comfort, construction, and budget advantages, thermally active surface systems make architecture more architectural by enabling new relationships within body, program, technology, material, and form. In an age when biology is increasingly the model for diverse forms of thought, thermally active surfaces in buildings finally acknowledge the physiology of the bodies that buildings are intended to enclose and support. The fabric of a building itself is no longer merely a passive container of space of ignored bodies, but an active agent in the performances of buildings and bodies. When structure, enclosure, and human comfort merge into one material/energy system, architecture gains new roles for itself.

Thermally active surfaces in practice
One recent example of a thermally active surface approach is a proposal for a pair of office buildings in downtown Denver. In addition to the typical constraints that determine much market-driven office space in North America, this pair of office buildings (about 100,000 square feet each) was limited to 65 feet in height due to a landmarked Beaux-Arts structure next door (Figure 19.17). Thus competing, air-based proposals were limited to four stories. By de-coupling the thermal loads of the buildings from its ventilation loads, the thermally active surface approach by AndersonMasonDale Architects with myself as a consultant, however, was able to insert another level of office space by altering the floor-to-floor height; removing most of the ducts and other equipment that typically occupy increasingly thick ceiling and floor plenums (Figure 19.18). Further, as roof top units were not an option in this historically sensitive context, the architects also opened up considerable floor space by removing fan rooms and duct chases. Taken together, these leasable gains significantly transformed the developer's pro forma. For instance, the building envelope budget was calculated as a percentage of the leasable floor space (Figure 19.19). With the extra level of leasable space, the architects can invest more design time and budget in the building envelope; a key effort in thermally active surface strategies (Figure 19.20). Further, budget otherwise spent on ducts and drop ceilings was re-directed towards a more robust precast concrete thermally active surface structure with an exposed plaster ceiling. The thermally active surface strategy is optimal for the developer in terms of maintaining unleased office space because such systems utilize a low-air temperature approach to heating, thus saving operating costs for the owner and because it can so easily be zoned. When these multiple advantages are conflated with less energy consumption, greater human comfort, and consequently, greater office productivity, the thermally active surface approach gained momentum in this case.

Figure 19.17 Exterior view of proposal

Figure 19.18a–b Air-based and water-based wall sections

Denver Office Building Floor Area Analysis

	Program Brief	
	Gross SF	Leaseable SF
Ground	20,287	14,991
2	23,954	21,896
3	23,954	21,896
4	23,954	19,791
5	0	0
Total	**92,149**	**78,574**

	Thermally Active Surface Approach			
	Gross SF	% Delta	Leaseable SF	% Delta
Ground	23,954	18.1%	17,160	14.5%
2	23,594	1.5%	22,218	1.5%
3	23,594	1.5%	22,218	1.5%
4	23,594	1.5%	22,218	12.3%
5	23,594	n/a	22,218	n/a
Total	**118,330**	**28.4%**	**106,032**	**34.9%**

Figure 19.19a–b Air-based and water-based floor area analysis

Figure 19.20 Exterior view of proposal

Conclusion

Matter is captured energy. When this fact is observed in practice, the efficacy of some of architecture's persistent assumptions such as layered construction and air-conditioning becomes suspect. This opens material practices to more integrated trajectories that are a mongrel of material and energy systems. This has formal potential not only for the shape of an individual building but the shape space as well that determines its behaviors, performances, and appearances of matter and buildings. This shifts the foci of design composition from the hegemony of visual appearance to more robust parameters that do not deny but transcend visuality as the only criterion of composition in architecture. Ultimately, design composition specifies how energy is captured and channeled in a building; how energy will pattern material and its performance. Yet, the specification of material in a building in turn specifies a pattern of external energy flows that shape often distant landscapes, economies, and lives. This chapter points to a paradigm of lower-technology, higher-performance buildings based on matter as captured energy. Such a paradigm demands that we peer beyond the surface of a shape and, finally, into the complex patterning that is actually responsible for the formation, appearance, and performance of architecture.

Notes

1   D'Arcy W. Thompson, *On Growth and Form* (Cambridge: Cambridge University Press, 1951), p. 16.

2   Norbert Wiener, *The Human Use of Human Beings: Cybernetics and Society* (Boston: Houghton Mifflin Company, 1950), p. 108.

3   Ralph S. Lillie, "The Nature of Organizing Action," *American Naturalist*, 72(742) (Sept.–Oct., 1938): 389–415 (on p. 390).

4   Luis Fernandez-Galiano, *Fire and Memory: On Architecture and Energy* (Cambridge, MA: The MIT Press, 2000), p. 56.

5   This view is developed in Kiel Moe, "Extra Ordinary Performances at the Salk Institute for Biological Sciences," *Journal of Architectural Education*, 61(4), May 2008.

6   Stuart Kauffman, *Investigations* (Oxford: Oxford University Press, 2000), p. 12.

7   Kiel Moe, *Thermally Active Surfaces in Architecture* (New York: Princeton Architectural Press, 2010).

Chapter 20
A Brise-Soleil without a Building

Hilary Sample
MOS

Our office actively exploits the strange to create performative physical properties of materials for the purpose of producing unexpected visual experiences in urban settings. Most recently, we have worked with employing unusual textures, luminescent surfaces, and natural membranes that become uniquely architectural where their structural geometries intersect. With *Urban Battery*, for the competition Flip-a-Strip held by the SMoCA in Scottsdale, Arizona, we proposed a large-scale urban intervention as a physical structure akin to a power station, a vertical greenhouse and a billboard, all rolled into one new type of enclosure (Figure 20.1). It double-functions as an object that shades the parking lot of the strip mall below and provides internal shading. As a structure that plays with shade, we investigated those forms, an attempt to advance Modern ideas especially as they relate to the role of the brise-soleil (Figure 20.2).

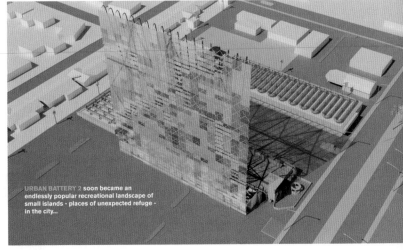

URBAN BATTERY 2 soon became an endlessly popular recreational landscape of small islands · places of unexpected refuge · in the city...

Figure 20.1 *Urban Battery,* view from street

Figure 20.2 *Urban Battery,* helicopter view

By definition, a brise-soleil performs the specific function of reducing heat gain within a structure by deflecting sunlight. Within that definition there are different categories of brise-soleils – each with different lineages (Figure 20.3). Le Corbusier first introduced the brise-soleil into his lexicon of Modern architecture with his unbuilt Algiers projects[1] (Figure 20.4). From there it can be traced through the wide-ranging work of other Modernists, whose work would be unrelated in almost every aspect, from Oscar Niemeyer, to Jane Drew and Maxwell Fry with their far-reaching projects in Africa, to Richard Neutra's lightweight models, to the pattern-based screens of Erwin Hauer. The brise-soleil has evolved from simple, fixed forms of vertical or horizontal louvers to sophisticated, computerized forms in projects like Jean Nouvel's *Institut du Monde Arabe* in Paris. Brise-soleils have become more accepted as a building feature since the early 1990s (Figure 20.5). This rich and varied history affirms the brise-soleil as a persistent architectural type.

Figure 20.3 1958 United Federal Savings and Loan Bank, brise-soleil in Reno, Nevada, demolished

Figure 20.4 Le Corbusier, *Carpenter Center*, Cambridge, MA, 1965

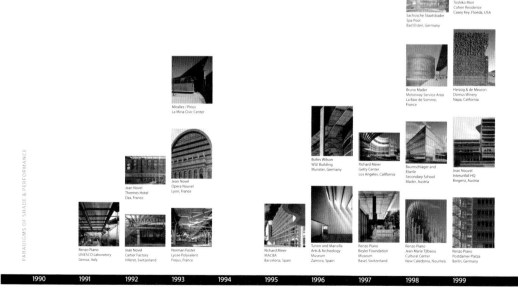

Figure 20.5 Timeline comparing façade treatments of shading either by man-made materials or the introduction of landscape as façade materials

A brise-soleil is an oddity in architecture, and this is what makes it interesting. It does not insulate the interior from environmental conditions such as air temperature, moisture, wind, dust and dirt, because no part of it actually encloses interior habitable space. It is typically applied in a uniform and monolithic manner which makes it appear to be integral to the façade, though it is structurally parasitic. As an outer boundary, it functions as the front face or image of a building, but it is actually screening the line of enclosure. It creates a weird space at the front of the building. Despite its limited performance as a thermal barrier or architectural enclosure, it is nonetheless significant as an object because it constructs a *material* boundary between the outside natural world and the environmental seal of the building that typically lies just behind it. In other words, it sits between the inside and the outside, as a mediating façade. Brise-soleils expand the distance between the inside and outside of the building. Such thickening of the façade could be seen as a performative act to further produce deep dark internal space. As an aesthetic object, appearing as a billboard-like figure, the brise-soleil as a form is as much a political act as it is a material one. As a political act, increasing the distance between inside and out, or further differentiating one type of space from another, office space from in-between space acts as a visual barrier, providing shading but also obscuring the view to or from the interior (Figure 20.6). It appears as a hard division between inside and outside, and it often visually masks what is going on behind it.

Figure 20.6 In-between space

A curious example of this can be found in 1960s American architectures, where lightweight metalized brise-soleils were novel and dominated major architecture works. Given the politics of a façade-as-mask, it is especially interesting that the brise-soleil was most often found on civic buildings. Looking back, its usage appears as cheap and shoddily constructed. It's a "fake" front. As an independent front façade, its fakeness plays with our sense of what constitutes the building envelope and what does not. As a mask, the desire of the brise-soleil is to intervene between architecture and nature or its surroundings. Their shape is oddly familiar – sometimes resembling a billboard, other times giant venetian blinds. They are more post-modern than modern perhaps. They are often broken due to maintenance failure, and of the brise-soleils that remain intact, often the fins are fixed and rusted in place, corroded, pitted, dented, or, worse, missing fins. The invention as a façade that was to be more like scaffolding and less like a building was economically a smart strategy. Like a billboard, the brise-soleil is more concerned with projecting an image to the urban environment than it is with the internal life behind it. To see out, one must always look on the oblique.

Though most early brise-soleils have been demolished, one of the most significant examples remains in Los Angeles. Richard Neutra's *Los Angeles Hall of Records* exemplifies the gradual shift in the Modern aesthetic from the desire for complete transparency – with all glass façades in homes and in offices – towards a screened surface (Figure 20.7). Oftentimes fully glazed spaces were uncomfortable – spaces were simply too hot or too bright to work in or, conversely, when glazing became dirty, up to 50 percent of natural light would be lost. In response to these conditions, the brise-soleil emerged as a physical remedy by providing shade, reducing the infiltration of heat, glare and brightness. In effect, it produced a better living and working environment. Careful not to replace the emerging advancement of large glazed surfaces, late Modernism went wild with covering up transparency with new forms of brise-soleils. At the same time, the brise-soleil emerged as an aesthetic problem as much as an environmental solution. Neutra developed a novel approach with a lightweight metal frame clad infilled with metal panels. (Verging on obsession, nearly every project that Neutra designed incorporated a brise-soleil in some shape or form.) With the *Hall of Records*, Neutra achieved a screen equal to the full height of the façade with its 125 ft fins (Figure 20.8). What is striking about Neutra's twist on Le Corbusier's original fixed screens is the operability of the formed aluminum louvers. The *Hall of Records*, built in 1962, was remarkable for its era as each full-height fin was connected to a mechanical eye on the roof-top. The entire system moved as the eye tracked the sun (Figure 20.9). It still works today, although it is in serious need of restoration. Neutra consistently used the brise-soleil as a passive cooling feature to simultaneously create a patterned façade, and by extension expanded a visual game between the internal architecture and the city.

Figures 20.7–20.9 Richard Neutra's *Los Angeles Hall of Records*

To focus on the exterior impact of the brise-soleil is to only tell half of the story. Over time, the brise-soleil sponsored the comforting idea that internal space could be protected from the exterior. It is important to underscore that the brise-soleil developed concurrently with advances in glazing. (It is only natural then that this lightweight, attached or supplement device would be subsumed back into the physical enclosure of the building as a double glazed wall.) Brise-soleil, while physically detached from the interior, screens it from intense light and visually divides the interior life from its external context. Until recently, the brise-soleil was rarely documented from an interior vantage point.[2] However, several contemporary artists have taken up the subject and have, through their works, demonstrated the potential of these screening devices to produce atmospheric effects on the interior. Germaine Kruip, an installation artist, and Luisa Lambri, a photographer, have produced projects that reclaim the subjects of nature and visual effects through the elementary forms of brise-soleil: fins and louvers. At the *Stedelijke Museum* in Amsterdam in 2004, Kruip's delicate insertions of small-scale, rotating fins covered with mirrors demonstrate the desire for shade, but the reflective fins bring in light and also surprising views of the city outside as they rotate (Figures 20.10–20.12). The piece reintroduces the urban panoramas that brise-soleils typically cancel out. The view is brought back through the rotating

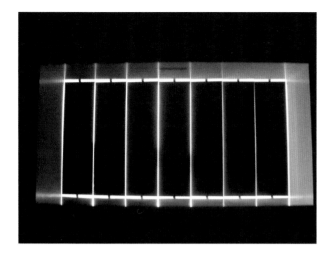

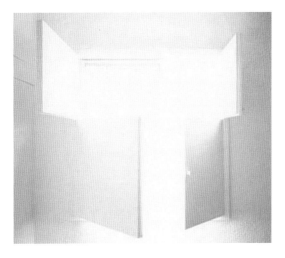

Figures 20.13–20.14 Luis Barragán's shutters

screens but, this time, the view is altered. Not only is it mirrored, it is also fragmented as the fins continuously revolve. In another piece, a series of colored screens transforms the light entering through the skylights – it becomes ethereal and beautiful, evoking the softness of morning light and delicate sunsets. Pink, orange, blue and gray light fills the interior space. No modern brise-soleil ever achieved this kind of sensuousness.

Using a different artistic medium, the photographer Luisa Lambri captures light effects through carefully focused frames of domestic windows. Her most celebrated images document Barragán's shutters (Figure 20.13). In the close-up photographs of the steel-frame windows, the brise-soleil appears to be missing, leaving the aluminum cladding exposed to the natural world beyond. It is as if the aluminum panels have dissolved or eroded away leaving the thinnest framing behind (Figure 20.14). The view from within exposes the desire to see beyond the brise-soleil, to reveal the city – as Kruip does with her fragmented and almost kaleidoscopic turning fins – or to reveal nature – as in Lambri's surprising panoramas. In Lambri's photographs there is marked interest in gaining access to nature. The aesthetic interest in brise-soleil proves it to be a dynamic device – all the more dramatic for its ability to both hide and reveal.

Rethinking the structural, material, and contextual opportunities of the brise-soleil as a type of architecture, drove the proposal for the *Urban Battery* (Figure 20.15). Prompted to intervene within the strip mall typology, we proposed, not a reinvention of the strip mall, but an addition to it. While the most pragmatic solution – from a developer's point of view – would have been to renovate the existing façades, making a Wild West storefront, we decided to take advantage of the competition as a chance to explore radical alternatives and potential futures wherein the strip mall plays an essential environmental role. *Urban Battery* acts as an energy producer: filtering air, housing oxygen-regenerating plants, sponsoring bike paths and public gardens, and storing bio-products within the structure. The proposal acts as a piece of urban infrastructure found in multiples throughout the flat urban context. The greenhouses worked in series as a system of wayfinders throughout the city as well as serving to provide a new energy source to local neighborhoods. The Scottsdale competition site lacks any healthy urban infrastructures, no community centers, no pools, no green space – it's a dead quadrant. *Urban Battery* reinvigorates it.

Figure 20.15 *Urban Battery*

As a design intervention, it presents an opportunity for urban renewal, both formally and also functionally. The greenhouse is comprised of lightweight materials (polycarbonate glazing, aluminet fabric and algae affixed to a structural aluminum frame) whose large form casts a shadow that covers the parking lot of the strip mall below, thereby cooling the brutally hot asphalt surface (such a distinct feature of our collective strip mall imagery) and making for a more amenable urban space (Figure 20.16). The screen wall recalls the ubiquitous urban billboard, a reference to Venturi and Scott Brown's *Learning from Las Vegas*,[3] as much as it references the lightweight aluminum brise-soleils made popular by Richard Neutra in the 1960s. At the same time, the structure is lined with an aluminum fabric that shields the interior from direct sun, allowing a gentler, more diffuse light to permeate the interior. *Urban Battery* is a thin, tall, and lightweight structure that is, in effect, a brise-soleil without a building (Figure 20.17).

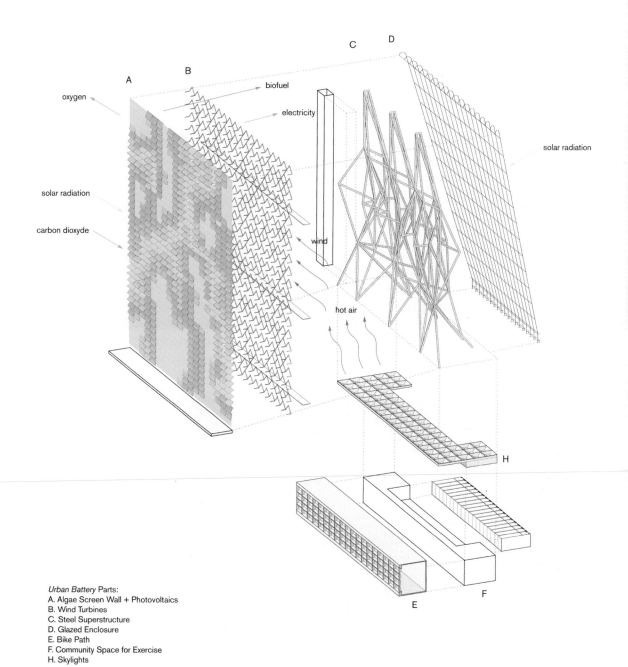

oxygen

solar radiation

carbon dioxyde

A

B

C   D

biofuel

electricity

solar radiation

wind

hot air

H

E   F

Urban Battery Parts:
A. Algae Screen Wall + Photovoltaics
B. Wind Turbines
C. Steel Superstructure
D. Glazed Enclosure
E. Bike Path
F. Community Space for Exercise
H. Skylights

Figure 20.16 *Urban Battery,* components

Figure 20.17 *Urban Battery*, night view

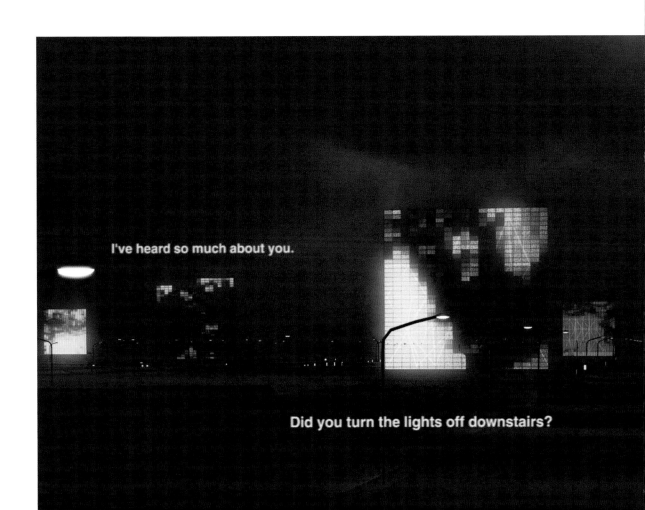

Today, we ask façades to be responsive to a complex array of environmental pressures. Brise-soleil, as a re-emerging type, must take on this task – operating as part of a larger mechanism for architecture and civic infrastructure. At the same time, the brise-soleil can capitalize on its historical image – it can be iconic as a result of *actual* efficiencies not just perceived advantages (Figure 20.18).

Notes

1   Le Corbusier's original invention of the brise-soleil occurred with the Algiers project, then at the Cité de Refuge, then the brise-soleil was adopted at the Ministry of Health and Education in Rio de Janerio, and later Le Corbusier used deep thick concrete fins in Chandigarh, and at the *Carpenter Center*.

2   David Leatherbarrow presents close-up photographs in his book, *Architecture Oriented Otherwise* (New York: Princeton Architectural Press, 2009).

3   Robert Venturi and Denise Scott Brown, *Learning from Las Vegas: The Forgotten Symbolism of Architectural Form* (Cambridge, MA: The MIT Press, 1977).

Figure 20.18 *Urban Battery,* serial deployment

"To grow algae it isn't necessary to convert any arable land, and it doesn't require good soil. Just flat land, carbon dioxide and sunlight."
http://www.renewableenergyworld.com/rea/news/story?id=47237, viewed on September 8, 2008. January 26, 2007, Making Biofuel from Pond Scum by Shelley Schlender.

Part VII
Matter Pedagogy

The integration of material practice with architectural education provides a unique vantage of experimentation. These projects represent practitioners who bridge between academia and practice pursuing clear agendas that synthesize a personal line of inquiry with a larger agenda of digital medias, materiality and academic pedagogy. Founded in an intense examination of the role of materiality in design education, the projects are design build installations, founded in a systemized process of integrated learning through making. Building out of specific tools, materials and budgets, their formal agendas are derivative of their constraints. Pushing the envelope of consideration, the infrastructure of the system in which they are produced weigh heavily upon their framing and outcome. The product is not simply the process or the object, but the transfer of knowledge associated with the exercise.

Jeremy Ficca
Lawrence Blough, GRAFTWORKS
Santiago R. Pérez

Chapter 21
Material Resistance

Jeremy Ficca

Resistances, those facts that stand in the way of the will.

(Richard Sennett)[1]

In 1505, Michelangelo was summoned to Rome to design the Tomb of Pope Julius II. Originally intended for Saint Peter's Basilica and consisting of nearly 40 free-standing figures, the version completed in 1547 was a ghost of the original proposal. Following Julius' death in 1513, numerous funding reductions and competing demands of Michelangelo's time led him to permanently stop work in 1523 on what were to be a series of enslaved figures that would form the base of the tomb. As a result, six slave figures were left unfinished and stand as a physical record of Michelangelo's process (Figure 21.1). While the sculptures provide insight to the techniques of the day, perhaps more striking, is the resulting imagery. It is one in which the slaves struggle to break free from not only their torments, but the very stones from which they are formed. The juxtaposition

Figure 21.1 *Slave,* Michelangelo

between identifiable human forms and rough hewn stone animate the figures in such a way as to suggest the slaves coming into a state of existence out of the stone. Michelangelo speaks to this as he describes his process as one that does not sculpt figures into stone but rather liberates them.

Sculpting natural materials is an inherently precarious proposition. The material characteristics that enrich the object under formation are the very things that present challenges to those working the material. In the case of Michelangelo's enslaved figures, one must have the skill to read and navigate the veins and pockets within the stone to ensure material integrity is preserved and vision achieved. In his seminal book *The Nature and Art of Workmanship*, David Pye refers to this negotiation as a workmanship of risk. In contrast to a workmanship of certainty, in which "the result is predetermined and unalterable once production has begun,"[2] risk relies upon acquired knowledge to address problems as they are uncovered. The stone quite literally, presents resistance to the act of chiseling. The skill of the individual working the material is directly related to their ability to work through the material resistance. This is not the result of sheer will, but rather an opportunistic response to those things uncovered. It is a form of enlightened improvisation. While, in the case of the enslaved figures, the risk is tethered to materiality, risk can also manifest through the tools and techniques employed. In essence, Pye's distinctions between certainty and risk speak to the very relationship between design and realization. This is inherently a negotiation between will and feasibility.

In the sphere of architecture, this relationship has, by necessity, typically been top-down with design largely determined prior to fabrication or construction. This is understandable, as the act of building is often a unique, complex assembly of a multitude of components and materials.[3] In light of the inherent costs, those with a vested financial interest in the process must mitigate risks and keep surprises to a minimum. As a result, there is an implicit bias towards resolution prior to fabrication and often a reliance upon low-risk conventions.

Increasingly advanced design, simulation and management tools such as building information modeling software promise an even greater degree of design resolution and efficiency before the commencement of construction. In the context of practice, the benefits of such tools have been made clear.[4] Streamlined information sharing and the ability to "see" every piece of the building are changing the ways architects collaborate and the extent to which a building is understood prior to construction. While this process remains novel in the construction industry, it has been utilized for quite some time in the aerospace industry as an attempt to remove all uncertainties prior to the costly endeavor of fabrication.[5] While an airplane and a larger building may share complexity, most buildings are typically one-off custom constructions with unique material conditions. As a result, the design processes are implicitly distinct. While the data may facilitate a streamlined process, and in the case of the airplane, lead to highly optimized engineering, it alone does not ensure a great or even good building by standards beyond measure. Ideally, in the case of architecture, the data of the virtual model is parsed through the expertise of the architect. Here, the distance between virtual design data and material reality is compressed through an architect's material sensibility, borne out of observation and engagement of material conditions and their associated limits. A classic example is that of precision. While software may allow absolute dimensional precision, only the architect versed in material reality will transpose intrinsic material characteristics such as dimensional variability to the virtual simulation. As such, the virtual design data is most useful when understood in relationship to the physical conditions it represents.

Digital fabrication technologies have been heralded as processes that extend the digital design workflow into the physical realization of built form and by extension, direct attention to the formal, tectonic and material potential revealed through computer-controlled equipment.[6] While use of the software in the design process may in the past have distanced the designer from the messiness of physical reality, emerging connections between software and hardware tools have extended the hand of the designer deep into the process of fabrication. Herein lies the paradox. Computing and digital material processing are perhaps one of the stronger connections to materiality. In the academic realm, the promise of such processes is a material awakening or, as Richard Sennett refers to, a material consciousness[7] whereby one develops an interest in physical things one can change. This active engagement of materiality prompts a reassessment of virtual design data that, for the young architect, are often devoid of material characteristics. The result is a materiality infused with the characteristics of its digital processing.[8] Here the presence of the digital is evident through geometric complexity, control and fidelity rather than a singular formal or aesthetic representation of digitally derived form.

Since its inception, the architectural design process has relied upon various forms of representations, simulations or proxies.[9] The sheer size and complexity of buildings do not allow the degree of full-scale studies common in other design disciplines. The design of a product, such as a chair, typically affords a degree of immediacy and direct material investigation not found in architecture. While mock-ups or material studies may be executed prior to construction, they generally have served as a test of prototypical conditions or occasionally a limited palate of options. Their execution is necessary to the process of construction but typically has not served as the catalyst for design advancement. As abstractions, material proxies may represent a limited range of material characteristics, but they often serve as a rendering of form rather than a tool to elicit fundamental material properties. As is the case with virtual design data, their utilization relies upon one's ability to project materiality onto an otherwise inert form. This, again, relies upon a sophisticated design process that is conscious of materiality.

Over the past decade, digital fabrication tools have grown exponentially in presence throughout the academy. It has been a veritable arms race among institutions to project themselves as among the architectural vanguard. The transformative potential of these tools is clear and the opportunities to explore complex physical form have been well documented, however, the material focus of such processes is very much emerging. The focus of our investigations resides in the pedagogical impact of the tool, specifically the value of a student's understanding that materials and processes present resistance and limits that affect the design process. This is a reciprocal relationship of negotiations, one that is both top-down and bottom-up.

Digital fabrication tools generally perform one form of action on a material and can be loosely categorized as subtractive or additive in which material is removed or combined. They are marketed and deployed based upon which of the two categories the tool falls within and subsequently, how it facilitates material transformation. Contrary to this condition is the industrial robot which, by itself, is not designed or biased toward a specific task or action on a material. Industrial robots have a significant presence in mass production settings such as automotive manufacturing as a measure to streamline production, increase productivity and improve safety. In this context, the robot has been used almost exclusively for highly repetitive tasks. Here, the time and associated cost to program the robot were outweighed by the productivity gains once the machine was operating. Other than occasional maintenance, the robot could predictably perform the task into the foreseeable future. The articulating arm industrial robot differs from most other digital fabrication tools in that it, in and of itself, does not bias a particular method of fabrication. The tool on the end of the robot dictates what the machine can or cannot do. While industrial robots have been deployed in industrial settings for quite some time, their use within the field of architecture is quite recent and has primarily been within the academy.

An ABB IRB 4400 industrial robot was acquired by the School of Architecture at Carnegie Mellon University as a supplement to existing task-specific digital fabrication tools. The IRB 4400 is a six-axis articulating arm with a reach of approximately 2 meters and an end-of-arm load rating of 40 kg (Figure 21.2). The robot work-cell was further outfitted with a rotary table that acts as a seventh axis, providing additional flexibility and reach for the robot. The first of what will be a series of courses taught to undergraduate architecture students, focused on the utilization of industrial robots in the field of architecture. The intent being that each course will be structured around a specific type of fabrication and architectural condition. A guiding principle for the research is a focus on the material and tectonic potential through the use of the tool. Subtractive processes, specifically multi-axis milling, served as the mechanical process, while the architectural screen served as the architectural condition. To this end, the robot was configured as a multi-axis subtractive tool with a high-speed cutting spindle mounted on the end of the robot arm, allowing for the cutting of foams, plastics and woods.

Significant differences exist between a milling robot, such as the IRB 4400 and traditional subtractive CNC equipment. Whereas most subtractive CNC equipment operates about three axis and tends to limit milling to one surface at a time, the industrial robot allows a substantially greater degree of carving options such

Figure 21.2 Six-axis industrial robot with milling spindle

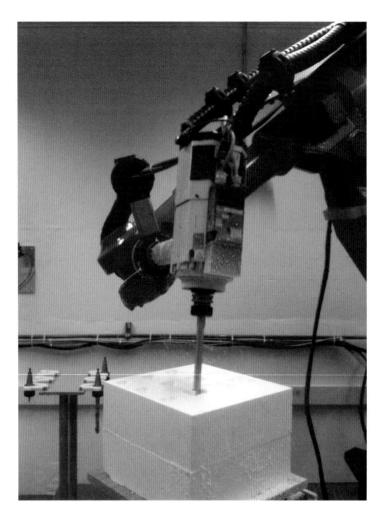

as undercutting, where the axis angle of the cutting tool varies from what is traditionally fixed at 90 degrees on three-axis CNC equipment. While industrial robots offer a significant degree of task and motion flexibility, they do not have the same degree of stiffness found with traditional subtractive CNC equipment such as milling machines or routers. As a result, the palate of potential robot carved materials tends to be limited to softer materials such as foams and woods.

The architectural screen both separates and connects the spaces and individuals on either side. As a surface, wall or object, the screen is defined by the relationships between material and void, across the screen and through its thickness. Here, one's attention vacillates between the screen, its implicit boundary and the resulting effects. Screening can be achieved through a permeable surface or object, or can be the result of a spatially loose assembly of components that leads to porosity at the joint. These distinctions speak to a geometric and tectonic logic that is potentially reliant upon subtractive or additive methods. The porous nature of the screen implies a degree of correlation between its two faces. This can be reciprocal or the resultant intersection between two distinct surface conditions and geometric systems. Initial investigations probed these conditions through the development of complementary, yet non-intersecting geometric systems and surfaces. The translucent properties of Corian were exploited to reveal a superimposition of the two systems (Figure 21.3). While the surface denied a literal visual connection, the relationship between surface geometry and tool trace were revealed when backlit. Slight variations in the sheet thickness resulted in a broad range of translucency throughout the ½" sheet thickness and spoke to the latent potential within a relatively thin piece of material.

- - - - - - - - - - - - - - - - - -

As the investigation proceeded, the influence of materiality shifted in light of the necessity to work with distinctly different materials on the robot. The maximization of thinness, associated with the use of Corian, shifted to the maximization of thickness offered through the use of foams. This additional thickness allowed for the development of spatial transformations through the thickness of the material. A focus on surfaces that were previously reciprocal yet non-intersecting evolved into a focus on the relationship between surfaces and perforation.

While the industrial robot offers a higher degree of milling flexibility, the considerations of how the machine will remove the material are far greater than found with traditional three-axis machines. Industrial robots, such as the IRB 4400 typically have more than one robot arm orientation for any given point in space.

Figure 21.3 Three-axis milled Corian, 12" x 12" x ½"

Robot orientation can be resolved by the robot controller software in real-time or planned in conjunction with the generation of robot instructions. If robot orientation is resolved by the controller, unpredictable robot motion may occur, leading to collisions between the robot and the milled material or any supporting fixtures or jigs. In light of these added levels of planning, initial use of the robot began as relatively simple operations and grew in complexity to match the learning curve. This was manifest through subtractive studies based on distinct collections of points, lines and surfaces and began with drilling and ended with mult-axis milling (Figure 21.4). In milling operations, material is typically carved through a progressive engagement of the bit tip with material. The added freedom of the robot offers alternative methods for subtractive milling. As robot milling progressed, attention focused on use of the length and edge of the bit as the cutting surface. This type of milling, referred to as swarfing, utilized the ability of the robot to tilt the bit about the z-axis and subsequently allowed for a substantial degree of geometric transformation along the z-axis (Figure 21.5). The axis of the bit acted as a rule line and could be traced through the material to develop a ruled surface. Closed boundary curve geometry was created at minimum and maximum levels along the z-axis. Tool-paths were calculated as straight lines between an equal number of points along both curves. The geometry and resulting voids could be transformative, allowing for spatially distinct or intertwined voids (Figure 21.6). While use of expanded styrene foam (EPS) in these investigations allowed for quick, rather inexpensive iterations of a thick material, it offered few compelling material properties beyond its insulation capacity.

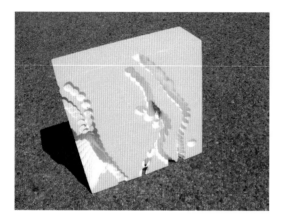

Figure 21.4 Six-axis drilled EPS foam 12" x 12" x 4"

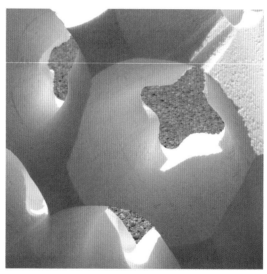

Figure 21.6 Swarf milling detail

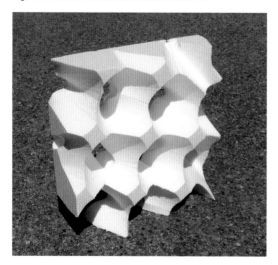

Figure 21.5 Six-axis milled EPS foam 12" x 12" x 4"

As work proceeded, there was a shared sense that materiality and the methods for processing material be explicitly addressed and expressed. This ambition moved the conversation of materiality beyond that of a proxy or simulation in which the immediacy of material characteristics may be sacrificed, into the realm of specific material properties and limitations. The understanding of material and process transformed from a single step subtractive workflow in which foam served as the proxy, into a multi-step process in which foam was utilized as a negative mold for subsequent casting (Figure 21.7). The potential for a thick, spatially varied screen was retained while the completed screen could be manifest through a range of cast materials. Casting materials were limited to those that were readily available and cost effective. High-strength cement and fast-setting plaster were deemed most appropriate for casting plasticity and structural viability. Initial castings were tube-like and relied upon simple one-part molds. They consisted of a ¾" thick ruled surface as the spatial envelope. Each casting contained a single void that was an offset of a perimeter hexagon and could be nested as a cellular system of components (Figures 21.8–21.9). While the physical strength of the initial castings was promising, they were deemed unsatisfactory due to the fact that reliable stacking and nesting could not be achieved without the use of an adhesive or mechanical fastener. Ideally, the system of components should be dry stackable, yet capable of producing a broad array of internal voids in response to particular performance criteria such as light transmission and airflow. By addressing exterior and interior surface geometry independently, rather than as offsets of the same surface, component nesting (exterior surface) and performative potential (interior surface) could be refined simultaneously under distinct criteria. A system of "ridges" and "valleys" along the outer surface allowed the components to reliably stack and nest without a secondary means of attachment (Figures 21.10–21.11). Furthermore, two-part molds allowed a greater degree of geometric transformation and facilitated a significantly thicker screen. An extruded hexagonal tiling system acted as the geometric basis for screen geometry and provided a substantial degree of rigidity through the packed nature of the pattern (Figure 21.12). Transformation points were subsequently placed across both sides of the surface and served as the basis for algorithmic transformations between outer and inner surfaces (Figure 21.13). As these transformations diffused across the tiled geometry, size, shape and directionality of openings adjusted in conjunction with a change in distance from the transformation points. The result is a dynamic range of spatial conditions that shift as one moves along the wall (Figure 21.14).

Figure 21.7 Milling and casting workflow
Figure 21.8 Prototype plaster cast, approx. 12" x 10" x 10"

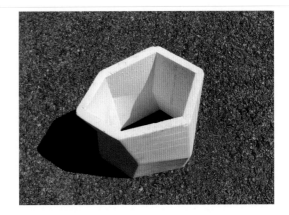

Figure 21.9 Prototype cement castings, approx. 24" x 24" x 20", combined

Figure 21.10 Component nesting

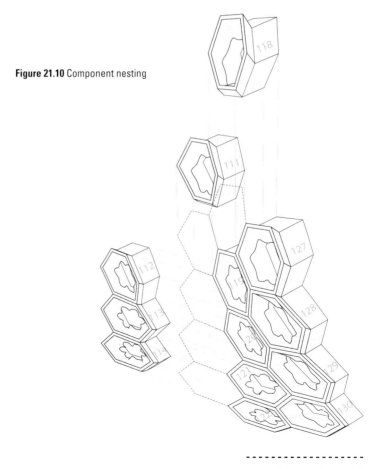

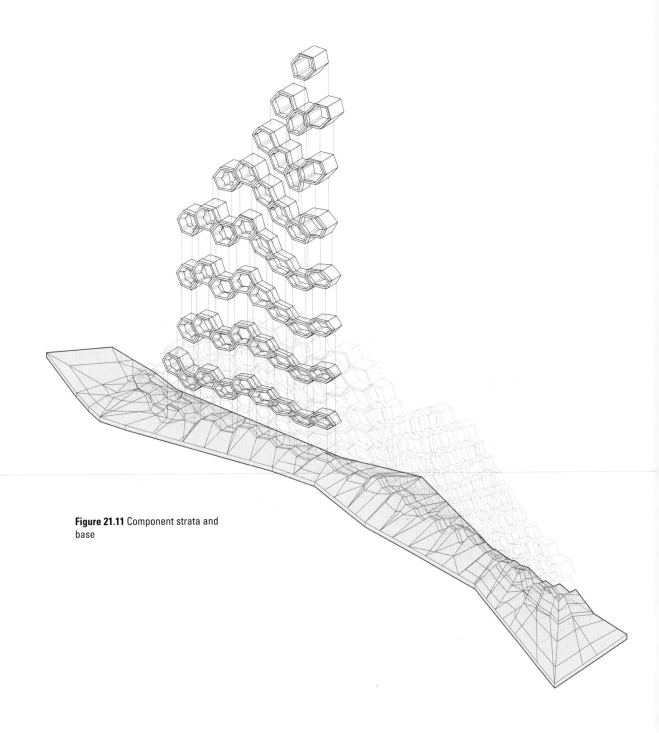

Figure 21.11 Component strata and base

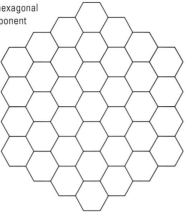

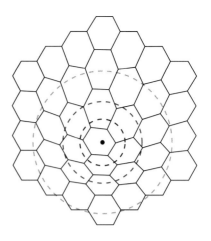

Figure 21.12a–e Distorted hexagonal
pattern and individual component

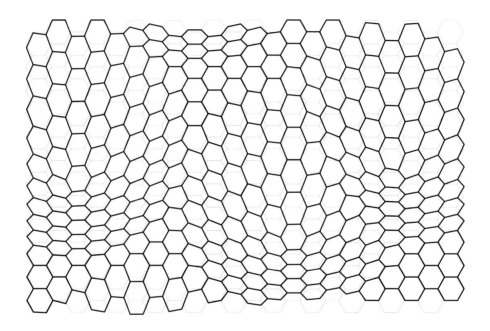

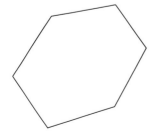

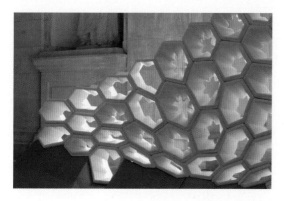

Figure 21.13 Installation detail

The physical manifestation of the screen resists simple associations and stands in contrast to typical perforated conditions. The screen is at once material substantial yet highly porous. The pattern of openings abides by a strict set of interrelated geometric transformations but is comprised of over 150 unique components. While the geometries are controlled and speak to their digital origins, the surfaces are decidedly textured and evocative of the multiple processes undertaken. As such, materiality is a manifestation of both analog and digital processes. The resistance presented by processes and materials necessitated recalibrations of intent and resulted in a complex set of translations between geometric systems, digital and analog processes and material characteristics. The resulting construction offers a material and tectonic language that is both reliant upon and evocative of emerging fabrication processes, while also referencing longstanding methods of material use and construction.

Acknowledgements

Instructor: Jeremy Ficca.
Students: Nelly Dacic, Jared Friedman, Puja Patel, Craig Rosman, Arthur Azoulai, Jaeeun Chung, Christopher Gallot, Spencer Gregson, Matthew Huber, Patrick Kim, Jaclyn Paceley, Giacomo Tinari, and Eddie Wong.

Notes

1   Richard Sennett, *The Craftsman* (New Haven, CT: Yale University Press), pp. 119–146.
2   David Pye, *The Nature and Art of Workmanship* (Cambridge: Cambridge University Press, 1988), pp. 4–8.
3   Stephen Kieran and James Timberlake, *Refabricating Architecture* (New York: McGraw-Hill, 2004).
4   Ibid., pp. 25–27.
5   Ibid., pp. 79–84.
6   Branko Kolarevic, *Architecture in the Digital Age: Design and Manufacturing* (London: Spon Press, 2003), pp. 29–54.
7   Richard Sennett, op cit.
8   Fabio Gramazio and Matthias Kohler, *Digital Materiality in Architecture* (Zurich: Lars Müller Publishers, 2008), pp. 7–11.
9   James Ackerman and Wolfgang Jung, *Conventions of Architectural Drawing: Representation and Misrepresentation* (Cambridge, MA: Harvard University GSD, 2001), pp. 8–36.

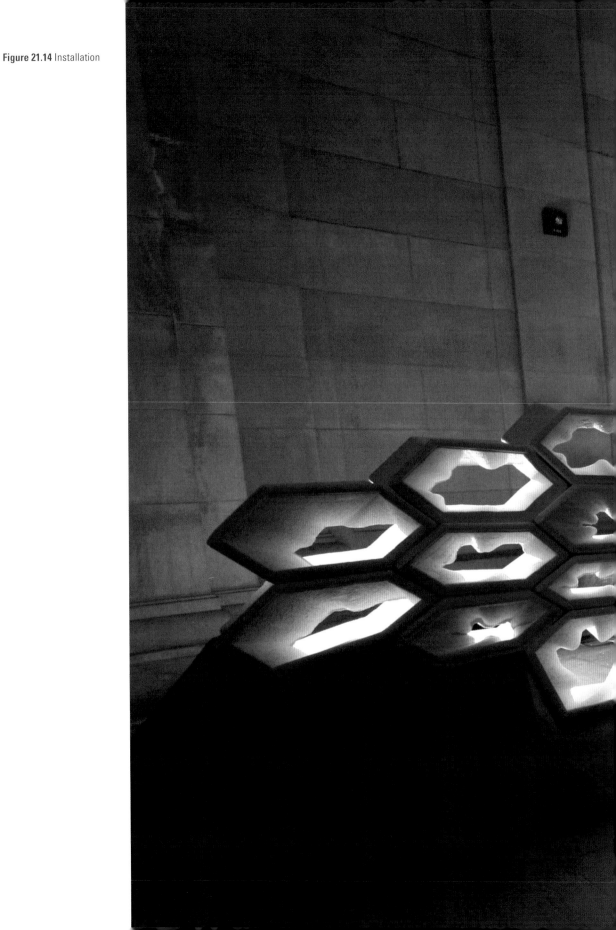

Figure 21.14 Installation

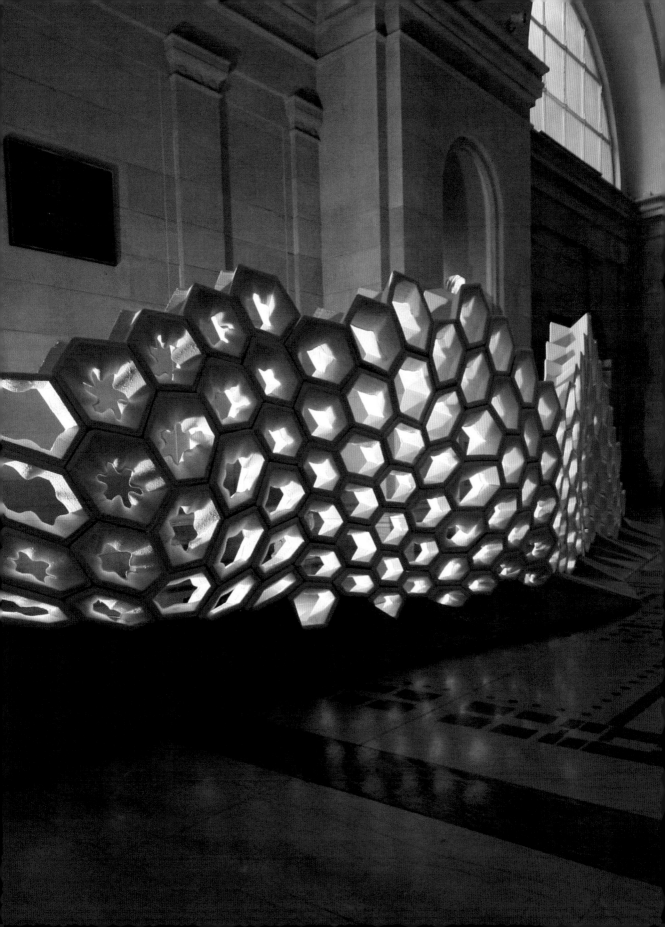

Chapter 22
Digital Tracery
Fabricating traits

Lawrence Blough

GRAFTWORKS

Provocation

In his remarkable essay "Drawn Stone," Robin Evans discusses stereotomy – the cutting of solids – through the technique of the trait. Developed in the sixteenth century,

> *Traits* were layout drawings used to enable the precise cutting of component masonry blocks for complex architectural forms, especially vaults. Thereby accurate fabrication of parts could be achieved prior to construction. *Traits* are not illustrations and yield little to the casual observer. They are orthographic projections, but they are not like other architectural drawings.[1]

Evans argues that this method was required only in extraordinary conditions and was at the limits of mathematical geometry, technical drawing, structural theory, practical masonry, and military engineering. More than an early form of shop drawing, the trait can be seen as both a representational and cognitive tool to marry complex form with the exigencies of construction (Figure 22.1).

Analyzing the highly complex fan vaults at Henry VII Chapel, Westminster (Figure 22.2), Evans writes that the apparently contradictory principles of structure and ornament are inseparable, having been developed through the geometric and jointed logic of the trait:

Figure 22.1 Layout drawing for a rear-vault, *L'encyclopédia Diderot et D'Alembert*

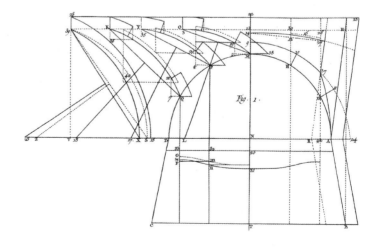

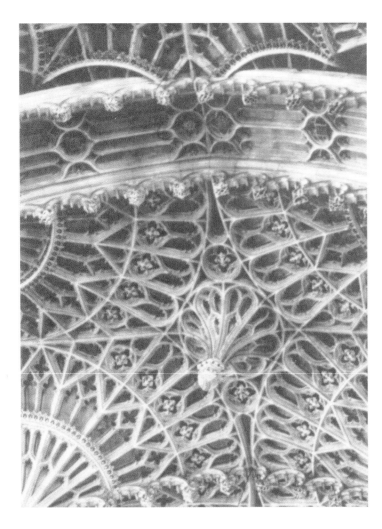

Figure 22.2 Fan vault tracery, Henry VII Chapel

The filigree of liernes and ring ribs is nothing more or less than the generator of the fans and the loci of their rotation repeated over and over. The pattern is a diagram in the way in which the surface was construed.[2]

He then goes on to argue that the components of the vaults were in all likelihood precut or prefabricated before being installed by the masons.

The extraordinary effect at Westminster can be described as the union between "construing" and "constructing" or the production of discourse and the act of building through the agency of the detail.[3] Details and by extension joints have been described by Frascari

as the minimum units of signification in the architectural production of meanings. These units have been singled out in spatial cells or in elements of composition, in modules or in measures, in the alternating of solid and void, or in the relationship between inside and outside.

If we look at the biological definition of trait as a genetically determined characteristic or quality that is physical (hair color or the shape of a leaf) or behavioral (nesting in birds or burrowing in rodents), details and joints can be also seen as the genetic material that constitutes a work of architecture. Architectural performance begins with these concepts of the trait, where parts to whole relationships are generative and catalytic, and feedback is developed between varying scales of material and spatial joints.

Recently, prototyping enabled by CNC technology has found its way into design practice where concepts can be quickly and economically tested through multiple design iterations that closely approximate the realities of one-to-one construction.[4] This has led to the promise of renewed research in tectonics and constructional techniques where the traditional concepts of craft and the joint that were once married to the hand can be rediscovered through the agency of mass customization. If we apply the lineage of the *trait* to these new ways of working, pedagogical approaches can be developed that extend the current interest in intricate surface, structural morphology and geometry towards a robust materiality rooted in componentry, the joint and part to whole relationships.

Many of the digital modeling techniques we have seen in the schools of architecture beginning in the 1990s strive for formal complexity at the expense of material and assembly related research. In a recent interview about one-to-one CNC fabrication, Fabian Scheurer of Designtoproduction suggests that architects typically confront fabrication only after their designs have been completed, not as an integral part of the process. Scheurer notes that, "All of this top-notch modeling software out there effectively hides the complexity of the geometry. But the complexity is back as soon as you try to break it down into segments and manufacture it."[5] Having consulted with Zaha Hadid and UN Studio on fabrication strategies, Scheurer's experience points to a gap between fabrication processes and design pedagogy.

An emphasis on component modeling and the joint can be seen in the work of Konrad Wachsmann and Pier Luigi Nervi. A common thread links this work that originates with Viollet-le-Duc and Structural Rationalism. These ideas would have an impact on architecture at the edges of the modern movement and are still influential today in work that embraces prefabricated constructional techniques and material research in the service of expressive tectonics.

The theoretical promise of Viollet-le-Duc's *Entretiens sur l'architecture* was "an unprecedented architectural code created out of the articulation of constructional logic."[6] As a reaction to Neo-Classicism, Viollet-le-Duc argued for the establishment of critical and interpretive play with regard to the past. It was not stylistic but was governed by unlocking the technical and constructive principles behind what was already built. His thesis suggests how emerging building technologies in concert with structural research could lead to a new tectonic expression in architecture. Art Nouveau, Jugenstijl, and the Arts & Crafts movements grew out of this approach and much of it resided in the study of structural and geometric analogs found in nature. The lineage of the tension between structure and ornament that Evans unlocks at Westminster is a marked quality of Art Nouveau, where the articulation of a structural logic is conflated with the continuity of the surface through elaborate tracery. This tendency can also be seen in the work of Wachsmann and Nervi.

Wachsmann's *Study of a Dynamic Structure* started as a research studio project at the Chicago Institute of Design in 1953 with the aim of producing a novel construction system using factory-produced components. Working as a team, the students developed interlocking "three-legged, wishbone-like members" that operate as both column and beam and connect at midpoint locations where the structure is horizontal[7] (Figure 22.3).

The joint becomes the generator of the project where the modules intertwine at nodes that provide vertical and horizontal contact and distribute the loads in converging diagonal lines. Also known as the *Grape Vine Structure* in Wachsmann's archive, the components are organized from the bottom up and aggregate into a complex 3D lattice that is analogous to a botanical system. The material for the modules was never defined although there is a study that shows the members as continuous tube or channel sections that could be made from steel or precast concrete. The study also shows that the modules could be broken down even further as triangular sections forming either corrugated sheet steel members or lightweight trusses. Thus, the part to whole logics would be consistent across scales of construction and jointed modules would be formed of jointed parts.

Nervi had been experimenting with prefabrication for long span structures as early as the mid-1930s but his great innovation began a decade later when he began developing ferrocement vault and dome

Figure 22.3 *Grape Vine Structure* jointed modules, Konrad Wachsmann

structures. Prefabricated pans were arranged on scaffolding with 4" channels between them where cement would be poured in situ, creating dense lattices. The pans were effectively material and formal joints where multiple variations in size and shape would develop a complex geometric tracery of voids creating lightweight thin shell structures. This is best seen in the coffered ceiling of the *Gatti Wool Factory* or the *Small Sports Palace* where the ribs map the flow of forces along the interior surface of the spaces (Figure 22.4). Nervi describes in

Figure 22.4 Prefabricated dome ceiling pans, P. L. Nervi

his book *Structures* that many of the forces were impossible to calculate without the aid of large-scale models.[8] Nervi used this method of material analysis throughout his practice to test and measure loads and stresses under various conditions. Partial full-scale models were also used to lay out and construct the prefabricated pan systems. Nervi was actively involved in prototyping across scales as a rehearsal for one-to-one construction – his methods of constructing are literally embedded in the surface of the architecture.

Pedagogy

The pedagogical heuristic of the *model* traces a line through the text and images being presented in two ways: (1) as a tool for conceptual thinking – both the drawing as *model* and the model as prototype marry the "cognitive-perceptive with the figurative-operative";[9] (2) as a working method to unlock material and structural performance – the scalability of the prototyping process becomes a rehearsal for the realities of one-to-one construction. Over the past three years, two model-based approaches using digital fabrication techniques have been tested in an undergraduate research seminar at Pratt Institute School of Architecture: component invention using analogs from nature specifically botanical models, and component mutation interrogating preexisting architectural systems.[10] The model-based approach emphasizes the development of part-to-whole relationships through jointed assemblies and privileges expressive tectonics as a means to confront scale and the exigencies of construction. Although 3D printing has proven itself to be a powerful tool to visualize complex form, its use has been discouraged because of its lack of materiality and its tendency to produce smooth surfaces with no tectonic differentiation. The laser cutter is the tool of choice because, by default, assemblies have to be made of modules. The limitations of the tool also demand that 3D form be geometrically constituted from sheet stock with a restricted size. Tectonic innovation using off-the-shelf materials was privileged over new material technologies.

The aim of the seminar was to interrogate digital prototyping as a working method and form of research that differs from classical "iconic" models of representation.[11] Working within two parallel forms of inquiry – the design/fabrication of laser cut wood models and the analysis of selective readings – the potential of contemporary digital modeling was exposed as a speculative practice that embraces iterative making as design intelligence. Critical to this method was the scalability of the prototyping process – each consecutively scaled model raises questions about material performance and constructional specificity.

Assuming that the two prevalent taxonomies of laser prototyping are the intricate surface (single cut and/or folded sheet) and the fuselage (framework of ribs forming tubes of space), a third alternative strategy was investigated – *digital tracery*. Using the logic of Gothic architecture's jointed 3D lattices as a departure

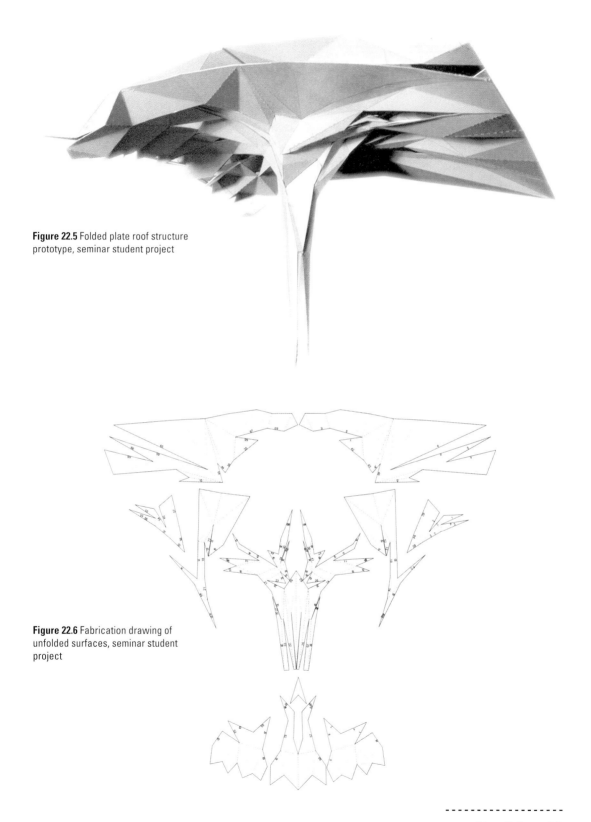

Figure 22.5 Folded plate roof structure prototype, seminar student project

Figure 22.6 Fabrication drawing of unfolded surfaces, seminar student project

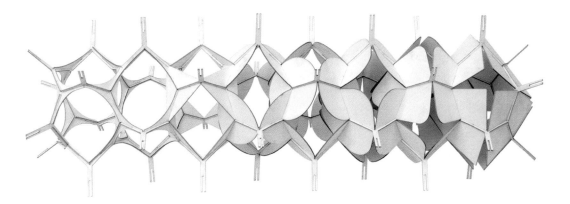

Figure 22.7 Jointed structure/skin prototype, seminar student project

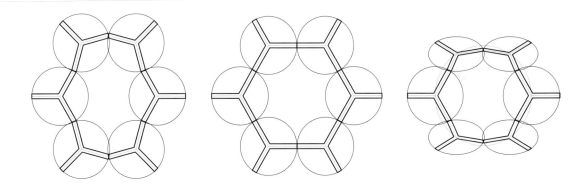

Figure 22.8a–c Projection drawings, student project

point, digital tracery marries the contour between column and beam to create surfaces that have the potential to both develop topological variation and confront the laws of gravity. Working in teams, students tested multiple design variations by fabricating ½" = 1'-0" scale jointed lattices and ¼ full-scale joint details using a 18" x 32" laser cutter. The intent was to limit the size of the components that form the lattices, so students would have to confront the economies of assembly and structure, while still maintaining the effects of continuity and lightness (Figures 22.5–22.8).

To begin the investigation, students were asked to independently analyze a particular botanical analog with an emphasis on organizational and geometric characteristics. From their research, students attempted to trap or intensify particular traits through notational drawing and detail modeling by developing simple modules of assembly and building complexity from the bottom up. Students then broke into teams to research techniques and fabricate prototypes to draw out larger organizational principles and structural details. Simple "programmatic" pressures in section such as compression vs. dilation, cantilever vs. vault, light vs. dark introduced variability across different scales of the assembly system.

Case study: *Textile Helix*

Out of five projects produced in the seminar, *Textile Helix* was selected for full-scale fabrication to be installation in the Siegal Gallery at Pratt Institute School of Architecture in the fall of 2009.[12] After the completion of the seminar in the spring, a team of two students performed an independent study over the summer to further develop their proposal and prepare the project for CNC milling later in the year. Following the logic of the seminar, the installation would be made of standard sheet stock material using a three-axis mill for economy. *Textile Helix* began with the seemingly simple idea to weave a surface out of a limited set of jointed parts that could form a continuous enclosure.[13] As the project developed over the course of the summer, it became clear that exigencies of full-scale construction would put demands on the concept in ways that smaller models could not address. From issues of material performance and tolerance, to geometry and assembly sequencing, the process proved to be far more complex and intense than anticipated by the design team. This, however, was in keeping with the pedagogical objectives of the seminar and provided critical research and development experience for the students beyond what is typically taught in the design studio.

Early studies of botanical models revealed typologies with spiral organizations that grew in plan and section. The students began by developing an analog parametric model where part-to-part relationships were constrained by the angle of intersection and dimension of offset to produce variations of a spiral surface. Slotted joints in each part formed the connections (Figures 22.9–22.10). Although early ½" = 1'-0' laser cut chipboard models were successful in demonstrating that the concept was workable, when a ¼ full-scale prototype of a series of components was built out of rigid plywood, the parts were distorting to such a degree that the joints were not closing. It was clear that the geometry of the smaller models was not as accurate as it appeared and the assemblage was able to make up for inconsistencies due to factors of scale and material behavior. The thinner material was bending at the local connections and the whole assemblage was able to flex, whereas the rigid material was less forgiving and demanded greater precision. The students had developed an organization out of only four parts and the goal was to try and maintain a limited set of components to produce complexity. It was agreed that if the project was to progress, a digital parametric model would have to be constructed to rationalize the geometry and to test if the concept was viable.

Ronnie Parsons and Gil Akos acted as parametric design consultants to help the team move the scheme from an analog parametric model to a digital one that was relational and adaptive.[14] Several significant parameters were developed by the team during the process of building the project digitally: (1) it was determined that the joint-to-joint slot connections be constrained to 90° so a three-axis mill could be used avoiding compound cuts; (2) a constrained component 3D assembly or "eight point lattice" made of four parts was developed where the relationship between lattice to lattice is maintained vs. part to part; and (3) the geometry of the organization had to change from a spiral to a helix, where the radius is constant allowing the assemblies and offsets to remain

Figure 22.9 Analog parametric model version 1
Figure 22.10a–d Morphology diagrams

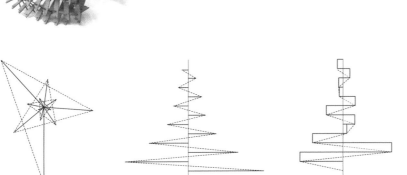
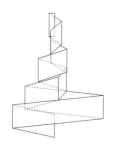

consistent – this prevented each lattice from being different which would have generated an enormous number of custom parts. After a process of trial and error, a parametric helix was built in Rhinoceros with Grasshopper producing a radius that could be modified (Figure 22.11). The component assemblies were then made to follow the geometry of the helix – each assembly rotates approximately 105° and is offset one to the other to produce the desired figure. Variations could now be tested quickly at two scales with all of the information updated in real time – the part profile and the radius of the helix could be quickly modified as long as the relationships within and between the eight-point lattice were maintained. This allowed the team to virtually test different levels of porosity, volume and scale and then output them to the laser cutter to produce geometrically precise prototypes out of flat stock material.

After a ¼ full-scale prototype of the complete organization was fabricated, Pat Arnett, an engineer at Robert Silman and Associates, helped the team evaluate the structure of the project. It was agreed that the geometry needed to be adjusted to form a "surface-active structure"[15] (Figure 22.12). Early in the process, the students had produced their models using no glue, relying on the tightness of the slotted joints to keep the surface together. Because the project worked both like a load-bearing wall in places and like an arch, Pat argued if the geometry was just right, in theory no mechanical connections would be required. By literally pushing and pulling the large physical model until it supported itself, the design team estimated how to modify the radius and height of the volume so it could work with gravity and use only the notched joints in the material to keep the components tight in a continuous chain.

Now that it was determined that geometry and assembly logics were performing structurally, the team could focus on refining the design of the project. Several issues needed to be addressed that had been suspended until the digital parametric model had proven to be workable: (1) how the organization was to meet the ground – a helix only touches the ground at one point; (2) part profiles – how they would be differentiated for ease of assembly and effects of porosity; and (3) how the project would be situated in the gallery – its height, diameter and larger surface logic relative to the human body in space. Several iterations were developed in the computer and then tested in a new ¼ full-scale prototype that ultimately became the last scale model of the whole organization before fabrication (Figures 22.13–22.14).

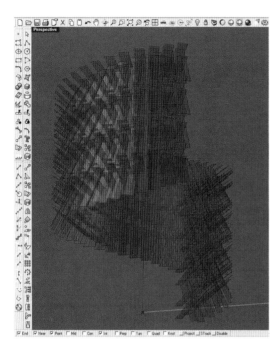

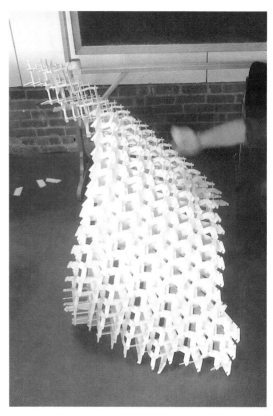

Figure 22.11 Digital parametric model version 2

Figure 22.12 Full-scale model version 3

The following developments identified above provoked the team to introduce other scales of feedback into the organization and pushed the project to incorporate variations in structural and surface effects. In order to negotiate the oblique intersection of the helix and ground plane, the four standard parts were adapted to become leg-like supports that rotate and become progressively smaller. Because all of the weight of the project was now being transferred to the supports, they were to be made of two layers of laminated plywood to resist bending. The supports buttress and lift the helix to produce a continuous transition from vertical to horizontal. They also allowed for a limited set of plate connections to be designed at the floor level. The logic of the profile of each part was determined by how it joins to the adjacent parts. Our engineer had given the parameter that a minimum of 1″ be maintained on either side of a notched joint and that a notch not exceed half the depth of the part. Excess material from each part was subtracted and the contour was tailored in the direction of the load path from connection to connection. The result was a much lighter assemblage with a greater level of aeration. Additionally, each of the components now had an identifiable contour to aid in the part to part sequencing during construction. Finally, variations in the larger aggregate that had appeared in the initial analog models were reintroduced. This included selectively removing areas of the component assemblies to create an opening in the surface of the helix. Describing the larger-scale load paths of the surface-active structure from arch to bearing wall, this operation also produced a threshold in the organization where one could pass through the surface of the helix from one side to the other.

With the final scheme approved by the design team, it was now the time in the process to verify that the jointed component assemblies worked at full scale to form an assemblage. It was the last time before final fabrication to reproduce the geometry that the digital models and prototypes had successfully simulated. Because each of the eight point lattices joined to their neighbors to form a network of connections, there was redundancy in the structure. The lattice assemblies also produced a thick wall surface because each constituted a 9½″ box when the components locked together. Our engineer confirmed that we could use ½″ plywood which

Figures 22.13–22.14 Full-scale model version 4

Figure 22.15 Assembly sequence diagram

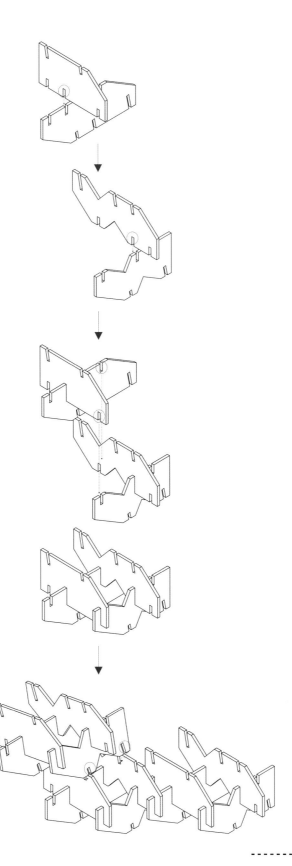

would be very light and cost effective. The team selected unfinished birch fin-ply for its strength, stability and appearance. Because the School of Architecture does not own a CNC mill, the components were made off site by Timbur, a fabrication shop in New Jersey.[16] Before an assembly chunk could be fabricated, a notch test had to be milled to evaluate the tolerance of the material and select the right joint dimension. Thus, .0075" of clearance was chosen from a range of notch sizes milled into two interlocking components. From discussions with the engineer, we wanted the joints to be as tight as possible to prevent cumulative "drift" in the assemblies but we also needed enough play so multiple interlocking components would fit together without splitting the wood or warping the lattices. A ¼" radius was also specified for the outside corners of all the parts for ease of handling (Figure 22.15).

The full-scale prototype of four lattices was successfully fabricated and assembled. To the team's relief, the geometry worked as planned and the joints fit properly with no distortion or warping (Figure 22.16). After a final tweak to one of the part profiles, the project was ready for final fabrication. Sizes of the components varied in length from 15" to 20" and in depth from 7½" to 4½". Because of the profile and size of the components, an extremely efficient nesting pattern was able to be laid out for each 4 x 8 plywood sheet resulting in very little material waste (Figure 22.17). *Textile Helix* would be 9'-6" tall at the highest point with an interior diameter of 6' but required only 12 sheets of material.

A team of three students with two faculty members supervising assembled the project in 20 hours. The project was built on the floor in vertical bands one lattice at a time (Figure 22.18). The friction joints, hammered together with a rubber mallet, proved to be extremely strong. As an allowance for safety, a small amount of carpenter's glue was applied to the inside of each notched joint. There was only one way that the components would fit together – the particular joint locations in each part along with the part geometry coded a set of instructions for their order of assembly. However, because of the complexity of the geometry, it was still not easy to locate where along the surface of the helix the assembly sequence was taking place. The ¼ full-scale

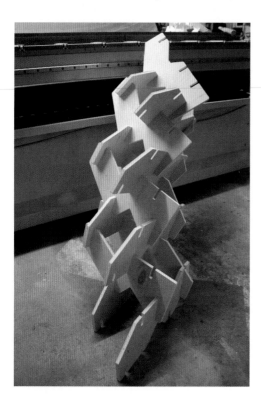

Figure 22.16 Full-scale prototype of four lattices

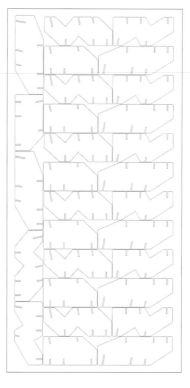

Figure 22.17 Part nesting pattern 4 x 8 sheet

Figure 22.18 Construction sequence 1

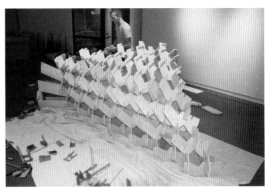

Figure 22.19 Construction sequence 2

Figure 22.20 Construction sequence 3

Figure 22.21 Construction sequence 4

model was an invaluable tool, where the team could literally count the lattices to determine how far along the full scale the piece was in the construction sequence, and how to plan for future developments in the process (Figure 22.19).

Because the helix formed a radius in section, the stacked vertical bands of lattices produced a partial arch (Figure 22.20). Early in the process of design development, the engineer thought that falsework would be required as a mold for the components to achieve the required geometry. During the construction sequence, however, the jointed components demonstrated that they were both self-jigging and self-aligning. Each part set up the location for the next and as soon as they were hammered in place, the correct geometry was formed with minimal shoring required. The redundancy in the system, along with the network of connections and the precision of the parametric model, allowed virtually no drift in the assemblage.

Once the arch progressed to where it could go no farther before it hit the floor, the helix was tilted up vertically and temporarily shored. A group of students were recruited to help lift and maneuver the project against a column in the gallery (Figure 22.21). One set of leg-like supports had been assembled as part of the arch and the project was positioned so that they supported half the weight of the helix along with shoring on the opposite side. Now the remainder of the helix could be constructed, terminating in the final set of supports at the floor. The completed organization was slid into the correct location in the gallery and blocking was added under the leg supports to prevent the project from moving or being pushed over. Because no screws were permitted in the gallery floor, the blocking was adhered to the floor with 3M VHB tape. The leg-like supports were screwed to the blocking from the sides, these being the only mechanical fasteners used on *Textile Helix* (Figures 22.22–22.25).

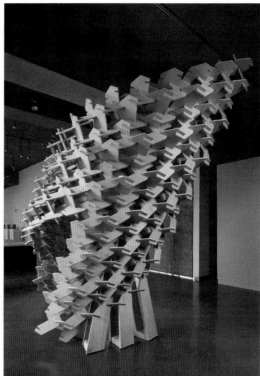

Figures 22.22–22.23 *Textile Helix* full-scale installation

Figure 22.24–22.25 *Textile Helix* full-scale installation detail

Stocktaking

One of the first impulses in the development of the fabrication research seminar was to foment cross-pollination between practice and academic research. The students would be exposed to one-to-one digital fabrication logics and collaborate with a team of professional design consultants to produce highly specific prototypes informed by material properties. The faculty, on the other hand, could benefit from the feedback of the student research to influence the work in the office – research that, although it took on a set of real-world parameters, was nonetheless unfettered by some of the debilitating resistances of practice. Following the development of *Hothouse Lily*, a digitally prefabricated installation designed and built by GRAFTWORKS, it was clear that this type of research could go much further if the ideas and processes could be fleshed out by teams of students in a focused learning environment. In order to continue the promise of the investigation, these ideas were developed into the fabrication seminar that ultimately led to the construction of *Textile Helix*. In light of this genealogy, it is productive to evaluate the success of the work by summarily comparing the two installations.

The genesis for this thinking began in 2005 as GRAFTWORKS' competition entry for the P.S.1/MoMA Young Architects Program, where the proposal was a finalist but was not selected for construction. After having seen the competition entry, Locust Projects, an alternative not-for-profit art space in Miami, approached GRAFTWORKS about adapting the YAP prototype into an installation tailored for their outdoor exhibition space. *Hothouse Lily* was constructed in the spring of 2008 and was open to the public for three months.[17]

The concept to produce a complex and flexible organization married to an economical construction system led to two intersecting trajectories in the development of *Hothouse Lily*. One was to design a system of digitally prefabricated components that could easily be assembled on site with unskilled labor. The other was to examine a botanical analog – the Victoria Regia – to unlock principles of structural morphology, organization, and adaptability (Figure 22.26). Restricting the material to 75 standard ¾" 4 x 8 plywood sheets, the intention was to assemble a temporary architectural installation from a limited set of jointed and sistered parts (Figures 22.27–22.28).

The structure of *Hothouse Lily* worked like a two-way beam system, where feedback from the particularities of the analog, site and program produced novelty in the organization. A structural lattice was supported on columns that were continuous with the contour of the beams, forming a forest of vault-like profiles. Contextual pressures such as the narrowness of the site, created opportunities for the structure to hang from the parapet of the exterior wall of the gallery. The requirement that the courtyard gate remain operable during the course of exhibition led to the development of a column-free space in front of the gallery where the lattice cantilevered over the sidewalk. These parameters provoked innovations, where spans up to 11' were achieved with ¾" plywood and up to 19' with two layers of laminated material.

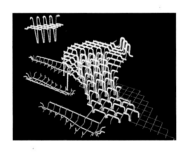

Figure 22.26 YAP laser cut structural lattice scale model

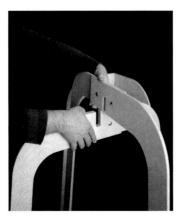

Figure 22.27 YAP full-scale joint prototype

Figure 22.28 YAP full-scale assembly prototype

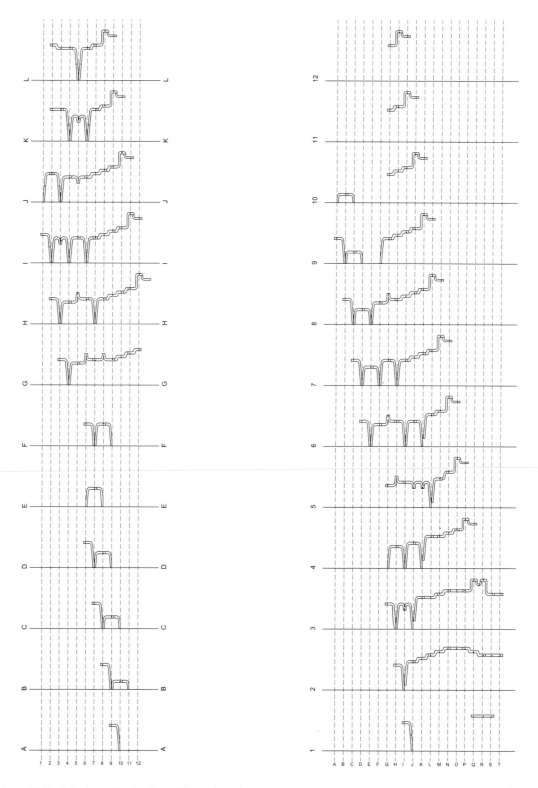

Figure 22.29a–b *Hothouse Lily* adaptive profiles, alpha and numeric

Programmatic layers registered three conceptual horizons in the courtyard – on top, inside and under the lattice. The project was constituted from a series of profiles that were tailored to accommodate a set of activities or perform certain functions. By adapting three component types, the organization in aggregate created a canopy for shade, a threshold/entry sequence to the gallery and spaces for different scales of gathering (Figure 22.29).

In is clear that the material processes first investigated with *Hothouse Lily* influenced the design and construction of *Textile Helix* in several ways: (1) both *Hothouse Lily* and *Textile Helix* were developed from flat stock material to produce 3D form; (2) both used an eight-point lattice as the minimal unit to constitute the geometric logic; (3) both used prototyping at multiple scales to test organization and assembly strategies; and (4) both used a limited set of jointed parts to develop structural surfaces able to produce variation from a single system. *Textile Helix,* however, pushed the work into new territory that points to the success of the pedagogical model of the seminar (Figures 22.30–22.33).

For one, the form and geometry were more complex in *Textile Helix* enabled in part by parametric modeling. The surface of *Textile Helix* also achieved a density of enclosure far greater then *Hothouse Lily.* The effect of the organization and redundancy of parts in *Textile Helix* approached the ornamental, where the continuity of the surface was conflated with the articulation of the assembly logic. Although density was produced in *Hothouse Lily* by adding a secondary system of components as infill, it never achieved the skin-like quality of *Textile Helix.* Some of this can be attributed to the difference in structural systems between the two installations – *Textile Helix* worked like a stacked load-bearing system of modules and *Hothouse Lily* like a beam grid system. Also, the part types were much smaller in *Textile Helix,* producing an intricacy of light and dark effects without having to supplement the system. Ultimately, the eight-point lattice assemblies of *Textile Helix* in concert with their joining principles can be seen as the *traits* of the project. Each part independently revealed very little about the whole, but when placed in relationship with the other parts and assemblies, they formed a code of constructional logic.

Figure 22.30 *Hothouse Lily* gallery

Figure 22.31 *Hothouse Lily* gallery entrance

Hothouse Lily was substantially larger in scale and scope compared to *Textile Helix*. Fewer part types were used in *Textile Helix* – this along with their size and profile created more efficient nesting patterns for fabrication with far less waste. The surface organization of *Hothouse Lily*, however, produced a greater degree of difference because it actively sought feedback from its context. This resulted in many more part types but it was able to produce more variability across different scales of the assembly. Where *Hothouse Lily* was actively grown and grafted onto the gallery courtyard, *Textile Helix* remained passive in relation to its site. Finally, *Hothouse Lily* was shaped by program in a more aggressive way. Whether it was working as a canopy, scripting the entry sequence to the gallery, or creating different scale spaces for the body, *Hothouse Lily* reconstructed the space of the courtyard while producing internal variation as a system. These types of site and programmatic inputs will be the focus of the next developments in the directed research, perhaps best approached through pairing the seminar with a design studio.

Figure 22.32 *Hothouse Lily* gallery courtyard

Figure 22.33 *Hothouse Lily* parapet connection detail

Notes

1   Robin Evans, *The Projective Cast* (Cambridge, MA: The MIT Press, 1995), Chapter 5, p. 179.

2   Ibid., pp. 236–237.

3   Marco Frascari, "The Tell-the-Tale Detail", in *Theorizing a New Agenda for Architecture: An Anthology of Architectural Theory 1965–1995*, edited by Kate Nesbitt (New York: Princeton Architectural Press, 1996), pp. 500–505, originally published in *VIA 7*, 1984. Frascari quotes Erwin Panofsky's description of the geometrical relationships in High Gothic as being arranged "according to a system of homologous parts and parts of parts." For a contemporary discussion of component assemblies as it relates to the evolution of the joint in current industrial fabrication, see Stephen Kieran and James Timberlake *Refabricating Architecture* (New York: McGraw-Hill, 2004), Chapter 4, pp. 93–101.

4   Michael Speaks, "After Theory", *Architectural Record,* June 2005, 72–75. Speaks argues for "design intelligence" through design prototyping based on what MIT Media Lab's co-director Michael Schrage terms a spreadsheet way of knowledge. The design process becomes less about producing a one-off building, and more about dynamically developing a product using contemporary business practices as a model. Because the prototype can be analyzed, adjusted and remade quickly throughout the design process, it "becomes a tool of innovation and not just a version of the final design." This way of working also allows architects to actively reengage with the complexities and logics of construction as a direct extension of their design practice.

5   Jeff Byles, "I Robot", *The Architect's Newspaper (New York),* December 5, 2007, 18–19.

6   Kenneth Frampton, *Modern Architecture, 1851–1915* (New York: Thames and Hudson, 1983) Chapter 3.

7   Konrad Wachsmann, *The Turning Point of Building* (New York: Reinhold Publishing Company, 1961), p. 194.

8   Pier Luigi Nervi, *Structures*, as quoted in Ada Louise Huxtable, *Pier Luigi Nervi* (New York: George Braziller, 1960), pp. 24–26.

9   Tomás Moldonado, "A Question of Similarity," *Ressegna 32 (Maquette),* December 1987, 57. Moldonado discusses the feedback between the act of drawing and the physical model where drawing is a type of cognitive model-making which anticipates the object and its construction. The productive tension between this form of construing and constructing he calls the cognitive-perceptive and the figurative-operative.

10   The fabrication research seminar "Digital Tracery" is co-taught with Aaron White. Student work from the seminar was exhibited in the show *Emerging Talents, Emerging Technologies* at the World Art Museum, Beijing, for the Architecture Biennial in 2006.

11   Moldonado, "A Question of Similarity," p. 57. Moldonado clarifies the difference between classical iconic model-making and drawing that represents a proposed building or object, and non-iconic models that are diagrammatic. Non-iconic production targets how an object works, its function and structure are important, not its form. He calls this class of models analogous and includes mathematical models as an example. Interestingly, prototypes – "models that serve to facilitate preliminary or final decisions about a product that will be mass-produced" – fall outside iconic production because "one can talk about prototypes in a construction-related industrialization system, but not in the case of traditional building." Although this article was written in 1987 before the introduction of digital fabrication into design practice, it is prescient in that it points to the shift in thinking that the discipline is taking in regards to mass customization and the blurring of the distinction between building and product. See Speaks, "After Theory."

12   The installation was exhibited as part of a new series on fabrication research showing both student and faculty work. It was funded in part from a Pratt Institute Faculty Development Grant and support from the Dean's Office, School of Architecture. Chelsea Lipham and Laura Wikesberg were

- - - - - - - - - - - - - - - - - -

the student team who designed and developed the project as overseen by Lawrence Blough and Aaron White. Alexander Drabyk and Joel Stewart helped assemble the project.

13   How do you begin? You begin with the wall. "The beginning of building coincides with the beginning of textiles. The wall is the architectural element that formally represents and makes visible enclosed space as such, absolutely, as it were, without reference to secondary concepts. We might see the pen – the fence of interwoven and tied sticks and branches – as the earliest partition produced by the human hand, as the most original vertical spatial enclosure invented by man." See Gottfried Semper, "Textiles: Technical-Historical," in *Style in the Technical and Tectonic Arts; or, Practical Aesthetics* (Los Angeles: Getty Research Institute, 2004), pp. 247–249.

14   Ronnie Parsons and Gil Akos teach advanced digital software and techniques at the School of Architecture as part of the Digital Futures Group.

15   Heino Engel, *Structure Systems* (New York: Hatje Cantz, 1968), p. 212:

> Structural surfaces can be composed to form mechanisms that redirect forces: surface-active systems. Structural continuity of the elements in two axes, i.e. surface resistance against compressive, tensile and shear stresses are the first pre-requisite and first distinction of surface-active structures. In surface-active structures it is foremost the proper shape that redirects the acting force and distributes them in small unit stresses evenly over the surface.

16   Timbur is owned and operated by Ezra Ardolino who also teaches at the School of Architecture. All of the faculty members involved had a stake in producing a successful installation with the aim of developing a model for future design/fabrication work at Pratt. This allowed for positive communication, collaboration and helped with troubleshooting in preparation for milling. Ezra produced the part nesting for fabrication and tool paths using CAD/CAM software. Only three sheet types were required for the component milling.

17   *Hothouse Lily* was part of the group show *Synthesthetics*, curated by Felice Grodin. The project was funded in part by a Pratt Institute Faculty Development Grant and support from Locust Projects. Lawrence Blough is the principal of GRAFTWORKS Design Research. Aaron White collaborated on the design and development of the installation. John Heida, Ben Howes and Eric Cooper were the design/build team. Nat Oppenheimer and Pat Arnett of Robert Silman and Associates engineered the structure.

Chapter 23
Towards an Ecology of Making

Santiago R. Pérez

Introduction

How can we develop an *extended rationality*[1] borrowing Aalto's terminology, transcending technical functionalism and aesthetic, formal speculation, into a unified *technical-humanist* material ethic of advanced fabrication?

A fundamental disjunction exists between the instrumental control and determination of form facilitated by the use of advanced computational methods, and the significance of the intuitive relation between MAKER, MATERIAL and FORM, in contemporary Craft and Fabrication. The present work expands upon the themes presented in the author's earlier essay, "Towards a New Tactility: Embodied Material Consciousness and MAKING."[2]

The *material experience* and engagement of contemporary form-making, as a confluence of aggregate material-component systems, must be critically examined to (re)establish the *act of making* as a form of critical reflection, theoretical inquiry, and resistance towards the globalizing tendencies of consumer culture and the aesthetic and technical instrumentality of parametric culture. The current proliferation of procedural, serial production and pattern-based surface systems must be examined within the larger cultural sphere of production, re-centering the designer and maker within a "rational-humanist" framework of "Critical Fabrication and Ecologies of Making."

From digital fabrication to "Fabcraft"

Recent advances in generative, algorithmic "bottom-up" methods of design have produced a new wave of form-production, inscribed by internal rules and scripting, leading to a plethora of component-based geometric systems, with aspirations toward the elegance and profusion of nature as a model for production. Parallel to this development, the rise of CNC and desktop manufacturing and prototyping has created a culture of material-logic and fabrication, encountering the tooling, processing and limitations of material systems, mediated by the "economies of excess" engendered by rapid prototyping.

The renewed interest in craft-based practices within the culture of advanced fabrication, stems not from a "pastoral" nostalgia for recovering lost material practices, but rather as an offshoot combining computational virtuosity, human skill and the material logics of rapid-manufacturing processes, increasingly available to the architect during both the initial design research phase, and into full-scale production of component systems (Figure 23.1).

Figure 23.1 Buffalo Bayou installation, Houston, 2008

Figure 23.2 Eames wood splint

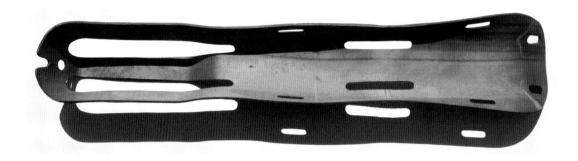

Twentieth-century designers and makers such as Eames and Prouvé understood the value of connecting material innovation with both available craft skills and advanced material processes, incorporating the "social life of materials" within emerging practice models (Figure 23.2). Prouvé resisted the title of "architect" or "engineer," preferring instead to be called a "Constructeur."[3] Both Eames and Prouvé represent a merger of techno-rationalist logics of production and assembly, with the poetics of intuitive form, reaching equilibrium that serves as a model for contemporary design and material systems.

Contemporary designers and makers must embrace emerging practice models expanding our understanding of material practice to include the rational, intuitive and social structures influencing the act of making, incorporating advanced fabrication technologies within an expanded social and technological network, or "Ecologies of Making."

Architectural production is increasingly subsumed within a (technical) culture of design computation and digital fabrication, founded upon the shift from analog, intuitive practices towards parametric, mathematical logic. The technical and aesthetic instrumentality of current digital practices has resulted in a homogeneity of forms, ironically produced under the banner of "continuous variation"[4] (Figure 23.3). Neutra, while developing his concept of "biorealism," understood the need for what he termed "Progressive Differentiation." In a prescient moment, he cautions against the loss of differentiation:

> A relatively evolved organism may also revert to a pitiful state of amorphousness. By this we mean a state without an organic logic of form, with undifferentiated texture and monotonous overall characteristics unfit to serve specific functions.[5]

Recent debates on "Post-Parametric" culture and "Critical Digital" practices, at Columbia and Harvard Universities, respectively, illustrate a shift away from the uncritical acceptance of (parametric) technology, towards a re-framing of these technologies within a culture of "Expanded Practice" and "Design Ecologies."[6] The focus of much media attention on parametric practices suggests an architecture of (seamless) continuous variation, effortlessly fulfilled by the promise of CNC fabrication and robotic production, eliminating the JOINT as an operative (pre-)condition of architecture, and material SKILL as an obsolete requirement of (pre-)digital, parametric and CNC production. The true promise of expanded practices, however, derived

Figure 23.3a–c Element/micro-module/
super-module

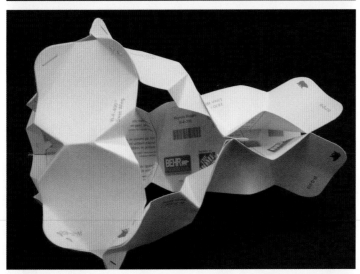

from the advent of "emergent" methodologies, could not be further from the de-materialization implied by the instrumentalism of parametric design. "Provisional," hybrid practices steeped in both the CRAFT (intuition) and SCIENCE (logic) of contemporary material practice are challenging the totalizing, instrumental tendencies of parametric culture, opening new territories for design and production.

The dual, hybrid nature of these practices absorb and re-integrate both traditional craft knowledge and advanced fabrication techniques, into a composite practice, influenced by, but not totally dependent upon, parametric determination of form and automated production of material. This dual practice may be seen as a form of "FABCRAFT."

The experience of making

The *gap* between computation and making today may be seen as a rapidly developing over-reliance on parametric instrumentality, at the expense of material invention and discovery. This gap has widened since the early promise of digital fabrication projects such as SHoP's *Camera Obscura,* combining a sense of craft, detail and spatiality with parametric techniques and advanced fabrication. The shift towards automated robotic assembly, in addition to automated material fabrication, further complicates and distances the maker from the experience of making (Figure 23.4). This profound shift requires the (parametric, robotically aided) architect to renegotiate the process of making with respect to the material, economic, legal and social implications of automated fabrication.

Figure 23.4 Welding Microliving frame, Houston, 2009

Figure 23.5a–c Forming/folding/assembling

> The demise of the skilled craftsperson is one instance in the ongoing transfer of economic and political power from those who work with their hands to the privileged class of "symbolic analysts" who manipulate information.[7]

One of the current underlying tenets of advanced fabrication culture, stresses the relation described in the equation:

CONSTRUCTABILITY = COMPUTABILITY[8]

This equation:

> should in theory increase the architect's control over the project and make building costs more predictable. However, it also renders the skilled building trades largely obsolete and reduces opportunities for taking advantage of serendipitous occurrences during construction, eliminating the sorts of chance happenings that artists, and many architects, often find enliven their works.[9]

In *Diminishing Difficulty*, Willis and Woodward question the claims of parametric culture, cautioning against the loss of imperfection, improvisation, craft skill, detail and material diversity implicated by the instrumentalization of design from a human-centered activity, towards a mathematical and computational impoverishment of making. One of the primary questions raised by their argument bears further scrutiny within the context of the experience and act of making:

> Coupled with the economic advantages of building with fewer but larger modular "chunks," does this suggest that building technology, following the COMPUTABILITY = CONSTRUCTABILITY equation, is leading us to buildings with fewer details and less variety in the ways they are made?[10]

The less publicized aspect of digital fabrication, and its corresponding "culture of making," countering this diminishment of detail, pertain to the multiple material systems and strategies that are being explored as a parallel development of digital and material culture (Figure 23.5). The confluence of FABCRAFT techniques is creating a renewed culture of open-source, shared knowledge, utilizing composite strategies of milling, mold-making and casting, among many techniques borrowed from traditional crafts to empower emerging practices. This new collective knowledge framework combines parametric workflows, traditional crafts and advanced rapid-prototyping and manufacturing into what may be described as MI or "Material Intelligence."

Material Intelligence (MI)

The slow, intuitive acquisition of material or "tacit" knowledge, as termed by Michael Polanyi, typical of traditional craft practices, must be re-engineered into a system coupling the logistics of machine-based production and material performance, with the contingent, secondary effects of (human) skilled intervention, engaging unforeseen processes. Contingent making and Material Intelligence tend to produce multiple systems of "lateral fabrication" (molds, tabs, connectors, etc.), enabling the designer to translate the ideal representation of (generative, emergent) form into the actual production of (component-based) material systems (Figure 23.6). Tacit knowledge must now be expanded to include both an intimate understanding of material, and an expanded proficiency working with complex material systems composed of both physical and digital logic and workflows.

This phenomenon I will describe as Material Intelligence, or MI. A comparison can be made between bottom-up component-based methodologies of design and making associated with MI and concepts borrowed from Robotics and Artificial Intelligence (AI).

Reaction-based or "emergent" behaviors in robotics built upon a bottom-up architecture, attempt to mimic the behavior of natural organisms. This type of framework in AI is known as "subsumption architecture."

> A subsumption architecture is a way of decomposing complicated intelligent behaviour into many "simple" behaviour modules, which are in turn organized into layers ... As opposed to more traditional AI approaches subsumption architecture uses a bottom up architecture. [11]

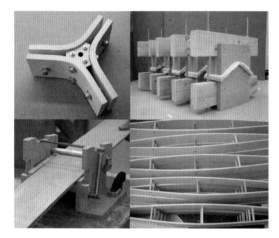

Figure 23.6a–e LATERAL FAB

Figure 23.7 *Tension* sculpture by Richard Sweeney, 2003

Reactive behaviors or "tropisms" emerge as a consequence of inhibiting or exciting networks of sensors and actuators, leading to complex adaptive behavior. Material Intelligence, by comparison, may be seen as complex reactive behavior among multiple component systems, with interacting material-logic, and the human, tacit intelligence subtly adjusting the material system (Figure 23.7).

Another useful tool for understanding the potential of twenty-first-century Material Intelligence is the concept of exaptation, coined by Stephen Jay Gould and mentioned by Reiser + Uemoto. The term "Exaptation" is used in the context of the critique of post-Darwinian "adaptationist" models of evolution. According to Gould, they are "useful structures by virtue of having been co-opted ... They were not built by natural selection for their current role."[12]

Critique of automatism versus embodied practices

A problematic relation exists today between increasingly automated digital production and fabrication, and "embodied practices" requiring the intervention of the hand and manual skill. Prior to the development of automated CNC or rapid fabrication practices, the role of the hand or manual intervention may be seen as a "maintenance function", ensuring consistent quality of identical elements. With the advent of computer numerical control, and the introduction of this technology within the flow of design, the proximity or direct manual involvement of the maker becomes intertwined with automated processes, combining both craft-based traditional production with advanced, continuously variable automated production. Innovation is increasingly dependent on both knowledge of (digital, generative) processes and material intelligence (Figure 23.8).

The tendency towards increasing levels of machine autonomy in a culture of technical rationality was critically examined in Heidegger's *Question Concerning Technology*.[13] More recently, Baudrillard's *System of Objects* confronts the problematic relation of man and automation:

> Automatism amounts to a closing-off, to a sort of functional self-sufficiency which exiles man to the irresponsibility of a mere spectator. Contained within it is the dream of a dominated world, of a formally perfected technicity that serves an inert and dreamy humanity. Current technological thinking rejects this tendency in principal, and holds that true perfectionism in machines – one genuinely founded on an increasing level of technicity, and hence expressing true "functionality" – depends not on more automatism but on a certain margin of indeterminacy which lets the machine respond to information from outside. The highly technical machine is thus an *open structure* [emphasis mine], and a universe of such open-ended machines presupposes man as organizer and living interpreter. But even if the automatizing tendency is repulsed at the highest technological level, the fact remains that in practice it is continuously pushing objects into a dangerous abstractness.[14]

The "Cybernetic" feedback loops between generative software and file-to-fab processes, without the contingent actualites of embodied practices, reduce design and making towards a molecular atomization of components, undifferentiated, without constraint or purpose.

The "endgame" of (generative) technical instrumentality has its roots in pre-digital practices, in the space-frame structures of Wachsmann, absorbing difference by means of the universal node or connector, atomizing architectural differentiation:

> In this context, the structure of a building increasingly becomes a geometric scatterplot of generic elements. The overall geometry of the construction is decomposed into an atomic structure, into the abstract basic elements of a generative system.[15]

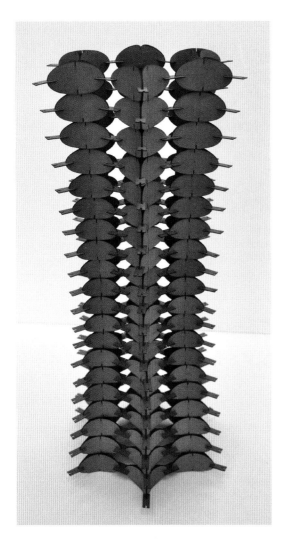

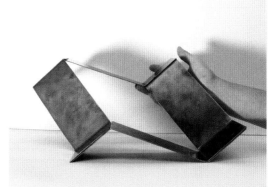

Figure 23.8 Variable iteration, 2010
Figure 23.9 Steel component, 2008

Material ecologies, skill, and resistance

Perhaps not surprisingly, the new vanguard of alternative practice makers are largely comprised of jewelry designers, furniture makers and artists who are adopting low-cost DIY strategies, utilizing desktop fabrication with home-built or kit CNC machines, by start-up companies like MakerBot Industries. These "Ecologies of Making" cross-fertilize niche cultures that were previously distinct, creating alternative design practices influenced by DIY, open source, hacker, and garage innovation, towards new models of expanded practice or "provisional economies."

The most fertile aspect of these new Maker Ecologies is the role of *play* as a form of resistance, both material and economic, against the homogenizing tendencies of contemporary (digital, parametric) culture. As Patrick Harrop, in *Agents of Risk,* has described it, "Play mediates the resistance of a medium whether it is language or matter. Even though one may begin an engagement with a subjective intention, it will only succeed if it provokes a reciprocal response from an *intentionality* embedded in the material"[16] (Figure 23.9).

The complementary roles of manual play and skill, as agents of resistance against technical instrumentality, lead to a "transcendent experience," a "natural coming together of hand, material, and form ... craft making is centered in material and its transformation through the hand as sensing agent."[17]

Within the present context of the "Architecture of Continuity," as Lars Spuybroek has termed it, how can we reframe the critical resistance of the "Tectonic", as approached through the agency of Craft, as introduced by Frampton's idea of critical architecture? Is there a middle ground, between the increasing elimination of the Tectonic within the contemporary architecture of continuity, and a nostalgic return to the pre-generative practices embodied by the normative notion of Craft?

The answer to this question seems intertwined between skill, and the human condition, as noted by Adamson in his *Thinking Through Craft*:

> Frampton shows how ... to think about craft skill ... as Dewey and Albers conceived it: not as a discrete set of techniques, but as a way of being within society. [He] reminds us that through the mechanism of skill, the builder engages with the internal forces of the material; these, in turn, provide a set of constraints that test and shape the building. *In the process, the material becomes the cultural.* [emphasis mine][18]

Another form of resistance implied in skill is the concept of "Slowing Down Time" to conform to repetition and boredom, as Pallasmaa suggests is an essential aspect of learning a craft:

> As the performance is gradually perfected, perception, action of the hand and thought lose their independence and turn into a singular and subliminally coordinated system of reaction and response. Finally, it is the maker's sense of self that seems to be performing the task, as if his/her existential sense exuded the work, or performance.[19]

How may we embody the role of (material) intentionality, resistance, play and skill, within a digital/generative culture of (detached) CNC production? The development of "Functional Ecologies of Making" suggests a hybrid practice drawing from both traditional craft practices and advanced digital production as a means towards a synthesis of MAKER + MATERIAL in contemporary expanded practice.

Figure 23.10 Microliving frame, Houston, 2009

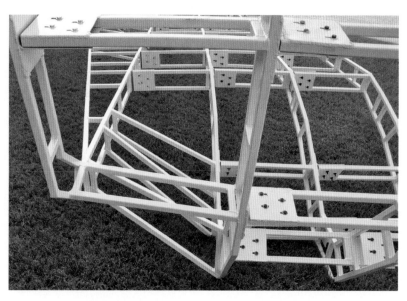

Ecological functionalism and functional ecologies

The architect and theorist Juhani Pallasmaa promotes a "paradoxical" reconciliation between the *primitive* and *advanced* aspects of architecture, as one of the primary tasks in the formation of an "Ecological Functionalism."[20] Framing the task of eco-functionalist architecture, he stresses the need to both return to functionalism, transcending metaphorical tendencies, towards a truly operative functionalism based on performance (Figure 23.10). Pallasmaa underscores the need for architecture to return to

> the aesthetics of necessity in which elements of metaphorical expression and practical craft fuse into each other again; utility and beauty are again united. An ecological way of life brings forth a concomitant ethical stance: an aesthetics of noble poverty, as well as a notion of responsibility in all its philosophical complexity.[21]

In comparing architecture with animal constructions, Pallasmaa attempts to re-unite reason and beauty, advocating an eco-functionalist realism, while supporting advanced practices: "Animal architecture teaches us that a proper way towards an ecologically sound human architecture, ... is not through regressing back to primitive forms of construction, but through extreme technological sophistication."[22] Within the context of advanced digital practices, this eco-functionalist approach begins to define the process and scope of fabricated assemblies towards a purposeful articulation of form as a responsive, performative and efficient assemblage of material. The intertwining of "tooling" towards both aesthetic, generative investigation, and operative ecological functionality becomes a paramount ethical goal of making, in this context.

A reversal of these terms brings us to the concept of FUNCTIONAL ECOLOGIES of making. The sculptor Richard Serra, in attempting to define and expand the relation of the artist to the act of making, proposed a "Verb List Compilation: Actions to Relate to Oneself."[23] Serra comments on the significance of this list on the act of making:

> So what I had done is I'd written a verb list: to roll, to fold, to cut, to dangle, to twist ... and I really just worked out pieces in relation to the verb list physically in a space. Now, what happens when you do that is you don't become involved with the psychology of what you're making, nor do you become involved with the after image of what it's going to look like. *So, basically it gives you a way of proceeding with material in relation to body movement, in relation to making, that divorces from any notion of metaphor, any notion of easy imagery* [emphasis mine].[24]

Serra's verb list was utilized in his early work, to intertwine the [physical] body with material, as in the act of throwing molten lead repeatedly, allowing a slow accumulation of material, coalescing into form. The evolution of Serra's work into large-scale steel forms required a distancing of the body and material, similar to the limitations of building in architecture. How then to maintain the proximity of the body within the expanded scope of material production in digital fabrication?

Michael Speaks, in *Design Intelligence*, invokes Spinoza and Deleuze, suggesting a redefinition of the body, viewing design as "dynamic and nonlinear, with a blurred distinction between thinking and doing."[25] Speaks promotes a more abstract notion of the body, having the "capacity to affect and be affected by other bodies. Bodies are more or less able, in other words, to affect change in their environment, depending on the degree to which they are capable of being affected by their environment."[26]

Manuel DeLanda takes this idea one step further, in attempting to define the relationship between properties and capacities, as they relate to variability and evolvability (Figure 23.11):

The main source of variability in material form does not come from properties but from *capacities* ... Capacities are different from properties in that capacities are always relational ... Properties are always subject to what might be called tendencies. The tendency of material entities at certain critical points of a condition allows a change from one set of properties to another. Properties can display a reportoire of variables. Therefore variability is everywhere, in properties and in capacities.[27]

DeLanda further distinguishes systems that support (mere) variability, from robust (biological) systems incorporating what he terms "Evolvability", or the ability to mutate both individual elements (downstream) and the substrate supporting those elements (upstream).

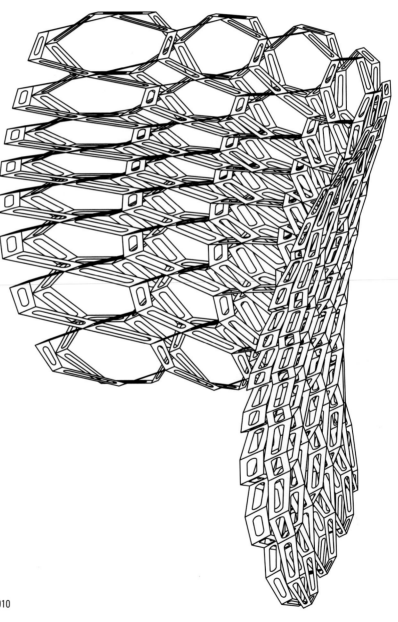

Figure 23.11 Variable structure, 2010

Case study 1: wood (bend)

> There is in nature, even below the level of life, something more than mere flux and change. Form
> is arrived at whenever a stable, even though moving, equilibrium is reached.
>
> (John Dewey)[28]

Matter may be viewed as both raw material, as essence, and also as a unit of measurement, a tool, towards understanding the relation between the body, force and material (Figures 23.12–23.14).

Laminated plywood has specific anisotropic characteristics, despite the effort to reduce the effects of wood grain by alternating the direction of individual layers. These qualities allow for the individual unit stresses to inflect the overall strength and performance of an aggregate assembly. The *bentwood CLOUD* installation on Houston's Buffalo Bayou investigates the relation between individual crafting of unit parts, and the collective assembly and performance of the aggregate system.

Structures of atmosphere

Jean Baudrillard, in his book *The System of Objects*, provides a critical catalog of the multiple classifications of the technical object within a consumer culture. Structures of atmosphere refers to "Form as Camouflage," as both obscuring and attempting to domesticate Nature as a contradictory impulse or idea within modern culture: "Naturalization, concealment, superposition, décor – we are surrounded by objects whose form comes into play as a false answer to the self-contradictory manner in which the object is experienced."[29]

Figure 23.12 *bentwood CLOUD* installation, Houston, 2008

Figure 23.13a–c Wood process, Houston, 2008
Figure 23.14a–v Steel process, Houston, 2008

Case study 2: steel (moiré)

One of two full-scale Microliving prototypes were developed in conjunction with a collaborative fabrication studio with William Massie. This project explored the confluence of flat-packed steel cartridges with a twisted steel façade, reconstituting the moiré patterning developed with the use of a parametric Rhinoceros GH model (Figures 23.15–23.17).

The material logics of information transfer reduce the essential data to a single act – the laser cut notch, calibrated to the correct angle for the maintenance of the overall twisted pattern effect. An extreme economy of means is thus achieved, however, this detail encounters the particular limits of twisting a thin metal sheet. Buckling effects were mitigated only through the direct understanding afforded by trial and error pre-stressing of the material. The steel sheets are placed into the precut slots and put in tension before spot-welding the connections. The project may be seen as an attempt to combine flat-pack techniques borrowed from furniture design, with a performative material logic derived from parametric patterning of the façade panels. Moiré effects (Figure 23.18) are "never quite hylomorphic nor morphogenetic; it is something that involves the application to something else. It is a measure, something that comes from outside and yet reveals the internal operations."[30]

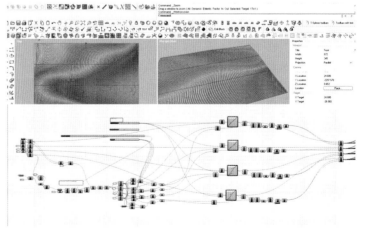

Figure 23.15a–c Microliving installation, Houston, 2009

Figure 23.16 Steel process, digital, Houston, 2009

Figure 23.17 Digital process, Houston, 2009

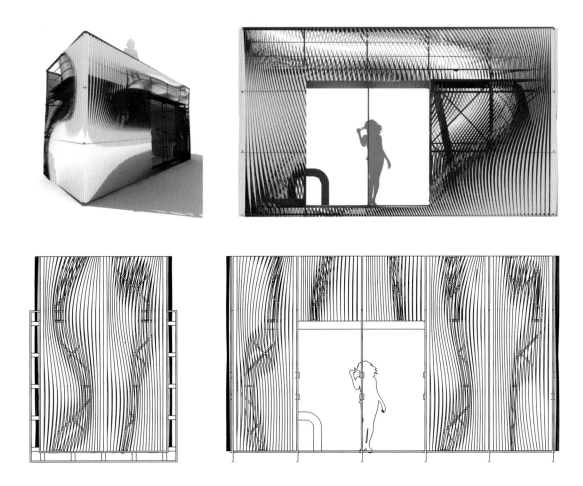

Figure 23.18a–d Digital model and moiré effects, Houston, 2009

Conclusion

The development of new, hybrid practices incorporating the potential of MI or Material Intelligence as a confluence of parametric logic and physical capacities is only just beginning to surface as a strategic position within FAB culture. These provisional practices encompass a much larger "space of flows" both informational, cultural and material:

> Provisional, which we might also call post-edge, practices, do not position themselves against mainstream social, political, or philosophical agendas. Their objectives are more opportunistic, pragmatic, strategic, and optimistic ... Provisional practices collectively are driving a broad range reformulation of critical practice, with the aim of bridging the too often separate disciplines of theory and building.[31]

Within this context, perhaps it is time to revisit the relation between *extensive forms* (actual, physical embodiments of complex processes) and *intensive processes*. Recent theoretical texts drawing on the work of DeLanda, Massumi and others, continue to be based upon the concept of morphogenesis as a driving process in the "Art of Assembly." A constructive, critical interpretation of these "machinic spaces" would posit the body not as a passive agent, a transmitter of form, but rather as an active agent, capable of "accurately describing the material formation of systems as well as insert ourselves into those same processes of formation."[32]

This chapter has attempted to describe the author's developing critical position with respect to the confluence of generative, parametric design culture, craft, and advanced fabrication. The intent has been not to establish an oppositional framework, but rather to conceptualize strategies for synthesis between the act of making, and procedural design methodologies. One possible mode of research stemming from this work considers Henry Dreyfuss' *Measure of Man and Woman*[33] and the "Space of Making" as a transformational force, examining the potential of networked systems of production, in relation to the body. A comparison between the robotic envelope or cell, limited by degrees of movement, and the transformation of the act of making in studio culture, will be the topic of future research.

Acknowledgements

With the exception of Figures 23.2 and 23.7, all of the works illustrated in this chapter were produced by my students at the University of Houston's College of Architecture, between 2006 and 2010. While the individual names are too numerous to list, I wish to thank all of those students whose intellect, sweat, determination and skill allowed a body of work to emerge and be actualized, contributing to "Towards an Ecology of Making".

Notes

1   Juhani Pallasmaa, "The human factor," in *Alvar Aalto through the Eyes of Shigeru Ban*, eds. Juhani Pallasmaa and Tomoko Sato (London: Black Dog Publishing, 2007), pp. 44–45.

2   Santiago R. Pérez, "Towards a new tactility: embodied material consciousness and making" in *Material Matters: Making Architecture* (proceeding of 2007 Fall West Conference of the Association of Colligrate Schools of Architecture), eds. Gail Peter Borden and Michael Meridith, 2008.

3   C. Dumont d'Ayat and B. Reichlin, eds., *Jean Prouvé: The Poetics of the Technical Object* (Weil am Rhein: Vitra Design, 2005).

4   For a critical perspective on variation, see Manuel DeLanda's essay, "Material evolvability and variability," in *The Architecture of Variation,* ed. Lars Spuybroek (London: Thames & Hudson, 2009).

5   Richard Neutra, *Survival Through Design* (New York: Oxford University Press, 1969), p. 344.

6   "Expanded practice" is the title of Höweler + Yoon Architecture/My Studio's monograph. "Design ecologies" is taken from *Design Ecologies: Essays on the Nature of Design*, eds. Lisa Tilder and Beth Blostein (Princeton, NJ: Princeton Architectural Press, 2010).

7   Ibid., p. 78.

8   Daniel Willis and Todd Woodward, "Diminishing difficulty," in *Harvard Design Magazine*, ed. William S. Saunders (Cambridge, MA: Harvard University Press, 2008), pp. 71–83.

9   Ibid., p. 73.

10   Ibid., p. 80.

11   "Subsumption Architecture," Wikipedia: The Free Encyclopedia. Wikimedia Foundation, Inc. 23 December 2009. Web. 11 March 2010. http://en.wikipedia.org/wiki/Subsumption_architecture.

12   Quoted in Reiser + Umemoto, "Atlas of novel tectonics," p. 194. The reference to "exaptation" is taken from Stephen J. Gould, "The Pattern of Life's History," in *The Third Culture: Beyond the Scientific Revolution,* ed. John Brockman (New York: Touchstone, 1996), pp. 51–73.

13   Martin Heidegger, *The Question Concerning Technology and Other Essays*, (London: HarperPerennial, 1997).

14   Jean Baudrillard, *The System of Objects* (London: Verso, 1996), p. 119.

15   The concept of atomization of material systems in architecture is paralleled by the notion of a "virtual particle." See Georg Vrachliotis, "Flusser's leap: simulation and technical thought in architecture," in *Simulation,* eds. Andrea Gleininger and Georg Vrachliotis (Basel: Birkhäuser 1998), pp. 63–80.

16   Patrick Harrop, "Agents of risk: embedding resistance in architectural production," in P. Beesley, W. Cheng, and R. Williamson, eds., *Fabrication: Examining the Digital Practice of Architecture,* Proceedings of the 2004 AIA/ACADIA FABRICATION CONFERENCE, 2004, p. 69.

17   Howard Risatti, *A Theory of Craft: Function and Aesthetic Expression* (Chapel Hill, NC: University of North Carolina Press, 2007), pp. 102–103.

18   Glenn Adamson, *Thinking Through Craft* (Oxford: Berg, 2007), pp. 100–101.

19   Juhani Pallasmaa, *The Thinking Hand* (Chichester: John Wiley & Sons, 2009), pp. 79–82.

20   Juhani Pallasmaa, "From metaphorical to ecological functionalism," in *Encounters,* ed. Peter MacKeith, (Helsinki: Rakennustieto, 2005), p. 189.

21   Ibid.

22   Juhani Pallasmaa, "Architecture of the essential: ecological functionalism of animal construction," Weblog, *Structure and Meaning in Human Settlements*, University of Pennsylvania. Available at: http://www.design.upenn.edu/arch/news/Human_Settlements/essential.html (accessed March 14, 2010).

23   For an online version of this verb list, visit the "UBUWEB Anthology of Conceptual Writing." Available at: http://www.ubu.com/concept/serra_verb.html.

24   Art:21 Interview with Richard Serra, "Charlie Brown." Weblog. *Art:21*. Available at: http://www.pbs.org/art21/artists/serra/clip1.html (accessed March 14, 2010).

25   Michael Speaks, "Design Intelligence: or thinking after the end of metaphysics," in *Versioning: Evolutionary Techniques in Architecture, Architectural Design Journal* (London: Wiley-Academy, 2002), p. 6.

26   Ibid.

27   See note 4.

28   John Dewey, "The Live Creature", in *Art as Experience* (New York: Perigree Trade, 1980), p.13.

29   Baudrillard, op. cit., p. 64.

30   Christopher Hight, "The moiré effect in architecture," in Lars Spuybroek, ed., *The Architecture of Variation,* (London: Thames & Hudson, 2009), p. 19.

31   Elite Kedan, J. Dreyfus and C. Mutter, eds, *Provisional: Emerging Modes of Architectural Practice USA,* (New York: Princeton Architectural Press, 2010).

32   For an overview of DeLanda's morphogenetic concepts, see the book review of *Intensive Science and Virtual Philosophy*, by Aron Pease. Electronic Book Review. Available at: http://www.electronicbookreview.com/thread/criticalecologies/morphogenetic.

33   Henry Dreyfuss, *The Measure of Man and Woman: Human Factors in Design* (New York: Whitney Library of Design, 1993, rev. sub. ed.).

Part VIII
Matter Sensations

The perception of matter through, formal, tactile, intellectual means provides a frame through which the engagement of the work is privileged above all else. The legibility and response on an instinctual level allow the language of the project to be evaluated. Deploying a sensorial spectrum of engagement from visual optics through tactile senses, the reading of the work becomes visceral and thus moves the discourse to an almost instinctual response. The intellectualization is not abandoned, but the formal organicism of the resulting object is privileged, not for its process or its complexity, its specific material or its tooling, but rather the collective perception of the object itself. The form, space, effect are all derivative of the method and intention. The result is an architecturalization that bridges from the highly theoretical to the purely formal with grace and ease.

Keith Mitnick, Mireille Roddier, and Stewart Hicks, Mitnick Roddier Hicks
Marcelo Spina and Georgina Huljich, P-A-T-T-E-R-N-S
Rhett Russo, Specific Objects, Inc.
Tom Wiscombe, EMERGENT
Warren Techentin, Warren Techentin Architecture

Chapter 24
Ana-Log Cabin

Keith Mitnick, Mireille Roddier, and Stewart Hicks

Mitnick Roddier Hicks

----

affect[2] |ə fekt| |ə fɛkt| |ə fɛkt|
verb [trans.]
pretend to have or feel (something); to put on a pretense of; to feign.

> There is rarely a pleasure without seduction, or seduction without illusion. Consider: sometimes you wish to seduce, so you act in the most appropriate way in order to reach your ends. You wear a disguise. Conversely, you may wish to change roles and be seduced: you consent to someone else's disguise, you accept his or her assumed personality, for it gives you pleasure, even if you know that it dissimulates "something else."
>
> (Bernard Tschumi)[1]

The history of architecture is animated by continually changing attitudes towards the role of construction in creating form and conveying meaning. Regardless of how something is built, its methods of assembly infer semiotic content upon its form. One may choose to discuss it, or not, but because construction is inherent to all architecture, each building or structure assumes a position of value towards its significance.

In a similar way, all architecture engages issues of representation in the creation of architectural experience. Because buildings stand up, occupy space and exist in light and shadow – they are experienced in

Figures 24.1–24.2 Installation views on and off axis

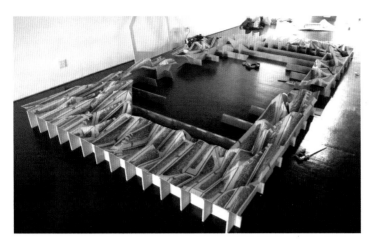

relation to culturally constructed notions about sensory experience that conditions the affects they produce. Buildings are like billboards that display images of perceptual effects, such as light and shadow in actual light and shadow, even when the billboard is blank, or its surfaces are peeled back to show how it holds itself up.

The advent of digital fabrication in architectural discourse has stimulated a return to the expression of construction as a primary generator of form. Much of this work tends to discursively bracket out the social and political factors to which architecture invariably responds. The majority of it is founded upon the explication of apparent geometric complexity, and construction systems, made sculptural in the context of gallery spaces. Work of this sort typically conveys the complexity of the processes through which it was conceived without being particularly complex in the way that engages extra-architectural ideas, issues and concerns. This is not surprising, given that the architecture that has historically employed construction as a primary formal determinant is generally associated with discourses about immediacy and perceptual experience and is, therefore, considered to be more *authentic*.

When we think about authentic architecture we imagine the Unabomber's cabin. Even though it is physically *just a cabin*, it embodies the complexity of the Unabomber's relationship to society. Its form is simple but the meanings it conveys are not. The Unabomber was fixated upon his own self-imposed isolation but he nevertheless felt compelled to express it to others by sending letter bombs back to the very society he had abandoned. In a similar way, the philosophers Thoreau and Heidegger *went away* to the woods to build cabins for themselves in which to forge philosophies founded upon essential notions about nature. More recently, Le Corbusier, the epitome of Modernity, built his rustic Cabanon-hut by the sea as a means of cutting through the very cultural attitudes towards which he was a major contributor. Each of these men built primitive huts to escape the world and to enforce a purportedly more direct connection with *nature* that was understood to be

- - - - - - - - - - - - - - - - - - -

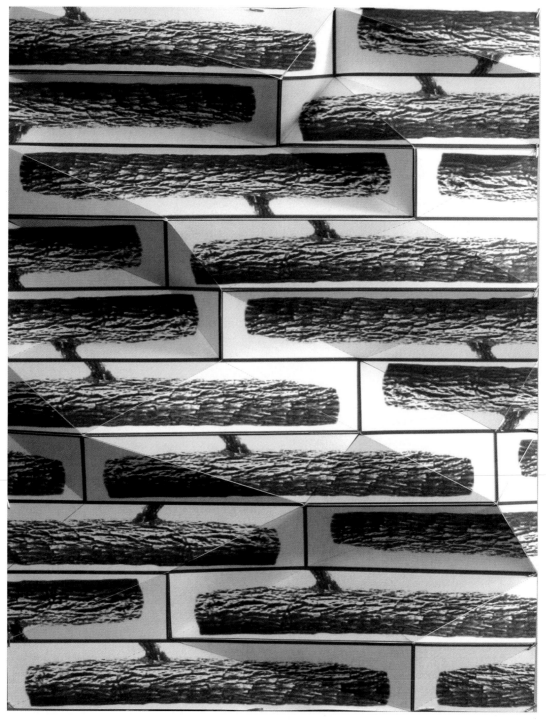

Figure 24.5

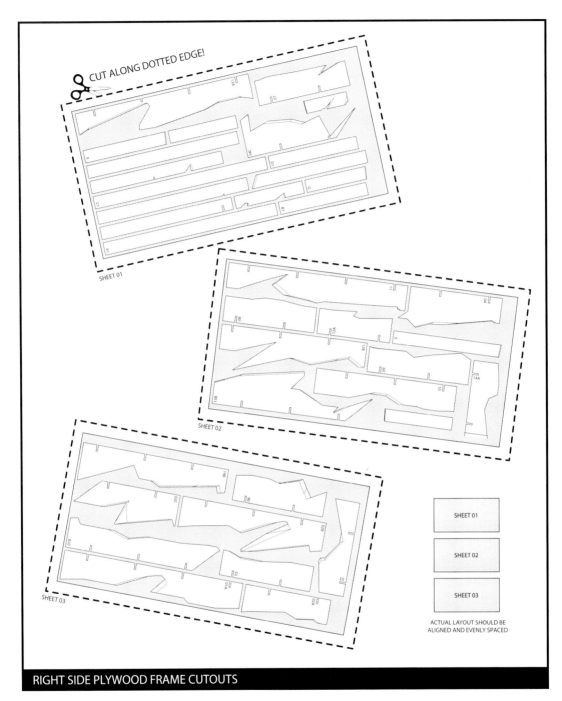

CUT ALONG DOTTED EDGE!

SHEET 01

SHEET 02

SHEET 03

SHEET 01

SHEET 02

SHEET 03

ACTUAL LAYOUT SHOULD BE
ALIGNED AND EVENLY SPACED

RIGHT SIDE PLYWOOD FRAME CUTOUTS

Figure 24.6 Plywood templates

Figure 24.7
Figure 24.8

free of the social circumstances in which the significance of their work as writers, philosophers and architects was upheld.

We see connections between notions about authenticity and the ways that many discussions about digital fabrication and parametric modeling make indirect claims about immediacy (by foregrounding process and the aesthetics of construction) and confuse the internal economies of their work (described in the langue of efficiency and optimization) with the larger and more complex economies in which architecture exists and performs. Discussions of this type of work tend to be limited to a fixation upon *how* they were made rather than *why* they were made and, because the structures are built at 1:1 scale, they are understood to be *real;* that is, they are not representations of some other construction, they *are* the construction.

In the *Ana-Log Cabin* project, we paired together aspects of the digi-fab discourse with questions about authenticity in order to make their relationship architectural. In addition, we added the idea and techniques of anamorphic projection as the antithesis of authenticity because it uses visual deception to question our expectations of reality rather than proffering immediate and essential notions about it. The image of the *Ana-Log Cabin* only coheres when viewed from a single fixed point in space (Figure 24.1). Like the Unabomber's cabin, the cabin-image can only be experienced by one person at a time, but as one walks around it, the visual mechanics of the inverted-cabin-image are revealed to be other than they appear from the idealized view; the parts do not reinforce the privileged experience of the whole, they subvert it (Figure 24.2).

Among the primary influences for this project was Marcel Duchamp's *Etant Donnés*. In this work, one looks through two peep holes drilled through a rustic barn door imported from a farm in the South of France. Through the holes, one sees a carefully constructed tableau of elements including the torso of a woman, a waterfall and a bundle of twigs. Though it is not open to public view, but was published in the annotated construction manual Duchamp made for the installation, the rear-view of the installation is a bundled together mismatch of cheap and irregular construction materials held together with tape and rubber bands. According to Duchamp, this "backstage" was not intended to be seen, but for us, this hidden *other-side* is an important foil to the precision and control engendered by the single privileged perspective through which the project is experienced. One side shows the effect and the other how the effect is achieved. It is this duality of independent views that contributes to the complexity of the work and interests us most about it.

Figure 24.9 Graphic surface

Figure 24.10 Detail

In *Ana-Log*, the back is like a jerry-rigged mess of plywood strips and two-by-fours (Figure 24.7) while the front is the image of a collection of uniformly stacked logs rendered as log-wallpaper (Figure 24.4). Cheap building materials take on the status of expensive ones through the care and complexity with which they are folded and assembled. The image of a building is pulled apart from the logic of its construction. Similar to the kit-of-parts Lincoln Logs toy, in which diminutive representations of logs are made out of actual logs, that is, they are at once actual pieces of wood and scaled representations of logs, the conceptual and optical doubling of material properties and codes may be used to articulate symbolic notions about the ideology of authenticity through representation, anamorphic projection and the exaggeration of parallax views.

Instructions for construction

1. In Rhinoceros®, construct a 3D model of the Unabomber's cabin, with historically given plan dimensions w x d, wall height h and ridge height h'. The plan forms the rectangle ABCO'.
2. Locate the privileged point of view P such that P is located on the line O'B such that B be located between O' and P. Set the distance BP at 15ft. Locate P at an eye-level elevation of 5ft.
3. Scale down the modeled cabin so that the height $h = 5\text{ft} - b$, where b is a base thickness of 15in.
4. $h = 45\text{in}$. Lift the cabin a height b above the ground.
5. Construct a rectangular hexahedron that fully contains the cabin, with two adjacent sides A'B and BC, coplanar with the elevations of the cabin extruded from AB and BC.
6. Draw the vertical Picture Plane running through B and perpendicular to O'P.
7. Draw the concurrent lines through A', A, B, C and C' that intersect at P. These lines intersect the picture plane at points K, L, B, M and N respectively (Figure 24.11).

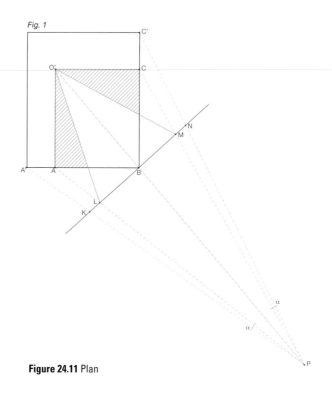

Figure 24.11 Plan

1. Determine the location of A' and C', such that the angles A'PA and CPC are equal.
2. Set the distances KL = MN = 12in.
3. Set the height of the volume at 105in.
4. Identify the points G, O and D at the top of the wall directly above A, B and C. G, O and D should each have an elevation at 5ft. Identify F as the ridge point located on elevation ABOG, and F' as the ridge point located on elevation O'CD. Draw the line connecting F' and P. The point at which it intersects plan BCD will be called E. Draw a line parallel to BC that runs through E. It will intersect the line running through BO in K. Draw the segment connecting F and K (Figure 24.12).
5. Create a wallpaper made of 3.75" x 23" wood logs. Apply it to both elevations, except for the triangle FKO and the adjacent polygon KODE.
6. Render the construction positioning the camera at P and the target at O (Figures 24.13–24.14).
7. Take the previous model. Draw the concurrent lines connecting A, B, C, D, E, F, G and O with P. Define each of the points *A*, *B*, *C*, *D*, *E*, *F* and *G* at the respective intersections of segments AP, BP, CP, DP, EP, DP, FP and GP with the Picture Plane. Note that B and *B* are coincident points. Draw the heptagon *ABCDEFG* (Figure 24.13). Connect points *A*, *B*, *C*, *D*, *E*, *F* and *G* with O'. Construct the seven triangular adjacent planes *AO'B*, *BO'C*, *CO'D*, *DO'E*, *EO'F*, *FO'G* and *GO'A* (Figure 24.15).
8. Using Cinema 4D®, project rendering back onto the construction using central projection method, locating the rendering on the picture plane and the origin of projection at point P.

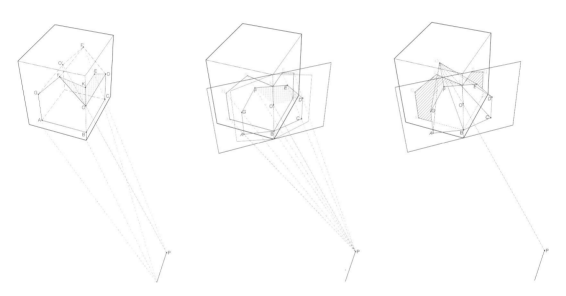

Figure 24.12 Form   **Figure 24.13** Projected figure   **Figure 24.14** Perspective

Figure 24.15 Geometrics

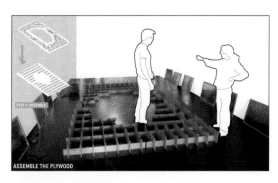

Figures 24.16–24.19 Assembly

Acknowledgements

Special thanks to Jason Chernak for his collaboration throughout. Project funded by a "Design through Making" grant, sponsored by the Taubman College of Architecture & Urban Planning, University of Michigan. Project installed at the gallery of the Los Angeles Forum for Architecture + Urbanism, Hollywood, California (www.youtube.com/watch?v=6qp_Ileln2A)

Note

1   Bernard Tschumi, "The Pleasure of Architecture," originally published as "Architecture and its Double" in *Architectural Design* 48, No. 2–3 (1978), 111-16.

Chapter 25
Composite Tectonics
From monolithic wholes to manifold assemblies

Marcelo Spina and Georgina Huljich

P-A-T-T-E-R-N-S

Composite: a material beyond material?

The relation between material and formal ethics has been at the heart of disciplinary discourse and discussion since the advent of Modernism. One could not imagine discussing modernity without referencing the experiential transparency of glass, the structural slenderness of steel or the expressive robustness of concrete. Not only is the relation between form and material inextricably linked, but also material is very much in support of explicit design agendas, which promoted such important values as continuity, stability, permanence and mass culture.

The ambition to liberate design from the ethics and traditions of material constraints, tectonic assembly and even on-site construction instigated a widespread interest and appeal for monocoque[1] construction and composites[2] in the past decade. Conceptually opposed to the traditional notion of tectonic implying assembly of parts, and certainly outside the encompassing axiom of "truth to materials or truth of materials,"[3] composites afford architects with the synthetic and artificial qualities of plastic infinite versatility. In her seminal essay "Plasticity at Work," Sylvia Lavin accurately characterized the disciplinary framework and recent history of plastic in architecture, expanding the social and cultural understanding of the material and its effects and arguing for the essential role of plasticity in a contemporary project.

As provocative and influential this argument can be for a whole generation of architects, it definitely does not lead to a single reductive conclusion, especially one that would simply equate building form with plastic. After all, can the discipline incorporate the concept of contemporary plasticity as an over-encompassing notion that would allow architecture to be conceptually and literally conceived like a solid and monolithic object?

On what the significance of composites is in contemporary design, there are clearly two well-established lineages with two very distinct responses. The first indiscriminately equates form with plastic and design with transformation. In fact, composites have become the ultimate material refuge for architects who do not know how else to fabricate and construct complex surface topologies. The process of reverse engineering that many of these projects have often to endure in order to achieve their desired formal effects is reminiscent of art fabrication and Hollywood set productions, wherein composite construction is used extensively. For these productions, anything goes into making what I would ultimately consider an image of a physical actuality. While some of the results emerging from this tendency are actually acceptable, their failure to engage and rehearse the full tectonic possibilities of their material medium often makes their architectural manifestation a caricature and their effects ephemeral.

A second, less explored and maybe more materially aligned lineage, and the one I am personally interested in, definitely acknowledges and takes advantage of the plastic properties of composites. However, and much like the Eames with their early fiber-glass lounge chair or advanced cars of today, this lineage does

----

not seek to subject an entire project to the pliability of composites. In addition, this lineage also acknowledges composite's potential for variable materialities, synthetic tectonics, and flexible assembly. This lineage seeks to integrate composites within a larger genre of materials and construction processes rather than segregate them as a single solution; therefore aspiring to a more robust tectonic form, one that not only can produce nuance effects but also sustain them over time.

Why composites?

Composites require advanced tooling and intricate molding. They have the ability to absorb and subsume systems, embedding discrete components within surfaces of variable thickness. They can take on the role of finish, structure and envelope in synthetic ways. They can contain and enclose MEP components, move and adapt, transmit or reflect.

Composites, as we have fabricated them,[4] are "composite" in the normal way (a fiber cloth and a resin matrix) but also through time and procedure. They can be made in many steps, as other connections, materials, subassemblies, or other components are added. In the end, simple or complex, all are in the rubric of composites. Therefore, the use of composites in design is both flexible, but also very demanding. Composite tectonics implies synthetic materiality and embedded forms of connection and assembly. Different from mechanical assemblies, which confound not only the building code but also the overwhelming majority of the building industry, the connections within composites are organically molded or built in.

When it comes to materiality, the versatility of composites lies in their capacity to produce highly synthetic qualities. Containing material micro particles inside a resin matrix, surfaces are able to both mimic and augment known material finishes while also producing new hybrid qualities.

Composites may not have a stable "truth" to their material constituency. Their truth is malleable and in their nature lies the potential for generating endless material character and effects. Whether these effects are real or fake is more a function of context than substance.

If one were to ask what then does a composite wants to be? The answer would be short and simple: Manifold.

Case A: *UniBodies* and synthetic materialities

UniBodies was an attempt to explore the material, formal and tectonic properties of FRPs (fiber reinforced polymers),[5] their anisotropic materiality and its capability of melding, fusing and embedding discrete systems and components (Figure 25.1). *UniBodies* examined composite shells in the production of small and intensive proto-architectures that inventively challenge the implicit distinctions between skeleton and skin – modular and monolithic, smooth and porous – while pursuing an advanced degree of technological, formal and material invention.

Materially, *UniBodies* explored the plasticity of composites. FRPs have the capacity to synthetically subsume systems. Furthermore, they imply an amalgamation of time and procedure. Based on a unique use of anisotropic components to heterogeneously assemble surfaces, every piece is made entirely of a variable combination of fiber cloth, resin matrix and flexible core materials. Core components such as core-mat (used in *UniBodies*) or balsa wood add local stiffness and add structural capabilities to the surface. *UniBodies* exploited the versatility of composites to produce artificial and intensive materialities. Variable degrees of translucency, viscosity, and surface profile were integrally molded and explored through pigmentation and resin fillings (Figures 25.2–25.5).

Figure 25.1 *UniBodies* MicroSection during polishing period

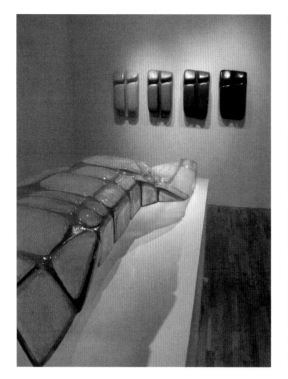

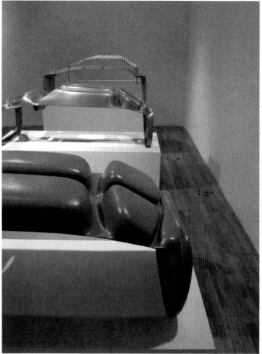

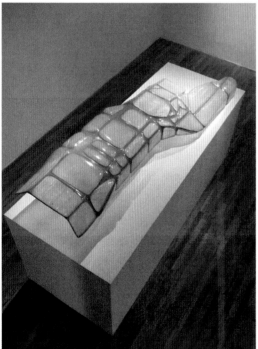

Figures 25.2– 25.3 Macro prototype
Figures 25.4– 25.5 *UniBodies* MicroSections

UniBodies I MacroSurface

In the Macro prototype, a skeletal armature is embedded within a resin shell, giving way to a dual reverberation process: a vein-like system of variable depth appears in the underside of the skin while its top creases and produces near cellular compartments. In the vein-like system, glass fiber material accumulates and stiffens while also gaining mass. In the cellular compartments, micro glass fibers are distributed within a resin matrix but without the cloth, which makes the caramel-like surface more viscous. Air bubbles are randomly formed in the surface, producing a further unevenness to its finish (Figures 25.6–25.9).

This partial absorption of one system by another where there is no longer as a result a duality within the body nor a total fusion of *a priori* discrete systems, but rather a synthetic, composite quality to the overall body amounts to a different but quite unique form of material behavior.

UniBodies I MicroSections

The MicroSections are sectional studies of the larger prototype. The objective of these pieces was to further explore surface partition, fenestration and their relation to several material finishes. Most of the objects use post-applied finish (shades of gray and white), which gives the surfaces a characteristic "orange peel" texture produced by the distribution of spray paint in the surface.

Figures 25.6–25.9 *UniBodies* MicroSections in-mold and post-applied finishes

Figures 25.10–25.11 MicroSamples

UniBodies I MicroSamples

The MicroSamples are direct studies and instances of synthetic qualities of material and procedure (Figures 25.10–25.11). Plastic, aluminum and stainless steel finishes are all produced through in-mold pigmentation. Altering the mold in direct contact with the resin produces a transition from smooth to coarse in the aluminum Sample.

In the remaining piece, aluminum particles were introduced into the resin matrix and applied in the first layer against the mold. Hence the aluminum particles are concentrated right towards the surface of the piece. While de-molding, the surface appears dull (similar to any metal casting), polishing brings the aluminum shine back. What appears to be a thick and heavy aluminum cast solid object is instead a thin and lightweight composite surface. The underside of it shows the heterogeneous fiber distribution in contrast to the glossy aluminum of the front (Figures 25.12–25.13). Due to the anisotropic nature of the material, areas of low aluminum powder distribution amount to patches of semi-translucency along otherwise continuous aluminum finish. Though actively sought and yet not entirely controlled, this kind of effect makes the material behavior of a composite surface all the more magic. The manipulation of material properties enabled by composites represents one of today's most powerful possibilities for material innovation. Despite their artificiality, and due to the uneven distribution of constituent materials, composites appear both real and natural. In a contemporary age obsessed with ultimate precision, composites can maintain a level of material roughness and tectonic imperfection that becomes not only desired but novel and fresh.

Figures 25.12–25.13 Aluminum MicroSection seen from above and underneath

Case B: *Chengdu Fluid Core-Yard* and manifold assemblies

In a completely different way, we used composite GFRC (glass fiber reinforced cement) for the torque-coffered surfaces of an office building in Chengdu, China (Figures 25.14–25.15).[6] The lightweight performance and durability of GFRC[7] make them an appealing alternative to concrete and metal for the construction of complex and articulated surfaces.

A diagonal wedge of circulation that dynamically cuts the plan and connects front and back organizes the building. A regular volume is subtracted from at its corners, generating similarly opposed structural cantilevers that produce a strong sensation of levitation in its mass. Coffered hyperbolic surfaces[8] connecting vertical walls and horizontal slabs further induce the sense of plastic obliqueness throughout the building, linking the front and back visually and physically (Figures 25.16–25.17). The repetition and inversion of the same hyperbolic geometry at opposite ends produce a sense of spatial reciprocity and strange symmetry (Figure 25.18). Subtly but substantially subverting the generic mass, the inverse repetition of the waffle parabolic surface creates a sense of *déjà vu* when rapidly moving in and out through the building.

Figures 25.14–25.15 Overall view of the building from back and front

Figures 25.16–25.17 Coffered surfaces in the front of the building

Figure 25.18 Second level plan showing projected coffering ceiling in cantilevers at opposing ends

Tectonics of assembly

In *Chengdu Fluid Core-Yard*, a standard panelized aluminum envelope is used to clad all flat surfaces of the building. The inset eye-like windows cavities and the coffered torque surfaces underneath the cantilevered volumes are constructed with GFRC. In both cases, their finish is matte plastic with cement coloration. All GFRC surfaces in the building are seamless. Mold making for these parts was done in the facilities of E-grow in Shanghai. E-grow uses wax as material for casting large molds (Figure 25.19). These solids are subsequently CNC so material is carved out and shaped very easily. As a result, formwork and later on precast components are produced rather quickly. As in all composite construction, parts are produced mostly off site, with on-site construction requiring only assembly and finishes.

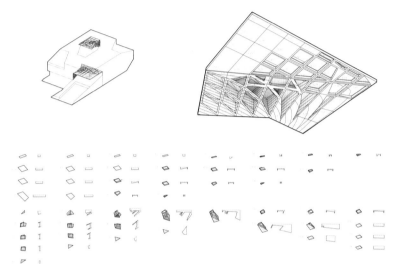

Figure 25.19a–c Drawings of component fabrication and assembly

The coffered surfaces were digitally subdivided and sectioned so as to produce small and manageable molds. Molds were used to cast GFRC coffers and flat components. These were brought to the site and installed there, with seams being erased with the application of the plastic finish.

Coffered torque surfaces

Using hyperbolic paraboloid geometry, the coffered surfaces occupy the underside of the diagonally opposed cantilevered volumes at the front and back façades (Figures 25.20–25.21). Rather than *a priori* system, the coffers are locally articulated. Indexing the movement of the surface from its Cartesian origin, the coffer cells gain depth as the hypar (hyperbolic paraboloid) shape moves away from the walls and towards the waffle ceiling. The function of these surfaces is to introduce a radically small scale of articulation in the most public areas of the building.

The spatial performance of these surfaces is to challenge the planarity and smoothness of the overall envelope, by means of concave surfaces that accentuate or distort perspective from and towards them.

GFRC surfaces are finished in matte plastic gray and they contrast quite a bit from the aluminum finish clad of the outer building surfaces. However, the interstitial placement of these surfaces and their proximity to the aluminum create light refractions that balance the reflectivity and coloration of the materials, hence attenuating their contrast. Despite their lightweight construction, discontinuity with the outer cladding and ornamental relation to the building's steel structure, the GFRC surfaces appear weighty, solid, cohesively integrated and structurally purposeful.

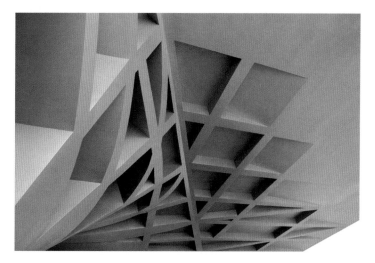

Figures 25.20–25.21 GFRC coffered
torque surfaces seen from underneath

Eye-like torque windows

The inset eye-like torque windows are another example of the versatility of composite assembly and its effects. Constructed through sections (as shown in assembly drawings, Figure 25.22) and applied directly onto a steel structure subframe, the resulting surfaces are entirely monolithic. Placed adjacently to the aluminum panels, the solid surfaces are perceived as both formally continuous and materially discrete. While material difference with aluminum panels is apparent, color refraction and reflection from one material to the other create a sense of overall consistency throughout, therefore challenging immediate tectonic readings of the building (Figures 25.23–25.27).

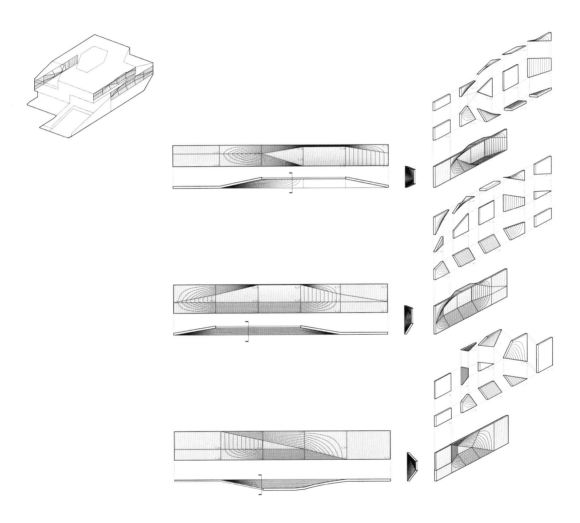

Figure 25.22 Inset eye-like windows' fabrication and assembly drawings

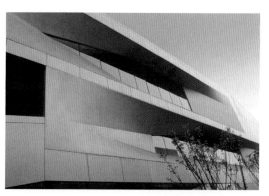

Figures 25.23–25.25 Close-up views and details of GFRC inset eye-like windows

Figures 25.26–25.27 Interior view and details of inner GFRC light well

Conclusion: from monolithic wholes to manifold assemblies

In exploring the use of composites in architecture, we moved from small-scale prototypes based entirely on formal cohesion, affluent materiality and viscous sensibility, to large-scale building volumes relying on formal effects of mass, plastic surface distortion and material economies. The shift implies a transition from the materially rich and coherent use of FRP to the materially abstract and locally assembled use of GFRC. Beyond the material specificity and scale shift, the conceptual deployment and effects produced by the use of composites had further resonances. It originated an even greater shift in the ontological understanding of the work: a healthy and welcome transition from monolithic wholes to manifold assemblies.

The first approach is concerned with producing overall cohesion by completely aligning form, structure and tectonics. We are still very attracted to this mode of cohesively conceiving form where material can be almost magically altered from opaque to translucent, smooth to coarse, dull to glossy, etc., or accumulated so as to respond to conditions of local stiffness and stress. However, we realize that scale, economy as well as availability of technology are crucial factors for building with composites. While it is true that "composites are poised to revolutionize the building industry" by streamlining material production, construction and assembly, it is also true that for the most part, building processes and materials are still very discrete.[9]

On the contrary, the latter approach is both tectonic and pragmatic since it implies allowing form to influence material decisions in more direct and local ways. Flat surfaces can be easily constructed (monolithic or panelized) because they imply no immediate complexity in their tectonic make-up. Complex surfaces can be treated independently of the whole and can be composite. Overall material cohesion or contrast can both be achieved according to the particular finishes of composites. Furthermore, the possibility of off-site fabrication and on-site assembly allows for greater flexibility of construction, while increasing plasticity in the expression.

Manifold assemblies imply that the tectonic whole is no longer materially rigid and monolithic but composite and varied: a complex assembly of discrete means of construction and fabrication customized for specific needs. This logic entails understanding the material and tectonic make-up of a building less as an organism and more as an ecology; a complex ecosystem where a series of diverse systems and components fuse and coalesce. Rather than having one formal system or ontology dictate a coherent material distribution throughout a building, material changes can induce the emergence of more figural relations, or even compositions between part to whole. By liberating figural parts from the material coherence of the whole, building tectonics can be both richer and intensive. I am not arguing here for a return to collage through tectonic means, but for a broader and extended understanding of material coherence in contemporary form.

Using composites in a less monolithic and dogmatic way represents a novel approach to contemporary form and tectonics. One that is not bound by the old ethics and principles promoted by modernism that advocates continuity of form, structure and truth to material, but rather by the ecological pragmatics and formal economies of today, the obvious fatigue of indiscriminate hyperarticulation and insidious fluidity, and a renewed sense of holistic form.

Notes

1   Although an infrequent approach to construction and design since its inception (i.e., monocoque or semi-monocoque construction is currently used in no more than 5 percent of contemporary vehicles), these structures imply a uniquely integrated process of fabrication, production and assembly capable of streamlining construction processes, while at the same time allowing an advanced degree of technological, formal, and material innovation.

2   The recent attention to composites stems from a contemporary ambition of generating continuity, structure and articulation within complex surface topologies. While modularity and aggregation constitute a rational and constructively feasible tectonic approach, the technical and theoretical need to continue a holistic and integral approach to architectural form, structure and assembly continues to haunt not only the discipline of architecture, but also the automotive, aeronautic, nautical, and even the product industry as well.

3   Sylvia Lavin, "Plasticity at Work," in Jeffrey Kipnis and Anita Massey, eds., *Mood River* (Wexner Center for the Arts, 2002).

4   As technically limited as it is, our practical knowledge of composites is indebted to Kreysler & Associates and Makai Smith for our incredible collaboration in producing *UniBodies*, and also in assisting with several academic research ventures at SCI-Arc.

5   Excerpt from Kreisler and Associates website: FRP (fiber reinforced polymer) includes hundreds of combinations of fiber, polymer and processes. This versatility is what makes composites unique. On the other hand, it's often difficult to decide what fiber, resin and process is best for a given application. Because FRP is strong, durable, and lightweight, it often has advantages over stone, bronze, steel, and other conventional materials. Its ability to be economically molded into complex shapes offers other unique advantages. FRP is the contemporary alternative providing designers with new and unprecedented freedom from material constraints.

6   All composite fabrication and assembly was carried out by Excerpt from E-grow, E-Grow International Trading Co., Shanghai, China. The accurate resolution of the project's complexity is partially due to their expertise.

7   GFRC stands for glass fiber reinforced cement, which is used for outdoor spaces and exterior walls. GFRC has a high A Standard for fire resistance, high strength, high toughness, waterproof, soundproof, heat insulation, corrosion resistance, ease of processing, and seamless large area, and is very different from normal GRC products. A special formula cement creates a low-expansion, high-strength precast concrete. As with all composites, surface finish is totally synthetic. Finishes can range from artificial stone, high-gloss, matte, terrazzo to different types of coating. (Excerpt from E-grow, E-Grow International Trading Co. Shanghai, China.)

8   While we are aware that their geometry lies in simple mathematical calculations, we often determine hyperbolic and saddle surfaces in loose and elastic ways. Due to their genealogy, these surfaces can be easily combined with other more relaxed planar surfaces. Precisely in this fact lies their capacity to produce spatial and continuous cavities within a more standard building organization, type or mass, or even figural networks when deployed externally. Hence they can generate interstitial regions that, though intensely distinct, are intimately connected with the building structure.

9   In the USA and for the most part, the composite industry is still a very craftsmanship-oriented field destined to producing racing boats for high-performance, lightweight bikes and motorcycles, auto parts and sophisticated art pieces. Kreysler and Associates in Napa Valley is one of the few exceptions.

Chapter 26
Alternative Forms of Malleability

Rhett Russo

Specific Objects, Inc.

- -

The role that material plays in architecture is complex, the same static matter that brings definition to our buildings, also gives rise to a dynamic set of forces. In architectural design, material selection and structural design have traditionally remained separate questions. A far smaller divide exists in other fields where material behavior plays a larger role in the development of form and structure. In craft-based practices, innovative designs are developed in response to the structural capacities of matter. This is a position that may seem contradictory or at odds with digital design methodologies, however, this is not the case. This sentiment can be traced back to the early nineteenth century and the Gothic revival of Viollet-le-Duc in the *Entretiens sur l'architecture*[1] and the subsequent development of structural rationalism. The advent of iron presented significant challenges to the historicist doctrines of the Ecole des Beaux-Arts. It was a new material that offered the possibility for new forms of structural expression.[2] Blacksmithing had been practiced for centuries in the absence of any scientific knowledge and during the early part of the twentieth century craftsmen began to play a much larger role in the detailing and implementation of metalwork through their intimate knowledge of the material. The Arts & Crafts movement and Art Nouveau were the result of an interdisciplinary collaboration between architects and craftsmen. In a similar way our work is branching out to address material applications in industrial design and architecture more directly. We are revisiting traditional processes equipped with new manufacturing possibilities and a new repertoire of digital tools.

Over the centuries craftsmen have developed techniques to work with the unique capacities of matter. Prior to the introduction of iron into architecture, significant developments had been made in the field of weaponry. In *The History of Metallography*, Cyril Stanley Smith carefully describes how different cultures developed knowledge and innovation through an intimate understanding of the materials' properties. He describes two parallel developments in the history of sword making concerning the Damask pattern, or *water pattern*, in the Damascus blade and the segregation of iron in the Japanese sword.[3] Both contain mixtures of different types of iron and in the case of the Damascus sword, the blade is superior to its predecessors, in its patterning, strength and flexibility. Intuitively, the Persians understood that the patterning of the blade was related to its strength. It was originally believed that these micro crystalline patterns were the result of forging, and this has been the subject of many conflicting theories. Most scholars agree that the pattern is a consequence of the crystallization, high carbon content, and the mixing in of impurities, such as slag[4] (Figure 26.1). The expertise behind the seventeenth-century Damascus blade eventually vanished and could not be reproduced. It represents a significant approach toward materiality that does not distinguish affect from performance. The intensification of the pattern is a reflection of its increased resilience. The source of differentiation in the blade is a singular development, or a *singularity*. It results from the intensive nature of the crystalline structure and it is propagated across multiple scales of organization. In this scenario the metalsmith develops the design from the intensive nature of the material.

- - - - - - - - - - - - - - - - - - - -

The Japanese sword makers took a different attitude toward materiality during the eighteenth century.[5] They refined the process by carefully fusing together various types of iron to make a *composite* (Figure 26.2). They formalized the mixing of the metal, and interspersed the crystalline structure by cutting and folding the steel. As their knowledge of the material grew, they began to assign the performative qualities of the iron to different regions of the blade. For example, the cutting edge became one kind of metal that was much harder, as opposed to the backbone of the blade, which requires more flexibility. Iron with different degrees of carbon was carefully distributed to different regions of the blade. The metalsmiths' innovation involved tuning the capacity of the material to its performance. The *degree* of the mixture has a direct correlation on the material's variability which in turn affects its performance. This relationship is at the core of material science and it is increasingly the barometer by which we evaluate the complexity of our designs, both large and small. The material's variability is dictated by the craftsman's understanding of the mixture, and its effect on the patterning and performance of the blade. Smith argues that material science progressed in small steps, from the production of material phenomena, to performance, through the craftsmen's intimate knowledge of the material's capacity. It is important not to overlook the role of malleability in this process. It is both an instrument and an objective of the design.

Figure 26.1 Persian sword, from the seventeenth century. The granular Damask

Figure 26.2 Manner of assembly of different steel pieces for final forging of the sword

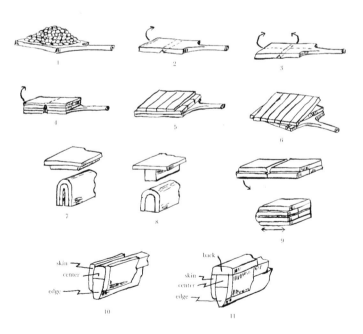

Plasticity

Plasticity is an important aspect of any design process and its relationship to matter is continually being revisited. There have been significant developments in the history of architecture, stemming from the study of minimal surfaces. Heinz Isler, Antonio Gaudí, Frei Otto, and Felix Candela, each developed innovative methods to rationalize the tensile and compressive forces of complex surfaces using membranes, masonry and concrete. Their work was inspired by an interest in the forces and structural capacities of bubbles, bones, and shells. Less attention has been given to the efficiencies of plastic surfaces, in particular, the organic tissue of plants and animals. The behavior of these surfaces is more difficult to codify. In contrast to minimal surfaces, these malleable surfaces buckle or fold, to achieve stability. It is generally accepted that plasticity plays an important role in the development of plants, bone and organic tissue, but the study of its role in the evolution of phenotypes is a rather recent undertaking.[6] The distinction between *plastic* and *elastic* requires clarification. Each process achieves equilibrium differently. *Elastic* behavior or pliancy is common in the tissue of organisms, these materials return to their initial shape after they are deformed. *Plastic* processes behave more like bubble gum, and they do not keep their shape. I am using *plasticity* to refer to the role that the material plays in the development of variability in the design.[7] It is also important to distinguish the difference between variability and variation. Variability is a feature of a system or material, which changes, often unpredictably and it is measured in degrees, while variation pertains to the formal differences, and the classification of types.[8] Factors associated with plasticity become increasingly evident in the design process when more than one material is involved, and this can occur when two materials fight for equilibrium at the same time.

Singularities: *Flabella* and *T-Stool*

When conceptualizing matter it is hard to imagine how any material process could be considered a singularity, but there are circumstances, like the Damascus blade where the internal capacity of the metal gives rise to multiple levels of organization. The term singularity does not refer to the number of materials, but instead to the distinct behaviors that result from a single path of development. A significant portion of our work that involves casting and forming has evolved through singular processes. In 2007, my partner Katrin Mueller and I were invited to participate in an exhibit entitled *Useless* at Project 4 in Washington, D.C. The show focused on industrial objects that had failed during the production process. We had been experimenting at the time with different casting methodologies that would allow us to cast forms in various states of equilibrium, and in response to the call we developed *Flabella I* (Figures 26.3–26.4). To study this we began by filling folded sheets with liquid to fill out the shape of an elastic membrane. Depending on how it was oriented, its center of gravity would change. The *Flabella* series represents a significant change in the way we approached the material's agency. We began to develop a more conservative approach toward variation. The character of the form we were after was a malleable response to the pressure of the plaster and the elasticity of the membrane. This should not be confused with form finding since we were not searching for an optimal form. In fact, prior to folding the membrane we did not know what the form would look like, and this resulted in numerous failures (Figure 26.3). Our interest stemmed from wanting to achieve a differentiated form through the plastic development of a singularity.[9] While we could not achieve this with the open forms of *Flabella I*, it was eventually accomplished in the design of the *T-Stool*. The resulting modularity of the stool is the product of buckling, and folding, a single, two-dimensional disc (Figure 26.5). We developed more precise methods for locating the placement of the folds, the tiebacks, to hold the exterior of the surface in place, and knockouts that would keep the internal surfaces separated enough that we could cast between them. Our success with the stool was due largely to the fact that we were able to develop a topological method of folding the membrane inward to produce internal modularity, while offsetting the pressure of the cast. We knew that we would eventually be limited by the weight of the material and its tendency to destabilize or break the mold. Any time we put pressure back on the mold, we were not able to capture the curvature cleanly and while the malleability was a virtue of the process, it often

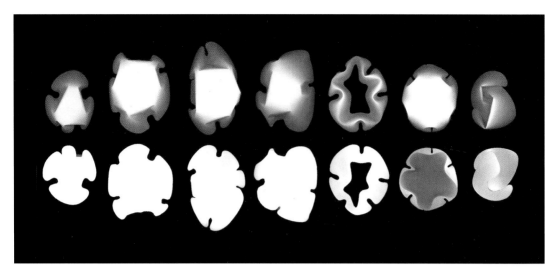

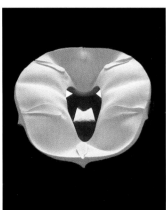

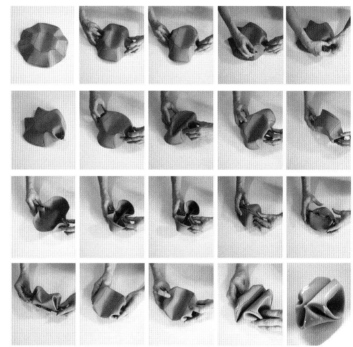

Figure 26.3 Initial membrane casts, top and bottom views

Figure 26.4 *Flabella I*, membrane cast, approx. 12" x 3" x 8"

Figure 26.5a–t *T-Stool*. The sequence of developing a flat disc into a buckled volume prior to casting

Figure 26.6 Membrane model for *Flabella 2* pinned in place prior to 3D scanning

resulted in unwanted dents and dimples. This presented us with a new set of problems that were more easily addressed with digital tools. Once we understood how the material would behave we abandoned the casting on *Flabella 2* and concentrated on the definition of the membrane in the computer (Figure 26.6). This process of transferring the physical mode into the computer was streamlined through the use of the 3D scanner.

In designing the *T-Stool*, we forced the singular nature of the surface to develop internally. The folding of the disc presented us with only a few possible outcomes once we took into account all the demands of the casting process. There was a level of complexity that could not be extricated from the materials, and without taking into account the material's variability, the definition of the work would not have been conceivable. At this stage we realized we were dealing with a system. In the process of designing through the material's capacity we reached a plateau where the collection of knowledge that led to its possibility was no longer distinguishable from the material's behavior, appearing as matter of fact when it was, in fact, highly complex.

Analog and digital craft

Most manufacturing software evolves in response to the particular demands of a material. In some cases the material's curvature cannot be described using rational geometry.[10] The need for standardization has generated a set of tools that are designed to produce a consistent response and insure quality control. It is easy to overlook this aspect of digital tools, but inadequate tools can easily sidetrack the design process. Consequently, many designers have either begun to script their own tools, work with animation software, or prematurely suspend the use of software in favor of physical models. Our focus has been on the latter primarily because we are interested in giving the material as much agency as possible in the design process and this keeps the homogenizing effects of any particular software at a safe distance. By situating the analog model as a protagonist to the instrumental bias of the software, we are able to continue to apply the tools in new ways, and this keeps the novelty of the material in play.

The fidelity of a material's behavior can be undermined by the changes in magnitude that exist between the scale of the models and the final scale at which they are built. That is to say, there are principles associated with a material's malleability that dictate how it behaves at different scales. This is the subject of very precise ratios. It requires careful judgment to identify how and when these discrete behaviors will contribute the right character to the design. It takes experience to pinpoint the material's behavior, since it varies according to the surface area, and a careful survey of the form to isolate the most elegant deformations. Take, for example, the membranes that we have been designing with; we did a lot of research to find a material that would meet our requirements. It needed to be able to fold, but not crease. It was only much later that we realized, by accident, that it was elastic and waterproof, and this allowed us to cast into it. We eventually stopped using folded surfaces and began focusing our research toward the construction of structural shells and, by extension, folded volumes. This seemingly small capacity had huge ramifications on the way we formulated our design process. The nature of the curvature that is associated with the material is unique and the curvatures are remarkably consistent but, they proved impossible to draw. This required us to change the way we used software and hardware. While we found it possible to replicate some of the curvature with NURBS geometry, the topological continuity of the volumes presented challenges to the piecemeal approach of building regions and stitching them together. It became tedious to maintain the tangency across the seams of the virtual model. The curvatures could not be reduced to an affiliated set of geometric arcs or lines without losing the plastic character of the model that we were after. The difficulty associated with describing the curvature was not only a difficulty in the computer, but it was also an issue in making the model. The material rarely behaves the same way, and because it is elastic, it buckles in places where we did not want it to. This is where we were willing to depart from the physical model and refine it digitally.

The most suitable software we found is used to design characters for video games. There are several things that distinguish it from the curve-based software. It is designed to address the malleability associated with the tone and muscular definition of bodies, and it allows the user to do this without using curves. Only surfaces, edges and points are used. Second, detail is conceptualized in a new way, by anticipating the computational demands that are inherent to video games, it allows polygons to be added only where they are needed. The result is low polygon counts and it allowed us to efficiently place polygons only in places where there is higher curvature or a need for more detail. For video game designers it represents a new economy for balancing surface detail with speed, but for us, it offers a medium for refining complex topology without breaking the form into pieces or sacrificing continuity. This represents a significant change in approach. Detail is not achieved by adding elements; instead it is a process of parametric refinement to a *single* topological surface. As a process, it closely resembles the plasticity that is afforded by the analog membrane and its ability to be modulated locally.

This software also tackles surface continuity in a novel way. To overcome the irregularities of the surface, the software relies on a smoothing algorithm to smooth out the facets of the polygons. A similar problem emerged in working with the membrane. If we built the models too large, the material would buckle, too small, and it was unable to form radii. This is an inherent problem in designing with malleable materials, whether it is the polygonal "skin" of a video game character or a membrane. The size of our analog models had a huge effect on the variability of the material and the degree of smoothness. As the size of the analog models changed, so did their character and precision. With the polygons, the degree of smoothness is a function, or strength factor, that functions independently of size. When it came to placing the polygons, we had to anticipate their placement, so we could manufacture the parts. It became clear that plasticity is not only an analog or digital problem. In both environments we relied on similar forms of craft, or technique, to define the wrinkles and folds that are common to membranes.

Composites: *Giant's Causeway Visitors Center* and *Flabella 2*

If the first material concept involved singularities, the second concept stems from the composite strategies that are particular to the materialization of the Japanese sword. In speaking about the behavior of composites, material scientist, James Gordon, offers the following assessment:

> It is scarcely practicable to tabulate elaborate sets of "typical mechanical properties" for the new composites. In theory, the whole point of such materials is that, unlike metals, they do not have typical properties because the material is designed to suit not only each individual structure, but each place in that structure.[11]

This is an important qualification because it suggests two things, first, that these structures require a careful understanding of the structural behavior and, second, that the continuous variation of the structure necessitates a more intricate and calibrated response.

Our first project to address the idea of a composite structural system began with a competition for a new *Visitors Center* at the Giant's Causeway in Northern Ireland in 2005. The causeway is a rock outcropping that extends into the sea, consisting of six-, seven-, and eight-sided basalt columns. The effect of seeing thousands of these elements grouped together in the landscape is remarkable and while they are crystalline in form, the landform has a plastic disposition. I was inspired by the variability of the geology and the level of definition that it gave to the landform. The design of the *Visitors Center* was developed from a lattice, of non-uniform, hexagonal tiles (Figure 26.7). The roof structure consists of a series of approximately 420 hexagonal tiles, encircling two courtyards, topped off with a bar and lantern that overlook the sea (Figure 26.8). The structural demands of the roof are heterogeneous; it is a mixture of lateral spans, a central vault, and a vertical tower. To meet the demands of each system, the tiles are conceived of as a composite that can be reoriented to negotiate the forces anywhere in the building. The roof tiles are organized laterally to intersect and form a space frame. In the lantern, similar tiles are stacked vertically into a load bearing system (Figure 26.9). The tiling made it possible to synthesize the tectonic with the stereotomic by sidestepping the distinctions that traditionally exist between metal and masonry systems. The tiles are deployed plastically, by definition, each region has the freedom to stretch in the

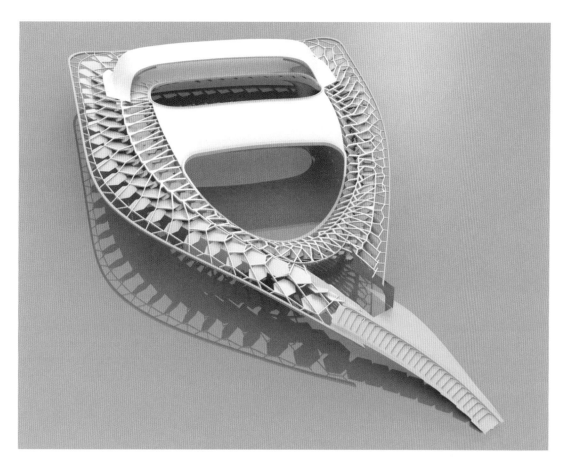

Figure 26.7 *Giant's Causeway Visitors Center.* 3D view of the roof structure

Figure 26.8 *Giant's Causeway Visitors Center.* Plan showing the structural tiles and the ceramic patterning

Figure 26.9 *Giant's Causeway Visitors Center.* Detail of the north face of the lantern

- - - - - - - - - - - - - - - - - - -

plane of the roof and respond to concentrated loads. The rules for mating the tiles together did not change. At least two edges of each tile are connected to the face of another tile while each row adjusts to meet the changing curvature of the roof. The exact mechanics of this relationship demanded that the structural tiles remain flat once they mated. This presented challenges in that the number of degrees of freedom was unique to each tile and this fluctuation did not obey any particular pattern. The structural continuity proved easier to resolve in the presence of physical models and the force of gravity.

As the structural patterns developed, the overlap and variation of the tiles revealed more intricate crystalline patterns. This variation was incorporated into the polychroming of each structural tile and the surface was subdivided into a series of ceramic tiles. This was the first time we had used architectural ceramics. There are seven "parent" patterns consisting of five glazes that vary to meet the shearing angles of each tile. It was important for this patterning to develop from the geometry of the tiling system and for it to have a correspondence to the tiles. The ceramic tiles reiterate the presence of the crystalline composite by extending the pattern throughout the lattice, giving it a directionality, and a visible grain (Figure 26.10).

Depositional techniques: ceramic and metal

Often the intelligence and rules of thumb that were applied to investigating the material at one scale do not apply to larger scales. The advantage of testing these ideas at the scale of industrial design is that these scalar transitions are not as pronounced. In some cases the techniques can be passed on to the next scale of production rather seamlessly as was the case with the *T-Stool*. There is no fast rule for achieving this, but it is clear that the concepts associated with composites and singularities are inherent to the way we conceptualize the role of matter in the design process and they help us identify which materials share the same capacities.

In our industrial design work we have continued to investigate depositional processes at larger scales. *Flabella 2* is being fabricated from multiple ceramic parts and the *T-Stool* will be electroformed in metal. Both techniques can be used to produce structural shells through the deposition of clay slip or metal. These processes have existed for centuries and are now being revisited with digital fabrication tools. Electroforming and electroplating are techniques that have existed for hundreds of years. These techniques were originally used by jewelers and in the last forty years they have gained the attention of the military for everything from intricate metal parts to relatively large complex fuselage components. Because of the distinctive undercuts we began to investigate methods to electroform the *T-Stool* (Figure 26.11). This process offers two distinct advantages.

The electroforming process does not require a mold and this affords the possibility of undercuts that would traditionally not be possible. Second, because the metal, either copper, nickel or bronze, is built up over a mandrel, one atom at a time, it retains excellent detail and requires no additional finishing and this makes it possible to have extremely narrow cavities. The folded topology that we began with can be fabricated and finished in one step with only slight modifications to the initial geometry. We are also able to engineer the thickness of the metal so that the minimum amount of metal is used to produce the required stiffness. The 3.5 mm shell will be slowly built up, atom-by atom, in a catalytic bath, over a three-week period, without the presence of any seams, it will closely resemble the initial topology.

The size, form and structure of *Flabella 2* present a different set of challenges (Figures 26.12–26.13). This ceramic and acrylic assembly developed as an offshoot of our research into casting hollow structural forms. The scale of this work has started to address the complexity of making architectural assemblies, in addition to ceramic glazes and color. There are inherent difficulties associated with architectural applications of ceramics that require the fitting together of multiple pieces, and one of these problems is the differential shrinkage that occurs during the drying process, the other is weight. Shrinkage can be minimized, but it cannot be eliminated in a studio environment. Rather than resorting to using the parts as cladding, we are investigating methods to make the parts work together in a composite assembly, and because it will need to be disassembled, careful consideration is being given to the placement of the seams and the design of the mechanical connections that hold the ceramic parts together.

Figure 26.11 *T-Stool.* Rendering of the electroformed stool, 90cm x 60cm x 45cm h, side view

Conclusion

The way we engage the capacity of material in the design process is directed toward the development of either singularities or composites, and this depends largely on the scale of the design. Whether building or instrument, both approaches apply. For us there is no pure science to the way that this is done, it begins with experiments until we arrive at a consistent level of craft. It is handled in the studio through the repetition of producing the models over and over. We embrace the fact that material behavior is dynamic and variable. There is no conception in the design process that the material is a static thing or that the form is determined from the outset, the process, like the form, is malleable. Material can be tempered, it can initiate change, it can be altered, and it can be dealt with on a composite level in dialog with the properties of other materials to reveal new forms of organization. These ideas run parallel to the idea of performance and similarly in the history of sword making, we see it happening, by design, within the atomic structure of the metal. It is an intimate process that allows us to develop the character of our designs in response to the intensive nature of material.

Figure 26.12 *Flabella 2.* Rendering of the ceramic assembly. Detail showing the ceramic glazes, EKWC, 2010

Figure 26.13 *Flabella 2.* Hollow ceramic prototype, top view, approx. 1m x 1m, glazed and unglazed ceramic, acrylic and metal, EKWC, 2010

Notes

1   Eugène-Emmanuel Viollet-le-Duc, *Lectures on Architecture*, Vols I & II, translated from *Entretiens sur l'architecture* (1877–1881) by Benjamin Bucknall (New York: Dover Publications, Inc., 1987).

2   See G. Kohlmaier and B. von Sartory, *Houses of Glass: A Nineteenth-Century Building Type* (Cambridge, MA: The MIT Press, 1986), p. 129. With the introduction of the iron spaceframe, the thickness to span ratio steadily decreased. Over a 230-year period, the ratio progressed from 1:19 in the Frauenkirche, Dresden (24m span/1.25m thickness) in 1722 to 1:1,570 in the Exhibition building Paris (205m span/13cm thickness) in 1956. The diameter to thickness ratio of an egg is 100:1.

3   See Cyril Stanley Smith, *The History of Metallography* (Chicago: University of Chicago Press, 1960), p. 45. The development of these composite blades began during the second century in Japan. The variety of effects achieved as a result of intermixing are named after living things; the *fish intestines effect* is described thus by Arai Hakeuseki: "If you cook a fish fully and remove its bones, the shape of its guts will be seen to be like the lines on a *snake-coiling* sword." This type of description is characteristic of materially oriented practices such as fashion, cooking and architecture.

4   Cyril Stanley Smith, op. cit., p. 16. In other swords the carbon content is roughly .01 percent. Analysis of the Damascus blade revealed a carbon content of 1.5–2 percent. There are also trace amounts of other materials that do not appear in other blades.

5   Cyril Stanley Smith, op. cit., p. 45. The *chi kang* "combined steel" method of forging is first recorded in AD1065. This method was also used during the eighteenth century.

6   See Mary Jane West-Eberhard, *Developmental Plasticity and Evolution* (Oxford: Oxford University Press, 2003), p. 34: "[Regarding evolution] ... Plasticity, or environmental responsiveness, is a natural property of living things ... any organism whose size, whether due to accretion or growth, is large enough to create internal environmental differences, such as those between the inner and outer regions of a clump of material, has the potential for regional internal differentiation. [When considering modularity and plasticity] ... plasticity is probably the more fundamental, for the ability to replicate, which distinguishes organic from inorganic nature, requires molecules which are interactive and precisely responsive – adaptively plastic."

7   Ibid., p. 35.

8   See Manuel DeLanda, "Uniformity and variability: an essay in the philosophy of matter," unpublished pdf. DeLanda argues that the variability of matter, in particular, iron, that had been studied for centuries by blacksmiths was quickly replaced with more uniform and predictable alloys during the nineteenth century.

9   See Mary Jane West-Eberhard, op. cit., p. 8. "The Cohesiveness Problem: Development as a Conservative Force versus Development as the Source of All Change." A belief in the stabilizing role of development is consistent with an equilibrium approach to evolutionary theory that begins with the Hardy-Weinberg equilibrium and treats the causes of change, such as mutation, selection, and drift as departures from equilibrium.

10   Gerald Farin, *Curves and Surfaces for Computer Aided Geometric Design: A Practical Guide* (New York: Academic Press Inc., 1988), pp. xiii–1. Farin describes the development of the Bézier curve and its application in the design of the Rénault. While it was developed in response to issues concerning quality control, it played an important role in defining the character of the car using curvature that could not be reduced to lines and arcs.

11   James Edward Gordon, *The Science of Structures and Materials* (New York: Scientific American Library, 1988), p. 18. This quote appears in Manuel DeLanda, "Uniformity and variability."

Chapter 27
The Art of Contemporary Tracery

Tom Wiscombe
EMERGENT

Figure 27.1 *Yeosu Oceanic Pavilion*

At the beginning of the twenty-first century, following the death of the "single surface" project in digital design, a sudden interest in tectonic discretization and componentry emerged. To some degree, this development can be attributed to the first generation of digital designers beginning to tire of virtual continuity in the form of endless blank surfaces, moving toward fine-grained surface articulation driven by material limits and available production methods. Since then, a huge amount of work has been undertaken in this area, with issues ranging from buildability and cost-effectiveness, to the aesthetic implications of CNC tooling, to the use of parametrics

to generate variable panelization across surfaces. Parametric discretization, in particular, has taken the discipline by storm, with its seductive implications of being an art form conveniently couched in an economic model – a perfect match of beauty and optimization. The problem is, parametric work tends to be immediately identifiable and therefore consumable. It is identifiable through its indexicality to the algorithms that drive it as much as to the industrial methods of production that underwrite it.

More compelling, perhaps, is the competing sensibility of a new generation of architects focused on surface features which exceed such limitations towards the transformative and the mysterious. This sensibility avoids the aesthetic and conceptual limitations of linear parametric gradients, recognizing that surface discretization as it relates to the expression of material limits is expedient but ultimately passé. A perfect example is the recent advent of "meta-seaming," or the articulation of seams as ornament, driven by affect, rather than as a one-dimensional index of the beginnings and ends of pieces of material. Meta-seaming puts form and material into a more complex relation; once a joint or seam is released from indexicality, it is free to obfuscate or enhance formal, ornamental, or even infrastructural features within surfaces. Meta-seaming logic can begin to break down the lock-step of seams and sub-structure into articulations in surfaces which can begin to do unexpected kinds of work in unexpected patterns. Meta-seams, like tribal tattoos, can shift between emphasizing underlying bone structure or musculature and expressing completely independent painterly effects.[1]

The meta-seam is a subset of what might be called *the art of contemporary tracery*. Tracery refers to the moment when a surface transforms into line, expressed as a negative seam, a slight protrusion, or deep relief, but also when lines pull off of surfaces entirely to become spatial armatures. It also invokes the issue of the trace, or vestige, which is when a pathway is just barely discernible from a smooth field, in a state of either appearing or disappearing, tensing or relaxing. The architecturalized trace is, however, not a map or diagram, nor is it symbolic; it is an exquisite form of becoming, of surfaces oscillating between dimensions. The sensibility of tracery is deeply embedded in the discipline, appearing in the transformation of the three-dimensional Classical column into the two-and-a-half dimensional pilaster, or as Gothic bundled columns spreading out into vault relief and window tracery, or as organic Art Nouveau surface relief flattening out into graphics in one area only to tense back up dimensionally in another.

Contemporary tracery can be lacy, branchy, cellular, or hybrid – a repertoire recently expanded through developments in generative computation. But more importantly, it must fade in and fade out of flatness and avoid indexicality. This is what distinguishes tracery from the structural expressionist ribs and lamella systems of Nervi as well as from Mies van der Rohe's decorative yet standardized mullions. Tracery doesn't languish under the need to express singular performative diagrams. Nevertheless, while it operates at the level of form

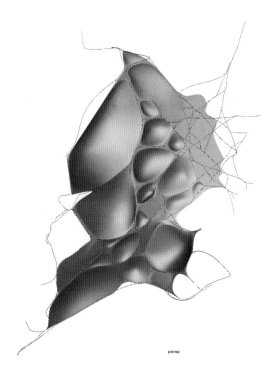

persp

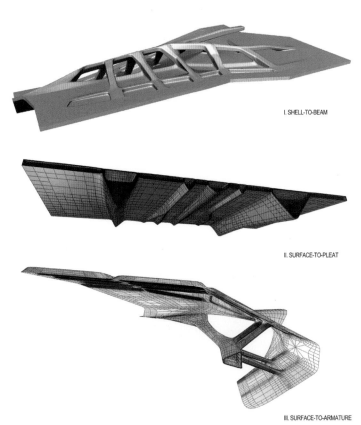

I. SHELL-TO-BEAM

II. SURFACE-TO-PLEAT

III. SURFACE-TO-ARMATURE

Figures 27.3–27.4 Surface-to-line tracery

and affect, this does not exclude it taking on other kinds of instrumentality. In fact, the cross-categorality of line and surface, depth and flatness, is most productive when it imbues aesthetic formations with other types of performance. The pleat, or becoming line of a surface, creates a bridge between technological and ornamental territories. The double-pleat, in addition to creating beam-like stiffness in surfaces, provides hollow poché spaces within which air, fluid, and light can flow. Adding performative dimensions to tracery is not an alibi, however. It is a way of increasing effects of ambiguity and delight by activating multiple ontological frameworks. Tracery is therefore at odds with Venturi and Scott Brown's concept of the "decorated shed," where ornament operates independently from all other architectural and tectonic concerns.[2]

Composite materials, hybrid systems, and goblin hands

The re-emergence of tracery within architecture is no doubt supported by developments in composite materials and hybrid systems. These include fiber-resin composites, impregnated membranes, glass fiber reinforced concrete, and other such super-plastic materials. Composite materials not only allow for smooth formal transitions between surface and line, but increase in capacity through such blending. Fiber-composite monocoque construction in automotive, naval, and aerospace applications is entirely dependent on patterns of pleats, warps, and bas-relief in surfaces for structural performance, thus forcing a feedback loop of visual and structural concerns. Fiber-composites are driven by intensive materiality in the sense that they are themselves organized by micro-tracery of fibers laid out according to force pathways as well as local build-ups of matrix and fiber. In terms of assembly, traditional hardware and substructure get thrown out the window in favor of seamless connections using structural adhesive and hidden lap joints. This means, ironically, that construction seams, made visible or invisible, are more likely to run against the grain of tracery patterns to maintain structural continuity.

Hybrid systems such as "beam-branes" and "beam-shells" are also tied to the language of contemporary tracery. These two systems hybridize shell or membrane surfaces with variable veining, allowing for wider application in asymmetrical or unbalanced conditions. Patchy, veiny patterns embedded in the surface can resist anomalous bending forces occurring in irregular membrane and shell morphologies. According to force analyses as well as aesthetic criteria, these patches can vary in depth or even pull-off and reconnect with other patches forming strange transitions between brambled vector-active systems and smooth surface-active systems. Another species of beam-brane is the "boom-brane," recently developed by my office. Boom-branes allow for the construction of huge bubble structures via networks of air-pressurized, double-pleated tracery. This type of tracery, which can also be stiffened in-situ using pre-preg technology, has the amazing characteristic of not spanning, per se, between supports. It inhabits the interior of the surface, rigidizing its peaks, valleys, or transitional moments, then fading back into flatness before reaching its perimeter. This engenders a radically different pattern and density of articulation in transparent surfaces compared to that forced by the heavy glazing and mullion systems of the last century. The leap is as game-changing as that between plate glass and iron frame

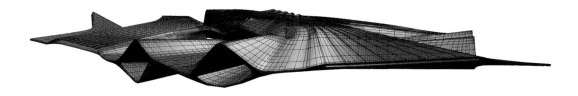

Figure 27.5 Hollows created by double pleating allow for latent infrastructural behavior

construction in the mid-nineteenth century and annealed glass curtain walls in the early twentieth century.

Fueling the desire for these kinds of technological leaps are new design techniques that allow for unprecedented control of geometry and formal transitions. Indeed, without the simultaneous evolution of digital design tools, offering advanced ways of modeling the in-between of line and surface, the art of tracery might have remained a lost craft. Subdivision surface modeling in particular has made it possible for architects to manipulate surface in ways not possible even five years ago. Invented by the entertainment industry in response to the problem of efficiently modeling goblin hands, subdivision surfaces are driven by the mathematics of non-uniform meshes, where areas of extreme articulation and areas of repose can inhabit a single surface patch. You certainly can't model fingers, veins, and wrinkles with NURBS lofting – the U and V logic will always end up producing things with indexical directionality, and local articulations will always fade off too uniformly.

Still, neither technique nor technology can explain the seductiveness of tracery. Tracery resonates along a disciplinary thread stretching back hundreds of years. This thread is characterized by a loose, fluctuating relationship between building technology, formal features, and painterly composition, synthesized in a wild array of experiments.

The excess of vault ribs and pilasters

Over the past two centuries, there has been a lively and revealing discussion as to the relation between what is ornamental and what carries loads in Gothic cathedrals. The debate began in earnest with Viollet-le-Duc's assertion in the mid-nineteenth century that vault ribs were not only structurally active but that the surface of the vault was merely infill and structurally passive. This view was attacked in the 1934 by Pol Abraham, who was convinced that the opposite was the case: that vaults were shell-active and that vault ribs were ornamental. It was a zero-sum duel of rationalist thinking. Not until the early 1970s was the debate at least provisionally settled by Jacques Heyman, who did finite element analysis on digital models of existing cathedrals. He found that shell and ribs exhibit differential, composite behavior, and it became suddenly clear that the terms of the debate had been flawed all along.[3] The flaw was the belief that vault ribs could be categorized at all, and more importantly, that the art of illusion was not as important as the truth of engineering. It is actually quite charming and ironic that it took an engineer to usher the discussion back to architecture.

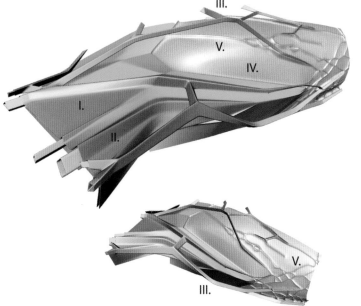

Figure 27.6 Tracery of structural pull-offs and "boom-branes" in the *Yeosu Oceanic Pavilion*

I. FIBER COMPOSITE SHELL

II. STRUCTURAL PLEATS

III. MOHAWKS
Stabilizing armatures for
ETFE membrane

IV. ETFE MEMBRANE

V. AIR BEAMS
Pressurized double pleats
in membrane

STRUCTURAL DIAGRAM

The "function" of the classical pilaster has similarly been the subject of much study and debate, although not in such techno-rationalist terms. The first pilasters were of course actual columns – called engaged columns – embedded in non-structural infill walls. The Roman temple Maison Carrée (Nîmes, 16 BC, Figure 27.7) has no pilasters per se, although the visual effect is that columns-in-space begin to merge with the surface of the infill wall towards the rear of the building. Later Roman architecture began to dissolve engaged columns into bearing walls, and the pilaster was born as architectural excess. Despite Wittkower's description of the pilaster as a "flattened column which has lost its three dimensional and tactile value,"[4] it seems unproductive to frame the discussion in terms of lack, even when thinking of Alberti, who pushed the pilaster so close to the surface of the wall that it almost ceased to exist. The pilaster, seen instead through Deleuze, is a becoming-column of a wall, a virtual spatiality emanating from flatness. This virtual phase-changing becomes all the more complex when the verticality of the pilaster and its link to gravity begin to dissolve in the Late Baroque period; in this case, pilasters become more and more broken down and overgrown through figuration and color effects alien to the classical orders. The mega-tracery of the pilaster is transformed into an atmospheric field of micro-traceries (Figure 27.8).

What the histories of the vault rib and the pilaster reveal is an evolutionary tendency toward exquisite excess rather than minima, despite their structurally instrumental beginnings. In the vault rib versus the vault surface, the excess is in the structural redundancy of the two systems combined through a unifying surface-to-line ornamental sensibility. In the pilaster, it is the cultural tendency to consume structural solutions and embed them in a painterly realm that is excessive. In both cases, it is the migration of behaviors between features, and the tendency of features to therefore become excess, that is key to their architectural effect. Mysteriously, the same phenomenon is everywhere to be found in nature, where such migrations generate endless weirdness and complexity.

Co-option and biological excess

Despite incessant arguments to the contrary – that species and ecologies are pure expressions of purpose – the reality of biological formations is far more messy. While it is true that species and ecosystems do work, they often do it in a non-optimal way. Features are built up over time through leaps of random mutation as much as refinement, creating inherent redundancies and excesses. This is what happens when you never begin with a *tabula rasa*, as nature never does (Figure 27.9). The hammerhead shark, for example, does exceptionally well as a species considering the massive disadvantages of the hammer-mutation, related to vision and hunting, and only minor advantages, related to increased surface area for electro-receptors. The hammer is not, contrary to popular belief, a navigational diving-plane driven by optimization. And this is not an exceptional case. Indeed, excess pervades every level of the biosphere and is a primary driver of the biodiversity that so intrigues us.

The phenomenon of co-option reveals how the de-linking of features and behaviors can produce astounding effects as well as do unexpected work. Co-option refers to the fact that behaviors tend to migrate between features over time: a classic example is that although bird feathers originally evolved for insulation, they were co-opted for flight. An even richer example is found in the keel-billed toucan of the Amazon rainforest (Figure 27.10). The male toucan has a gigantic colorful beak which was always assumed to be the singular result of sexual selection pressures. Recently it was discovered, however, that although the beak was originally adapted as sexual ornament, it has since been co-opted as a vascular, controllable thermo-regulator for the bird.[5] The beak's exquisite formal and color features do not index its ability to collect and exhaust heat, but they are nonetheless critical for the character of the bird.

Muddled together, feature upon feature, mutation upon mutation, species develop complexity, not despite, but because of, excess. Contemporary tracery, in the same way, is a productive muddling of line and surface, technology and ornament. Combined with ambiguous materials and unnatural color and lighting effects, the architecture of contemporary tracery engages through its indeterminacy and irreducibility.

Figure 27.9 Behaviorally ambiguous tracery in agamid lizard skin. Megachannels route water to the lizard's mouth, while the additional layers of micro-articulation and color variegation have no discernible purpose according to biologists

Figure 27.10 Migration of behaviors between features in the keel-billed toucan

Projects

Prototypes I–III

These three prototypes are part of recent research concerned with unpacking the spatial and ornamental potentials of airflow, fluid flow, and glow, often considered to be "minor" forces in architecture. Based on chunk logic rather than layer logic, these prototypes are intended to be manufactured and delivered as fully integrated three-dimensional assemblies embedded with all internal infrastructural systems. They are to be constructed of formed fiber composite and polycarbonate materials assembled with socket connections and structural

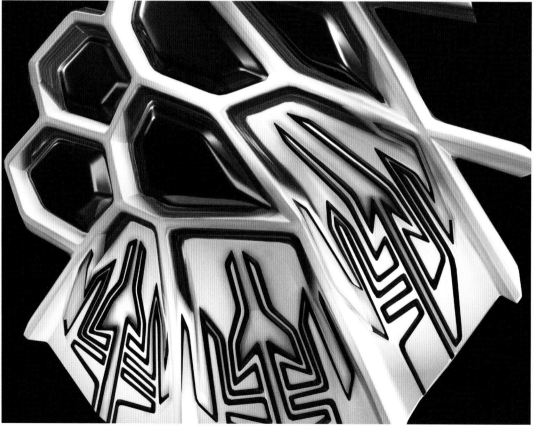

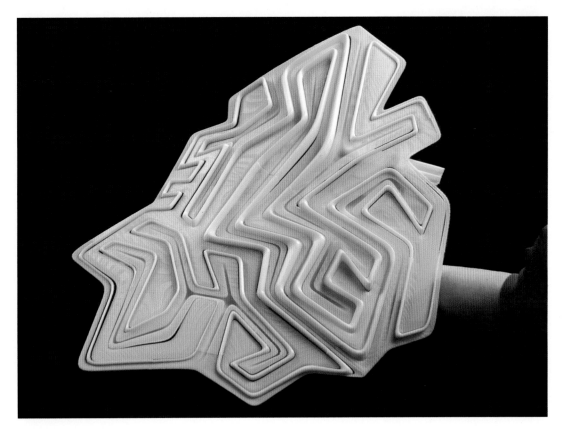

Figure 27.11 *Tracery Glass*
Figure 27.12 *Thermo-Strut*
Figure 27.13 *Lizard Panel*

adhesive, as well as more normative materials such as plate steel. They feature embedded solar thermal and photovoltaic systems, algae photo bioreactor coils, radiant cooling systems, and grey water capture systems.

Prototype I: Tracery Glass
Tracery Glass reconsiders stained glass in contemporary architecture. Rather than dematerializing glass, this glass is not only not glass (it's polycarbonate), it is highly characterized by embedded technology which does both ornamental and physical work. It allows views, but through layers of light, relief, coils, PV panels, and gradient color patterns (Figure 27.11).

Prototype II: Thermo-Strut
Thermo-strut intertwines welded-up plate steel beams with fiber composite shells embedded with solar thermal tracery. In armature conditions, the solar thermal system is interiorized and receives solar exposure through transparent apertures, while in surface conditions, it spreads out as patterns of relief and color (Figure 27.12).

Prototype III: Lizard Panel
Lizard Panel, based partially on the skin of the Australian Agamid Lizard, is a puzzle-piece system with socketed structural and mechanical members for continuity. It is characterized by a lacy, meandering pattern of algae PB pipes for energy generation as well as deep channels which collect gray water from rainfall. Algae and gray water systems are interwoven in a way that produces emergent structural behavior (Figure 27.13).

Figure 27.14 *Batwing*

Batwing

The prototype is intended as a re-examination of the threshold between architectural surface and infrastructural tracery. It is based on manifold geometry which incorporates structural, mechanical, envelope, and lighting system behaviors. This is not to say that any one of these systems is "optimized" in terms of functional prowess – the formal and ambient spatial effects of fluidity, translucency, glow, and silhouette are all as important for the overall effect of the piece. The intent is to establish a link between the sensate realm and infrastructural flows in architecture. This is different than simply expressing structure or expressing building technology, making it legible. *Batwing* is not the inside-out *Centre Pompidou*, which exports technology to the building exterior without transformation. It is an intensive set of transformations which reveal and obfuscate behavior.

The design sensibility of *Batwing* is driven by two types of surface transformation: the pleat and the becoming-armature. Pleats operate in terms of providing structural rigidity and directed airflow across the surface while also creating a seductive ornamental patterning. The armature transforms the envelope system into a duct system which provides supply air as well as structural continuity between envelope components. Deep pleats become air diffusers, featuring an embedded cooling meshwork of micro-capillaries used for cooling or heating of passing air. Based on the principle of water-to-air heat exchange, this cooling system heats or cools through local radiative transfer rather than relying on "central air" (Figures 27.14–27.16).

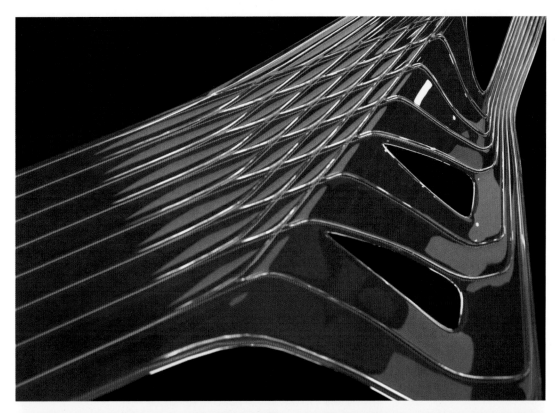

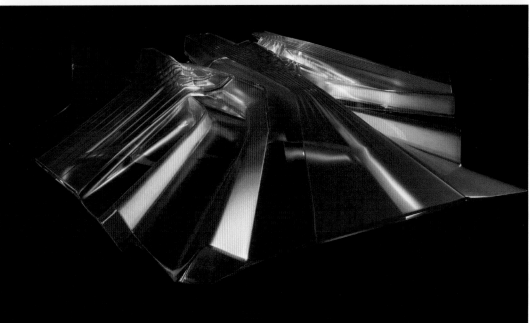

Figures 27.15–27.16 *Batwing*

Taipei Performing Arts Center

This project, an international competition submission from 2008, weaves the three performing arts theaters together by way of an elevated concourse, creating a unified whole. The concourse is a bridging element which acts as circulation for the theaters but also as a commercial and cultural zone which includes lively urban activities. It is articulated as a hanging, cantilevered massing which is porous to the urban space below.

The morphology of the project is based on patterns of armatures and pleats which form an intricate ornamental network. Armatures are woven together to create the circulation and structure of the concourse, forming deep spaces and views from the plaza into the building as well as from the building down into the plaza and out into the city. Micro-pleats track along the armatures but also spread out along surfaces, changing in depth and number, and occasionally fading out into flatness. Sensations produced by this fluid tracery are heightened by a gradient of color which is most intense on the interior but fades out to the exterior of the building (Figures 27.17–27.19).

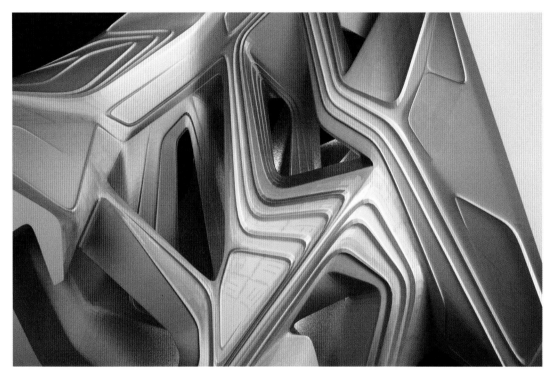

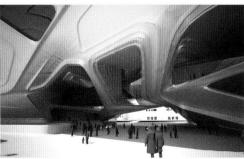
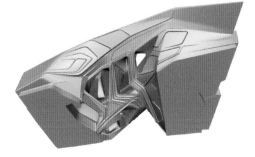

Figure 27.17–27.19 *Taipei Performing Arts Center*

Flower Street Bioreactor

The point of departure for this project was to engage the nascent cultural paradigm shift from thinking about energy as something which comes magically from distant sources to something which can be generated locally in a variety of ways. The goal was not, however, to simply express material processes or feats of engineering, but rather to create a sense of delight and exotic beauty around energy technologies through excess.

The project, a commissioned piece of public art in Los Angeles, is an aquarium-like photo bioreactor inserted into the façade of a renovated building, containing green algae colonies that produce biofuel through photosynthesis. The aquarium is made of thick transparent polycarbonate, molded to create intricate relief with haptic effects for passers-by. This relief tracks along with and supports an internal lighting armature which is based on the "Bio-feedback Algae Controller" invented by the biofuel company OriginOil. This new type of bioreactor uses tuned LED lights which vary in color and intensity to support algae growth at different stages of development, maximizing output. According to OriginOil, "This is a true bio-feedback system ... the algae lets the LED controller know what it needs as it needs it, creating a self-adjusting growth system." This system is powered by a sinuous solar array that winds up into the branches of an adjacent tree. At night, the piece generates a simultaneously urban and jungle effect: glittery reflections on plastic combine with an eerie élan vital of glowing organic material (Figures 27.20–27.22).

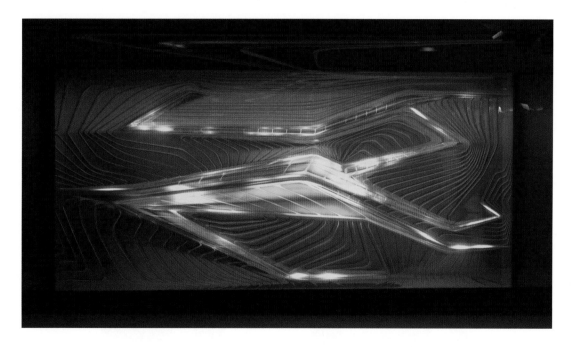

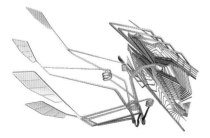
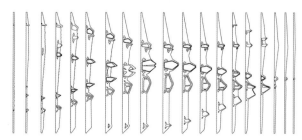

Figure 27.20–27.22 *Flower Street Bioreactor*

Novosibirsk Pavilion

This pavilion design is the result of research into grid-stiffened shells. Grid-stiffened shells (a.k.a. gridshells), prevalent in 1950s and 1960s engineering masterworks by Nervi, Otto, and Candela, were part of a lineage of experimentation into material intelligence and analog shape computation leading all the way back to the Gothic era. These structures were characterized by form-found curvature and uniform patterns of relief. These solutions were, however, often limited by their tendency toward minima and rational expression of material limits. The gridshell is newly relevant today, re-invented through non-uniform patterns of relief and non-indexical materiality.

This design is based on the simultaneous response of pattern to surface curvature and force pathways, generating a highly varied, non-linear structuration. Variability in pattern morphology, density, and depth allow for a localized structural tuning which would be impossible with invariant pattern logic. Limitations of traditional form-finding, where structures tend toward funicular forms, are lifted, and more complex, unbalanced surface shapes begin to be possible. The result is "beam-shell" logic, or a hybrid of shell behavior and beam behavior, where the build-up of forces in shells can be relieved through the introduction of vector elements.

Massive scale shift between neighboring cells in the surface pattern is critical to the design. Competing forces of curvature and stiffness reinforce this heterogeneity, which is consciously distant from linear parametric gradients (Figures 27.23–27.25).

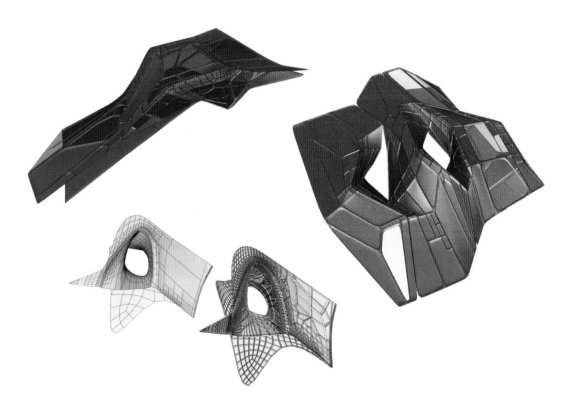

Figures 27.23–27.25 *Novosibirsk Pavilion*

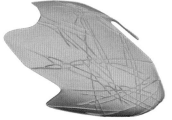

Yeosu Oceanic Pavilion

This project is the result of a collaboration between EMERGENT and KOKKUGIA, intended to capitalize on both shared sensibilities as well as individual expertise. It is an exploration of messy computation in the sense that the project is the result of moving in and out of the realms of designing and scripting. It represents a loose, open-ended way of working that biases effects over self-justifying processes.

The Pavilion is intended to be the centerpiece for the Yeosu 2010 Expo, a space which celebrates the ocean as a living organism and the co-existence of human culture and ocean ecosystems. In the design proposal, the building object and its territory enter into a feedback loop. The role of the architect is expanded to include the active re-organization of matters and energies around and underneath the building, where the species selects its environment as much as the environment selects its species.

Tectonics and color

The building is based on an aggregation of soft membrane bubbles merged together with a hard monocoque shell. The two systems are characterized by patterns of surface articulation which are specific to their materiality. Nevertheless, features tend to migrate, hybridize and become redundant. Deep pleats and mega-armatures that create structural stiffness are generally associated with the fiber-composite shell, while fine, double-pleated air-beams spread over and stabilize the vaulted ETFE membranes. Pull-off armatures (a.k.a. "Mohawks") transgress thresholds between shell and membrane, creating structural and ornamental continuity between systems.

As much as the project is driven by mathematical hierarchies, material logics, and ornamental sensibilities, it is also driven by color features. Color is used to visually intensify transformations in structural behavior (for instance mega-armatures tend towards purple/pink while Mohawks tend towards orange/yellow). Nevertheless, color gradients are neither 100 percent indexical nor are they completely smooth; they are coherent yet glitchy. No longer a secondary effect in architecture, color is used as an active, substantial source of architectural excess (Figures 27.26–27.29).

Notes

1   D. Leatherbarrow and M. Mostafavi, *Surface Architecture* (Cambridge, MA: The MIT Press, 2005).
2   Robert Venturi and Denise Scott Brown, *Learning from Las Vegas: The Forgotten Symbolism of Architectural Form* (Cambridge, MA: The MIT Press, 1977).
3   K. D. Alexander, R. Mark and J. F. Abel, *The Structural Behavior of Medieval Ribbed Vaulting* (London: Society of Architectural Historians, 1977).
4   Rudolf Wittkower, *Architectural Principles in the Age of Humanism* (New York: WW Norton & Co., 1962).
5   G. Tattersall, D. Andrade and A. Abe, "Heat exchange from the toucan bill reveals a controllable vascular thermal radiator," *Science,* July 24, 2009.

Figure 27.29 *Yeosu Oceanic Pavilion*

Chapter 28
The Sideways Rocker Project

Warren Techentin

Warren Techentin Architecture

The concept for the chair began when my wife and I had twins. Books suggest a rocking chair be included in a child's nursery so that infants may be rocked to sleep. And we used an Eames rocker which would have been perfect except for the fact that we discovered our twins each preferred to be rocked side-to-side, rather than front-to-back. Why, we mused, are there no side-to-side rocking chairs? And so the project began – an attempt to make one for the babies.

Research uncovered other sideways rockers, but mostly one-off custom endeavors. There seemed to be a hole in the market which for some reason had not been explored. A touch of hubris, a dollop of naïveté, and sheer exhaustion from newborn twins emboldened solutions for this new sideways rendition of the popular rocking chair typology which could be mass produced. Why stop with my children? Why not help babies around the world get to sleep in the same way my twins preferred? It seemed like the perfect opportunity to enlist parametric design software to help design a chair that could not only be "printable" in a variety of materials from fabrication shops all over the world, but customizable as well – allowing a small office to sell directly from a website. An interface could be developed to allow simple manipulation of the form online to customize shape definitions, materials, and colors. This future business model would be developed over time as part of an ongoing process.

After many iterations of the parametric model – deciding on proportions, solidity, weight, material, breathability, references, and even "grippage" (a word coined here to describe the ability of the chair to hold the butt firmly in place), a prototype was built out of plywood. Wood offered a relatively cheap material and traditional associations of "warmth." The Version 1 prototype was meant to flush out problems of the production process in addition to being the default version of the future business plan.

What began as a 5-axis milling project based on the lamination of 3" thick pieces of plywood, eventually needed to be converted to the use of a 3-axis machine due to a series of unexpected results from the process. The chair was based on a grid of holes – providing lightness, breathability, and the perceived comfort of an upholstered surface. These holes telescoped in all orthographic directions throughout the body of the chair. Ultimately based on the curvature of the rocker base, the resulting subtle curvatures throughout the interstices were something we liked a lot, but it meant we were milling a warped grid with all the grid extensions at angles relative to the milling bed. We had designed the grid extensions too thinly and chatter from the 5-axis machine caused some of these extensions to snap off. Most of these extensions could be easily rejoined, but on occasion we needed to re-mill the individual pieces that had snapped off. This required time-consuming re-mapping of the milled surface. By using the 3-axis machine, better and faster sweeps of the bit could occur without the grid extensions snapping off, but the grid extensions then did not meet dead-on once mated with their opposing piece. This effect ultimately led to "jaggy" y-axis curvatures and resulted in improvisational post-glue-up sanding which inevitably produced a slight but noticeable irregular rocking curvature. In other words, we got a bumpy ride. In addition, we experienced unexpected "released tensions" of the milled 3" plywood which

led to further tinkering of the pieces upon glue-up. To resolve the bottom bumpiness of Version 1, the bottom surface was re-mapped and scribed to incorporate small, wood "rocker-sleds" which corrected the rocking experience, smoothing the curvature and creating a soothing ride. What we had imagined as a simple process was complicated in practice by the characteristics of the plywood and the nuances of the machine.

Version 2 is now in the design and production process and will ultimately produce a prototype that makes a more complex version of the chair milled with a 5-axis machine. This version pushes the design to respond to user-defined preferences and includes modifications that respond more specifically to the curvature of the back and butt. It will resolve the issues of irregular rocking curvature that arose in Version 1 by changing the striation of the plywood from vertical to horizontal. This will allow the bottom rocking surface to be milled at one time instead of pieced together. The curvature of the bottom, in theory, can then be milled perfectly. The thicknesses will be re-assessed, and joints will be incorporated into the digital model. An added benefit of this horizontal striation process will allow the "upholstered" seat to produce irregular figuration patterns resulting from the topographic excavation of the plywood perpendicular to the layer striations.

Two more versions are planned. Versions 3 and 4 will include a variety of "bonus" features and will experiment with high-density foam and rubber systems instead of wood. In Version 4 we want to experiment with casting instead of milling, creating an inverse relationship of the pieces to the millwork. Those materials are yet to be determined. After these versions are produced and the final material types have been determined for production runs, it is hoped that babies everywhere will sleep soundly.

Figures 28.1–28.11 *ParaChair, Iteration 1.2,* various photographs of the prototype under construction at Machine Histories

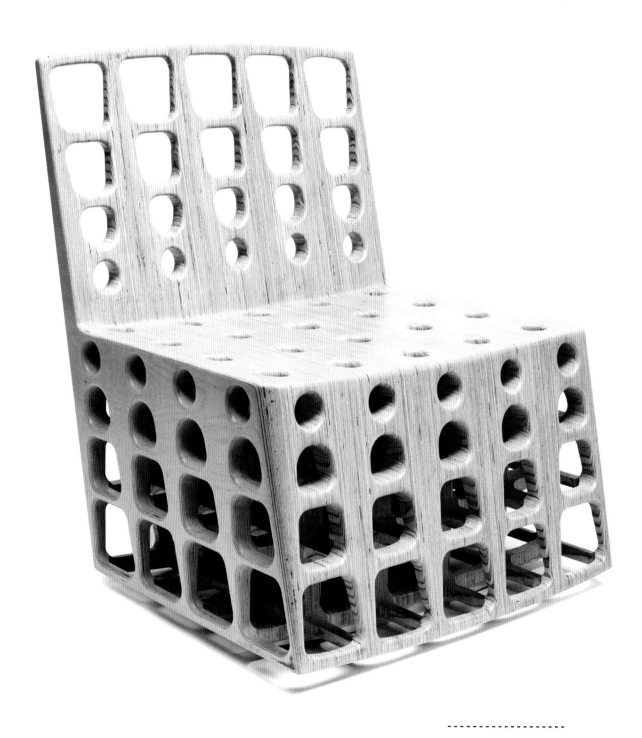

Figures 28.12–28.15 *ParaChair, Iteration 1.2,* first full-scale
prototype designed and built in collaboration with Nima Payan
and Machine Histories

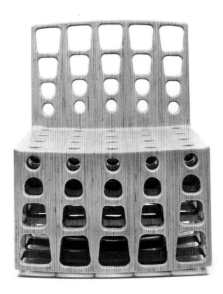

Part IX
Matter Surface

Engaging the surface directly, matter surface becomes interpreted as a responsive approach through design, effect and object on skin. At the scale of the material unit and the scale of the holistic skin as a contiguous reading, the direct translation of a simultaneously localized and collective system is energized with multiple overlaid responsibilities, both performative and effectual. These functional activators are derivative of the material and the process and then systematized to the field. The repetition of the unit, coincident with the localized fabricated individuation of the piece, aggregated through a system of construction and joinery, creates a surface that is familial, but unique. Contiguous and systematically repetitive, the variation and subtlety of the calibrated process allow for the incremental deviation. The parameters of the system and the effect of the surface define the architecture and the experience. The space becomes uniquely shallow as the surface engulfs the subtlety of perception through its legibility and depth. The architecture is the systematized process of its conceptual assembly.

Thom Faulders, Faulders Studio
Andrew Kudless, MATSYS

Chapter 29
Diachronic Growth

Thom Faulders

Faulders Studio

> How smart is a rock? ... Although it may appear that nothing much is going on inside a rock, the approximately 10^{25} (ten trillion trillion) atoms in a kilogram of matter are actually extremely active. Despite the apparent solidity of the object, the atoms are all in motion, sharing electrons back and forth, changing particle spins, and generating rapidly moving electromagnetic fields. All of this activity represents computation, even if not very meaningfully organized.
>
> (Ray Kurzweil)[1]

Time-based representation has successfully integrated high-speed differentiation and responsive production throughout building design and drawing processes. Yet, there is a disconnect typically between the diachronic state of virtual conceptualization and the fixed material stasis of the constructed outcome. Could a building, or at least its primary tectonic elements, continue to develop and mature by processes of dynamic material growth, beyond phases of initial construction? And what role could this diachronic materiality – that of occurring or changing along with time – serve in reinforcing a larger conceptual and functional intentionality of architectural realization?

Typical project development relies on efficient construction methodologies and turnkey exigencies. As capital for exchange, buildings require a synchronic completion effort – that is, precise and time-specific – in order to deliver a finished product to an intended end user. Cost campaigns and commercial immediacy further demand that buildings are handed over as completed objects for cultural, institutional, or private consumption. Yet, though it is obscured, a building's material life is never fully arrested. In an ongoing entropic battleground, buildings attempt to continually resist the non-stop wear from repeated occupancy use, degradation from weathering, ultra-violet decay, and an astounding array of other disruptive forces working to smooth, flatten, and debase the architectural intention. Seen in this way, architecture's material presence is never entirely static, complete, or fully synchronic, but is instead an active arena of material-based resistance and survival. In the profession's collective design effort to insure that this "state of play" remains imperceptible and unobtrusive, architects and clients bargain for time through an elaborate material specification process, hoping to insure their buildings survive unchanged, unaffected, and forever new (Figure 29.1).

In *The Selfish Gene*, Richard Dawkins conceptualizes that all living matter – from simple cellular life forms to the human body – can be classified as "survival machines" for colonies of information-bearing genes.[2] Whether stationary and designed to take advantage of solar rays via photosynthetic capacities, as in plant life, or mobile and agile for nutrient-seeking animal life, all biotic matter has evolved materially (and selfishly) in order to keep the genes replicating healthily and continually. Accordingly, evolutionary innovation for various behaviors, including the ability to quickly act and react in defense for survival, to successfully seek nutrients, or to proactively attract mates, might simply be considered material developments that insure the longevity of a biotic safe haven for these information-rich genes. For example, the visual pattern creating the optical effect of a false mouth on a trigger fish (*balistapus undulatus*) evolved not as decorative excess, but as an efficient and

----

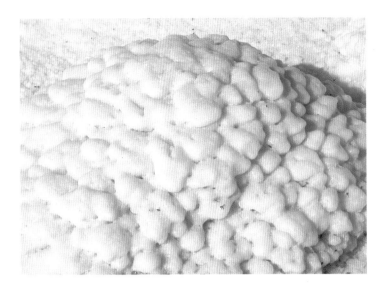

Figure 29.1 Close-up view of salt deposits on Robert Smithson's *Spiral Jetty* in 2003

innovative means to insure gene-pool longevity. Through deception and masquerading (I have a big mouth and I will eat you), or for mating and securing colony replication (presuming big mouths are seductive to other trigger fish), it could be argued that it is phenotypically and materially easier to evolve a pigment-based false mouth than to genetically reshape a small mouth into an actual large one. This anthropomorphized deceit (patterns don't technically "lie" of course, they are simply functional patterns) helps to insure the security and ongoing succession of the trigger fish as a genetic project.

While these evolutionary survival techniques are specific to plant and animal life, there is perhaps a shared ethos for survival in our own constructed habitat through sheer "phenotypic" inventiveness. For biotic life, this inventiveness insures the ongoing survival of the species; in case of our buildings, to insure the functional relevance and continued advancement of tectonic typologies. For instance, large structural steel bridges are continually exposed to the corrosive processes of oxidation. While in continuous contact with atmospheric moisture and accelerated with the presence of water, this non-stop proliferation of rust (typically red oxides) creates an ongoing state of diachronic degradation. This would seem to fully subvert the idea for our continuing to build bridges with steel, especially those that span bodies of salt water. Yet, in order to address this fact, a rather extreme material bargain emerges: all structural surfaces are forever coated with paint (which also degrades and erodes), or else the structural framework will fail through intrusive corrosion. Each bridge spanning the San Francisco Bay (Bay Bridge, Golden Gate Bridge, Carquinez Bridge, etc.) employs a full-time staff of painters and paint-strippers to continually coat, scrub, or touch-up its structure with this pigmented layer of brushed-on and labor-intensive weatherizing protection. Working year round, for every year since initial construction and throughout its projected future life, layers of protection are applied to insure structural integrity and functional survival, and therefore confirming the lasting infrastructural relevance of the typology. In some ways, one could argue that this is an even more heroic effort than the initial construction, as the battle to stay ahead of corrosive failure demands an extensive and time-intensive process, in perpetuity. These bridge projects can never be "finished," and their typology for deploying exposed steel frameworks relies on this simple yet extreme reliance for this secondary (and ultimately costly) diachronic building practice.

Defensive similarities can also be found in serviceable demands that maintain weather-stripping functionality on curtain wall envelopes on all large-scale buildings. The use of polyurethane and silicone-based sealants and caulks form a final barrier against the penetration of climate forces, as well as prohibiting the internally regulated interior climate from inefficiently leaking outward. Just as important, the inherent pliability of the weather-stripping acts as a flexible buffer between panels, allowing the overall architecture to flex with lateral wind loads or temperature variations without crumbling its protective envelope. Yet, with the effects of open exposure and compounded degradation, the soft substances of sealant must be serviced and replaced intermittently throughout the building's life cycle. This soft system remains a critical tectonic component for the longevity and survival of the building type. Like steel bridge painting, its replacement process is a part of the overall diachronic agreement of the curtain wall typology. And while this rubberized network is the keystone of protection that allows the curtain wall application to function, its architectural expression remains mostly hidden as an unspoken detail of functional necessity.

While all buildings need upkeep and renovation, these two diverse typologies – the exposed steel bridge and the exposed curtain wall systems – exist *only* by their tectonic functioning reliance on this integrated diachronic stewardship. Furthermore, unlike many other architectural building types that aesthetically evolve through an ongoing engagement with the forces of change, the typical bridge and the high-rise generally resist any aesthetic change or any form of evolutionary architectural transformation or growth. Like the pristine maintenance program for a high-end automobile, they strive to remain synchronic, that is, in the "non-event" state of original perfection.

Saline solutions

In contrast to the elimination of material change, the *GEOtube* proposal seeks to address the following question: how might a building harness diachronic material phenomena into a productive and proactive tectonic relationship? As a case study, *GEOtube* engages in a negentropic relationship with physically emerging crystalline processes, and reverses standard tectonic degradation (salt + moisture + structure) towards an increased state of usefulness and viability. *GEOtube* is a speculative proposal for a new 170-meter-tall, iconic tower for the city of Dubai in the United Arab Emirates (Figure 29.2). Non-programmed in terms of office or residential demands, an international call for proposals was intended to define a new tower design strategy (much like the Eero Saarinen-designed Gateway Arch in St. Louis completed in 1965) that would represent the city as a regionally vital and globally relevant metropolis. As is well documented, the city of Dubai continues to undergo rapid urbanization and massive construction programs at an unprecedented pace, and is a global

Figure 29.2 Street view rendering of *GEOtube*

"poster child" representing a synchronic, vast, and delirious form of urban growth. In response, a core idea of the *GEOtube* proposal is to set in motion a discernible architectural contrast: within this context of immediacy and globally imported architectural stylization, this 43-storey tower would slowly "grow" its building skins on site using local mineral deposits.

In stark contrast to its manufactured metropolitan emergence, the city of Dubai is situated in one of the most unique natural environments on earth. The world's highest salinity for oceanic sea waters are found in the adjacent Persian Gulf (also known as the Arabian Gulf), as well as the Red Sea, which borders the Saudi Arabian land mass to the west. Typical salt content for the world's oceans is 35 parts per thousand (35 0/00). In the Persian Gulf and the Red Sea, the content of salt is elevated to approximately 40 parts per thousand (40 0/00), enough of an increase to alter the effects of buoyancy when swimming along its beaches. This is due to high evaporation rates in the region from elevated temperatures, the low influx of fresh rainwater and rivers, and to the narrow inlet connecting to the ocean. Dubai's regional coastal plains, called *sabkahs*, are geological formations of salt flats created by the presence of extreme temperature and humidity conditions combined with extraordinary water salinity. Varying climate conditions and temperature swings cause thermal contraction at night and expansion during the day, generating a unique polygonal surface cracking common in the *sabkah* planes. Local deposits of primarily halite, gypsum, and aragonite form some of the major subsurface hydrocarbon reservoirs found throughout the Middle East.

Sodium chloride (NaCl), also known as common salt, table salt, and halite, is a chemical compound most responsible for the salinity of the world's oceans, and as well is the major extra cellular material of many multi-celled organisms. Salt is the only rock humans eat, and its intake is an absolute physiological necessity for bodily survival. Historically, wars contesting the control of the limited, naturally occurring salt stocks, and in addition for the control of accessible trade routes, have been as critical to the flux of regional and world geopolitics, as are contemporary technological, political, and militarized efforts to control the flow of petroleum-based resources. Of equal strategic importance was the dependence on salt as a vital food-preserving resource, a fact not to be underestimated prior to the recent technological advancements of refrigeration and canning. In combating today's global environmental degradation, it is generally acknowledged that the harmful effects of man-made pollution are lessened in coastal areas. As an atmospheric presence, salt molecules produce a healthy air saturated with negative ions. This concentration is naturally higher along wave-churning coastlines, where salt water aerosols are dispersed into the air, and effectively mitigate one of the harmful disruptions of industrially produced airborne pollution, which generates an overabundance of positive ions.

Constructing through evaporation

By deploying evaporative processes for the construction of its surfaces, *GEOtube* presents a new kind of tower. Continually moistened with salt water from the adjacent Persian Gulf coastline, its massive, highly visible building faces are entirely grown – diachronously and slowly through salt crystallization processes – throughout the entire life of the building, rather than constructed as a timely turnkey operation. Its primary visible presence is in continual formation as a mineral ecology, and is never fully completed. It is created locally, in contrast to the usual importation of building materials to the city. By its very nature of accreting its surfaces with mineral salt – typically corrosive to building tectonics – *GEOtube* engages in an uncontrolled mineralization technique that challenges the boundaries separating disruptive materiality (unintended results will emerge) from predictable intentionality (quarried stone gloss). As the water evaporates and salt mineral deposits aggregate, the tower's appearance transforms from a grayish transparent mesh into a highly reflective and vibrant white opacity, emerging in contrast from the very same environmental processes that formed the arid *sabkha* planes.

In our effort to more fully replicate and analyze the fundamental material crystallization processes, a series of small-scale "salt cultures" were grown in the studio. Rather than immerse the metal mesh in a saline solution and leaving the liquid to fully evaporate (which would mimic a traditional industrial salt pond process), the screens were misted with the saline solution daily. As is evident in Figures 29.3–29.6, the crystallization build-up transforms the original, transparent mesh into a visually opaque solid surface. This can also be rendered translucent depending on the natural or artificial lighting conditions (the solid salt skin culture is the result of a continuous 30-day saturation and drying period). At the full building scale, various studies would be required to determine the optimum scale and size of solid/void relationships of the mesh.

Figures 29.3– 29.6 Salt crystallization growth study

    For the design of the tower, the salt water is directly supplied to *GEOtube* via a newly proposed 4.62km underground aqueduct. This incoming water is further distilled on site via solar evaporation in order to naturally increase saline saturation levels, and is subsequently filtered for impurities prior to being pumped to the top-level holding cistern. Using gravitational forces to passively distribute this saline liquid throughout *GEOtube*, the water is periodically misted (night-time during warm months) onto the skin mesh via the exo-skeletal piping system in its distributed network of nozzles, each directed towards the inner mesh layer. The salt water easily evaporates with atmospheric temperatures ranging from 24 degrees Celsius in winter to over 41 degrees Celsius in the summer (75–106+ degrees F). Aiding in the evaporation are the prevailing on-shore northwesterly winds during the day (*shamal*), and the offshore southeasterly winds during the night.

    The *GEOtube* structural system is a redundant structural lattice comprised of two layers: the inner layer is sheathed with the salt-layered mesh, and the outer layer remains open and contains the salt water dispersal system. The layers are interconnected with lateral structural bracing via the wind tube openings. Appearing like

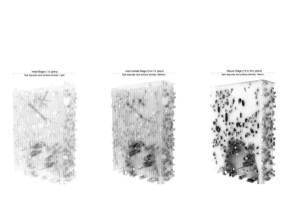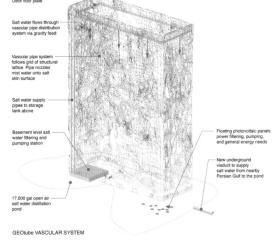

Figure 29.7a–c Diagrammatic renderings show the evolutionary salt build-up on the exposed inner core of *GEOtube*

Figure 29.8 Water distribution diagram

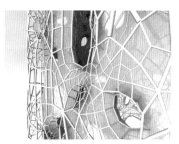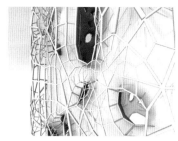

Figures 29.9–29.11 Close-up sequence showing transformation of exposed inner building surfaces through the crystalline build-up of salt

a stone ventifact, these wind openings are irregularly sized and spaced throughout *GEOtube*, and function to bring air into the interior open core. Placed with non-uniform alignment, these openings create asymmetrical air flows, current differentials, and variable wind eddies, that further assist in the overall evaporation of the salt surfaces on the inner core. The variably sized structural steel tube framework is coated fiber-reinforced polymer (FRP), an emerging material technology used to both strengthen and protect structural members and other large-scale elements. FRPs are non-corrosive to most chemical, environmental, or ultraviolet degradation factors, and presently offer a high-performance, lightweight material option to contemporary infrastructural and building practices.

Surrounding the outside base of *GEOtube*, and extending into the inner core area, the open-air salt water distillation pond contains 17,000 cubic meters of water. Powering the pumping of water to the above-ground cistern, photovoltaic panels float upon the pond's top surface via a custom pontoon system, providing a total surface area of 2041 square meters. These energy-absorbing "lily pads" are tethered to the bottom of the pond with enough slack to allow for random movement and clustering, and are wired to the energy grid via a system of flexible conduits. Regional rains are minimal, averaging only 80mm per year. When rains do arrive, they constructively aid in cleansing and washing away loose crystals and foreign airborne particles that cling to the salt skin. More forcefully, the well-known annual sandstorms (Al-Haffar, Barih Thorayya, Al-Dabaran, etc.) similarly provide a constructive role in scrubbing down rough edges and loose particulate matter. These naturally occurring "exfoliating" processes play a vital role insuring the formation of a strong and durable salt skin capable of lasting for many decades. In addition, *GEOtube* requires minimal human maintenance, similar to the necessities of window washing for large-scale buildings and structures. This process will mitigate potentially dangerous stalactites from surface areas prone to excessive water accumulation and dripping.

Chemical building blocks

When salt is dissolved in water, the sodium and chloride atoms are pulled apart by the water. As water molecules evaporate (hydrogen and oxygen evaporate more readily than the salt atoms), sodium and chloride atoms rejoin and form dried, crystalline deposits. This simple molecular process occurs abundantly in nature, and is easy to harness and reproduce in artificially controlled environments, such as in the relatively low-tech manufacturing of table salt in open evaporation ponds. By engaging with this fundamental molecular process, *GEOtube* engages in a form of on-site material production that is the result of an out-of-control dynamic exchange. This disrupts the normative condition that fosters an architectural legibility that is materially inert, isolated, and fixed. As an environmentally produced proposition, *GEOtube* is more mineral rather than vegetal, grows through geomorphic accumulation rather than biotic regeneration, and appears grotesque and rugged through layers of accretion rather than lush with soft foliation. It embraces unruly material-building processes that are typically considered corrosive to buildings and other machines of technology. Still, *GEOtube* aligns itself within the wider spectrum of environmentally engaged architecture, and its ultimate mandate is to broaden the lens of ecological architectural discourse by challenging what it is that constitutes "useful nature" in the creation of buildings and cities. As a hypothetical proposal, *GEOtube* directs its "natural act" towards the creation of a regional cultural contribution, and purposefully resists the temptation to limit its ecological conceptualization solely under the guise of planetary protectionism (Figures 29.9–29.17).

Notes

1   Ray Kurzeweil, *The Singularity is Near* (New York: Viking Press, 2005).
2   Richard Dawkins, *The Selfish Gene* (Oxford: Oxford University Press, 1976).

Figure 29.12 Render view looking up the north face of *GEOtube*. Solid surfaces are created through crystal growth

Figure 29.13 Close-up view of exterior surface and structure

Figure 29.14 Site plan

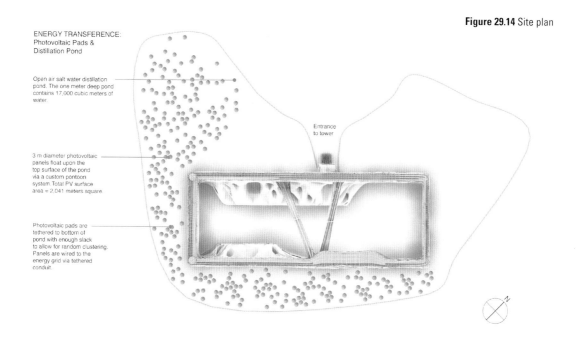

ENERGY TRANSFERENCE:
Photovoltaic Pads &
Distillation Pond

Open air salt water distillation
pond. The one meter deep pond
contains 17,000 cubic meters of
water.

Entrance
to tower

3 m diameter photovoltaic
panels float upon the
top surface of the pond
via a custom pontoon
system. Total PV surface
area = 2,041 meters square.

Photovoltaic pads are
tethered to bottom of
pond with enough slack
to allow for random clustering.
Panels are wired to the
energy grid via tethered
conduit.

Figure 29.15 Interior view

Figure 29.16 Night view
Figure 29.17 Night view close-up

Chapter 30
Bodies in Formation
The material evolution of flexible formworks

Andrew Kudless

MATSYS

- -

Born from the complex negotiation between liquid mass and tensile constraint, flexible formwork castings resonate with material energy. Hard as stone yet visually supple and fluid, the pre-cast architectural assemblies produced using flexible formwork techniques suggest integrative design strategies that acknowledge the intricate associations between form, fabrication, and material behavior. This tripartite synthesis between geometry, making, and performance has emerged as one of the central themes of contemporary architecture and engineering. Borrowing ideas of morphology from biology and physics, twentieth-century architectural innovators such as Antonio Gaudí and Frei Otto built a legacy of material practice that incorporated methods of making with material and geometric logics. The emergent effects (and affects) produced through these highly integrative practices serve as the basis of much of the research and design at MATSYS. Building on the flexible formwork research of Miguel Fisac in the 1970s, the *P_Wall* series by MATSYS explores the use of digital tools in the generation and fabrication of these bodies in formation.

Diagrams of force

Biomimicry, the study of natural processes for design inspiration, has been a popular topic in the last decade of contemporary architectural design. However, one of the most overshadowed concepts fundamental to biomimicry is the importance of physics in our understanding of the natural world, both organic and non-organic. That is, underlying every process of formation, from the geologic to the biologic, is a complex network of physical principles that guide the organization of material systems. Although we often hear of the importance of genetic information determining the morphogenesis of life forms, these genetic processes must still play by the rules of the physical world. Put another way, the software (code) still has to run on the hardware (physical reality).

In the early twentieth century, D'Arcy Thompson, the noted scholar of mathematics and zoology, attempted to communicate this concept in his book *On Growth and Form*.[1] Although a proponent of evolutionary theory, Thompson was uneasy with the "black box" approach that many then (and now) use to explain complex living systems. Thompson felt that although evolution certainly contributed greatly to the morphology of forms, the physical environment was a more fundamental factor. Philip Ball, a contemporary science writer summarizes this issue:

> D'Arcy Thompson brought to the fore the issue of exactly how such forms come about through the action of physical forces. It just wasn't a question of ensuring that evolutionary biology obeys physical and chemical laws; he felt that these laws play a direct, causative role in determining the shape and form of biology. Thus he insisted that there were many forms in the natural world that

- -

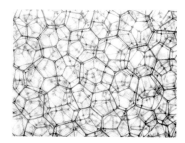

Figure 30.1 D'Arcy Thompson based his research on studying the emergence of order in simple, non-organic materials systems such as soap bubbles. He would then extrapolate how the principles governing these systems can be seen in more complex systems such as bees' honeycombs, cells, and tissues. Frei Otto extended this research to the architectural scale at his Institute for Lightweight Structures

Figure 30.2 The *Multihalle*, Mannheim, Germany, 1969. Designed by Carlfried Mutschel and Partners with Atelier Warmbronn, Frei Otto, Ewald Bubner, and Ove Arup and Partners

one could, and indeed should, explain not by arguing that evolution has shaped the material that way, but as a direct consequence of the conditions of growth or the forces in the environment.[2]

Thompson developed this thesis through countless examples demonstrating how simple physical principles such as surface tension, gravity, and pressure inform the organization of matter both organic and non-organic (Figure 30.1). He argued:

> The form, then, of any portion of matter, whether it is living or dead, and the changes of form which are apparent in its movements and in its growth, may in all cases alike be described as due to the action of force. In short, the form of an object is a *diagram of forces*.[3]

Although some of Thompson's specific theories proved wrong over time, his fundamental concept of the importance of force in the development of form provided the conceptual and technical framework for the great material practitioners of twentieth-century architecture.

Practice, practice, practice

The research and work of these material practices run both in parallel and counter to the mainstream Modern movement. Although working at the same time and with similar materials, these architects, engineers, and fabricators resisted the prevalent Fordist principles in favor of the development of non-standard production techniques that sought a higher integration between form, fabrication, and material performance. Unsatisfied with the Modernist tendencies towards mass-production and abstract formalism, these practitioners experimented rigorously with new material systems and, like Thompson, looked for relationships between form and force that could be used productively in the design and construction of new architectures.

The members of this group of twentieth-century material practitioners span the geographic and material spectrum. In contrast to the emerging "professional" architect, these practitioners were inveterate experimenters who constantly engaged in the development of new technical, formal, and constructive techniques.

Bridging the divide between architect, engineer, and fabricator due to their intensive research and experimentation, many of these practitioners have become associated with particular material systems and techniques: Gaudí (masonry arches), Otto (pneumatics, cable nets, gridshells), Dieste (brick shells), Fisac (pre-cast concrete beams and skins), Isler and Candela (thin-shell concrete), Torroja and Nervi (folded concrete shells), etc. (Figure 30.2). A central methodology of all of these practices was the use of Form-Finding, an experimental process that uses the self-organization of material under force to discover stable forms. The most famous example is Gaudí's use of hanging chains to find optimum curves for his stone and brick arches. However, Frei Otto and others developed dozens of techniques that allow designers to quickly test systems of great formal and material complexity. Although often these techniques are used to prototype structures at a smaller scale, the fact remains that these forms emerge not from abstract ideas, but from the interplay of "top-down" constraints put in place by the designer and the "bottom-up" negotiation between material and force. That is, there is a synthesis between code (the design parameters) and force in the material system and this synthesis could be called the craft of material practice.

Risky business

Usually far outside the model of the straight-laced professional architect, the members of this group were experimental craftsmen at heart. Walking the line between architect, engineer, and fabricator, they resisted the de-skilling of labor through mass-production strategies and instead developed their work through intensive material and technological experimentation. Like all experimental research, the work was risky and often pushed the limits of material performance and craft. Through intensive experimentation, these designers extracted knowledge about new technologies, materials, and processes and converted this knowledge beyond raw engineering and into works of fine craftsmanship and architecture.

It is this focus on the craft of architecture that most distinguishes these designers from others. Without risk, there is no innovation and these designers pursued a risky practice that relentlessly pushed the material, technological, and formal possibilities of architecture. The designer, thinker, and maker David Pye developed this concept of craft and risk in his seminal book *The Nature and Art of Workmanship*:

> If I must ascribe a meaning to the word craftsmanship, I shall say as a first approximation that it means simply workmanship using any kind of technique or apparatus, in which the quality of the result is not predetermined, but depends on the judgment, dexterity and care which the maker exercises as he works. The essential idea is that the quality of the result is continually at risk during the process of making; and so I shall call this kind of workmanship "The workmanship of risk": an uncouth phrase, but at least descriptive.[4]

Unlike the dry rationality of the mainstream canon of Modernist work, the material practices of the twentieth century crafted an architecture that was unsettling in its vitality. That is, the work was often not "crafted" in the sense that it was clean, resolved, and precise. Rather, the craft of their work lay in its acceptance of risk as an essential byproduct of innovation and life. Columns leaned and branched, walls folded and rolled into roofs, surfaces bore the marks of their making. Traditional notions of Form (or in Sanford Kwinter's term "the merely formulistic"[5]) were resisted in their work in favor of the emerging ideas of "formation," the inseparability of form, growth, and behavior in all systems.

Grotesquely sublime

The work of the Spanish architect Miguel Fisac exemplifies this trajectory of the twentieth-century material practice. Working in post-war Spain, Fisac hovered between architect, engineer, and fabricator and focused on the rigorous development of pre-cast concrete structural beams and façade systems. Known mostly for his long-span concrete roofs of the 1950s and 1960s, Fisac's later work in the 1970s and 1980s concentrated on the use of flexible formwork in pre-cast concrete façade modules. Fascinated by concrete's fluid nature, Fisac began using plastic sheeting and metal wire in his formwork. The flexibility of the plastic sheeting, constrained by the metal wire, allowed the finished panels to resonate with concrete's inherent fluid properties.

Fisac first began thinking about these ideas early in his career during the *Teacher Training Center* project in Madrid in the 1950s (Figure 30.3):

> I then started to think about concrete – which I considered the best building material – and wanted to reflect its fluid condition in some way, set it apart from the remaining materials that arrive solid on the construction site. Stone is carved, brick is pressed in a mold, but concrete is a material that is poured in a doughy state. With that in mind, I decided to make molds for the canopy with strings and plaster which, after some nine days, we removed leaving those soft contoured shapes. This was the beginning of a research that led me years later to the flexible formwork.[6]

It wasn't until the *Mupag Rehabilition Center* project (1969–1973) that Fisac began fully exploring the use of flexible formwork (Figure 30.4):

> After a decade making exposed concrete, I realized that something was not right, because the concrete took on the texture of the planks, as if it were wood; so I decided to give it an expression of its own, because if it is a material you pour on site when it is still soft, it should have a final appearance resembling that fluidity. While I was building Mupag, I asked the foreman to use a wooden mould and to tie up some wires like those you use to join the reinforcing bars; we put plastic on top of it and set the steel mesh between two concrete lifts of about 3cm; when we removed the formwork it looked great, a smooth and bright surface as if it were still soft.[7]

Not only did the use of the plastic sheet produce a quilted surface curvature that resonated with the concrete's fluid fabrication, but also the plastic sheeting formwork itself was inexpensive, easy to construct, and less wasteful than traditional wood formwork. Fisac continued to develop these techniques; however, not everyone has appreciated the new forms that were expressed in the façades (Figures 30.5–30.6). Kenneth Frampton, commenting on Fisac's entire body of work, barely noted Fisac's flexible formwork projects with the exception to call them "grotesquely textured 'plastic' surfaces" and to indicate they were a distraction from his larger focus on the structural capacity of concrete.[8] However, others, such as Mohsen Mostafavi, place Fisac's surface experiments in the context of the informal and its ability to talk to things *in formation* rather than the cold rationality of idealism. Mostafavi states, "Fisac's explorations with surface, linearity and curvature imbue his work with a sense of the monstrous and the imperfect ... Fisac rejects the ideality of pure and rational order."[9] Like Gaudí and Otto, Fisac was not interested in purely rational structuralism, but in the ability of emergent material forces and new construction techniques to literally inform form. These forms, grotesque to some, offer a new approach to the aesthetics of architectural form. Impure, imperfect, and complex, Fisac's pre-cast undulating façades point to a certain resonance between form, growth, and behavior that is beyond the domain of the designer.

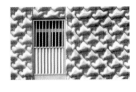
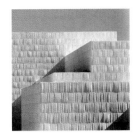

Figure 30.3 *Teacher Training Center*, Madrid, Spain (1954–1957) by Miguel Fisac

Figure 30.4 *Mupag Rehabilitation Center* (1969–1973) by Miguel Fisac

Figure 30.5 *Centro Social de las Hermanas Hospitalarias*, Madrid, Spain (1985–1986) by Miguel Fisac

Figure 30.6 *Centro Cultural,* Castilblanco de los Arroyos, Seville (2000) by Miguel Fisac

Informal form: *P_Wall (2006)*

MATSYS was established in 2004 on the desire to build on the legacy of the material practices of the twentieth century through the use of new digital fabrication and generative tools. At the time, I was infatuated with the control these new tools provided in the development of complex systems. However, the more I scripted, the more I saw the need to return to first principles and rediscover the material resonances that most inspired me in the work of Gaudí, Otto, and the others. More often than not, scripting in design is used to facilitate complex, but completely deterministic processes. After a particularly demanding project that involved a great deal of (deterministic) computational design and fabrication, I sought a research project that would engage my interests in informal forms and emergent processes. Inspired by Fisac's work, I began a three-month initial research phase to simply understand the techniques and processes of flexible formwork.

The first prototype was a complete failure, or so I thought at the time (Figure 30.7). Using a small wooden mold and an elastic fabric skin, my desire was to form a perfect funnel shape by pulling and constraining the fabric at the center. The result was anything but perfect. Covered in wrinkles, cracks, and blemishes, the cast form fell into the "monstrous" category for which I was initially unprepared. After weeks of work, experimenting with various elastic fabrics, plaster mixes, and increasingly complex molds, I began to realize that I was less interested in achieving a pre-conceived "perfect" formal idea and the initially grotesque became not only acceptable, but also desirable. That is, through the process of inventing more and more complicated ways to attain an ideal form, I realized that the imperfect was more interesting as it emerged on its own through very simple constraints.

This idea was then developed into a proposal for a wall installation at the Banvard Gallery at the Ohio State University. The goal of the project was to use computation to develop a constraint system that would negotiate the complex material forces between the flexible formwork and the fluid plaster slurry. Through months of experimentation, it was determined that the point constraint spacing in the fabric formwork was critical to the formation of surfaces. The spacing of these constraints determined if the cast pieces failed through two ways. As the weight of the plaster slurry expands the elastic fabric, the ratio between the elasticity of the fabric and the weight of the slurry is critical. If the points are placed too close together, the fabric is over-

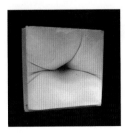

Figure 30.7 First experiment with flexible formworks, MATSYS

constrained and resists sagging. This lack of sufficient sagging results in very thin cross-sections of the dried plaster forms which tend to be brittle and weak. On the other hand, if the spacing between points was too large, the fabric could become overloaded with the slurry weight, causing the fabric to rip out of the constraint points. This would immediately lead to massive (and explosive) blowouts, ruining the fabric and wasting time and materials.

After a series of empirical tests to determine the appropriate minimum and maximum spacing of constraint points, a computational script was developed that would allow the user to create gradient fields that undulated between high and low densities of constraints (Figure 30.8). This script did not determine the overall form, but rather helped guide the fabrication to a position of acceptable risk. That is, the use of the scripted constraint points allowed me to gain a certain amount of generalized control over the areas of high and low density while still allowing the forms to self-organize at a more local level. I could not predict specific results but I could predict the larger pattern as well as know that the forms were emerging (mostly) within tolerances that would not completely endanger the casting process.[10]

The script used a very simple, "brute force" algorithm to place the constraint points. Using a grayscale image as a guide, the script would sample the pixel luminance at random points and translate that value into an acceptable distance to the closest constraint point. The script would then compare this specified test distance with the actual distances between the test point and every other point already determined. If the point was within the acceptable minimum or maximum range, it was added to the list of constraint points. If there was already another point within the test distance, a new random point was tested elsewhere and the process would begin again until a specified total number of constraints were found. Although more sophisticated techniques could have been used (such as spring systems) that could have been faster or more efficient, the basic script

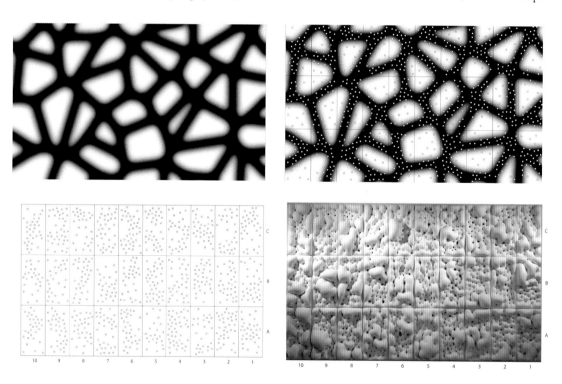

Figure 30.8a–d Process diagram (from top) an image was made that roughly sketched areas of high or low density of desired constraint. The image is then processed by a script to convert it into the desired number of constraint points located within the required minimum and maximum allowable tolerances. The pattern is then divided into 30 modules measuring 18" x 36" each. Each module is cast from using the specified point pattern and then assembled into the larger wall

Figure 30.9a–d Fabrication sequence (from left): base constraint point template, lower support frame, upper fabric frame, cast panel in mold

performed well enough to locate roughly 1000 constraint points.

The final mold design consisted of three main components (Figure 30.9). The first component held the constraint points (vertical wooden dowels) in place according to the locations determined by the script. The lower wooden support frame was then positioned around and above this constraint template, locking it into place. Finally, an upper wooden frame with a taut elastic fabric was lowered into place on the lower frame. The dowels would push the fabric surface above the top surface of the upper support frame. Any fabric above the surrounding frame would be above the "waterline" of the plaster (like islands in the sea) and would appear as holes in the final cast surface. As the plaster was poured in, the fabric expanded under its weight. The more plaster was poured in, the more the fabric would expand until the weight of the plaster reached equilibrium with the elastic tension in the fabric. That is, under a certain threshold based on the strength of the fabric, the surface would expand in proportion with the load of the plaster. Beyond that threshold, the fabric's elasticity was surpassed and tears would occur in the fabric. Similar to blowing up a balloon or soap bubble, the surface expands until the material (or surface) tension is too great.

Appearing inflated and soft, the hard plaster wall resonated with the energy present in its making (Figures 30.10–30.12). As adjacent areas of the fabric surface expanded under the weight of the fabric, they slowly began to form creases, wrinkles, and folds in the surface. The complex forces at play informed even the constraint points: although fixed from below, the dowels often began to lean towards the larger loads in the surface, attempting to find equilibrium. Although the wall surface appears complex, the process simply relied on the self-organization of the two materials (plaster and fabric) to find a balance with each other based on a limited amount of design parameters.

Figure 30.10 *P_Wall (2006)*, front view

Figure 30.11 *P_Wall (2006)*, oblique view

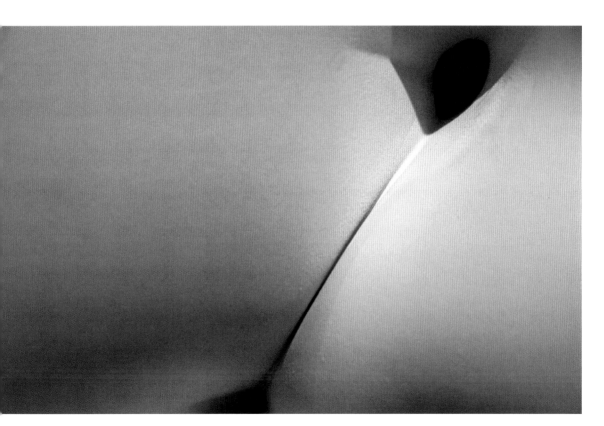

Figure 30.12 *P_Wall (2006)*, detail view

From object to field: *P_Wall (2009)*

In 2009, the San Francisco Museum of Modern Art commissioned a new version of the wall for inclusion in their permanent collection and for exhibition in *Sensate: Bodies and Design*. This new work was dramatically larger than the original wall. At 45 feet long and 12 feet high, the new wall was four times the size of the 2006 wall. This new opportunity allowed me to look back at the work of 2006 and rethink several areas of the design.

The dramatic difference in gallery dimensions greatly informed the design of the new wall. At 45 feet long, the new wall had moved further from the scale of an object on a wall to actually becoming the wall itself. Unlike the 2006 wall, the new wall was sited to take up the entire length and height of the gallery wall, essentially transforming the intentionally nondescript traditional gallery wall into an undulating contemporary body alive with irregularities, informalities, and energy. This scale shift led me to think about the wall more as a field than object. The shifts in constraint density in the original wall were related to the module size; each module contained both high and lower densities. The larger size of the wall at SFMoMA required a shift in scale from the singular module to the aggregation of multiple modules. Using the same constraint point script but

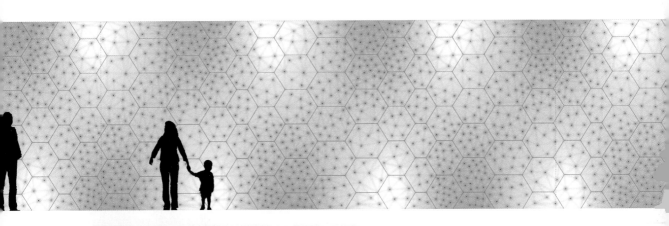

Figure 30.13 *P_Wall (2009)*, elevation

Figure 30.14 *P_Wall (2006)*, oblique view. The horizontal edges of the modules break up the continuity of the surface when viewed from the side

Figure 30.15 *P_Wall (2009)*, oblique view. The hexagonal pattern of the modules creates a more continuous landscape surface when viewed from the side

with a source image with more gradual shifts between light and dark pixels (which translate into low and high densities of constraints), the overall depth of the wall could be controlled gradually between deep (white) and shallow (black). Arrayed on the wall, the slightly differing average depths of each module created large areas of the wall that either protruded or recessed from the gallery visitor, a series of undulating coves and overhangs (Figure 30.13).

Although much longer and higher, the gallery space at SFMoMA was much shallower than the Banvard Gallery at Ohio State University. The SFMoMA gallery was only 8' deep compared to the 30' depth at OSU. Where the main view of the wall at OSU was frontal, it was oblique at SFMoMA. This difference in orientation between the viewer and the wall led to the second major change from *P_Wall (2006)*. As one moves from the frontal view to the oblique view, the gaps between the modules become less noticeable and the entire wall appears as one seamless landscape. However, in the 2006 wall, the use of the rectangular modules prevented the horizontal seams from disappearing in the oblique view (Figure 30.14). By moving to a hexagonal module, there was always one module interrupting the alignment of the horizontal seams that allowed the individual models to almost disappear in primary direction of view. Furthermore, the use of four different hexagonal module sizes (S, M, L, and XL) disrupted the seams in the diagonal sightlines as well as break up the rhythm of the modules in the frontal view (Figures 30.15–30.17). Unable to quickly perceive the actual rhythm of the module sizes (a repeating octave from XL to S and back to XL), the viewer focuses on either the larger or smaller spatial effects (Figures 30.18–30.20).

On the technical side, *P_Wall (2009)* made several material, fabrication, and assembly improvements on the 2006 wall design. Although simple and easy to make, the casting plaster used in 2006 was brittle. Not only were the panels heavy, but they were also delicate. By adding a higher density and strength plaster to the

Figures 30.16–30.17 *P_Wall (2009),* front view

Figures 30.18–30.20 *P_Wall (2009),* detail view

normal casting plaster as well as chopped fiberglass strands to the plaster, the plaster modules were much less prone to damage. In addition, perlite aggregate was added to the slurry that allowed the weight of each panel to be cut by almost half. The design of the molds was also improved to make their disassembly, cleaning, and reassembly each day much faster. As the wall was composed of 150 unique modules and 6 modules were cast every day, it was essential that it was fast and relatively easy to transition between separate pours. Finally, the hardware that allowed the modules to be hung on the wall was improved to make the wall's assembly on site more efficient.

Entropy and life: *P_Wall (Weathering)*

In the context of a museum or gallery, the two walls have a different reading than Fisac's flexible formwork projects in the 1970s and 1980s. Henry Urbach, curator of the Architecture and Design department at SFMoMA described the project as, "a radical reinvention of the gallery wall. Typically smooth, firm, regular and, by convention, 'neutral', the gallery wall has shed its secondary status to become a protagonist in the space it lines."[11] However, despite their "reinvention" of the traditional gallery wall, the projects still had to adhere to the restriction put on objects of art in museums or galleries. That is, despite the wall's sensuality, the museum viewer was not permitted to touch it, and it remained a visual artifact out of the very tactile reach it evoked. This separation between object and user is not something architecture often confronts. Architecture is, almost by definition, a thing in constant physical contact with humans whereas Art often exists at a more formal, and mostly visual, level of interaction.

This issue became even more poignant when I began to reflect on the maintenance of the walls. During fabrication, I was constantly blowing dust, dirt, and even spiders from the crevices and holes of the panels (Figures 30.21–30.22). After installation, the museum preparators were on constant vigil, looking for handprints left by museum visitors snatching a touch when the security guard's back was turned. As a reaction to this situation, I wanted to create an alternate vision of the wall free of protection from both human contact and natural weathering. The *P_Wall (Weathering)* project visualizes how I suspect the wall would age over several years outside (Figure 30.23). The *P_Wall*'s surface encourages the deposition of soot, the growth of moss, the nesting of birds. Its surface is not optimized for cleaning and it would slowly accumulate an emergent community of organic and non-organic life. Although some have described this process as entropic, the tendency of a system to lose energy and deteriorate, it could also be described as heading in the opposite direction; the wall's properties encourage the emergence of life across and through its surface.

Figure 30.23 *P_Wall (Weathering)*

Figures 30.21–30.22 *P_Wall (2009)* The wall's creases accumulated seed pods, dirt, and spiders during the fabrication process

Corporeality

Unlike many of the material practitioners of the twentieth century, the *P_Wall* projects do not use the self-organization of materials under force to create building systems that are about material optimization, lightness, or efficiency. However, they do share a more fundamental interest in the integral relationships between form, fabrication, and performance. This last word, "performance," is often too simply understood in its technical sense relating to structural and or environmental performance. However, architecture also has to perform culturally, economically, politically, and aesthetically. The *P_Wall* projects are successful in how they use the capacity of material self-organization to connect the worlds of organic and non-organic life. The undulating surfaces of the walls resonate with viewers because the same underlying physical principles are at work in both the wall and their own bodies. At a basic level, the human body is an elastic skin surrounding a dynamic fluid interior. As we gain weight, the skin grows and stretches; as we age, the skin's elasticity decreases and we gain wrinkles. The wall's surface, its subtle bulges and sensual creases, formed through a similar negotiation between a fluid weight and an elastic skin. The walls resonate with the visceral energies that form our own body's geometries. Its corporeal nature is not designed, but emerged from complex material forces wrestling with simple design parameters.

Notes

1 D. Thompson, *On Growth and Form* (Cambridge: Cambridge University Press, 2000).
2 P. Ball, *Shapes* (New York: Oxford University Press, 2009), p. 12.
3 Thompson, *On Growth and Form*, p. 11.
4 D. Pye, *The Nature and Art of Workmanship* (Bethel: Cambrium Press, 1995), p. 20.
5 In Sanford Kwinter's essay, "Who's Afraid of Formalism?" he states,

> The form problem, from the time of the pre-Socratics to the late twentieth century is, in fact, an almost unbroken concern with the mechanisms of formation, the processes by which discernible patterns come to disassociate themselves from a less finely-ordered field ... What I call true formalism refers to any method that diagrams the proliferation of fundamental resonances and demonstrates how these accumulate into figures of order and shape.
> (S. Kwinter, "Who's Afraid of Formalism?," in *Phylogenesis: FDA's Ark*, Barcelona: Actar, 2004, p. 96)

6 *AV Monographs,* 101 (5–6, 2003), p. 40.
7 Ibid., p. 100.
8 K. Frampton, "Tectonic Talent," *AV Monographs,* 101 (5–6, 2003), p. 9.
9 M. Mostafavi, "Curved Calligraphy," *AV Monographs*, 101 (5–6, 2003), p. 15.
10 Although the script helped minimize the chance that the forms would neither expand too much (and cause tears in the fabric) nor too little (and cause breaks in the plaster), there was always a degree of uncertainty in the process. With the number of independent variables in play (directionality of the fabric, natural inconsistencies in the strength of individual wooden dowels, etc.), it was difficult (and not desirable) to completely eliminate risk in the process. In order to fabricate the 30 panels that make up the 2006 wall, 32 panels were fabricated. One failed after casting because a number of thin sections happened to align and a crack formed across them when the panel was transported. Another panel dramatically failed during the casting process when a wooden constraint point snapped and punctured the elastic fabric, flooding the workspace with gallons of wet plaster.
11 H. Urbach, extended label text for the *P_Wall (2009)* project at the *Sensate: Bodies and Design* exhibition at the San Francisco Museum of Modern Art.

Figure Credits

All figures are credited to the individual authors, firms and organizations unless otherwise noted. The editors and publishers would like to thank the individuals and organizations that gave permission to reproduce material in the book. Every effort has been made to contact and acknowledge copyright holders. The publishers would be grateful to hear from any copyright holder who is not acknowledged here and will undertake to rectify any errors or omissions in future printings or editions of the book.

Figure 1.10
Credit: Vidal Sassoon Collection 1972, Christopher Brooker, stylist

Figure 3.22
Credit: Luke Gibson Photography
Figure 3.25
Credit: Luke Gibson Photography
Figure 3.39
Credit: Luke Gibson Photography
Figure 3.40
Credit: Luke Gibson Photography
Figure 3.41
Credit: Luke Gibson Photography

Figure 5.1
Credit: Photo by Anja Franke
Figure 5.25
Credit: Photo by Anja Franke

Figure 10.1
Credit: "The Yorck Project: 10.000 Meisterwerke der Malerei." DVD-ROM, 2002. ISBN 3936122202. Distributed by DIRECTMEDIA Publishing GmbH. The work of art depicted in this image and the reproduction thereof are in the public domain worldwide. The reproduction is part of a collection of reproductions compiled by The Yorck Project. The compilation copyright is held by Zenodot Verlagsgesellschaft mbH and licensed under the GNU Free Documentation License
Figure 10.3
Credit: "The Yorck Project: 10.000 Meisterwerke der Malerei." DVD-ROM, 2002. ISBN 3936122202. Distributed by DIRECTMEDIA Publishing GmbH. The work of art depicted in this image and the reproduction thereof are in the public domain worldwide. The reproduction is part of a collection of reproductions compiled by The Yorck Project. The compilation copyright is held by Zenodot Verlagsgesellschaft mbH and licensed under the GNU Free Documentation License
Figure 10.5
Credit: In 1965, Gordon Moore sketched out his prediction of the pace of silicon technology. Decades later, Moore's Law remains true, driven largely by Intel's unparalleled silicon expertise. Copyright © 2005 Intel Corporation
"Moore's Law Original Graph." Graph. Intel.com. 2005. 26 March

2010   <http://www.intel.com/pressroom/kits/events/moores_law_40th/Images_Assets/Image_Usage_Guide_Readme.pdf>
Figure 10.6
Credit: Great Sandune National Park, © Kentaro Tsubaki

Figure 12.2
Credit: © KieranTimberlake; photo courtesy of KieranTimberlake
Figure 12.3
Credit: Photo © Eliott Kauffman; courtesy of KieranTimberlake
Figure 12.6
Credit: Image courtesy of Decker Yeadon LLC
Figure 12.7
Credit: Image courtesy of Decker Yeadon LLC
Figure 12.8
Credit: Image courtesy of Decker Yeadon LLC
Figure 12.9
Credit: Image courtesy of Decker Yeadon LLC
Figure 12.10
Credit: Image courtesy of Decker Yeadon LLC
Figure 12.11
Credit: Image courtesy of Decker Yeadon LLC
Figure 12.12
Credit: Image courtesy of Decker Yeadon LLC

Figure 13.1a–d
Credit: Photos courtesy of OMA
Figure 13.2
Credit: Photo courtesy of OMA
Figure 13.3
Credit: Image courtesy of Zaha Hadid Architects
Figure 13.4
Credit: Photo courtesy of Iwan Baan
Figure 13.5
Credit: Photo courtesy of Peter Morgan
Figure 13.7
Credit: Image courtesy of Greg Lynn FORM
Figure 13.8
Credit: Image courtesy of Gnuform
Figure 13.9
Credit: Model images courtesy of Gehry Partners, LLP
Figure 13.10
Credit: Photo by Albert Vecerka, courtesy of IAC
Figure 13.11
Credit: Image courtesy of Reiser + Umemoto
Figure 13.12
Credit: Image courtesy of the late Jan Kaplicky
Figure 13.14
Credit: Photo courtesy of murmur

Figure 14.1
Credit: Juintow Lin
Figure 14.2
Credit: Diasy Yu, Paul Vu, instructor: Axel Prichard-

Index

400360